NATIONALIZING BLACKNESS

PITT LATIN AMERICAN SERIES

Billie R. DeWalt, Editor

NATIONALIZING
BLACKNESS

Afrocubanismo and Artistic Revolution
in Havana, 1920–1940

ROBIN MOORE

UNIVERSITY OF PITTSBURGH PRESS

Published by the University of Pittsburgh Press, Pittsburgh, Pa. 15261
Copyright © 1997, University of Pittsburgh Press
All rights reserved
Manufactured in the United States of America
Printed on acid-free paper
10 9 8 7 6 5 4 3 2 1

Library of Congress Cataloging-in-Publication Data will be found at the end of this book.
A CIP catalog record for this book is available from the British Library.

Illustrations from the following collections, journals, and archives are reproduced by permission: the
Biblioteca Nacional José Martí; the Centro Odilio Urfé; the Museo Nacional, Palacio de Bellas Artes;
the Museo Nacional de la Música; the Oficina del Historiador de la Ciudad de la Habana; *Bohemia;*
Estudios Afrocubanos; Juventud Rebelde; and the personal collections of Francisco Bacallao, Alicia
Castro, Lázaro Herrera, Hilda and Raquel Rivero, and Avelina Alcalde Valls.

En el susurro del palmar
se siente el eco resonar
de una voz de dolor que al amor llama

Oh, patria mía
¿quién diría que tu cielo azul
nublara el llanto?

— ELISEO GRENET

CONTENTS

PREFACE

Because ethnography and history are inevitably influenced by the "positioning" of the author, I feel it necessary to make a clean breast of things by describing some of the attitudes that contributed to the development of this project. In part, my decision to conduct research in Cuba was informed by the belief that Cuba is being treated unfairly by the United States government and its current foreign policy. This is true despite a recognition that Cuba is far from an ideal socialist state and that freedom of speech and other basic human rights are frequently infringed upon by authorities. My research represents an attempt to revitalize dialogue between our two nations and to raise consciousness about the needs and lives of the Cuban people. It also represents a reaction to the existing literature on Cuban music that too often avoids the politicization of popular culture, especially concerning racial issues.

Perhaps the most central goal of the project as initially conceived was to determine how the music of a "despised" minority—African descendants in the Americas—has become so central to national identity in various countries that continue to discriminate against them. I have not accomplished that goal to my satisfaction, but research in Havana taught me a great deal about the complexity of analyzing popular culture and provided specific examples of how subaltern expression enters national consciousness and discourse. I intended my work to address issues of ideology, hegemony, and resistance, and to study interactions between the state and cultural elite ("the system") and the black working classes. I hoped to provide insights into the formation of modern conceptions of self and nation in Cuba and the manner in which Afrocuban culture first affected them. I also intended chapters 2 through 7 (each a separate case study) to explore perceived gaps in Cuban cultural history by focusing on "nonsubjects" or unexplored aspects of relatively familiar subjects.

My reasons for choosing a historical project were twofold. First, the majority of critical North American publications on Cuban popular music in recent years (Robbins 1989, Manuel 1991b, etc.) focus on the period from 1959 to the present and offer few insights into earlier decades. I intended to redress this imbalance. More important, I wished to discuss somewhat controversial topics with interviewees involving racial discrimination and thought they might be more willing to talk openly about past experiences rather than those of the present. Government-sanctioned publications until recently maintained that racism did not exist in socialist Cuba (e.g., Serviat 1986); any statement challenging such pronouncements can still potentially result in complications for those who make them. Everyone agreed, however, that racial tensions existed in the early twentieth century, and for that reason the 1920s and 1930s seemed a more feasible period to investigate. I hoped that interview subjects would be more willing to allow their commentary to be taped and that I would have license to cite them directly without betraying their trust.

As so often occurs, I found it impossible to complete the project exactly as planned. Various obstacles immediately presented themselves. The lack of previous studies on many of my envisioned topics meant that even a superficial analysis required tremendous effort. The fact that I did not receive a major grant for dissertation field work—difficult to obtain in the best of times and more so in the case of Cuban research—limited my time and resources. Despite the official position maintained by the U.S. Treasury Department that academic research is not subject to regulation by the current economic embargo, my experience leads me to believe that government policy actively discourages such work in Cuba. All major granting agencies that receive federal support, for instance (Fulbright-Hays, the Organization of American States, the National Endowment for the Humanities, the National Science Foundation, and others), would not even consider my requests for funding in 1992. Excursions I had hoped to make to parts of Cuba other than Havana Province to conduct interviews often proved impossible. My thanks to the MacArthur Foundation for partial funding of three research trips to Havana between 1992 and 1995, to Aline Helg and Gerard Béhague for their crucial assistance with funding, and to the Rockefeller Foundation for postdoctoral support.

One of the most problematic aspects of the project, however, was not directly related to funding, but instead involved the difficulty of representing the black working-class musical experience of sixty years ago. Most well-known performers of that period had died. Among the few that were alive and agreed to be interviewed—and/or their relatives—consciousness of racial antagonism varied widely. Some maintained that Afrocuban performers of the 1920s and

1930s had never been the subject of discrimination, while others gave detailed accounts of humiliations, police brutality, and repression. Cristóbal Díaz Ayala has suggested that this discrepancy may be due in part to the political beliefs of interviewees, in addition to differences in personal experience. Those favoring the socialist government and its representation of Cuba's racial past may tend to remember the pre-1959 period as more repressive and discriminatory than those critical of current policies.

Because I was often forced to rely on second-hand accounts of musical life, I found it especially difficult to evaluate the ideological significance of the national appropriation of black street musics among working-class blacks themselves. Did they feel more "Cuban," more accepted as a result of the popularization of *sones* and the reauthorization of *comparsas,* for instance? Did they feel cheated, as if the acceptance of their cultural expression served only to hide their continuing social, educational, and economic marginalization? I discuss these issues briefly, but not to the extent I would have liked. Reading newspapers and magazines, listening to '78 records, and examining other archival material, I found it much easier to discuss hegemony from the "top down" by citing the published works of white middle-class composers and critics, as well as those of the black middle-class community. Some attitudes of working-class entertainers (as expressed musically, lyrically, or in interviews from the past) are included, but many questions remain. Much of my project thus analyzes dominant artistic discourse; perhaps others will be able to complement it by giving more attention to voices "from below."

In choosing interviewees, I often relied on the advice of friends who knew which individuals could provide information and where to find them. Havana has not published a telephone directory or similar guide since the mid-1970s, so conducting interviews there is not merely a matter of looking up an address and stopping by to chat. In a number of cases, I could not contact excellent candidates simply because no one knew how to locate them.

Among those who could be found and did offer their time and insights, I extend special thanks to musicians René Alvarez, Antonio Arcaño, Francisco Bacallao, the Castro sisters of La Orquesta Anacaona, Florencio Hernández Cuesta, Lázaro Herrera, Reynaldo Hierrezuelo, Senén Suárez, and Joseíto Valdés; retired cabaret worker Gilberto Arango; authors Walterio Carbonell, Tomás Fernández Robaina, Radamés Giró, Zoila Lapique Becali, and Rogelio Martínez Furé; musicologists Leonardo Acosta, Victoria Eli Rodríguez, Ligia Guzmán, María Teresa Linares, Raúl Martínez Rodríguez, Nefertiti Tellería; the staff at the Museo Nacional de la Música, including Pepe Piñeiro and Marco Antonio, as well as CIDMUC staff members Ramona Vidal Glez, Armando Núñez, and Tomás Jimeno; Centro Odilio Urfé director Jesús Gómez Cairo; Alberto Faya, musical director of the Casa de las Américas; composer Hilario González; dancers Natalia Herrera, Adelaida Mora, and Julio Rey; film ethnographer Serafín Quiñones; radio personalities Eduardo Rosillo and Oscar Luís López; Rodolfo de la Fuente and other staff at Radio Rebelde, as well as those at CMBF and Radio Habana Cuba; art historian Ramón Vázquez Díaz; and Avelina Valls, niece of Jaime Valls; and comic theater historian Eduardo Robreño.

Thanks also are due to Esteban Morales and Marité López Tamargo, at the Centro de Estudios Sobre Estados Unidos (CESEU) in Miramar, who assisted me during my first visits, and to radio journalist Cristóbal Sosa, who transcribed many of my interviews and furthered my investigation in other ways. Since returning to the States I have been especially grateful for the assistance and commentary offered me by Gerard Béhague, Aline Helg, Cristóbal Díaz Ayala, Leonardo Acosta, Rogelio Martínez Furé, Aurolyn Luykx, Alira Ashvo-Muñoz, and Peter Manuel. Their insights have added greatly to this project. Suzanne Silagi is to be thanked for her help in touching up period photographs and illustrations.

While it might seem unnecessary, I include many quotations in the original Spanish as well as in translation. This serves as an important means of analyzing the ideological position of their authors toward Afrocuban culture. I subject them to a fairly close reading, and thus the authors' original words may provide additional insights that cannot be fully conveyed in translation.

My study does not represent "traditional" musical analysis in certain respects. Although music is discussed in order to define genres and to describe processes of stylistic change, it is not my sole focus of study. Few transcribed examples of music have been included because the project concerns musical discourse and ideas about music even more than the notes themselves. In each section I present music and dance as central subjects yet I have tried to link these expressive forms to visual art, poetry, and stage works whenever possible, in an attempt to provide a more holistic view of Cuban culture. Such an approach necessarily entails devoting less time to all subjects and runs the risk of appearing superficial. Each chapter could easily become a full-length study. Nevertheless, I hope that my analysis, however introductory, will stimulate debate and suggest new avenues for research among those interested in artistic expression in Cuba and elsewhere.

NATIONALIZING BLACKNESS

INTRODUCTION

One of the most remarkable features of the evolution of
popular musics is its association, in numerous cultures
worldwide, with an unassimilated, disenfranchised,
impoverished, socially marginalized class. . . . They share a
common status on or beyond the periphery of stable,
"respectable" society. . . . It is paradoxical that these
marginal misfits in their milieu of bars and brothels
should be so crucial in the development of new musical
forms, especially since the genres they create are often
destined later to become celebrated as national
expressions . . . why should so much creative energy be
associated with despised and isolated social groups?
—Peter Manuel, *Popular Musics of the Non-Western World*

For at least sixty years, Cuban intellectuals, politicians, and artists have
defined their culture and society in terms of creole or mulatto imagery.
The mulatto nation metaphor refers to a physical process—the racial mixing
of Caucasians, Africans, and indigenous peoples over the centuries—but, more
important, a cultural one involving the fusion of once distinct systems of language, religion, artistic forms, and other expression into a unique composite.
Liberal middle-class representatives of what is often referred to as the "critical
decade" of modern Cuban ideological development, roughly 1920–1935, were
among the first to promote images of Afrohispanic cultural fusion. Such attitudes, which continue to be voiced by leaders today, including Fidel Castro
and other prominent Communist Party figures (Ralson 1991, 75; Casal 1989),
have their roots in the writings of authors such as Fernando Ortiz, Alejo
Carpentier, Juan Marinello, and Emilio Roig de Leuchsenring from the late
1920s.

The first qualified valorization of Afrocuban arts by the intellectual elite
and their acceptance as the valuable heritage of the entire nation date from the
1920s and 1930s (e.g., Carpentier 1976, 91; Ortiz 1934, 205). In an important

1

sense, the opinions of these authors were fundamental to the formation of modern Cuban thought. They demonstrate a significant break with previously held conceptions of Cuban society, from which African-influenced culture was almost entirely excluded. Much as Hobsbawm describes the turn of the century as decisive in the formulation of modern thought in many Western European nations (1987, 4), the decade associated with Carpentier and his contemporaries is essential to the way Cuba is currently "imagined."

Many factors contributed to this ideological shift. The 1920s was a period of tremendous upheaval and unrest in Cuba, to such an extent that the beginnings of cultural change are largely obscured by more visible events. The island experienced a severe depression after World War I. Underemployment and poverty were exacerbated first by the dramatic deflation of world sugar prices in 1920, then by the U.S. stock market crash of 1929. Tariff legislation passed in the United States in an attempt to protect North American sugar, coffee, and tobacco growers further aggravated matters (Pérez 1988, 393). Material desperation among Cuba's agriculturalists and urban working classes led to a constant succession of strikes and activism that disrupted what remained of the economy. Economic conditions in turn threatened the political stability of the administration of Gerardo Machado (1924–1933), already in disfavor for altering the constitution and unjustifiably extending presidential term limits. Beginning about 1928, Machado began to brutally suppress all opposition groups in a bid to maintain power. By the early 1930s, his policies had contributed to a mass polarization of sentiment culminating in civil war.

The war against Machado and his defeat in 1933 gave rise to strong nationalist sentiment. Anger over the previous administration's support of North American foreign policy, viewed as having contributed to Cuba's economic crisis, became more focused and intense. During the conflict and for a short time after its resolution, the country's intellectual elite attempted more actively to promote uniquely Cuban cultural forms. The sudden prominence of African-influenced music and dance in Cuba owed much to these events. The arts of socially marginalized blacks, for centuries ignored or dismissed by Cuba's middle classes, took on new significance as symbols of nationality.

From about 1927 through the late 1930s, an Afrocubanophile frenzy pervaded the country, affecting the attitudes of the white majority toward the noncommercial expression of Afrocubans themselves and inspiring Afrocubanist works among their own ranks. This *afrocubanismo* "moment" influenced virtually all domains of art, elite and popular. It inspired the poetry of Emilio Ballagas, José Tallet, and Nicolás Guillén; the paintings of Eduardo Abela, Jaime Valls, and Wifredo Lam; the novels of Alejo Carpentier; the musical theater of Ernesto Lecuona, Rodrigo Prats, and Gonzalo Roig; the symphonic compositions of Alejandro García Caturla, Amadeo Roldán, and

Gilberto Valdés; and the phenomenal national and international popularity of Cuban *son* and commercial rumba bands.

Cuban artists did not decide on their own to associate black street culture with a revised sense of *cubanidad* (Cubanness). On the contrary, their interests derived from international artistic trends, assimilated in many cases while studying abroad in Madrid, Paris, or New York. The 1920s precipitated a crisis in European bourgeois art internationally, from which many maintain it has never recovered (Hobsbawm 1987, 219). This was a time of fundamental change in the commercial music of nearly all Western countries, driven partly by technological innovation in the form of radio broadcasting and sound recordings, partly by the nature of the capitalism itself and a desire to expand markets into minority communities and overseas, and partly as a result of growing wealth and increased numbers among the working classes.

The most obvious manifestation of such changes in the production and consumption of music involved concession to blue-collar and non-Western aesthetics on an unprecedented scale. This was the era of the tango, the "jazz craze," "bohemian" Paris, the Harlem Renaissance, the primitivists, the fauvists, naive *kunst*, and a host of related movements drawing inspiration from non-European traditions. The arts of the "people without history," or at least certain conceptions and representations of them, became fashionable even among the elite. From today's perspective, the 1920s can be seen as a crucial first step in the gradual democratization of music making, paralleled by the emergence of genres such as calypso and samba, and presaging later developments such as rhythm and blues, salsa, and reggae.

In terms of Cuban music, one has only to refer to collections of sheet music and piano rolls, descriptions of public dances, or listings of radio programming in Havana before 1925 to realize the extent of musical change that occurred in following years. Compositions from the earlier period closely resembled popular songs of middle-class Europe. Examples include the *criollas* and ballroom dances of Luís Casas Romero such as "Estela,"[1] the *danzones* of Antonio María Romeu and Cheo Belén Puig, and the habaneras and *canciones cubanas* of Eduardo Sánchez de Fuentes (1974). Although genres such as the *criolla, canción,* and *danzón* were considered the epitome of Cuban expression at the turn of the century and do have some distinct stylistic attributes, their uniqueness relative to European popular music pales in contrast to Afrocuban genres that achieved national popularity in subsequent decades.

As a further indication of the extent of musical change, consider early record production. Díaz Ayala (1981, 112) provides a listing of Cuban recordings in the RCA Victor catalogue of 1923. Of the approximately 145 titles, most are listed as *danzón, vals, criolla,* habanera, or as dialogues from the *teatro vernáculo* (comic theater). The artists featured on these '78s tend either to be semiprofessionally trained *trovadores* (troubadours) such as Eusebio Delfín, Manuel Corona, and Alberto Villalón, whose repertories were heavily influenced by European art song, or classically trained singers such as Adolfo Colombo (tenor) and Conchita Llauradó (soprano). Musical representations of Cuba's blacks, *guajiros* (Hispanic peasants), and other working-class groups are largely absent. Within ten or fifteen years, however, genres prominent in the 1923 Victor catalogue were fading from popular memory, having been largely supplanted by *sones, guarachas,* stylized congas, rumbas, *afros,* and other Afrocuban-inspired compositions.

The stylistic trends of the *afrocubanismo* movement are not without precedent. If one considers Cuban working-class forms that never achieved mass commercial prominence, syncretic Afrohispanic artistry has a venerable history dating back at least to the seventeenth century (Agüero y Barreras 1946, 119; Urrutia 1935b, 9). Thus the period around 1930 represents a tentative valorization of influences long suppressed. Music and dance have always been among the most democratic of the arts in Cuba, representing forms of expression accessible to minorities that appeal to listeners across class and racial boundaries. As opposed to painting, sculpture, literature, or poetry, they require little or no institutional training, do not presuppose literacy or formal education, and do not generally involve the purchase of expensive materials. In Cuba, as in the United States and elsewhere, music and dance have served as a means of real and symbolic empowerment for those who would otherwise have no voice. They have also provoked violence and repression by those opposing such empowerment.[2]

The fact that for sixty years African-derived stylistic influences have been central to national musical production makes the study of music history in Cuba particularly rewarding. Given the past (and present) overrepresentation of Afrocubans themselves in musical vocations, music history affords insights into issues of discrimination and racial conflict. The extent of social stratification becomes evident by studying where and when particular sorts of musical performance were (and are) permitted or prohibited, and by whom. Bigotry and racial bias are manifested in discussions of Afrocuban street music in the popular press. In some cases, bigotry is evident even in the musical works of composers favoring the national acceptance of Afrocuban genres (see the reactions of the black middle class to *afrocubanismo* in chapter 7). The broad appeal of European-derived music among Afrocuban performers, and the resultant stylistic conflict in their compositions between African- and European-derived influences, directly allude to larger issues of cultural dominance and assimilation.

Perhaps most important, the study of music provides information on the construction of Cuban identity, past and present. As Faya (1993) and others

have noted, music and dance are crucial to definitions of the
as highly visible "primordial" referents that define Cubans ag,
against "them" (Geertz 1973, 259). Music offers a means of stu
of ideological unification wherein the oppositional expressi
transformed discursively and practically into "everyone's music,
ers of the mid-twentieth century eventually appropriated particular genres of
Afrocuban music for the nation, yet they were hard pressed to do so, given the
long-standing bias against them. African-derived culture in an abstract sense
may have been essential to dominant conceptions of *cubanidad* beginning in
the 1930s, but in many of its traditional forms it continued to be condemned
as backward, lewd, or primitive, as it is sometimes even today. An appreciation
for the inconsistencies between 1920s *afrocubanismo* as an ideology embracing
black expression discursively and the extent to which traditional Afrocuban
arts were actually accepted is vital in evaluating the significance of the period.
Even more important, the mass acceptance of certain forms of black music
and dance by Cuban society did not necessarily imply greater social equality
for or empowerment of Afrocubans themselves.

Outline and Theoretical Issues

This study investigates changing conceptions of race and nation in Cuba in
the early twentieth century, and how such changes affected artistic production
among various social groups. In a theoretical sense, it attempts to align musical scholarship on Cuba more closely with recent studies in anthropology and
other social sciences, especially as related to issues of nationalism, collective
cultural expression, and ideological formation. Although I discuss various decades to contextualize the analysis and provide a sense of historical continuity,
I focus primarily on the 1920s and 1930s. These years are most relevant for
having witnessed, in the words of Fernando Ortiz, "the dances of the rabble
accepted by aristocrats in their palaces" (1965, xiv). I am particularly interested
in how African-influenced musical forms and mass-mediated images of
Afrocubans first entered the national mainstream, and in their relation to
changing conceptions of *cubanidad*.

Afrocuban musics achieved national recognition through the efforts of two
primary groups. Professional, conservatory-trained musicians and other members of the (typically white) Cuban "culture elite" created representations of
blacks and black music "from above" that had a tremendous impact on commercial and noncommercial production in theaters, symphony halls, motion
picture soundtracks, nightclubs, cabarets, and published sheet music. Working-class and underclass Afrocuban performers affected music making on a
national level by forming carnival bands, popularizing syncretic genres such

as the *son,* performing music and dance for tourists, and perpetuating more directly African-derived musical traditions associated with traditional rumba and *santería* ritual.

Cuba's growing black middle classes also contributed to the nationalization of Afrocuban culture. Influential figures such as Ignacio Villa, Eusebia Cosme, and Rita Montaner mediated in an important sense between "the street" and "the elite," disseminating stylized genres of Afrocuban music similar to those written by the white middle classes, yet interpreting them differently. The emphasis here on a conceptual binary opposition between Hispanic/elite/dominant and African/popular/subaltern has the advantage of creating a sense of two distinct cultural and musical worlds in Cuba existing simultaneously in conflict, which has some validity in my experience.

A related concern is the more general process by which the artistic expression of marginal social groups gains acceptance by an entire society. Given the centrality of this mainstreaming phenomenon to musical production in Brazil, the United States, and other countries, surprisingly little attention has been devoted to it by music historians. Cornel West (1988) suggests that a cooptation/appropriation dynamic should be considered the "most salient feature" of popular music history in the industrialized world. Yet in Cuba, as elsewhere, issues of cooptation tend to be overlooked. Authors proclaim the virtues of "Cuban music" as a monolithic construct, or *"nuestro acervo musical"* (our [common] musical heritage), but fail to recognize the inevitably contested nature of all national culture. Walterio Carbonell deserves mention as an exception, having alluded to some of the more overtly problematic aspects of Cuban nationalist ideology beginning in the late nineteenth century.

Carbonell points out that the nationalization of subaltern expression represents a contradiction of sorts for traditional Marxist scholarship.[3] Subaltern groups have good reason to interest themselves in the music of the privileged, as involvement with "high" arts serves as a mark of distinction and can aid in attempts to transcend one's own social class (Bourdieu 1984). The overwhelming popularity of working-class musics among the middle classes and the elite, however, is more difficult to rationalize. Explanations for this phenomenon have been resolved in many respects using Marxist models derived from Gramsci that place greater emphasis on the role of concensus building and the legitimization of authority. An acceptance of oppositional artistic forms can further the interests of dominant factions by obscuring social division. Leaders of young and/or emerging nations, especially, have a strong need for cultural symbols with which to legitimize and naturalize the state. Factors associated with the economic "base" also affect processes of mass appropriation. Demographics, political instability, financial crisis, foreign relations, and technical innovation can all contribute to changes in conceptions of group identity. They create the initial need for reevaluating discourse pertaining to the "us" of a nation and the place of minority ethnicities within that construct.

In the mid-twentieth century, the nationalization of once marginal music typically resulted in its stylistic transformation. This tendency underscores the bounded nature of much commercial music making and helps us to recognize that taken collectively it defines an aesthetic space in which certain types of expression are permissible and others are not. Whereas more recent genres such as reggae, soul, and rap have been commercialized and mainstreamed with relatively few stylistic changes, early commercial blues, calypso, and (Puerto Rican) *plena,* as marketed on sheet music and '78 records, demonstrate a high degree of stylization relative to traditional musics of the same name and period. Their commercial variants represent a fusion of working-class styles with those of the North American and European middle classes. Afrocuban popular music of the 1920s and 1930s was similarly transformed, as manifested in the stage rumba compositions of Jorge Anckermann (n.d. 7), the salon congas of Eliseo Grenet (n.d. 3), and Yoruba dance music *(danza lucumí)* as conceived by Ernesto Lecuona (1955).

An awareness of such change and its relation to class and racial tension enables theorists to directly politicize musical style. Jones (1964) discusses this issue briefly, while Bourdieu (1984), Keil (1984), and Feld (1988, 1993) continue to theorize its scope and significance. They recognize that although the music of various groups may be "arbitrary" in a stylistic sense, it is not neutral politically, but rather serves to perpetuate complex power relations in the society of which it is a part. The musical landscape in modern urban societies, rife with ethnic conflict and class stratification, often manifests such division in sound. National music traditions might best be viewed dialogically as a jumble of interpenetrated "conversations," some more dominant than others as a result of their social positioning.

For Keil, a central aspect of musical mainstreaming in earlier decades involved what might be described as a stereotyping-reappropriation dynamic. In his model, the arts of the subaltern are musically "edited" by dominant groups into a form compatible with their own aesthetic norms or stereotypical notions of the "other." The "other" in turn accepts (and in some cases even perpetuates) these new representations as a means of gaining access to the commercial market but eventually transcends them, developing new and more oppositional forms of expression that more accurately reflect the subaltern's own social experience. Dynamics of this sort are evident in the successive popularization of jazz, blues, and R&B in the United States, the controversy they first aroused, and their eventual mass acceptance in somewhat altered form. Similar developments can be seen in the history of Cuban genres from the *contradanza, danza,* and *danzón* of the nineteenth century through the emergence of *son* and commercial rumba in the 1930s. As Lipsitz (1990) and Fiske (1989) suggest, ethnic and class divisions in modern society are inscribed in the products of popular culture.

In both a metaphorical and a tangible sense, popular music demonstrates conflict over the interpretation of social experience and of one's relationship to that experience (Fiske 1989a, 28). Popular culture's meanings are created through an ongoing dialectic between the commercial object and various "readings" of it by others. This is true regardless of whether the object originates from "below" or "above." Popular culture serves as an important means of defining individual identity—ethnic, racial, or otherwise—and the position of that identity relative to others. Especially in the culture of repressed minorities, these constructions reflect an opposition between conformity to dominant views of themselves and an assertion of their own.

Unable either to fully integrate or to extricate themselves from a culturally hostile environment, dominated minorities "accustom themselves to a bifocality reflective of both the ways that they view themselves and the ways that they are viewed by others" (Lipsitz 1990, 135). As in the case of music associated with the Caribbean steel drum, many genres of Afrocuban popular expression represent a site of mediation between distinct aesthetic systems and are thus able to satisfy the aesthetic preferences of "the culturally split neo-colonial subject" (Diehl 1992, 44).

An additional goal of this study is to demonstrate the frequently close relationship between social and cultural change, and by extension the potential contribution of cultural study to all disciplines in the humanities and social sciences. Cultural history has too often been shortchanged as an analytical focus, obscuring such relationships. This is true in two senses. First, ethnomusicologists themselves often reject the option of historical work in favor of ethnographic and other synchronic analysis. When they do conduct historical studies, music specialists generally confine their investigations to fact-gathering from scores and treatises rather than interpretive analysis, and thus do not reflect new trends in interdisciplinary scholarship (e.g., Widdess 1992). In a broader sense, many traditional historians tend to disregard cultural history as a primary or even secondary focus of study. Although ever more exceptions can be cited (e.g., Thompson 1967; Spence 1984; Bynum 1987), popular culture remains an underrepresented topic within the discipline.

The case of Cuba is typical. Luís Aguilar, Jules Benjamin, Ramón Ruiz, and (especially) Louis Pérez, for example, have contributed significantly to the literature on early twentieth-century Cuba, but their work remains largely focused on political, economic, and social issues. The same can be said of most historians living in Cuba, where this tendency is, if anything, more pronounced. Part of the reason for the lack of culturally oriented studies of this period stems from the abysmal state of research on modern presocialist Cuba generally. The comparatively ample materials available on nineteenth-century Cuba, and from 1959 to the present, contrast noticeably with a scarcity of research on the early Republic. In Cuba, the decades immediately preceding 1959 are considered "problematic"; several researchers mentioned to me that sensitive issues raised by publications deviating in any way from official Communist Party history created the possibility of political complications for the author. And while a number of books specifically on music deal at least in part with the 1920s and 1930s (e.g., Rodríguez Domínguez 1978; Calderón González 1986), they tend to be anecdotal and are of limited historical relevance.

The perceived escapist and superficial nature of much popular culture undoubtedly contributes to its continuing underrepresentation in scholarly work. On an overt level, for instance, it is difficult to link the subject matter of love ballads such as Nilo Menéndez's "Aquellos ojos verdes" from the early 1930s to the labor activism and political killings of the same decade. The apolitical content of most popular song in a lyrical sense has long been recognized by culture theorists, including Theodor Adorno, who dismissed such entertainment as a "musical opiate of the masses."

Recently, however, critics have suggested that it is precisely these discrepancies that may be the most interesting aspects of popular music. They argue that it offers potentially unique insights into the historical experiences of individuals as subjectively perceived rather than the "objective" truths typically studied by historians. For Erlmann (1991, xviii), popular song reveals "little-known layers and niches of consciousness that help to shed light on the nonmaterial, subjective forces and symbolic practices" that shape society. Fiske also urges critics not to treat "fantasy" and "reality" as mutually exclusive concepts. He emphasizes that the reality of any given moment is based on personal experience and that social relations can never be experienced objectively, as they have no a priori meaning in themselves (1989b, 124). Popular culture in this sense provides a means of analyzing the consciousness of the past, allowing the researcher to contrast macrosocial processes with the lived experience of the people.

Another contribution that the study of culture can make to Cuban history is to shed new light on racial discourse. Prior to the mid-twentieth century, belief in the biologically based superiority of the Caucasian race was widely accepted in most Western countries and justified actions taken against other groups. However, such ideas have been discredited in recent decades and replaced by justifications of racial discrimination based on particular readings (or misreadings) of the cultural practices of so-called minority groups. "Racial" bias is thus frequently the result of reactions to patterns of speech, dress, behavior, musical production, and other cultural expression; the negative attitudes derived from such readings are then "mapped" cognitively onto the physiological features of the same group.

Many demographic and social factors also affect the way dominant groups perceive the subaltern—for instance, the century-old associations in postslave societies between blacks and poverty, lack of education, crime, and violence—but this does not detract from the importance of culture as a site in which racial bigotry is justified and maintained. In many cases, the extent to which minority groups are accepted by the society they live in depends upon the degree to which they are able or willing to distance themselves from their unique cultural heritage. Music and related forms of expression thus constitute a primary source of information on racial conflict. Biased attitudes about music are part of an ongoing social dialogue on race and must be understood as a component of the larger phenomenon manifesting itself as racial segregation, discrimination, and overt physical repression.

This study is divided into seven chapters. Chapter 1 includes a brief discussion of conceptions of race in Cuba and the prominence of racial terms in everyday discourse today. It provides an overview of major political and historical events from the late nineteenth century through the 1930s, emphasizing the contested place of blacks and mulattos within Cuban society. Attention is given to segregation and exploitation of nonwhites, white supremacist discourse, and attitudes toward Afrocubans among the major political parties. The influence of Afrocubans on musical production before the mid-1920s is also discussed, as well as middle-class reactions to such influence. An appreciation for racial history, although not always linked to music and dance performance, helps to contextualize artistic developments and underscores the ironies surrounding the popularization of Afrocuban music in later decades.

Chapter 2, also primarily on the pre-1920 period, concerns the history of the Cuban blackface theater as an antecedent to *afrocubanismo* and related movements. Blackface productions are significant in that they represent the first form of commercial entertainment in which stylized versions of Afrocuban music and dance gained national popularity. The fact that the role of the comic black man *(negrito)* was invariably performed by a white actor in blackface, and that such entertainment tended to ridicule blacks and black cultural expression, however, reflects again an ambivalence toward Afrocubans.

Chapters 3 and 4 provide case studies of two musical genres created by Afrocuban working-class groups themselves and the changing attitudes toward them by municipal authorities, professional middle-class composers, and liberal intellectuals. Chapter 3 contains an overview of *comparsa* ensembles associated with street parades and carnivalesque celebration. It begins with early accounts of *comparsas* as described by observers of Kings' Day (Día de Reyes, 6 January) slave festivities of the nineteenth century. It examines the controversies surrounding the incorporation of these African-influenced musical groups into integrated carnival events of the twentieth century. (Before the Wars of Independence, carnival had been almost exclusively for white participants.) In a theoretical sense, chapter 3 addresses the relevance of Bakhtinian models in evaluating the meaning of carnival.

The term *African-influenced*, used here and throughout the book, does not imply support of the Herskovitzian position that particular genres of cultural expression derived from Africa have preserved their original forms. I refer to modalities unique to Cuba that are heavily influenced by African aesthetics but also by the expression of Spain and other sources. The form and content of Afrocuban street music has changed with emerging conceptions of blackness and self. *Africanness* and *blackness* are thus transitory notions that can be defined only within specific contexts. They represent a "cultural construction," to use the terminology of Linnekin (1992).

Chapter 4 includes a brief history of urban *son* music in Havana from its popularization in that city around 1910 through its mass commodification by white and black artists in the 1930s. This genre is the antecedent of modern salsa and remains the most frequently heard music in Cuba today. Early associations between *sones* and "degenerate" African cultural retentions, prostitution, and the most marginal of Cuba's black underclasses led to public denunciations and its suppression by authorities. By the late 1920s, however, the same music had become discursively transformed into the epitome of national expression. Technological changes in the music industry had an important effect on the gradual acceptance of the *son*.

Chapters 5 and 6 analyze several distinct forms of middle-class music inspired by Afrocuban street genres that gained national recognition in the late 1920s. Chapter 5 discusses musics whose primary scope of influence was Cuba itself. I describe the social and political turmoil associated with the late twenties and thirties in more detail and the relationship of such events to domestic artistic trends. I then examine the influence of Afrocuban themes in Cuban *zarzuelas* (light opera); salon sheet music compositions based loosely on rumba, *son, guaracha,* and other street musics; and the jazz-influenced dance band repertoire. Theoretically, chapter 5 elaborates on the relationship of popular culture to nationalist movements.

Chapter 6 critiques the term *transculturation* as employed in Cuba since the 1940s. It examines how stylized Afrocuban music of the *machadato* period was popularized internationally as a result of the commercial "rumba craze" and how it changed in the process. Beginning about 1928, prominent Cuban artists such as Justo Azpiazu, Moisés Simons, Rita Montaner, Carmita Ortiz, and Julio Richards performed stylized rumba before audiences in Europe, the United States, Latin America, and elsewhere. The music they promoted was reinterpreted by foreign artists, which in turn affected the development of 1930s tourist entertainment in Havana. Finally, Afrocuban performers themselves penetrated the tourist industry beginning in the 1930s and began disseminating their own images of black street culture.

Chapter 7 focuses on the elite compositions of the Minorista vanguard. This exclusive circle of painters, composers, and poets served as the intellectual center of the *afrocubanismo* movement and was extremely influential on subsequent generations of artists. Strangely, the Minoristas (as they called themselves) never managed to generate significant interest in their artistic creations. Drawing on modern aesthetic paradigms in Europe, their works remained stylistically unintelligible to most of the population. I explore some of the contradictions surrounding Minorista ideology: a desire to create new nationalist artistic forms that would express the sentiments of all Cubans, yet an unwillingness to embrace popular aesthetic conventions, African- or Hispanic-derived.

The conclusion suggests parallels between Cuban and North American music history and discusses trends in Cuban arts since the late 1930s. I note the increasing prominence of conservatory-trained composers who have consciously avoided Afrocuban themes in their work, rejecting the precedent established by the Minoristas. The 1920s and 1930s are thus characterized as a moment of relative thematic interpenetration of academic and popular arts, with both middle-class and street performers incorporating similar imagery into their work. Later decades gave rise to a widening gap between the style of "high" and popular culture that began to close only in the 1960s. The conclusion notes the strong influence that African-influenced music continues to exert on popular genres today. Appendixes provide reproductions of municipal and national legislation pertaining to music that has not been published elsewhere, as well as lists of prominent *conjuntos de son* from the 1930s and examples of *afrocubanista* poetry.

1

AFROCUBANS AND NATIONAL CULTURE

Throughout the long transition into agrarian capitalism
and then in the formation and development of industrial
capitalism, there is a more or less continuous struggle over
the culture of working people, the labouring classes and
the poor. This fact must be the starting point for any
study, both of the basis for, and the transformations of,
popular culture. The changing balance and relations of
social forces throughout that history reveal themselves,
time and again, in struggles over the forms of the culture,
traditions and ways of life of the popular classes.
—Stuart Hall, "Notes on Deconstructing the Popular"

Racial categories are central to the construction of collective identity in
Cuba, as in much of Latin America, and one cannot fully appreciate the
meaning of nationality without considering them. Countless terms and common phrases are used in Cuba to segment and structure perceived racial difference. In contrast to the political sphere, where discussion of blacks and other
minorities is relatively uncommon, Cubans' predilection for discussing race
among friends and family members seems especially significant. Such concern
among all Cubans is undoubtedly the result of the large percentage of the population with a racially mixed background. In recent decades, the number of
Cubans with at least some African ancestry has reached over 60 percent; even
in the 1920s it was at least 30 percent (Moore 1988, 36; Hagedorn 1995, 30).
Increases in the percentage of Afrocubans relative to Caucasians reflect in part
declining infant mortality rates among blacks after 1959 and the fact that most
of those who fled the island in the early 1960s were white. Studies of demographics in Cuba are generally unreliable, as census takers tend to accept Cubans' own self-designation as to whether they are "white," rather than apply-
ing more objective criteria.

Over the centuries, a mixed population has emerged in Cuba that is sensitive to subtle physical differences. Aside from the overarching classifications of

negro, mulato, and *blanco* (black, mulatto, white), Cubans make further distinctions that betray a strong bias against physical features considered African-derived in favor of those of European origin. Racial terms heard in everyday conversation include *mulato adelantado* ("evolved" mulatto), used to describe light-skinned mulattos with predominantly Caucasian features; *mulato blanconazo* (very white mulatto), a mulatto with so few African-derived physical features as to pass for white; *jaba'o,* a person of light skin color but overtly Negroid features; *trigueño* (wheat-colored), a relatively light-skinned mulatto or Hispanic with *pelo bueno* ("good" hair); *negro azul* ("blue" black), a Negro so dark that the skin appears to have a blue cast; and *indio* (Indian), a mulatto with physical features and/or skin tone that suggests descent from the island's indigenous population.

In addition to subcategories such as these, many other terms refer to specific physical attributes, such as *pelo malo* and *pasa* (bad hair, raisins), derogatory terms for kinky, Negroid hair; *bemba* (thick lips), associated with Africans;[1] *nariz buena/mala* (a good or bad nose), judged again on a perceived African- or European-derived shape; as well as phrases such as *adelantar la raza* (to evolve the race or species) or *blanquear* (to whiten), used by blacks who hope to produce lighter-skinned children through relationships with Caucasians. These terms, which also appear in song lyrics and other artistic expression, underscore the importance of race in Cuban society and illustrate the persistent negative attitudes toward manifestations of African ancestry in a country that ostensibly takes pride in being "mulatto."

Paradoxically, Cubans encode their national identity in figures such as the Caridad del Cobre, a dark-skinned female saint, and often express pride in syncretic cultural forms fusing African and Hispanic traditions. Since the 1830s, black women and especially the racially mixed *mulata* have been symbols of sensuality and sexual desire. In the writings of Cirilio Villaverde, Francisco Muñoz del Monte (a Dominican), and countless others, one finds a "symbolic privileging" of *mulatas* despite their repressed status in real social terms (Fernández de Castro 1935, 43; Kutzinski 1993, 7). These and other contradictions are reflected in the varied usages of *"negro"* and *"negra,"* which serve equally as terms of endearment or of derision. *"Negra"* can be used by a white father to refer to his white daughter, for instance, implying only affection and a high degree of familiarity.[2] Alternately, the term can be used in a relatively neutral fashion to address a younger black person who is unknown to the speaker (black or white) and in this case implies only a lack of deference (Fernández Robaina 1994). Finally, *"negro/negra"* can be used as an insult to emphasize race and the low status of blacks relative to Hispanics and other Caucasians.

Racial labels such as *"trigueño"* and *"chino"* (Chinese man or woman) are employed in a similar fashion. *"Chino"* is especially ambiguous, given that what appear to be Asian facial features are associated both with the descendants of Chinese immigrants brought to Cuba in the late nineteenth century as well as the heavy-lidded eyes of some Congolese Africans. The term can thus refer to either or both groups, or can be a generic complimentary nickname for a friend or lover.[3] The diverse meanings of blackness in Cuba, and other racial constructs, have never been thoroughly analyzed, though scholars are beginning to address them (e.g., González 1992; Kutzinski 1993; Wade 1993). They result from centuries of interracial conflict and the ambiguous position of Afrocubans within Cuban society as a whole.[4] Wade in particular discusses the complexity of racial study and notes a contradictory "double dynamic" apparent throughout Latin America involving both pride in African-influenced culture and persistent racial bias and discriminatory policies (1993, 7).

Most authors describe Cuban history in terms of successive waves of colonial domination, beginning with the Spanish explorers and continuing in economic form under the United States and the Soviet Union. Colonial practices in the Caribbean, from the sixteenth century on, were among the most brutal in all of Latin America. As a result of overt military campaigns of extermination, enslavement, and exposure to new diseases, most of the country's indigenous population died within the first seventy-five years of contact with Europeans. Siboney and Arawak musical forms, such as the sacred *areíto* (a communal ritual incorporating drumming and dance), were outlawed during the sixteenth century and had little effect on the cultural expression of the island after that time (Ortiz 1965, 72).

Although it was one of the earliest colonies to be established, Cuba soon lost much of its significance for Spanish authorities. With the discovery of gold in Mexico and Peru, and of other territories with more economic potential, expansion of the Cuban colony slowed. The island's only strategic role during the seventeenth and eighteenth centuries was as a way station for Spanish armadas carrying valuable cargoes back to Europe. As late as 1750, Cuba had only about 150,000 inhabitants, primarily Hispanic, which were concentrated in the provinces of Havana, Matanzas, and Santiago.

This situation began to change dramatically toward the end of the eighteenth century. As a result of revolution in Haiti and new markets in the United States, vast commercial opportunities opened up for Cuba. Prior to the 1790s, Haiti had been the largest producer of sugar in the Americas. Following the outbreak of war on that island in 1791 and the collapse of its plantation economy, global demand for sugar rose dramatically, as did sugar prices. Cuban investors took advantage of declining sugar exports from the French Caribbean by expanding their own production. Their decision had dramatic consequences for all facets of Cuban society. From 1790 to 1839, real income in Cuba increased by a factor of fifty (Aguilar 1972, 2), and the colony was transformed in only a few decades from a small, isolated territory to one of the wealthiest parts of the empire.

While many Latin American colonies were reducing or eliminating legal shipments of slaves from West Africa to the Americas during this period, the importation of slaves to Cuba reached unprecedented levels. Africans had been brought to Cuba since the late sixteenth century, but until the 1790s they represented only a small proportion of the population. By 1811, however, more than 320,000 blacks and mulattos lived in Cuba, accounting for more than 54 percent of all inhabitants. This trend reached its peak in 1841, with slaves and others of African descent comprising 58.5 percent of all Cubans (Paquette 1988, 298). In 1853 the importation of new slaves was officially prohibited, yet trafficking continued for at least another decade. The continuation of illicit shipments contributed to an unusually strong African cultural presence in Cuba in the early twentieth century. Significant numbers of slaves born in West Africa took part in the Wars of Independence (1868–1878, 1879–1880, 1895–1898), for instance, and were still alive at the turn of the century.

Yet another factor contributing to the strong influence of African culture in the late nineteenth and twentieth centuries was the formation of *cabildos de nación* with the consent of Spanish authorities. Africans and their descendants organized and directed these black societies, whose members came from different ethnic regions; slaves from areas controlled by the Yoruba, Bantu, Egba, Oyo, Ife, Mandinga, Carabali, and other groups maintained distinct *cabildo* societies (see Castellanos and Castellanos 1987). The advantages of the *cabildos* to colonial authorities were twofold. First, they provided support for recently arrived Africans *(bozales)*, helping them to learn Spanish and adjust to their new environment. Second, they maintained separate ethnic identities among the slave population, and thus decreased the likelihood of mass uprisings or conspiracies. Unintentionally, the *cabildos* proved fundamental in the perpetuation of African cultural forms in Cuba, including language, religious practices, and traditions of music and dance.

Slave Culture and Afrocuban Music in the Nineteenth Century

Carbonell notes ironically that the religions and expressive arts of Afrocubans in the nineteenth century, which most historians consider marginal to Cuban history, were for many years the culture of the majority (1961, 10). From about 1800 to 1850, the African population remained significantly larger than the European, with a proportionately central role in artistic expression. Relatively little documentation exists on slave culture, however; this reflects both a lack of interest in African-derived arts on the part of Cuban colonial society and the fact that a majority of slaves lived in rural, agricultural areas in relative isolation. Slave culture in nineteenth-century Cuba, as in most other American colonies, was not considered "culture" by colonial settlers (Quiñones 1992). In many cases, foreign visitors listened more attentively to the music and dance of the slave population and contributed more to our present knowledge of them than Cubans themselves.[5]

A number of Afrocuban slave genres emerged or gained prominence during the mid-nineteenth century. These include *tahona* and *yambú* dances, the *baile de maní,* and other precursors of the present-day traditional rumba; sacred song and dance associated with *santería,* and related, ceremony; and the *tango-congo* and *abakuá* music and dance performed by street revelers in Día de Reyes or Kings' Day celebrations (see chapter 3).[6] Also, syncretic Afrohispanic dance musics developed that became popular among working-class Cubans of all races. These dances, some of which are described by Sánchez de Fuentes, were performed primarily in brothels and taverns (1928, 83). The choreography and musical characteristics of most, such as the *caidita* (little fall), the *cachumba,* the *cangrejito* (little crab), the *repiqueteo,* the *famboá,* were never described in detail by contemporary observers and have apparently been lost. Others such as the *contradanza* and *danzón* achieved popularity in a modified and "more decent" form among the Cuban middle classes and thus survived into the twentieth century. Much more is known about their history.

The rapid demographic "blackening" of Cuba from 1800 to 1850 did not go unnoticed by Hispanic intellectuals. Increases in the black population raised justifiable concerns that Cuba would be prone to racial violence in its attempts to control slave labor. Colonists had only to consider the example of their nearest neighbor, Haiti, whose independence was initiated through a mass slave revolt in 1791, to recognize the reality of such a possibility. The psychological impact of the Haitian revolution and the mass influx of slaves into Cuba created hysteria among much of the Hispanic community and intensified sentiment against the continued importation of slaves (Kutzinski 1993, 5).

José Antonio Saco, a prominent essayist and social critic of the 1830s, served as a spokesman of the white urban middle classes. He supported abolition and encouraged white emigration from European countries to counterbalance the demographic effects of the slave trade (Helg 1990, 39). An early nationalist figure as well, Saco frequently clashed with Spanish authorities. While he opposed annexation to the United States and championed a Cuba free from oppressive colonial mandates, Saco did not conceive of Afrocubans as part of the emerging nation (Sánchez Roca 1960, 5). Obsessed with the abstract notion of an entirely white/Hispanic Cuba, Saco and contemporaries such as Domingo del Monte and Luz Caballero were unable to accept the possibility that Cuba might someday be comprised of both blacks and whites as equal citizens.

Colonial Repression of African-Derived Culture and
the Emergence of Afrocuban Dance Orchestras

Just as they perceived a physical threat from the black underclasses, representatives of dominant society tended to view Afrocuban artistic expression as a potential threat to national culture. At best, such expression was dismissed as a *"cosa de negros"* (something blacks do), but more often it was openly condemned as an influence that would carry the Cuban people "back to a barbarous phase of [cultural] prehistory."[7] As early as the 1790s, colonial authorities began to take this possibility seriously enough to regulate music and dance performance.

Municipal decrees restricting drumming and related activities affected both music making in the slave barracks and that of free blacks in the street (Leal 1980, 49). Police and legislators systematically suppressed overtly African-influenced genres such as the traditional *rumba yambú* and *columbia* (Martínez Rodríguez 1977, 2). They concentrated most of their efforts on Afrocuban religious ritual and secret *ñáñigo* brotherhoods, however.[8] From the late 1860s, colonial authorities targeted *ñáñigo* societies because they often served as clandestine centers of revolutionary activity. Police records from the 1880s provide detailed descriptions of raids on *ñáñigo* meeting halls, as well as the confiscation and destruction of musical instruments, dance costumes, and other ritual objects.[9]

Many free working-class and middle-class Afrocubans in the nineteenth century also became well known as performers of European music. The practice of free blacks forming European-style dance bands and playing minuets, quadrilles, rigadoons, and related genres for primarily white audiences has a long history. In the late sixteenth century, performers such as Teodora and Micaela Ginés, sisters born in the Dominican Republic, became famous because of the popularity of their *orquesta de baile* in Santiago (Agüero y Barreras 1946, 120). Dance orchestras constituted an important site of racial interaction, and the vocation of orchestral musician was one of the few in which blacks could work alongside whites. Although not all ensembles accepted blacks and mulattos in the early nineteenth century, many white orchestras employed them as bassists and *timbal* or percussion players.

By the 1830s, Afrocubans had become part of middle-class musical life, both by joining integrated groups and by forming their own. Indeed, the most respected Afrocuban ensembles came to be more sought after for dance events than those of whites (Díaz Ayala 1981, 38). Prominent black and mulatto musicians of the mid-nineteenth century include internationally renowned violinist and composer Claudio Brindis de Salas (1800–1872), who formed the orchestra La Concha de Oro; clarinetist Juan de Dios Alfonso, director of the Orquesta Flor de Cuba; and violinist Tomás Buelta y Flores (1798–1851).[10] A few of these figures, such as Buelta y Flores, amassed considerable personal wealth during their careers and possessed numerous slaves as well (Orovio 1981, 69). Black and mulatto orchestra musicians occasionally came from affluent families and were trained in music conservatories, but more typically they learned to read and perform music as soldiers in military bands (Acosta 1992). The *pardo-moreno* (black-mulatto) distinction maintained by the Spanish military in organizing military battalions and brass bands was reflected in a distinction between *pardo* and *moreno* orchestras of the day.

One reason why Afrocubans figured so prominently in nineteenth-century middle-class musical performance was that most white Cubans considered music making to be a servile profession "beneath their station." The youth of Cuba's haute bourgeoisie and middle classes, who comprised the majority of those who could afford a formal musical education, chose not to become involved with the arts. They followed more prestigious careers in the clergy, government, law, medicine, or other professions (Lapique Becali 1979, 25). Musicians tended to be paid less than other white-collar professionals, contributing to their lower status. In general, musical labor straddled a cognitive boundary between white-collar and blue-collar, elite and common, in the minds of many (Carpentier 1946, 137). What for upwardly aspiring Hispanic Cubans seemed an uninteresting career option, however, held tremendous appeal for Afrocubans. The fact that Cuba's white middle classes often chose to avoid careers as musicians explains the overrepresentation of Afrocubans in orchestras and other performance ensembles.

By the 1830s and early 1840s, so many Afrocuban musicians were performing European-style music that even in this context they were perceived as a threat; their preeminence inspired appeals by Serafín Ramírez and other critics for white Cuba to take back control of national music making (Agüero y Barreras 1946, 119). José Antonio Saco voiced similar concerns in 1832: "Among the enormous evils that this accursed race [the black population] has carried to our land . . . is that of having distanced the arts from our white population."[11] Conservatives condemned the subdued Afrocuban musical influences found in certain mid-nineteenth-century ballroom genres such as the *contradanza* and *danza*. Such influences typically took the form of the inclusion of the *güiro* (gourd scraper) or similar hand-held percussion in the ensemble and the prominence of rhythmic patterns and improvisations performed by the *timbalero*. In some cases, controversy over these "Africanisms" reached such proportions that despite their popularity among younger dancers they were banned in societies and clubs (Martínez Furé 1994).

In the wake of furor over the Escalera conspiracy in 1844, which greatly heightened racial tensions, the popularity of Afrocuban musicians decreased dramatically for nearly a decade.[12] The event, which had precedents in movements organized by José Antonio Aponte in the 1810s and slave uprisings in Matanzas and other areas, represented the culmination of years of anxiety on the part of Cuban slaveholders over the potential threat represented by Afrocubans, enslaved or free (Franco 1963). Spanish authorities made over four thousand arrests in conjunction with the investigation of this ostensible plot to foment slave rebellion, primarily among free blacks. Hundreds of blacks were put to death directly, and others died after being tortured to solicit confessions.[13] The distinguished poet Ambrosio Echemendía escaped punishment for his alleged role in the affair only through the intercession of influential white friends (Fernández de Castro 1935, 33). The poet Plácido (Gabriel de la Concepción Valdés)[14] and band leader Pimienta, by contrast, were quickly condemned to death; others such as Buelta y Flores and poet Juan Francisco Manzano fled into exile. Claudio Brindis de Salas was imprisoned and tortured under Governor O'Donnell (Carpentier 1946, 152); other lesser-known artists and performers, including Esteban Peñalver, Ulpiano Estrada, and Bernardino Vázquez, received similar sentences (Deschamps Chapeaux 1971, 115). La Escalera suggests that even free blacks at this time did not enjoy the rights of citizens and that in the minds of many they too represented a liability to Cuba.

The Emergence of *Costumbrismo* in Nineteenth-Century Cuban Art

The strong presence of Afrocubans in the early 1800s led to their increasing representation in all cultural production. Parodies of slave mannerisms are prominent in Cuban literature and visual art created by whites in the 1830s. Imitations of *bozal* speech—the manner in which recently arrived African slaves pronounced Castilian Spanish—are frequently found in popular fiction. Early examples include the writings of José Victoriano Betancourt, especially *Los negros curros* and *Los negros del Manglar* (Fernández de Castro 1935, 44). Conscious misspellings of words used to parody slave dialect also appear in editions of popular music from this period (Carpentier 1946, 231). Other allusions to blacks and African-derived culture appear in song titles of popular *contradanzas* and *pregones*,[15] although the published scores themselves reveal few if any Afrocuban musical influences. Examples include the *contradanzas* "Tu madre es conga," "Los ñáñigos," "Los negros catedráticos," and "El mulato en el cabildo" (Lapique Becali 1979, 42). Manuel Saumell (1817–1870), considered by many to be the first nationalist composer in Cuba, lived in the barrio

of Guanabacoa, which was renowned for its strong Afrocuban cultural presence. His popularity derived from the *contradanzas* and other music he composed using primarily European-derived musical elements with frequent title
references to Afrocuban culture. Even in the mid-nineteenth century, Saumell's
pieces demonstrate that emerging conceptions of Cuban nationalism were
intimately linked to conceptions and interpretations of blackness.

The works of nineteenth-century *costumbrista* painters also incorporated
Afrocubans as parodic subject matter. This movement, which depicted perceived comic elements in everyday Cuban life, has its origins in late eighteenth-
and nineteenth-century artistic trends in Europe of a similar nature exemplified
by the work of Balzac (Portuondo 1972, 52). Some of the first examples of
costumbrista art in Cuba include early sketches and essays in the *Papel periódico
de la Habana*, and works such as *Escenas cotidianas* (1840) by Gaspar Betancourt.
Influential *costumbrista* painters include Eduardo Laplante, well known for
his engravings of life on sugar plantations and for cigar *marquillas* (fancy labels) depicting romantic interactions between *mulatas* and Spanish colonists
(see Kutzinski 1993).

Even better known are the works of journalist and painter Víctor Patricio
Landaluze (1828–1889). Like many *costumbrista* artists, Landaluze was born in
Spain. His tendency to ridicule what he considered unique and laughable in
Cuban society was a source of embarrassment to members of the *isleño* bourgeoisie, who took pains to avoid these subjects in artistic expression (Castellanos
1990, 28). Landaluze is especially interesting as an early representative of Cuban nationalist art, despite his strong allegiance to Spain and his conservative
political views. As Portuondo points out, "This man, who was a decided enemy of [Cuban] independence and other progressive political movements . . .
was also the initiator of Cuban painting."[16] Some suggest that the works of
Landaluze directly anticipate those of the *afrocubanismo* vanguard of the 1920s
and 1930s (Castellanos 1990, 13). Whatever his status, Landaluze provides some
of the best visual documentation available on Afrocuban expressive arts in the
nineteenth century and of Cuban society generally (see illustrations).

Afrocubans, Nationalism, and the Wars of Independence

Afrocubans achieved greater recognition as members of the Cuban nation in a
rhetorical sense during the Wars of Independence because of their central role
in the armed struggle against Spain (Fernández de Castro 1935, 48). Blacks and
mulattos, although comprising only about a third of the population in the late
nineteenth century, turned out in large numbers to join the insurgents and
represented over half of all troops deployed (Scott 1985, 112). Some maintain
that as many as 75 percent of the soldiers in the Liberation Army were black or

mulatto (Despaigne Chueg 1939, 11). Even among the senior commissioned ranks of the Liberation Army, over 40 percent of the posts were held by Afrocubans after 1895 (Pérez 1988, 160). The many famous black and mulatto war heroes invoked by politicians in the postwar Republic, such as Antonio Maceo, Quintín Banderas, Flor Crombet, and Guillermón Moncada, established their reputations as combatants and strategists in the wars against Spain. The heroism of these and other Afrocubans put significant strain on dominant and exclusionary conceptions of "white nationalism" among members of the Cuban bourgeoisie who had initiated the rebellion.

Much disagreement existed among the white planter elite regarding Afrocubans and their place within the nation. When Carlos Manuel de Céspedes and others reluctantly made the decision in the late 1860s to liberate their slaves and asked them to join in armed rebellion, they did so against the wishes of many of their peers (Carbonell 1961, 93; Scott 1985, 48). The inclusion of Afrocubans in the Liberation Army is generally seen as having accelerated the end of legal slavery in Cuba, but it was far from a noncontroversial act. Landowners in Oriente, where the revolution began, tended to be the most marginal of the white elite and felt poorly represented by Spain. They were more willing to risk their lives and property than those living closer to the capital. Ironically, Cuban blacks also fought on the side of Spain in revolutionary conflicts, apparently hired as mercenaries (Fernández de Castro 1935, 48).

As might be expected, racial tensions remained high within the ranks of Cuban troops even after revolutionary leaders had accepted the presence of Afrocubans (Helg 1995, 69). Black military promotions became a subject of considerable controversy, with white soldiers openly refusing to serve under black officers in many instances (Betancourt 1940, 10). Perhaps the most divisive moment came in 1878 with the Pact of Zanjón, a peace accord that temporarily suspended hostilities. This treaty, which received the overwhelming support of the planters, offered tax reforms to Cuban landholders and greater representation of Cuban interests in Madrid, but offered emancipation only to those slaves who had served in the revolutionary army. To most Afrocubans, the agreement was entirely unsatisfactory. Their anger over Zanjón led to the Protest of Baraguá, a de facto mutiny within the revolutionary forces in which large numbers of primarily black and mulatto soldiers led by Antonio Maceo refused to accept the accord and lay down their arms.[17]

León (1991b) describes the development of Cuban nationalism as composed of two phases: the early nineteenth century through the early twentieth, and the 1920s to the present. He refers to the turn of the century as the end of a predominantly "white nationalist" era. In these years, the Afrocuban presence was accepted only in low-profile occupations subordinate to those of the overwhelmingly white middle classes and the elite (Zea 1986, 1345). After the Wars of Independence, however, Afrocubans could never again be easily dismissed by state officials. Plantation owners who had initiated the revolution and who eventually triumphed with the help of their slaves found themselves living with the consequences of their actions. By accepting Afrocubans as soldiers, they had implicitly accepted them as equal members of the free Cuban Republic they intended to create.

Many authors have suggested that the intervention of the United States in the conflict after 1898 may have been inspired by racial tensions. Cuban civic leaders continued to ask for (and eventually received) North American military aid in the late 1890s after the insurgents had achieved a clear military advantage. This suggests that instead of protection from Spain, white landowners actually wanted protection from their own army. They feared what the victory of a predominantly Afrocuban military force would mean for their country and hoped to avoid challenges to the established racial hierarchy (Arredondo 1939, 32).

Controversy Over the *Danzón*

The Cuban *danzón,* a ballroom dance genre, is the most important musical form associated with the Wars of Independence. Its rise to national prominence represents a cultural revolution of sorts that paralleled the armed rebellion against Spain. Although primarily derived from European traditions, *danzón* remained controversial for many years as a result of its strong associations with Afrocubans and Haitians. The genre can be viewed as symbolizing Cuba's early attempts to define itself in cultural terms that tended to exclude Afrocuban expression. Considered by many to be the first form of national music (e.g., Faya 1993), the *danzón* may have developed as early as the 1850s among the black urban poor of Matanzas.[18] By the early 1870s, however, it had been appropriated by members of middle-class black social clubs and transformed into a "respectable" ballroom dance.

Stylistically, *danzones* are descended from *bailes de cuadros* (square dances) popular among the Cuban middle classes beginning at the turn of the nineteenth century such as the *danza* and *contradanza*. Carpentier suggests that the overall sound of the *danzón* is virtually identical to that of these earlier genres (1946, 237). All are performed in duple meter by orchestras of European instruments such as the violin, acoustic bass, clarinet, trombone, and cornet (Schloss 1982, 1), as well as the *timbal,* which plays a constant rhythmic pattern. The most common timbal pattern consists of a *cinquillo* (five-note) figure followed by four quarter notes, as illustrated in figure 1.

Choreographically, *danzones* are performed by a couple holding each other in a loose embrace—a practice that was still uncommon in mid-nineteenth-

FIGURE 1

century Cuba and accounts for some of the early reactions against the genre (Castillo Faílde 1964, 87). Four distinct dance steps, the *paseo, cadena, sostenido,* and *cedazo,* are performed in succession over eight-measure phrases. Unlike many Cuban dances of the twentieth century, ballroom *danzón* choreography demonstrates little African influence, with the upper body remaining immobile and most steps involving motion from the knee down only.[19]

The most heated years of controversy over the *danzón* in the Cuban press were the 1870s and 1880s, as the dance grew more popular throughout the island. Critics denounced it for various reasons; commentaries in newspapers such as the *Diario de la Marina,* the *Aurora del Yumurí* (both conservative Spanish-owned publications), *La Voz de Cuba,* and *El Eco de Las Villas* attacked the *danzón* as "diabolical" and "contrary to Christianity" (Carpentier 1946, 237) because of its associations with prostitution and "improper" racial mixing. They characterized its dance steps as "lascivious," a degenerate form of *tango africano* slave dances (Castillo Faílde 1964, 144).

In the wake of its popularization in Havana by bandleader Miguel Faílde, the *danzón* was also criticized for its possible origin among *abakuá* groups. Although *abakuá* traditions do not seem to have affected the *danzón* musically or choreographically, it is likely that Faílde and many of the musicians in his orchestra were members of such brotherhoods (Lapique Becali 1993a). The occasional black and mulatto orchestras attempting to perform *danzones* with non-European hand percussion such as the *güiro* (gourd scraper) or *chéquere* were condemned for bringing "savage" Africanisms into the ballroom.

All of these objections resulted in municipal prohibitions against *danzón* performance in various cities during the late 1880s (Martínez Furé 1994), as well as the refusal of some black and white social groups to allow *danzones* to be played in recreational events. Though minimal by today's standards, the perceived African influences in the *danzón* represented a serious threat to middle-class Cubans in the nineteenth century. Acceptance of the *danzón* was equated with beginning a process that would result in the "deformation" or "miscegenation" of (European-derived) Cuban culture. As one observer remarked, "We began with the *danza,* then came the *danzón* . . . soon it will be the rumba, and, as is only natural, we'll all end up dancing like *ñáñigos.*"[20] Musical commentary of this sort makes clear that the ostensible acceptance of Afrocubans as members of the nation during the struggle for independence did not imply an acceptance of African-influenced cultural forms; these continued to be condemned.

Although *danzones* achieved greater acceptance in later years, middle-class attitudes toward the genre remained ambivalent through the early 1890s. Young society girls reportedly fled the dance floor if they heard a *danzón* and would wait for the the next *danza* or waltz (Martínez Furé 1994). These attitudes shifted, however, with the end of the War of Independence and the formation of the Republic. Beginning in 1898, with the U.S. military occupation, Cuba was inundated with North American music and dance, including the two-step, fox-trot, and turkey trot. In the context of high nationalist sentiment following the war and this barrage of foreign culture, the *danzón* seems to have taken on new meanings. After independence, it was increasingly accepted rather than condemned as lewd or foreign. References to its origins among the black population of Matanzas all but disappeared.

By the 1910s and 1920s, composer and musicologist Eduardo Sánchez de Fuentes flatly denied any influence of Afrocuban culture on the *danzón*, stating on various occasions that "no African elements of any sort" contributed to its formation (1928b, 167). He described the *contradanza* in a similar manner, emphasizing its stylistic roots in England and France and failing to mention that it had arrived via Haiti with black and mulatto immigrants in the 1790s (1928a, 32). Sánchez de Fuentes's generation had witnessed the development of several new Afrocuban dance genres that posed significant challenges to contemporary notions of "equitable balance" between African and Hispanic stylistic influences (Grenet 1939, xxx). The subdued Africanisms of the *danzón* compared favorably with *comparsa* or *son* music among conservatives, for instance, and made the former much more susceptible to discursive appropriation.

The history of the *danzón* is important in interpreting mainstream attitudes toward the twentieth-century Afrocuban musics that constitute the primary focus of this study. It demonstrates that controversy over "Africanisms" is not unique to modern Cuba. It further suggests that cyclical processes involving an initial rejection of syncretic Afrocuban culture, and later its nationwide appropriation, have some precedent. Time and again, the reactions of the Cuban middle classes reflect two distinct "readings" of emerging syncretic genres. The fusion of African-derived stylistic traits, imagined or real, with European forms are condemned by some as *"atraso"* (backwardness) and accepted by others as uniquely Cuban.

These opposing views result from a contradiction inherent in Cuban popular music: the genres that best symbolize the nation through the fusion of African and Hispanic characteristics are those of poor blacks and mulattos, and are therefore the sorts of expression least acceptable to the Hispanic elite as national symbols. The tension between an elite bias against African-influenced expression and a simultaneous attraction to it as a symbol of nationhood have defined the parameters of controversy surrounding popular music to the present day. Fundamental shifts in the attitudes of Cubans toward Afrocuban expression have typically occurred in moments of crisis involving civil war and economic collapse. This suggests that ideological reformations of the nation-state result from conscious strategies on the part of civil leaders to create more inclusive constructs of "the people," to create unity out of divisiveness.

Afrocubans and National Culture in the Early Republic

It is surprising in a socialist country like Cuba that so little history "from below" has been written to document the personal experiences of the working classes and other marginal groups. Few oral histories of any sort exist, and even fewer concentrate specifically on the lives of Afrocubans.[21] Information of this sort in many cases can only be collected painstakingly through interviews and by studying popular literature. Regarding political and economic history, however, much more is available to the researcher. Cuba in the early twentieth century consisted of a small, largely white creole elite in urban areas, with most of the population living in relative poverty in the countryside. Their lives had changed little since the 1850s. The census of 1899 shows that Cuba had a population of about 1,600,000, 66 percent of whom described themselves as white, 33 percent as black or mulatto, and 1 percent Chinese (Helg 1990, 47). These figures varied according to province. Blacks and mulattos comprised as much as 43 percent of the population in Oriente by 1919 and only about 20 percent in the Havana area (Arredondo 1939, 84). The relative decrease in the Afrocuban population by 1899, relative to that of midcentury—when slaves and others of African descent comprised 58.5 percent of the total population (Paquette 1988, 298)—is attributed to the fact that most slaves brought to the island were male and could not marry. Afrocubans also died in battle or as a result of dislocation and malnourishment during the revolutionary period.

The turn of the century witnessed gradually accelerating urbanization, with ever larger numbers of the rural population migrating to the cities in search of employment, education, and a better life. Demographic shifts began involuntarily during the Wars of Independence, when Spain's Governor Weyler ordered the relocation of farmers into garrison towns as part of his campaign to isolate and identify *mambi* rebels. Following independence, trends in urbanization were further propelled by voluntary migration and by land sales in

Cuba. Sharecroppers found themselves displaced as the land they farmed and lived on was sold to North American and European entrepreneurs (Fornet 1967, 65). Small landowners, who often lacked the capital to invest in these enterprises, opted to sell their property and move to Havana or Santiago.

Foreign investment in Cuba reached dramatic proportions in the first decades of the twentieth century. Despite an ostensible desire to help the new Cuban economy thrive and expand independently, North American bankers often proved unwilling to lend money to landowners. Investors preferred instead to wait until private farmers went bankrupt and then buy them out at relatively low prices (Pérez 1986, 65–69). The utter destruction of elite-owned plantations and industries, which formed a central part of the strategy of revolutionary forces under Maceo and others, helped to win the war but left the country economically devastated, with little capital or equity with which to rebuild. U.S. officials had long sought economic control of the island, and they used the United States' military intervention in the war to justify mass economic intercession at its conclusion (Benjamin 1990, 7, 32).

During the four years of U.S. military occupation after the defeat of Spain (1898–1902), North Americans controlled all facets of Cuban government and heavily influenced foreign policy with regard to trade and investment. Between 1896 and 1911, land purchases and other sales to North Americans quadrupled from $50 to $205 million (Aguilar 1972, 24). The portion of the sugar crop produced by U.S.-owned mills increased from 15 percent in 1906 to 48 percent in 1920 and 75 percent by 1928 (Pérez 1986, 188). Cuba through the early 1930s epitomized the capitalist's dream come true by providing inexpensive land, allowing the importation of cheap labor from neighboring islands such as Haiti and Jamaica, and setting no legal limits on the extent of foreign monopoly over industry. Whether one considers mining, utility companies, railroads, banking, agriculture, shipping, or other major areas of Cuban commerce, it is apparent that from the first years of "independence" Cuba was dominated by North American economic interests. In this sense, it remained colonized to an even greater extent than it had been under Spanish rule.

Racial Conflict in the Early Republic

Racial issues did not figure prominently in political debate of early twentieth-century Cuba, but to the extent they did appear, discussion tended to invoke the writings of the white intellectual and revolutionary José Martí (1853–1895). A progressive thinker on many fronts, Martí advocated the acceptance of Afrocubans as equal members of society and actively collaborated with black Cubans such as Rafael Serra (1858–1909) while in exile in the United States. Martí tended to express his views in idealized rather than objective form, however, and because he was killed before independence it remains unclear how his views would have translated into public policy. Martí's writings can hardly be criticized for the goals of racial harmony they promote, but they do strike the reader as naive; they abound with flowery rhetoric but lack substance. This was undoubtedly due in part to their function as political propaganda for the insurgency.

Martí asserted that as a result of the common struggle against Spanish oppression, white Cuban soldiers had overcome the biases inherited from three centuries of slavery. Avoiding the fact that controversies over racism continued to surface within the revolutionary army, Martí declared that the country no longer needed to fear domestic racial warfare. "The sublime emancipation of the slaves by their masters" during the Wars of Independence, he writes, has "erased . . . all of the hate of slavery"; the souls of dying revolutionaries, black and white, have "risen together in the air over the battlefields of Cuba" and are joined as one.[22] Far from curbing racial divisions in the new Republic, Martí's commentaries were often used by early twentieth-century politicians to deny allegations of bigotry and to suggest that the revolution had solved such problems.[23] In retrospect, Martí might have better served his country by recognizing and addressing objective social problems rather than confining himself to idealism.

Whereas most Latin American countries expelled large numbers of Spanish citizens following independence, the percentage of Spanish nationals living in Cuba grew significantly in the early 1900s. This was due in part to the exclusion of Cubans from the (U.S.-dominated) peace accords with Spain and the resulting inability of insurgents to seize colonial goods and property. It was also partly the result of an unwritten policy of "whitening," which Cuban officials supported by subsidizing the arrival of new immigrants from Spain and the Canary Islands. Between 1898 and 1916, approximately 440,000 Spanish-speaking settlers came to live in Cuba either from Spain itself or former colonies. By 1929 this figure had increased to 900,000 (Helg 1990, 56). At the same time, laws restricting immigration from Asian and other non-Caucasian countries were strengthened. The arrival of so many new citizens glutted the already competitive job market and led to racial conflicts on many occasions, as newly arrived Spaniards received jobs more quickly than black Cuban nationals. In a country already infamous for chronic unemployment, Afrocubans found themselves competing at a disadvantage with more and more unemployed whites and fewer jobs.[24]

As a result, the first decades of the twentieth century resulted in growing disappointment and frustration among blacks and mulattos. After three decades of nearly continuous armed conflict against Spain, in which their contributions had proven decisive to independence, they found themselves in the same marginal position. Pensions and compensation were not readily granted to any veterans, especially Afrocubans. The newly formed Cuban Congress, comprised overwhelmingly of white delegates, refused to offer token government positions even to prominent blacks such as General Quintín Banderas. Administrative posts had special importance in a country with little domestic industry and in which taxation and federal revenues comprised much of the wealth under the control of Cuban nationals. Moreover, United States transitional authorities exacerbated racial tensions by excluding blacks and mulattos from positions of authority in the newly formed national army (Pérez 1988, 211).

For all these reasons, but especially because of their exclusion from government and lack of employment options, Afrocuban *mambises* began to protest. Their complaints first erupted in violence during the August Revolution of 1906. More typically remembered as an event inspired by the fraudulent re-election of President Tomás Estrada Palma, the August Revolution was racially motivated as well, with Afrocubans comprising over 90 percent of the insurgents (Arredondo 1939, 58). Cuban officials openly rejected any prospect for peaceful mediation, correctly assuming that U.S. armed forces would be sent in to settle the disturbance and protect national business interests. Seventy-year-old Quintín Banderas, a central figure in the uprising, was assassinated in his sleep by soldiers under orders from the Estrada Palma administration (Pérez Rodríguez 1988, 1:159). Following the suppression of this rebellion, the United States organized and trained a new Cuban military force, the *ejército permanente,* to help national forces "maintain order."

During the first decade of the century, Afrocuban soldiers and intellectuals largely abandoned the hope of achieving their integrationist goals by cooperating with existing political parties. Any lingering faith in fair representation disappeared after the national elections of 1908, in which not a single black candidate was elected to public office (Helg 1990, 55). In response to these events, activist Evaristo Estenoz formed the Partido Independiente de Color (PIC) as a means of empowering the Afrocuban third of the population. The party grew rapidly and by 1910 boasted 20,000 members, posing a significant challenge to the established Conservative and Liberal Parties. After 1910, authorities took the threat of the PIC seriously enough to harass and jail its leaders, and to denounce members as racist for joining a party that promoted the interests of a minority over those of the country. Ironically, Martín Morúa Delgado, the only Afrocuban senator of his day, was the author and sponsor of a law passed in 1910 that formally prohibited the formation of political groups on the basis of race and thus made the PIC illegal.

Estenoz and his supporters were unwilling to accept the demise of the PIC and staged a revolt in May 1912 in Oriente, where public sentiment strongly favored the party. Taking advantage of the newly formed national army trained and supplied by the United States, President José Miguel Gómez sent troops to the area to crush the rebellion. Their ruthless tactics resulted in the death of over four thousand blacks and mulattos, the majority illiterate farmers without firearms. Helg describes this massacre, known as the Guerrita del Doce (Little War of 1912), as a deliberate "racist repression aimed at terrifying blacks and mulattos and keeping them out of political power" (1990, 56). In this sense it was quite successful, as organized political protest by Afrocubans ended abruptly and did not emerge again for decades. At the height of the conflict, government representatives are said to have paid five dollars for every black male cadaver brought to Santiago, with no questions asked about his identity or his involvement in the protests.[25]

Afrocuban Cultural Repression in the Early Republic

The political events of 1900–1920 have their analogue in the cultural realm. Various forms of overt repression of Afrocuban culture had existed in colonial times, but a de facto "war on Africanisms" became much more pronounced after the 1880s. This period coincides wtih the abolition of slavery in 1886 and an attempt by emancipated blacks to further integrate themselves into society. Cultural forms practiced for centuries by Afrocubans suddenly became more visible and as a result more threatening. Because the constitution of the new Republic ostensibly afforded blacks and mulattos rights and privileges equal to those of whites, culture came to serve as an important social marker and as justification for maintaining racially based social hierarchies. As Leal states, it was only after the "black [was] 'free,' potentially equal to the white, that it was necessary to find new methods of discrimination that would demonstrate his savagery, his incapacity to achieve the status of the rest of the population" (1982, 234).

Discourse about Afrocubans at the turn of the century became more accusatory and antagonistic, with cultural expression the focus of public controversy. Assertions of the inherent racial superiority of whites are found in the writings of even relatively liberal Cubans (e.g., Castellanos 1914, 341); blacks were commonly likened to apes or described as "a race vegetating in childhood" (Helg 1990, 48). Denunciations of this type continued into the 1930s (Urrutia 1935a, 8). Social groups such as the Liga Blanca de Cuba and El Orden de los Caballeros—a Cuban chapter of the Ku Klux Klan—were formed with the express purpose of "whitening" Cuba demographically and culturally, and extricating blacks and mulattos from every facet of national life (Kutzinski 1993, 146; Urrutia 1935b, 20).

The suppression of Afrocuban cultural expression by police and other municipal authorities took various forms. African-derived religion became a target of officials who pronounced it a "social pathology" brought by slaves to the Americas, a manifestation of the psychological inferiority of blacks. Prominent figures of the 1910s such as Fernando Ortiz called for the total prohibition of *santería* worship (Moore 1994, 34–36) in order to purge the nation of "degenerate" cultural practices. Police captain Rafael Roche Monteagudo devoted his entire career to this goal, seeking out houses in which worship services were taking place, arresting those involved, and confiscating or destroying altars, iconography, musical instruments, and ceremonial costumes (Roche Monteagudo 1925, 882–90).

Perhaps because of the practice associated with a few Afrocuban religious sects in Cuba (most notably *palo monte*) of using human bones in their rituals, African-derived religions were often falsely accused of involving child sacrifice. Chávez Alvarez (1991) documents this phenomenon and cites half a dozen well-publicized trials through the late 1920s in which blacks were convicted and in a few cases put to death for allegedly kidnapping and killing white children.[26] In most cases, investigations revealed that the murders had actually been committed by whites who mutilated the bodies in various ways to implicate black suspects. Performers asked to play religious music at *toques de santo* (Afrocuban religious events) were forced as a result of public hysteria to wrap or otherwise conceal their instruments, as the mere possession of such "artifacts of witchcraft" could mean incarceration (Martínez Furé 1966, 45).

Authorities additionally targeted *ñáñigo* ceremonies, alleging that *ñáñigo* groups were nothing more than criminal organizations. *Náñigo* societies were officially outlawed by the new Cuban government in 1903, just as they had been under colonial rule (Kutzinski 1993, 5). Police in many instances intervened in street celebrations involving music and *diablito* masked dancing, a tradition derived from nineteenth-century Epiphany celebrations (see chapter 3); offenders were incarcerated or fined, and all "attributes of *ñañiguismo*" destroyed (Roche Monteagudo 1925, 73, 890).

Rumba musicians and dancers often received similar treatment from police (see chapter 6), as did performers of other Afrocuban secular musics entirely unrelated to either *santería* or *ñáñigo* ceremony, such as *coros de clave* and *conjuntos de son* (see chapter 4). In 1922, only a few scant years before the onset of the *afrocubanismo* movement, the administration of Alfredo Zayas (1920–1924) passed comprehensive legislation that prohibited Afrocuban gatherings involving drumming and dance (see appendix). Because of the affront they were believed to represent to the moral values of the white middle classes, and because of the associations between such activity and the "theft, abduction, or murder of [children] of the white race," Zayas banned all performances of rumba, *santería,* and *abakuá* ceremony, as well as other African-influenced expression. The extent to which this legislation was enforced remains unclear. The mere wording of the prohibition, however, describing Afrocuban artistic forms as "symbols of barbarity," testifies to the extent of cultural intolerance at that time.[27]

Cultural Evolutionism and Early Publications on Afrocubans

As we have seen, two interpenetrating discourses about race permeated Cuban literature in the early 1900s. The first consisted of intellectuals who conceived of racial evolution in Darwinian terms, suggesting that blacks and other non-Caucasians were mentally and physically inferior to whites because they had not yet "evolved" to the same extent as Western Europeans. Discourses of this type were promoted by Oswald Spengler and other nineteenth-century intellectuals later associated with the Nazi Party in Germany, and also by Italians such as Enrico Ferri, Cesare Lombroso, and Alfonso Asturaro, who heavily influenced Cuban academics (Le Riverend 1973, 12).

A second discursive position that became more prominent in Cuba from the late 1910s based racial pronouncements on psychological or cultural criteria. It suggested that in physical terms blacks and members of other races were the potential equals of Caucasians, but their traditions and modes of behavior were heavily influenced by an earlier "stage" of cultural development. The best means of integrating minorities into Cuban society, from this perspective, was to suppress African-derived expression and to inculcate "superior" Western middle-class norms and values. Judgments of this sort by intellectuals justified and perpetuated the campaigns of "de-Africanization" in Cuba. Several authors who came to epitomize the early struggle to valorize Afrocuban arts and whose later works and activism promoted their greater appreciation—most notably, Fernando Ortiz—began the study of Africanisms primarily in order to facilitate their eradication.[28]

Before 1935, the investigation of subjects related to the black population was effectively taboo for most middle-class Cubans; academic literature of the day contains little discussion of them. Israel Castellanos figures prominently among the few who commented on Afrocubans. Born in 1891, Castellanos dedicated himself from an early age to the study of anthropology and related subjects, and began publishing in the 1910s (Abascal 1930). Like his contemporary Fernando Ortiz, Castellanos became involved in "racial criminology" as a result of exposure to works such as Lombroso's treatises from the 1870s (Le Riverend 1973, 12). Much of his research was an attempt to draw correlations between "deviant behavior"[29] and perceived physical anomalies among incarcerated blacks in Havana (Castellanos 1914a; 1914b; 1916). (Deviant behavior to Castellanos consisted of involvement in African "witchcraft" as well as acts of robbery or other forms of violence.) His studies contain charts giving detailed measurements of the body parts of over a hundred Afrocuban subjects, including the size of lips, earlobes, and women's breasts, nose width, shape of the forehead, and estimated size of the skull cavity. Such measurements proved to Castellanos that blacks bore a marked physical resemblance to the Neanderthal ancestors of Europeans, and that their bodies thus provided indications of retarded evolutionary development. Castellanos depicted blacks in general as physically, mentally, and morally inferior to Caucasians (1914a, 334; 1916, 7).

In a similar manner, Castellanos asserted that particular forms of artistic expression such as dance could be used to distinguish between the races and their respective states of evolution from primate ancestors. By analyzing the rhythms of dance music, the cadences of body movement, emotional attitudes manifested by dancers (almost certainly a veiled reference to the expression of sexual desire), and the parts of the body emphasized in dance, he argued, "one can distinguish between inferior and superior races" (1914b, 152). Masked *diablito* dancing was cited as an example of a vulgar tradition representing premodern civilization (1916, 66). Afrocubans in the twentieth century had "advanced" culturally as a result of their exposure to Western civilization, Castellanos suggested, but their parents and grandparents who danced in slave barracks did little else than twitch involuntarily to the loud, irregular pulsing of drumbeats. "The miserable slaves [danced] like barbarians," he wrote; "African dance of the *barracones*, because of its selvatic movements, might better be described as irrational leaping. . . . When slaves [hear the sound of the drum] they lose control over their own persons."[30] In the best interests of the Afrocuban population, Castellanos called for a national campaign of reeducation to help those with little exposure to European traditions learn more about them:

> We must elevate the moral [and cultural] level [in Cuba, and] educate the
> unrefined mental processes of those who continue holding fast to the barbarous
> foundations [of black life] whose influence makes such tenebrous habits
> continue. . . . [We] must subdue [those] incapable of adapting themselves to the
> juridic confines of civilized nations.[31]

Although in later years Castellanos asserted his opinions less aggressively, he remained critical of Afrocuban culture. He continued to use adjectives such as "primitive" and "barbaric," for example, when referring to Día de Reyes celebrations (1927, 37). Even during the heyday of *son* and other Afrocuban musics in Havana, he suggested that "the music of blacks . . . has been judged, even by the least severe critics, as more deafening than beautiful" and that "the majority of their instruments tend to make noise rather than agreeable sounds."[32] To Castellanos, the drum was a primitive instrument, derived from the same sorts of feeble mental processes that led to traditions of scarification and witchcraft among slaves and their descendants. The study of Afrocuban music and dance interested him not as an investigation of contemporary artistic forms, but an instantiation of the living past. He considered such expression important despite its unappealing qualities because it contributed to a fuller understanding of cultural "advance" in Cuba away from "degeneracy" and toward "civility."

Another central figure in early Afrocuban studies was Fernando Ortiz, whose attitudes toward Afrocuban cultural practices changed much more than those of Castellanos (see Moore 1994). Before the early 1920s Ortiz's writings demonstrated a disdain for African-influenced expression. His earliest work, *Los negros brujos* (The black witches) from 1906, condemned *santería* as a grave social affliction; similar pronouncements can be found more than two decades later in his studies of teeth filing as well as of musical traditions among African descendants (1920; 1929a). As with Castellanos, Ortiz's interest in Africanisms stemmed initially from a desire to better understand and remedy the social ills of the nation perpetuated by blacks. He considered cultural "atavisms" to be gradually disappearing as Afrocubans gained exposure to Western culture and wished to document the process.

Aside from conducting independent research, Ortiz worked actively in the 1910s for the Cuban government and established himself as a witness for the prosecution of Afrocuban religious leaders (Helg, personal communication). Later in life, Ortiz's attitudes toward Afrocuban culture changed significantly. He fought against racism in Cuba, founded the Society of Afrocuban Studies, and published several detailed studies of Afrocuban music in the 1950s that for the most part valorized such traditions. These latter works are widely known and have led to the overwhelmingly positive evaluations of Ortiz in recent years. Far from being noncontroversial, however, most of Ortiz's publications are replete with troublesome ideological implications. The intellectual trajectory of Ortiz's career metaphorically echoes the struggles of the entire nation to reposition their collective identity relative to black culture and to accept Afrocuban expression as Cuban.[33]

Segregation and Job Discrimination in the 1920s and 1930s

Segregation and employment discrimination also had an impact on Afrocuban musical production and performance of the 1920s and 1930s (see Arredondo 1939; Betancourt 1940; de la Fuente 1995; and Helg 1991). One of the most pervasive forms of discrimination was that associated with employment. Blacks as a rule enjoyed access only to blue-collar jobs as bricklayers, farmers, tailors, shoemakers, bakers, dockworkers, agricultural wage laborers, or soldiers. Even when soliciting blue-collar workers, however, many employers preferred to hire whites. Classified ads in the *Diario de la Marina* from 1927 include job announcements for cooks, chauffeurs, gardeners, porters, maids, seamstresses, and other domestics that specifically request *españoles, peninsulares,* or "blancos con un tiempo en el país" (whites who have lived some time in the country).[34] Other, slightly more prestigious manual jobs such as typesetting and working as a streetcar conductor were typically off limits to Afrocubans. Companies generally declined to justify their hiring practices or, in the case of streetcar employers, explained that many "society women [that is, white women] have expressed their repulsion at the possibility of entering into physical contact with black hands while paying their fares."[35] The only easily available jobs for Afrocubans as a result were the most menial and poorly paid, such as janitorial work, newspaper vending, working under short-term labor contracts available during the annual sugarcane harvest, and "invented" occupations such as shoe shining or street hawking.

In terms of white-collar employment, the market was even more difficult to penetrate. Of the 1,345 lawyers listed in the national census of 1907, for instance, only four were black or mulatto (Arredondo 1939, 59). Though they constituted approximately 25 percent of the population of Havana Province, Afrocubans in that same year made up less than 6.5 percent of the region's white-collar professionals; by 1919, the figure had risen to only 8.9 percent (Schwartz 1977, 63). In addition, they tended to be paid less for white-collar work than whites (de la Fuente 1995, 156). Census data analyzed by de la Fuente demonstrates that in 1929 blacks and mulattos remained significantly underrepresented in all preprofessional university programs, with their proportional representation never more than 55 percent of what it should have been, given overall demographics (ibid., 153).

Betancourt suggests that overt prejudice was not generally the most difficult barrier to white-collar employment for blacks and mulattos. Rather, he feels that white dominance tended to be perpetuated by the nepotistic practices of business owners who gave jobs to relatives and friends before other applicants.[36] In this way, established hierarchical patterns of social positioning according to race were perpetuated without concerted policies of discrimination. While Betancourt may be correct, the tangible results of such informal preferences differed little from the impact of racial barriers established by law. Through the 1930s, blacks were "systematically denied" access to all important posts of public administration other than the police force or the army (Betancourt 1940, 9). They rarely found work as nurses, pharmacists, or in the health industry, and they were virtually never hired to work in banks, retail stores, radio stations, utility companies owned by U.S. business interests, and many other enterprises (de la Fuente 1995, 155; Betancourt y García 1936, 9; Portuondo Calá 1937, 12; Rocillo 1993; Martínez Furé 1994). The combined effect of these limitations was to force Afrocubans to support themselves in the few areas of the job market not explicitly denied to them, including entertainment. Understandably, they were also highly overrepresented in illicit activities such as robbery and prostitution.

Examples of segregation and discrimination can be found in other facets of Cuban social life. Many of the wealthier districts of the city, including Miramar and Vedado, had unwritten policies of excluding black residents (Betancourt y García 1936, 9). Although ostensibly available to all, hospitals in Havana offered beds and services to eight white patients for every black or mulatto (Arredondo 1939, 59). Most of the larger hotels in Havana and other cities refused to accept blacks and mulattos as patrons. These included the Plaza and Sevilla Biltmore Hotels on the Prado, built and controlled by North American investors (Martínez Furé 1994, 7), as well as other Cuban-owned establishments including the Hotel Nacional in the Vedado district and the Royal Palm, San Rafael, Bristol, and Saratoga Hotels in Centro Habana (Bacallao 1994). The Hotel Lafayette in Habana Vieja refused a room to mulatto singer and composer Miguel Matamoros early in his career (Rodríguez Domínguez 1978, 51). Segregated policies remained in effect in a number of Cuban hotels through the 1950s.[37]

Many oceanfront venues in western Havana, Varadero, and other parts of the island reserved their beaches exclusively for white swimmers.[38] Public parks and central plazas in major cities, including Santa Clara, Ciego de Avila, and Trinidad, were also notorious for policies of segregation (Fernández Robaina 1992). Sometimes such practices led to violence; on 7 January 1934, for instance, a race riot broke out in Trinidad over the exclusion of blacks from Céspedes Park. It resulted in the death of mulatto journalist Félix Justo Proveyer and the destruction of black middle-class businesses and property (Arredondo 1939, 64). While segregated schools did not exist legally, racial separation was maintained by private schools that charged more for matriculation than most Afrocubans could afford (Hirrezuelo 1994). Public schools during the Republic thus became predominantly black schools and were poorly funded. Economic necessity forced many black and mulatto children to leave school at an early age to help support their families, which in turn contributed to their lack of education and marketable job skills as adults.

Alternative Politics and the "Black Problem"

Politically, the twenties and thirties continued to be a period of disenfranchisement for Afrocubans. Although José Armando Pla and a few labor activists emerged who attempted to consolidate black votes, their efforts produced few tangible results (Marinello 1936, 7). An awareness of discrimination re-

mained acute, however; journalist Gustavo Urrutia, one of the first Afrocubans
to be given a weekly editorial column in a major Cuban newspaper beginning
in the early 1930s, complained, "The Republic has not been able to fulfil its
social and economic promises [to the population of color]. That lovely revolutionary plan [of the 1890s] has been frustrated . . . [and] in practice everything conspires together for the discouragement and extinction [of blacks]."[39]
The established parties, the Conservatives and the Liberals, largely avoided or
denied racial issues, as they had done since independence.

Alternative political groups including the right-wing ABC Revolutionary
Party and the Communist Party, both founded in the 1920s, did make racial
issues somewhat more central in their respective platforms. Such changes did
not necessarily bode well for Afrocubans, however, and neither organization
initially included blacks or mulattos as prominent members. Martínez Furé
(1994) suggests that ABC representatives were open Nazi sympathizers, advo-
cating the demographic "whitening" of the nation through stricter immigration policies and the repatriation of Haitian and Jamaican migrant workers—
accusations borne out in some respects by their literature (see *Doctrina del
ABC*, 107). Jorge Mañach, a central figure both among the ABC intelligentsia
and in the Cuban literary world, considered Afrocubans to be mentally inferior to Hispanic Cubans for unfortunate historical reasons and did not support their inclusion in Cuban political activity until they managed to "*superarse*"
or "make advances" (Fernández Robaina 1994).

The Cuban Communist Party through the mid-1930s expressed a desire to
end the exploitation of Afrocubans in the workplace but did not apparently
envision them as part of the nation. Leaders advocated instead the relocation
of all blacks and mulattos to the province of Oriente and the creation of two
separate countries on the island, with black and white citizens, respectively.
This resolution, made during the meeting of the fourth Communist Congress
of the Confederación Nacional Obrera de Cuba and published in *Masas* magazine beginning in June 1934, termed their racially separatist policy *autodeterminación nacional* (national self-determination) (Arredondo 1939, 82; Serviat
1986, 117). The new "black territory" was to consist of the municipalities of La
Maya, Caney, Cobre, Guantánamo, Palma Soriano, Baracoa, Santiago, and parts
of Bayamo.

Segregation and Discrimination in the Entertainment Industry

Policies of discrimination affected Cuban cultural life in numerous ways. All
prominent hotels provided entertainment for their guests, but in the 1920s
and 1930s hotel managers almost never hired Afrocuban performers. In later
decades, it became more acceptable for Afrocubans to perform in major hotels

for white audiences, although they still could not rent rooms (Herrera 1993). Many club and cabaret owners in Havana also discriminated against clients on the basis of race. Cabarets in general were classified as *de primera, segunda,* or *tercera* (first, second, or third class), based on the number and quality of the acts they presented and their prices. Nearly all first-class cabarets refused entrance to blacks and mulattos as patrons through the 1950s, and frequently as performers as well.[40]

Second- and third-class cabarets, by contrast, were much more lenient in accepting black performers and clientele, and in some cases featured and were frequented primarily by them. A majority of the smaller and less prestigious cabarets were located either in Habana Vieja near the docks of the bay or on the beachfront areas of Marianao, renowned centers of prostitution as well as of music and dance (see chapter 6). Colonial authorities had officially desegregated Cuban theaters beginning in the 1880s (Leal 1980, 50), but for economic reasons most spectators on the ground floor in the early twentieth century tended to be white. Blacks, mulattos, and poor whites who wished to view events generally sat in the gallery. Bandleader Antonio Arcaño (1992) mentions that as a rule theaters would not hire black musicians to play in their house orchestras; at least none worked in the Encanto, América, and Riviera Theaters, where he performed regularly in the 1930s and 1940s.

Private clubs and social organizations, which provided another important source of income for musicians and entertainers, often refused to hire Afrocubans. Many different kinds of clubs existed in early twentieth-century Havana, the most exclusive being the Havana Yacht Club, the Miramar Yacht Club, and the Country Club. These institutions, located in expansive buildings in the high-rent areas west of Havana and frequently on stretches of beachfront as well, never admitted nonwhite members and rarely contracted black performers (Bacallao 1994). Segregation was so rigidly enforced at the Havana Yacht Club that Fulgencio Batista himself is said to have been refused membership the 1940s (Fernández Robaina 1993).

Slightly less prestigious venues for the upper middle classes but with similarly segregated policies included the Vedado Tennis Club, the Casino Deportivo, and the Club Náutico. *Sociedades españoles,* social institutions organized by the region in Spain from which one's family emigrated, represented yet another location off-limits to Afrocuban performers through the late 1920s; they were only rarely amenable to hiring them in later years (Quiñones 1992). The *sociedades* controlled tremendous financial assets and played a significant role in Cuban social life. In many cases, they boasted tens of thousands of members and organized music and dance events weekly. Among the largest were the Centro Gallego and Centro Asturiano (the Galician and Asturian Centers), located in massive buildings on either side of Havana's central park; others included the Centro de Dependientes, the Asociación Canaria, the Centro Vasco, and the Casino Español, all in downtown Havana.[41]

For their part, the Afrocuban middle classes organized their own exclusive social organizations known as *sociedades de color*, or simply *liceos*. Some of these groups, such as the Club Atenas[42] and the Minerva, catered primarily to Havana's black elite. They accepted only university graduates as members, maintained strict dress codes, and charged fees that were prohibitive even for most middle-class Cubans (J. Valdés 1994). Less exclusive *sociedades de color* existed in Havana as well, however. These included the Unión Fraternal,[43] the Antilla Sport Club, the Sociedad El Pilar, the Jóvenes del Vals, the Club Danzario, and the Club Las Águilas (Acosta 1993, 34).

In general, the music promoted by all *sociedades de color* consisted of heavily European-influenced genres. They regularly organized performances of what is today referred to as *"vieja trova"* repertory, popular song patterned after the arias of Italian opera. They encouraged involvement in Western art music among their members and contributed numerous performers to the Orquesta Sinfónica and Orquesta Filharmónica, both established in the early 1920s.[44] Frequently the clubs organized dance events featuring *danzón* orchestras (also known as *charangas*) such as the Orquesta Urfé, the all-female *charangas* of Dora Herrera and Doña Irene, the Orquesta Gris, and the Orquesta Aragón. (Some of these are discussed in chapter 4.) While white and integrated *danzón* groups existed in Cuba through the 1940s and beyond, most of those performing for the Afrocuban community consisted exclusively of black and mulatto musicians. Except for some percussionists, Afrocuban *danzoneros* represented a privileged group, having received formal musical training in Western-style conservatories, most typically the Escuela Municipal de Música in the Reina district or the Conservatory of Guanabacoa (Góngora Echenique 1928).

Far from wholeheartedly accepting a diversity of Afrocuban-influenced music and dance for their own recreational activities, the *sociedades de color* frequently forbade the use of drums or performance of genres such as *son, comparsa*, and rumba. In this respect, they were often less willing to compromise than their white counterparts, especially in later years after these genres had achieved national popularity. The Club Atenas, for instance, established a Comisión de Orden that monitored, among other things, the sorts of dance moves performed by guests and the instruments used in the band. It specifically forbade conga drums well into the 1940s (Martínez Furé 1994). Joseito Valdés remembers that his *charanga* was chastised for having brought drums to a performance in the Unión Fraternal during the same period; those in charge of the event only grudgingly permitted their use after the *conguero* agreed to sit behind a curtain (J. Valdés 1994). As late as the 1950s, *sociedades de color* refused to permit the performance of mambos, requiring instead only *música suave* (gentle music).

Working-class musical venues were also segregated. As in the southern United States, owners of dance halls often divided the floor with a rope, forcing blacks and mulattos to dance in an area separated from whites (Fernández Robaina 1992; Helg 1991, 5). Within Havana, the only public social areas where blacks, mulattos, and whites of all classes could mingle with some freedom were the smaller cabarets and clubs mentioned earlier, small local theaters, brothels, "dance academies" (see chapter 4), and the large beer gardens *(cervecerías)* of companies such as La Polar and La Tropical, which catered to the working-class community (Martínez Furé 1994). Even in these places, Afrocuban musical traditions involving drums and other percussion instruments were typically not allowed, gaining acceptance only gradually in the 1930s. Those working-class Afrocubans who could afford to listen to music at all—in theaters, beer gardens, and elsewhere—had to content themselves with accepted European-derived genres rather than the music of their own community. Private homes and street corners were thus the only haven for many forms of Afrocuban expression, even those of an entirely secular nature. Culturally and socially, working-class Afrocubans existed in a repressive environment that limited their actions and blocked their further integration into the national collectivity. Paradoxically, it was this bleak reality of racial division during the late 1920s and 1930s that gave rise to the domestic and international popularization of Afrocuban syncretic musics.

2 MINSTRELSY IN HAVANA

Music and Dance of the *Teatro Vernáculo*

〰〰〰〰〰〰〰〰〰〰〰〰〰〰

> We still lack a Cuban theater addressing interracial
> problems, in which the personification of people of color
> is not solely that of the funny white man with the face of a
> black charlatan and buffoon . . . but instead a stage on
> which the black can speak on his own, say "what comes
> from inside," and with his language, in his way, in his
> inflections, representing his emotions, even the most
> painful.[1]
> —Fernando Ortiz, prologue to Rómulo Latachañeré,
>   *El sistema religioso de los afrocubanos*

Of the wide variety of popular music in late nineteenth- and early twenti-eth-century Cuba, the history of song and dance performance within the *teatro vernáculo* (comic theater) is one of the most poorly documented traditions, rivaled in its obscurity only by the tourist cabaret. The importance of the *teatro vernáculo* to the development of Cuban popular music can hardly be overemphasized. Established as a distinct artistic form as early as the 1860s, it dominated all other kinds of commercial entertainment through the 1930s and maintained its popularity in slightly altered form through serial radio and television broadcasts into the 1950s and beyond.[2] As the first commercial form in which working-class Afrocuban music and dance were prominently repre-sented, and the first to (occasionally) address issues of racial discrimination, the comic theater was crucial in the formation of a new cultural identity for the nation that accepted African-influenced expression as Cuban. As such, it represents a precursor to the *afrocubanismo* movement of the 1920s and 1930s.

Conversely, by disseminating frequently derogatory images of black street culture and artistic expression, conceived and performed almost entirely by white Cubans, the popular theater also attests to the racial prejudice common in the early years of the Republic and the extent to which Afrocubans them-selves remained marginalized from most commercial music. More abstractly, the *teatro vernáculo* might be theorized as a forum of symbolic negotiation, a bounded artistic space in which concepts of *cubanidad*, derived from Hispanic- and African-derived cultural influences, as well as others from Europe and the United States, were slowly defined in the national consciousness. The meaning of Afrocuban stylistic influences in the comic theater varied greatly between the mid-nineteenth century and the mid-twentieth century. While initially little more than objects of derision or a source of comic relief, Afrocuban music and dance came to play increasingly important roles in the action of the *sainete* (one-act theatrical sketch) and to be associated with the national struggle for self-expression and liberation from colonial dominance.

Origins of the Genre

The Cuban comic theater—variously called *teatro bufo, teatro criollo, teatro vernáculo,* or *teatro de variedades*—developed largely from Spanish-derived theatrical forms such as the *tonadilla,* but was also influenced by French and North American theater.[3] The popularity of its antecedent forms in Havana and other urban areas of Cuba dates from the eighteenth century (González 1994). However, both the genre as a distinct entity and the parody of blacks and black street culture with which it is associated have their origins in the mid-nineteenth century. This was one of the most vigorous periods of the slave trade, when Cuba had the highest percentage of black and mulatto in- habitants relative to whites, a ratio of about 58 to 42 percent (Paquette 1988: 298).

Almost invariably, the action of the *sainete* took place in a working-class neighborhood or the central patio of a large urban tenement *(solar)*. As the plays tended to be short, they allowed for little character development and relied instead on established character types. In the earliest years, there was significant variation in the protagonists of the comic *sainete*, but by the late nineteenth century the characters had grown more standardized. They included the *negrito,* or comic black man, the *mulata,* or light-skinned black woman, and the *gallego,* or Spanish shopkeeper-businessman, with the occasional in- clusion of other figures such as the drunk, the policeman, the Chinese immi- grant, or the *negra lucumí* (the black "witch").[4]

The popularity of parodic representations of Afrocuban music and dance on the theater stage was paralleled by developments in other nineteenth-cen- tury arts. The first incorporation of comic black figures into Cuban literature in the works of *costumbristas* (writers of local genre sketches), as well as the paintings of Victor Landaluze, date from this era. Bartolomé Crespo y Borbón, a Spanish immigrant and early *costumbrista,* first parodied African-influenced speech in written form, creating a stylized literary version of the *bozal* dialect. Francisco Fernández also deserves mention as the creator of the *negro catedrático* or pretentious, semi-educated black.[5] Like Crespo y Borbón and Fernández, many other *costumbristas* who began as novelists or short story writers wrote for the comic theater after its popularity had been established.

Ironically, several of the best-known fictitious black characters of the *costumbrista* movement, such as Creto Gangá created by Crespo y Borbón, first appeared in print in the 1840s during the Ladder conspiracy (La Escalera), one of the most tragic moments in the history of Cuban race relations. The fact that many early *costumbristas* were Spanish-born suggests that foreigners, however biased their perspective, were often more willing to admit to a qualified interest in black cultural forms than their *isleño* compatriots. This trend continued into the early twentieth century. Spaniards Regino López and Federico Villoch became national celebrities for acting in and managing the Teatro Alhambra, an establishment for male patrons only and one of the most famous theaters featuring comic *sainetes* in Cuba's history.

The comic theater skyrocketed to popularity in the late 1860s. With the onset of the Ten Years' War (1868–1878) and the armed struggle for independence, it became increasingly recognized as an important form of national rather than Spanish-derived cultural expression. In just eight months, from May 1868 to January 1869, seven *teatro vernáculo* troupes formed in the Havana area and generated tremendous public interest (Díaz Ayala 1981, 63). The close association between these theatrical ensembles and the Cuban independence movement, as well as the extent to which overt political satire added to their appeal, were not lost on colonial authorities. At the opening of a controversial work by Juan Francisco Valerio in 1869, Spanish troops entered the theater and began firing indiscriminately into the crowd (Carpentier 1946, 252). Authorities banned all *teatro vernáculo* performances in mid-1869. This prohibition remained in effect until the Pact of Zanjón was signed in 1878, bringing a temporary end to hostilities.

Spanish officials never entirely banned theatrical production in Cuba again, but they did place significant restrictions on the content of stage shows, forbidding *sainete* authors from criticizing the government or discussing sensitive political issues. Policies of censorship seem to explain an increasing reliance on allusion and allegory, rather than overt political critique, in subsequent productions (Leal 1980, 75). The power of the comic theater as a political weapon despite colonial censorship is apparent when one considers the number of well-known writers for the stage, such as Miguel Salas, who were forced into exile after 1878 as a result of conflicts with authorities over the content of theater scripts (Robreño 1961, 27).

One common means of using the comic theater to make subtle political statements during the Wars of Independence was to employ racial characters as national symbols. From the late 1870s on, proindependence playwrights used depictions of Afrocubans and Afrocuban culture to refer to Cuba through their iconic and indexical associations with the island. In a similar fashion, figures such as the *gallego* represented Spain and Spanish colonial authorities. This gradual semiotic shift is difficult to analyze, given the lack of documentation on nineteenth-century popular culture—and the fact that such political references were outlawed. Nevertheless, it was crucial to dominant conceptions of *cubanidad* that emerged in subsequent decades. A combination of political censorship and rising nationalist sentiment during the 1895 revolution led to the inscription of the *negrito* and *mulata,* especially, with meanings never intended or foreseen by earlier *teatro vernáculo* authors. Afrocuban characters continued to serve as objects of public ridicule, and yet for the first time they also represented Cuba itself.

The importance of political commentary continued into the twentieth century in productions of the Teatro Alhambra. Examples include *El ciclón,* a work based on the events of the August Revolution of 1906; *La casita criolla* (1912), which concerned the racial violence of La Guerrita del Doce under President Miguel Gómez; *La isla de los cotorros* (1923), which made reference to the intentions of many in the United States to annex the Isle of Pines; *La reelección,* discussing the scandalous fraud associated with the Zayas administration in the 1920s; and *La intervención,* a commentary on the possibility of another U.S. marine landing in Cuba in the wake of the political violence of 1933.[6]

Many of the songs from the early twentieth-century theater that were re-edited as salon sheet music reveal similar topical and political content. One example is the Anckermann fox-trot "La danza de los millones" (1916), whose title refers to the spiraling global price of sugar throughout the decade. Another is "Siembra la caña" (1913), a stage parody of the Afrocuban *comparsa* songs incorporated after the 1910s into the political campaigns of politicians such as Mario Menocal. (See chapter 3.) Severe censorship of theater productions existed during the Republic as well, and comic actors were frequently harassed by police if their satires became too critical of the current administration (Arredondo 1981, 77, 120). Harassment and torture included detainment, peltings with stones, and in some instances being forced to drink toxic substances such as airplane fuel at gunpoint. These practices continued under Batista in the 1940s.

Although theatrical troupes toured throughout the island, especially during the *zafra* or sugarcane harvest, when workers had more money to spend on diversions, the center of such production was the Havana area (Hierrezuelo 1994). In the nineteenth century, comic theater shows tended to be presented in large, well-known establishments, with ticket prices high enough to limit the audience primarily to the white urban middle classes. (In 1899, for example, the average salary of a farm worker fluctuated between twenty and twenty-five pesos a month, while a ticket for a show featuring a celebrated performer often cost six or seven pesos.)[7] Plots of the early *sainetes* tended to be parodies of well-known light opera libretti, such as *La Duquesa de Haití,* based on Offenbach's *La Grande Duchesse de Gérolstein* from 1867.

By the late 1910s, however, with a modest increase in economic prosperity throughout the island, small theaters had opened all over Havana featuring smaller troupes, less extravagant performances, and more reasonable prices. Comic theater sketches alternated in these venues with short silent films, vocal performances, and other forms of entertainment, creating an ambience similar to that of turn-of-the-century North American vaudeville (Arredondo 1981, 65). The prominence of black and mulatto character types on stage meant that themes of poverty, unemployment, and interracial romance were sometimes incorporated into the comic theater.

Such was the popularity of the *teatro vernáculo* that virtually all of the well-known composers from the early twentieth century (Rodrigo Prats, Gonzalo Roig, Eliseo Grenet, and Moisés Simons, among others) began their careers conducting orchestras or writing music for productions of this sort. Prominent orchestras such as the Orquesta Hermanos Lebatard (many of whose members later formed the Lecuona Cuban Boys) first began playing in theaters and only later became famous in cabarets for the performance of jazz-influenced Cuban dance music.[8]

Racial Characters in the *Teatro Vernáculo*

Because of its reliance on stereotypes determined primarily by race, the one-act stage comedy represents a fascinating forum in which to analyze the ambivalent attitudes toward Africanisms and "blackness" on the part of middle-class and elite Cuban society. As in North American minstrel shows, Afrocuban characters in the Cuban theater were played by white actors who darkened their skin by using a combination of burnt cork and glycerine, typically wearing wigs as well (Arredondo 1981, 32). Afrocubans were systematically denied employment in the theater as late as the 1950s, and there are few well-known Afrocuban actors even today.[9]

In the turn-of-the-century theater, figures such as the *negrito, mulata,* and *gallego* became invested with archetypical power, figuring as central tropes for seventy or eighty years. As Linares (1992) notes, the popular theater effectively reinforced associations held by the largely white audience between Afrocubans and a wide variety of largely negative personal characteristics, including greed, lechery, stupidity, incompetence, wanton sexuality, and deceit. Most stage presentations tended to naturalize the degraded position of blacks in Cuba, presenting their poverty, lack of formal education, and miserable living conditions as the result of personal shortcomings rather than larger social processes. Conversely, some of the depictions of Afrocubans and their arts in the theater, especially in the twentieth century, can be viewed as racial critiques by authors sensitive to the oppression of blacks.

The Stage *Negrito*

Many variations of the *negrito* were incorporated into the *teatro vernáculo* in addition to the *negro catedrático* and *negro bozal,* already mentioned. These include the *negro calesero* or coach driver–slave, the *negro guarachero,* or fun-loving black, and the *negro jaranero,* or black troubador (Linares 1992). Each figure is associated with a distinct mode of dress and behavior. Some of the character subtypes date from the mid-nineteenth century, while others rose to prominence only after the Wars of Independence.[10]

The earliest references to the *negrito* as part of musical and theatrical performances appeared about 1812; author and playwright Francisco Covarrubias (1755–1850) is generally credited with one of the first representations of this character type (Leal 1980, 31). The nineteenth-century stage *negrito* (performed by a white actor for white audiences) might be considered the antithesis of the public images presented in Día de Reyes processions and other forms of non-commercial art performed largely by and for Afrocubans themselves. If the latter constituted a black "counterdrama," a form of cultural resistance, the stage *negrito* certainly represented an example of transformed or coopted artistic expression, the dominant society's perspective on Afrocuban culture. Leal writes:

> If Afrocuban forms of expression [such as the *Día de Reyes*] "represent" the black through black eyes . . . then white authors created its opposite in the *negrito,* that is to say, in the black character represented by white actors, for a white public, performing in Spanish or in *bozal* speech . . . and of course representing the point of view of the slave [and postslave] culture. It is in this way that the *negrito* has penetrated deeply into our history, altering [the perception] of the black so that he serves as a source of derision and ideological mockery.[11]

Afrocubans were the primary source of inspiration for parodic character types of the comic theater, although *guajiros* and other poor Hispanic Cubans, as well as Chinese workers, were also caricatured on occasion. Generally, the stage *negrito* occupies the lowest social and cultural rung relative to other figures, even in twentieth-century productions. His economic position is tenuous at best, his occupation depicted as subservient, criminal, or nonexistent. The *negrito* tends to be lacking in cultural development. His speech is deformed, his thought processes slow—attributes thought to be comic (López 1979, 695).

Yet from a musical perspective, the *negrito*'s role is pivotal, as it almost invariably involves song and dance as a central component. Of the hundreds of recordings of comic musical sketches derived from the *teatro vernáculo* made in the first decades of the twentieth century, a majority involve the performance of a *negrito*.

An example of this type of recording is the *diálogo y pregón* "El melonero" (The melon vendor) (Monteagudo 1924). The dialogue is mostly spoken, but it begins and ends with a stylized *pregón* or street cry as the *negrito* hopes to attract customers by describing the quality of his produce. The sketch involves interaction between a black man selling melons from a street cart and a *mulata* who happens to walk by. (The *negrito* is typically depicted as a hustler, trying to cheat customers and making sexual advances to all *mulatas* and light-skinned women.) Many of the most common themes used in representing the *negrito* are evident in this dialogue. They include the use of *catedrático* speech, involving the mispronunciation of complex words ("*síbala*" instead of *sílaba*, syllable; "*asquidente*" instead of *accidente*, accident; and "*si me enterio*" instead of *si me entero*, if I find out about) to ridicule the character. As in all comedy, punning, double entendres, and other word games play a prominent role in the dialogue. In "El melonero," the vendor asks the *mulata* if she is certain she doesn't want *el jamón*, a ham—by implication, a penis—instead of *el melón*, a melon. His song, consisting of a four-phrase diatonic melody over sustained, arpeggiated chords on the piano, is a highly stylized composition, much longer and more harmonically complex than the *pregones* used by actual street vendors.

Another black character type featured prominently in early twentieth-century recordings of *teatro vernáculo* material is the *negro calesero*. The *calesero*, a gaudily dressed coach driver–slave who inevitably believes himself to be extremely good-looking, is a common subject even in the mid-nineteenth-century *costumbrista* paintings of Landaluze. *Caleseros* and derived character types remained favorites into the 1930s both in the comic theater and in the somewhat more prestigious *zarzuela* (light opera, musical) performances associated with the Nacional and Regina Theaters.[12]

Perhaps the most famous musical sketch of all time featuring a *calesero* was written by Ernesto Lecuona in 1927 as part of the *zarzuela La niña Rita o La Habana en 1830*. It featured Rita Montaner in blackface as the coach driver–slave, a light-skinned Afrocuban female playing a *negrito* male.[13] The combined alteration of gender and racial identification in Montaner's role alludes to the semiotic complexity of Cuban theatrical performances and their many possible meanings for audience members. A modernized version of the same *calesero* scenario recorded by *teatro vernáculo* actors is the *diálago y canto* "El Ford" (Espígul 1916). The sketch portrays a *negrito* chauffeur, driving his employer's Ford, who makes advances to a passing *mulata* and invites her for a drive in the car. The interaction ends in a song with humorous lyrics that make obvious allusions to sex while discussing the automobile (for example, "Now, woman, now I'm getting up to speed . . . faster, faster . . . oh, the machine has blown out!").

Blackface theater was so popular and so widespread in early twentieth-century Cuba that it is impossible to mention all of the well-known white actors who based their careers on stylized depictions of Afrocubans in this way. Individuals such as "Tabernilla," Pepe Serna, Chicho Plaza, Rafael de Arango, Sergio Acebal, and Ramón Espígul stand out as important *negrito* actors of the period.[14] Arquímedes Pous, another influential actor who played such roles, is an interesting case in that rather than mocking Afrocubans, he is considered a champion in the fight against racial discrimination in Cuba. Born in Cienfuegos in 1891, Pous moved to Havana in search of work and education, and at age fifteen began his acting career in the Teatro Actualidades. Like many white performers, he came from a working-class background; he found that a stage career provided a relatively prestigious and potentially lucrative means of employment in a country known for chronic work shortages.

Pous was more successful than most other contemporary *negritos* for a number of reasons. One was his ability as a dancer; Rey (1994) reports that he was one of the few white actors capable of dancing various distinct forms of rumba based on the choreography of the traditional *columbia, guaguancó,* and *yambú.* Another reason for Pous's popularity was that, after forming his own company and beginning to write his own material in the early 1920s, he consistently presented plays that addressed important racial issues. These included scenarios, presented in *sainetes* such as *Del ambiente* (About the place) and *La canción del mendigo* (The song of the the beggar), in which an orphaned black boy is taken in and raised by a white family, only to be thrown out when he falls in love with a white woman (Robreño 1961, 39).

The issues of racial discrimination found in Pous's works were nothing new in Cuba, but they had never been brought into public discussion by being incorporated into popular theater shows. By 1923 Pous and company were performing regularly in the Teatro Cubano in Havana, as well as touring abroad in Mexico, Puerto Rico, the Dominican Republic, the United States, Canada, and Spain (Rego 1985, 17). Pous hired some of the most successful actresses of the day to tour with him, such as Luisa Obregón, Mimi Cal, Margot González, and Conchita Llauradó. Other works performed by the ensemble include *Oh, Mr. Pous* and *Habana-Barcelona-Habana,* both from 1924, as well as more musically based presentations such as *La clave de oro* and *Pobre Papá Montero,* the latter scored by Eliseo Grenet.[15] At the height of his career, in 1926, Pous died suddenly of appendicitis while on tour in Puerto Rico.

The Stage *Mulata*

As in the case of the *negrito,* many distinct subtypes of the *mulata* figure existed by the early twentieth century, including the *mulata de rumbo,* or "loose" woman of the street; the *mulata borracha,* or drunkard; the *chismosa,* or gossip; and the *sentimental,* or maudlin *mulata* (Martínez Rodríguez 1987). It is worth noting that a few actresses also became famous for interpreting roles of black women *(negras)* as well as mulatto women, although this was less common. Blanca Becerra, for instance, delighted audiences with her impersonation of a *negra lucumí,* or Yoruban woman from Africa, associated with "witchcraft" and divination (see illustrations). In general, the *negra* character type is distinct from the *mulata* in that she tends to be older and not as sexually appealing.

The *mulata* as cultural construct has a long history in Cuba. In novels, popular song, and in the theater, discourse about *mulatas* is perhaps more common than that of any other subject.[16] Many of the country's best-known literary works, such as Cirilio Villaverde's *Cecilia Valdés* (first published in 1839) adopt as their principal theme a love triangle involving a white man and black man and their competition for the attentions of a *mulata.* Novels such as these inevitably depict tragic stories of love restrained and eventually thwarted by social convention. From the seventeenth century on, the *mulata* has been frequently represented in song as well, with figures such as Michaela and Teodora Ginés, María Belén Chacón, María la O, and Amalia Batista becoming nationally recognized *mulata*-icons because of the popularity of compositions depicting them lyrically.

The construct of the *mulata* that most directly affects her portrayal in the *teatro vernáculo,* however, derives not from "high" art, but rather from the image found in *guarachas* and other songs of the nineteenth-century underclasses. These musical forms, along with the *danza, contradanza,* and other middle class–derived genres, gained popularity in *casas de cuna,* the nineteenth-century predecessor of *academias de baile* (see chapter 4). *Casas de cuna* were essentially centers of musical entertainment where white men went to socialize and/or sleep with women of color and where such women often sought to become involved with white men. The establishments played a central role in both interracial and interclass mixing in nineteenth-century Cuba and gave rise to a "mythology of the urban slum" (Carpentier 1946, 233), which provides the ideological underpinnings of most *teatro vernáculo* performances.

In the *guaracha* and related genres, the *mulata* appears above all as the object of sexual desire, the epitome of wanton carnal pleasure. She is viewed as the source of familial discord, a "danger" to married men, who pursues physical gratification to the point of self-destructiveness. The *guaracha* transforms the socially oppressed and marginal condition of black and mulatto women at the turn of the century, suggesting that they were only interested in sex. In 1882, A. O. Halloran provided many examples of this ubiquitous motif in his collection of lyrics from over 120 *guarachas*. An excerpt from "La negra del manglar," for instance, is typical:

> I'm made of sugar, for love
> And I'm made of fire, for pleasure
> Come, come and look at the *negrita* from the ghetto. . . .
> My waist is flexible, my heart a volcano
> How many men will despair over my lovely figure.[17]

Another example is entitled "La mulata":

> The mulata is like a piece of bread
> Which should be eaten warm
> Because if you let it cool off
> Not even the Devil would take a bite.[18]

Metaphorically associating the *mulata* with food is a common poetic device. Other means of depicting the *mulata* in song include giving detailed descriptions of parts of her body as she dances, especially the hips, breasts, and shoulders (Hallorans 1882, 100–01); descriptions of her in first person as she sings *pregones;* and occasionally as she sings about marital infidelity or the difficulties of interracial marriage.

The first actresses to depict the *mulata* in the comic theater—primarily white women—include Petra Moncau, Blanca Vázquez, and Pilar Jiménez, all of whom appeared for most of their careers at the Teatro Alhambra (Robreño 1961, 39). These early figures were generally trained singers who included comic sketches about the *mulata* in their repertory of material but who were more generally known as performers of light opera. One important exception is the turn-of-the-century figure Lina Frutos, discussed below. Famous *mulatas* of the twenties and thirties, by contrast, came more often from working-class families and had little or no formal training. These included Luz Gil, Blanca Becerra, and Candita Quintana. Some of these women were white but darkened their skin artificially when they performed as *mulatas;* others were actually light-skinned *mulatas* and accepted as such. In the tradition of the *guaracha,* musical sketches and dialogues depicting *mulatas* tended to emphasize the association between women of color with promiscuity and forbidden desire. López writes,

> As in the case of the *negrito,* [the *mulata* in the comic theater] is associated with the "lower" cultural and economic strata of society. In some instances she allies

herself with the *gallego* character in the hopes of improving her economic conditions; in other cases she identifies with the *negrito* by virtue of their similar values. . . . In terms of ideas about the role of women in society, this genre . . . [perpetuates the stereotype of] the mulata as sexuality incarnate; . . . it is with this characteristic of the *mulata* that the genre reinforces and legitimizes [dominant masculine ideology]: on the one hand, respect for the "señora" or wife, and on the other the liberation of sexual instincts outside of marriage.[19]

The career of white actress Luz Gil is typical of that of many *mulata* actresses between 1900 and 1930. Gil was born in Veracruz, Mexico, about 1893. Her mother died when she was still a baby, and her father left her to be raised by a reluctant relative.[20] Never fully accepted into her adopted home, Gil left at an early age and tried to support herself as a maid and by doing other odd jobs. She had virtually no formal education and could not read or write until she began teaching herself as an adult. The move to Cuba in 1912 seems to have been one of desperation, representing an ongoing search for employment common to the poor in much of Latin America. Shortly after arriving, Gil was contracted by the Molino Rojo, a theater that first opened in 1908, famous for its pornographic cabaret-style entertainment. She remained at the Molino Rojo for about a year, and then in 1913 joined the company of the Alhambra, making her debut opposite the well-known *negrito* Sergio Acebal in the *sainete Los habitantes de la luna,* singing "Oye mi clave" by Jorge Anckermann.

Both singing and dance interpretations were central to Luz Gil's increasing popularity as a performer (Hevia 1946, 33). She had a strong, if untrained, voice and was allegedly one of the first women to dance a stylized version of the Afrocuban *son* on stage, moving only her shoulders and not her hips, which made the genre somewhat less "scandalous" to audiences of the day.[21] Later, with her career established, Gil was able to perform in *zarzuelas* and other middle-class stage productions, such as those of Ernesto Lecuona and Gustavo Sánchez Galarraga in the Teatro Nacional. In the thirties and forties, Gil toured with acting troupes in Mexico and Spain and performed on Cuban radio shows after 1938. Her success made her one of the few actresses who achieved a measure of financial security later in life.

Among the archival recordings available for study, the comic dialogue "Mala gandinga" by Sergio Acebal provides a good example of *negrito-mulata* interaction (Acebal 1918). The title of the dialogue literally means "bad guts," but this phrase is used among Afrocubans to refer to those with a "bad heart," or evil intentions. "Mala gandinga" is a parody of a famous Spanish couplet, "Mala entraña" (Cristóbal Díaz Ayala, personal communication). It begins as spoken dialogue but later shifts to song as the *negrito* expresses his dismay at what he considers unfair treatment and infidelity by his lover. In a musical sense, the recording has little to do with traditional Afrocuban expression; the piano accompaniment sounds more like vaudeville or dance hall music from the United States and Europe than any inherently "Cuban" genre. The *negrito* begins the sketch alone, waiting in his apartment for the return of the *mulata,* with whom he was apparently living informally. When she arrives, he begs her to stay with him from now on and to stop being so casual about their relationship. The *mulata* in this sketch, as in many others, is portrayed as fickle and superficial, unwilling to commit to any single lover and most probably engaging in relationships with the *gallego* of the sketch or other white Cubans as well.

The *Gallego*

Although it is beyond the scope of this study to discuss the *gallego* or white Galician Spaniard character in detail, he deserves mention in that he tends to be the least musically inclined of all three. The *gallego* seldom dances or sings and generally makes a fool of himself if he tries to do so. In this sense, he serves as a sort of nonmusical counterpart to both the *negrito* and *mulata,* making their abilities seem all the more impressive by his incompetence. In virtually all other resepects, however, the *gallego* is depicted as superior to other characters. He is generally a successful businessman, with more education and social graces than the blacks and mulattos he interacts with. The *gallego* occasionally lacks attributes such as wealth or education, but never possesses less than the *negrito* and *mulata* (López 1979, 693). He never engages in illegal activity and is more often an exemplary citizen. Sometimes the Spanish accent of the *gallego* is parodied, but not not his vocabulary per se.[22]

The *gallego*'s only significant character flaw aside from a lack of musicality is his notorious attraction to *mulatas.* Whereas many white Cubans, even today, do not find darker Cuban women attractive, the *gallego*'s penchant (on and off the stage) for intimate involvement with darker *mulatas* and *negras* is notorious. One example of the countless rumbas, *diálogos,* and *cantos* of the comic theater that involve interaction between a *mulata* and *gallego* is Jorge Anckermann's sketch "Sin pan y sin luz" (Anckermann 1918). This recording, like "El melonero," also begins as spoken dialogue between a *mulata* shopper and *gallego* store owner, but later switches to song as the *mulata* begins to complaining about the scarcity of food in the shop. "Sin pan y sin luz" is an interesting historical document, reflecting the difficult living conditions for many Cubans after World War I.[23] The scenario resolves itself with the *gallego* agreeing to provide all food items requested by the *mulata* if she will kiss him (and by implication provide other sexual favors). Aside from these overt meanings, the *mulata* in this sketch metaphorically represents the needy Cuban nation and the *gallego* the corrupt national government, such as the notorious administrations of Mario Menocal and Alfredo Zayas (Cristóbal Sosa, personal communication). By viewing the comic dialogues of the *teatro vernáculo* both from the perspectives of racial bias and political critique, one becomes more aware of the complexity of this artistic form. The comic theater can be seen as simultaneously repressing and empowering particular factions of Cuban society by using music, dance, and humor as its semantic vehicles.

Afrocuban-Inspired Music and Dance in the *Teatro Vernáculo*

Although the music associated with the Cuban comic theater has never been studied closely, it is clear that most of it tended to be performed by small orchestras patterned after those of European theaters and dance halls. Instruments such as the cornet, violin, clarinet, acoustic bass, keyboard, and *timbal* or snare drum were most commonly found in theatrical ensembles. Whereas Afrocuban traditions served as the primary inspiration for many musical and choreographic sketches in the comic theater, the percussion instruments associated with such music in its traditional form appear to have been unacceptable to most audiences. Instruments such as the *tumbadora* or conga drum, the *bongó*, the maraca, and the *güiro* were considered indicative of African cultural *atraso,* the atavistic relics of a prehistoric past. Fernando Ortiz comments on this inconsistency:

> White [Cubans], despite not being able to resist the sound of [Afrocuban] rhythms and dances, did not [always] adopt their drums. [They chose not to] both because they were difficult to play and because they did not want to "lower themselves" by playing a "black instrument," that is to say (using the criterion of that time) an instrument of a vile people, of barbarians and savages.[24]

A simultaneous attraction to Afrocuban musical forms as parodic entertainment and an unwillingness to accept the instruments and timbres associated with their traditional performance led to a tension that was resolved through a process of stylistic transformation. Afrocuban genres remained the musical mainstay of the *teatro vernáculo* but were radically altered relative to their noncommercial counterparts. Genres such as *rumba, comparsa,* and *clave,* initially played by the largely illiterate urban underclasses, were performed at the turn of the century by conservatory musicians on instruments such as the violin and acoustic bass and sung by formally trained vocalists. The new music represented a fusion of middle- and working-class expression, with that of the middle classes considerably more prominent.

The Guaracha

The *guaracha* was the most prominent musical form in *sainetes* during much of the nineteenth century, and its history is intimately linked with that of the *teatro vernáculo* (Linares 1992). However, nineteenth-century *guarachas* differed from the fast, *son*-influenced music that bears the same name today; initially the term seems to have described any sort of moderately paced vocal duet between a *mulata* and *negrito* emphasizing bawdy humor. *Guarachas* played a central role in theater sketches and were danced both as part of the course of the action and during intermissions.

Guaracha costumes had a tremendous impact on the Cuban entertainment industry, an effect as significant as that of the musical genre itself. According to Robreño:

> [*Guarachas* of the nineteenth century] had a completely distinct rhythm, and are what we might describe as a musical dialogue between the *guaracheras* and *guaracheros,* the men dressed in their billowed shirts and shiny boots, the women with a scarf wrapped around their heads and another draped over their shoulders, displaying those colorful ruffled gowns that even today we see in the [Cuban entertainment] performed on television.[25]

During the "rumba craze" of the late 1920s and early 1930s, hardly a musical group or exhibition dance couple could be found on the island who did not dress themselves *"a la guarachera."* The ruffled vests and sleeves of these garments, as well as the long flowing "tails" sometimes worn by female dancers, came to be associated with commercial rumba during this period to such an extent that their origins in the comic theater were obscured. The very terms *guaracha* and *rumba* in the music of Cuba's cabarets and theaters had become synonymous by the early twentieth century, having lost their earlier associations with distinct commercial and noncommercial musical forms.

Ironically, the costumes associated internationally with show rumba and other forms of ostensibly Afrocuban music and dance seem to have been an invention of white nineteenth-century playwrights (Lapique Becali 1993). They developed primarily as satiric commentary on the clothing of *negros curros* (flashy dressers) and other urban, subcultural Afrocuban groups who were considered to dress outlandishly. In a complex process of multiple imitation, free Cuban blacks of the 1800s imitated the speech and styles of dress of Spanish *ladinos* (black Andalusians) and were in turn imitated by blackface comics.[26] Linares explains:

> The *curros* were groups that appeared in Havana that tried to imitate the first blacks that came as slaves directly from Spain. . . . They [*ladinos*] spoke in a very accented Spanish and used a romantic form of address; . . . they dressed in tight

pants and deerskin slippers, with . . . a ring in their ear, a plumed hat in the style
of Córdoba and a large ruffled silk shirt with a neck scarf. It was a style of dress
very similar to that of the Andalusians. In the theater they started to reproduce
the outfit and exaggerate it, adding lace cuffs to the sleeves.[27]

Virtually every conceivable type of Afrocuban music and dance has
influenced the comic theater since its inception. These include genres as diverse as European stage renditions of the *tango-congo,* the nineteenth-century
parade music of slaves performed on the Día de Reyes;[28] songs from twentieth-century *comparsa* groups, as well as those transformed into political campaign music for white politicians; stylized *clave* compositions recreating the
music of Afrocuban choral ensembles from the turn of the century;[29] and
pregones such as "El melonero," "El tamalero" (The tamale seller), "Maní tostao"
(Roasted peanuts), and others.[30] In many of these recordings, the traditional
forms have been so changed stylistically that the genres cannot be musically
distinguished. They can be recognized as *claves, pregones, comparsas, sones,* and
the like only by lyrical references.

One topic of research that deserves inquiry is the effect of stylized Afrocuban
music in the *teatro vernáculo* on the evolution of popular dance repertory in
Cuba. The relation between these two bodies of music has never been discussed by Cuban musicologists, but my investigations suggest that their mu-
tual influence was considerable. The use of the *timbal* (and later the *paila*) in
commercial music, for example, which has proved so fundamental to the sound
of salsa bands, was incorporated into commercial music in nineteenth-century ballroom *charangas* and in orchestras of the comic theater at roughly the
same time. Only later (beginning in the mid-1920s) did Afrocuban dance bands
such as the Sonora Matancera begin to use the *timbal* instead of the *bongó* in
popular *conjuntos.* Similarly, the use of secondary bell patterns typically performed by the *timbalero* during the "hottest" or most rapid sections of dance
band charts seems to have first appeared as a commercial musical device in the
recordings of jazz-influenced orchestras who began their careers in theaters
imitating *comparsas* and other Afrocuban groups. See for example the four-
volume CD release on Harlequin, *Lecuona Cuban Boys* (HQ CD 7, 11, 21, 26).
Afrocubans and other working-class musicians later reappropriated these same
sounds.

Although music and dance were the primary Afrocuban cultural forms inspiring theater works, virtually any topical issue in the press that concerned
Afrocubans could serve as the subject of a new farcical *sainete.* One chilling
example is the popularity of comic dialogues and music written about the
brujería or "witchcraft" scare of the 1910s and 1920s, in which dozens of
Afrocubans were falsely convicted of abducting white children to sacrifice in

African religious ceremonies.[31] Recorded examples of such material include "La brujería" by the Alhambra impresario Regino López, which was first featured in a *sainete* by the same name (López 1919). This dialogue, which involves interaction between a *gallego* and *mulata,* consists of increasingly fervent entreaties by the Spaniard that the *mulata* agree to an intimate relationship with him. He eventually threatens to denounce her as a witch to force her compliance.

The Stage Rumba

Of the various Afrocuban musics used in theatrical performances, the stage rumba was one of the most frequently performed by the turn of the twentieth century.[32] The initial incorporation of the rumba into *teatro vernáculo* shows probably occurred in the 1860s, at the beginning of the Ten Years' War (Lapique Becali 1993); playwright Antonio Enrique de Zafro from Seville is said to be among the first to compose *sainetes* that included a rumba in the finale (Leal 1980, 47). Yet, as mentioned, to discuss the *guaracha* and rumba as distinct theatrical genres is somewhat misleading, especially after 1900, because the terms were often used interchangeably to refer to any sort of up-tempo musical composition (with or without dance accompaniment) that parodied Afrocuban cultural traditions. Cabaret rumba music of the 1930s also derives from the comic theater and from the music of Cuban circus troupes such as Santos y Artigas, which also featured comics in blackface (Rey 1994).

To a greater extent than other Afrocuban genres, some rumbas of the *teatro vernáculo* represent a loose adaptation of traditional street rumba. Their melodies and lyrics, especially, were often taken directly from popular compositions,[33] arranged with a harmonic accompaniment, and performed by orchestral instruments rather than traditional Afrocuban percussion (Villoch 1945, 37). The *timbal* or snare drum is said to have been the most important accompanying instrument in many rumba sketches written for dancers (Sánchez de Fuentes 1923, 64), imitating with strikes both on the head and the shell of the drum the polyrhythmic and polytimbral sounds of a traditional rumba ensemble.[34] Despite the fact that the *timbal* was a European-derived instrument, even its incorporation into the theater as a means of parodying Afrocuban drumming remained controversial for many years (Ortiz 1952, 261).

Conservatory-trained composer Jorge Anckermann (1877–1941) wrote the most famous theatrical rumbas performed at the Alhambra. An amazingly prolific composer, Anckermann wrote over 700 musical works for theaters that included the Martí, Actualidades, Payret, Tacón, Lara, and Alhambra (Piñeiro Díaz 1977). Born in Havana to German parents, Anckermann studied music with his father and by his late teens had established himself as a nationally recognized composer and conductor.

Recorded examples of Anckermann's rumbas include "Cubita de mis amores" and "Mercé" (Anckermann n.d. 4, 7). Both pieces use few if any percussion instruments and are composed in the style of *son*-influenced dance hall tunes. The lyrics of "Cubita de mis amores" mention instruments associated with the *son* (and not with traditional rumba), including the *güiro* and *bongó,* implying that the song was probably written in the mid-1920s during the early popularization of that genre. "Mercé" is a more jazz-influenced composition. On the recording I heard, the vocal duet features the voices of Blanca Becerra and Adolfo Colombo, accompanied by piano and violin. The duple meter of the piece and its heavy accent on the fourth beat of each measure stylistically allude to the anticipated bass of the *son* even more overtly than "Cubita de mis amores." Lyrically, "Mercé" features picaresque lyrics with marital infidelity as their central theme.

Other recorded examples of theater rumba include "Las mulatas del Bam-Bay" by Arquímedes Pous, a *diálogo y canto* sung in *catedrático* speech with intentionally poor vocal production by Conchita Llauradó and Pous himself (Pous 1917). They are accompanied only by the piano. These examples illustrate the diverse musical influences contributing to the body of music that came to be called rumba in the comic theater and the difficulty of defining the genre as anything more than a discursive space in which numerous musical practices were synthesized and transformed.

An interesting function of theatrical rumba was to unite the entire company of actors for a brief moment at the end of the *sainete.* The final music and dance sequence, which generally took place in the patio of a *solar,* brought the characters together in happy revelry, despite their frequently antagonistic relations during the stage play itself. As Soloni describes it, "All differences overcome, everything is resolved and someone proposes to forget all of their troubles with a rumba."[35] Afrocuban cultural forms in this case directly mediated racial conflict on stage. Rumba served as a ritual act by means of which all actors became friends once again, and optimistic closure was attained even after the most problematic of scenarios. The racial tensions obscured in this way continued to exist, both in the *sainete* and in Cuban society itself, yet the spatial unification of characters and their involvement in a common dance activity functioned as an important means of ideological unification.

Rumba dance of the nineteenth-century comic theater, as in the case of rumba music, is by no means simple to define. It is clear that various dances, including a version of the Afrocuban *papolote,* promoted by Alhambra artist Luisa Herrera in the 1890s, gained considerable popularity for a few years. No known sources exist that describe her stage interpretations. *Teatro vernáculo* artists of the 1890s also tended to dance versions of the *rumba yambú,* a distinct subgenre associated with mimetic choreography. The slower pace of the *yambú* may have aided its early acceptance by the public at a time when rumba in general was widely considered to be offensive even in "Europeanized" form. Villoch describes stage *yambú* as "a monotonous dance, simple, a kind of march along the whole length of the salon, with the dance couple holding each other by the hands"; he notes that the primary venues featuring such entertainment were the Tacón, Irijoa, and Capellanes Theaters.[36]

Other early entertainers who became exponents of stage rumba include Lina Frutos and Pepe Serna, actors and dancers who performed for the most part in the Alhambra from the 1890s through the 1910s. They were highly controversial in their day. Frutos is said to have caused a scandal in Havana by incorporating certain African-derived pelvic movements into her performances, despite the fact that she typically performed in floor-length dresses. When Frutos danced with Pepe Serna, their act seems to have been loosely based on the male-female interactions associated with the *guaguancó* (see chapter 6). Few descriptions of their rumba performances are available either, aside from the metaphor-laden commentary of theater impresario Federico Villoch:

> [Rumba performed by couples in the theater] is a dance influenced by creole indolence, the heat and ardor of natives of interior Africa . . . with stylistic touches of the Andalucian bolero and the spiral contortions of flamenco, all of which is enveloped in a highly voluptuous atmosphere, reinterpreted with the elegance of [traditional] rumba communicated by the rhythmic shaking of the shoulders, the slow and gentle undulation of the waist and hips, and the movement of the arms, flexible tentacles that hold and agitate the colored silk scarf, an inseparable complement of the female dancer.[37]

Villoch reports that much theater rumba beginning in the late 1910s was stylistically distinct from that of earlier decades, demonstrating the influence of North American forms such as the charleston and other jazz dances.

Although Pepe Serna scarcely appears in material written on the Cuban *teatro vernáculo*, he may have been pivotal in the development of twentieth-century rumba shows performed on stage. A white *ñáñigo* (member of a predominantly Afrocuban secret society) from Matanzas, and thus completely familiar with genres of music such as the *rumba columbia* performed by initiates (Rey 1994), Serna was one of the first to bring the virtuosic and physically taxing movements of traditional male solo rumba to the theater. According to some reports, he was virtually the only blackface dancer (he was a *negrito* actor) respected by traditional Afrocuban *rumberos* (Robreño 1994). Serna performed in *guarachero* costumes, sometimes sporting a straw hat *(sombrero de jipijapa)* and neck scarf as well. The scarf served as stage prop, an object that he would pick up with his teeth after a series of spins and masterful contortions (Robreño 1994). Authors suggest that Serna's flamboyant style helped create what would become cabaret exhibition rumba, or *rumba de fantasía,* beginning in the late 1920s. In the words of Villoch, writing in 1945,

> What contortions and epileptic shaking was performed by Pepe Serna.... Serna gave the [theatrical] rumba a strange and nervous aspect, dancing it with a quivering in the entire body.... He never left anyone disappointed, this much-applauded and popular *rumbero* of the Alhambra theater; [his] is the same crazy, disjointed rumba, totally unhinged, with which [renowned dancers of the 1930s and 1940s] are triumphing in dance shows and cabarets. Pepe Serna should be credited, indisputably, with the creation of the modern [commercial] rumba.[38]

As in the case of Lina Frutos, Serna encountered significant critical opposition to his presentations and provoked a flurry of letters published in contemporary newspapers that rudely questioned the artistic value of his routines. Controversy over Serna underscores the extent of stylistic transformation of the music called rumba in the *teatro vernáculo* and the inability of audiences in Havana to condone the traditional genre on stage, although they had been enjoying stylized parodies of the same music and dance for decades. Serna's public assertions, as one example, that the rumba should be considered a legitimate and valuable form of Cuban expression were rebutted by an anonymous writer in *La Antorcha:* "The rumba cannot be a form of Cuban art, because rumba is something which only appeals to those persons completely lacking a refined familiarity with the beauties of the art [of music] which Chopin and Schubert so prodigiously knew how to elaborate."[39]

Opposition to the incorporation of the rumba into theater shows grew sufficiently to warrant the creation of "morality inspectors" who were given the task of attending all major productions and assessing their "social value." The activities of such inspectors were regularly reported in the "Por las oficinas" section of *El Diario de la Marina,* a column relating municipal decrees and ordinances. Examples include an article published on 26 January 1913 in which Inspector Francisco J. Sierra mentioned having attended a performance at the Teatro Payret where an artist named Zarzo sang and danced a rumba. Though it was not blatantly immoral, Sierra reported, nevertheless it "should be prohibited because that kind of dance which is not representative [of Cuba] or of national expression should be taken off all theater stages."[40] His suggestion was answered a week later in a memo from the municipal authorities authorizing "decent" rumbas in theaters as long as they did not demonstrate "lewd movement."[41]

Statements in the press underscore a fundamental ambivalence, then as now, toward the rumba. The same genre that in parodied form could serve as a centerpiece of the comic theater—one of Cuba's most popular forms of entertainment since the onset of the Ten Years' War—became the subject of contention and scorn if presented on stage as it was actually danced on the streets of Havana. Genres such as rumba served to represent both national expression, the unique heritage of all Cubans, and at the same time a West African heritage distinct from that of the majority that was excluded from Cuban culture as conceived by middle-class society. Performances of Afrocuban arts in the theater thus provide disturbing examples of racial conflict in early twentieth-century Cuba and help to articulate specific points of ideological strain in the imagined whole of the nation.

Conclusion

Rine Leal writes that the comic theater reflected "the colonial agony" of Cuba, that "below the mask of the smiling black [was hiding] the grimace of national frustration."[42] While this commentary is perceptive in light of the genre's popularity during the late nineteenth century when Cuba struggled for independence, one might add that the *teatro vernáculo* represented and perpetuated both patriotism *and* oppression, emerging nationalist sentiment and long-standing racial biases against Afrocubans of both sexes. If read as a cultural text, the comic theater sends a confusing mixture of messages as a result of its popularity among various classes and social groups from the 1860s on, given the distinct meanings such entertainment had for those groups. And such ambivalence is precisely what contributed to the commercial success of this genre. It is safe to assume that polysemy and multiplicities of meaning are a prerequisite of any artistic form that becomes popular in countries such as Cuba, rife with cultural, racial, and other divisions. Much as Manuel suggests in the case of modern salsa (1991, 159), we must view depictions of Afrocuban expression in the comic theater as metaphorically instantiating and alluding to a number of oppositions within Cuban society—region versus nation, black versus white, commercial versus noncommercial, elite versus working-class, and African versus Hispanic.

Music and dance performance in the Cuban comic theater played a crucial role for nearly a century as a locus of social and ideological mediation. This mediation occurred on a macro level through the gradual appropriation of stylized forms of Afrocuban artistry by dominant social groups, and their presentation in the theater as the expression of the country as a whole. Afrocuban music and dance became increasingly associated with national identity in the twentieth century and were viewed less as mere parodic commentary on the cultural forms of the Afrocuban underclasses, as their early authors had intended. In a more specific and performative sense, the mediation of social conflict in the comic theater can be seen in the ritualized behavior of actors such as the *negrito, mulata,* and *gallego,* and the resolution of all *sainete* dramas in the boisterous revelry of the rumba dance. Mediation in this form helped to portray *teatro vernáculo* entertainment as light-hearted and "fun," regardless of the gravity of the issues or political content of the stage play itself, and to symbolically reintegrate Afrocubans and Hispanic Cubans back into the same national collectivity.

③ COMPARSAS AND CARNIVAL
IN THE NEW REPUBLIC

Four Decades of Cultural Controversy

ᗰᗰᗰᗰᗰᗰᗰᗰᗰᗰᗰᗰᗰᗰᗰᗰᗰᗰᗰᗰ

A considerable body of literature exists on carnival festivities both in Western Europe and the Americas that interprets their significance from
the perspective of class and racial conflict. Authors such as Bakhtin depict carnival as a period in which social norms and conventions are suspended and/or
inverted, allowing subaltern participants a "temporary liberation from the prevailing truth of the established order" (1968, 10).

Carnival has been described as a "counterdrama" or "counternarrative," a
reformulation of conceptions of self and society by those typically denied access to the official apparatuses of representation (Leal 1980, 30). Fiske similarly
describes it as a sphere of resistance to orthodox norms created by means of
loud music, drinking, dancing, and gratification of the body in unconven-
tional ways (1989, 81–83). Attali emphasizes the symbolic polarization of Lent
and carnival, the former representing the established order, the latter chaos
and anarchy (1989, 21).

While these models provide useful insights into the history of Cuban carnival and its cultural relevance, they may overstate its rebellious qualities while
failing to articulate the more complex and contradictory relationships that
typically exist between any expressive modality and the social groups that create and perpetuate it. Carnival celebrations in modern capitalist societies cannot invariably be described as "symbolic violations" (Hebdige 1989) but more
frequently manifest both resistant and accommodational characteristics, depending on the moment in question (Lipsitz 1990, 236). Averill notes that the
potentially revolutionary qualities of carnival may justify intervention by the
state or other elite factions to regulate it in some way (1994, 219). Others pro-

pose that carnival be viewed as a means of social control, an institution that despite its apparent antiauthoritarianism serves dominant interests by functioning as a sort of "pressure release valve" for subaltern groups (e.g., Gross 1980).

Clearly, carnival can have many meanings, depending on the participants, the locations, and the particular contexts and functions of the celebrations. I use the term *carnival* in this chapter to refer both to Kings' Day (Día de Reyes) slave processions and to pre-Lenten traditions of European origin. European carnival dates back for centuries in Cuba and is still observed today. Kings' Day parades existed only in the nineteenth century, but they continue to affect modern celebrations through the enduring popularity of *comparsas,* the Afrocuban carnival bands associated with them.

From the mid-nineteenth century on, a combination of overt physical repression and government ordinances regulating *comparsas* (which received strong support from both the white and black middle classes) effectively transformed Cuban carnival into a less than pristine example of underclass resistance. Beginning in the 1910s and 1920s, the formation of Afrocuban *comparsa* bands for the sole purpose of electing white politicians to public office and the diffusion of stylized carnival dance music by white performers, both in exclusive ballrooms and in the blackface theater, further demonstrate how the cultural expression of marginal groups can be appropriated and transformed by others. Nevertheless, to the extent that *comparsas* have been allowed to participate in pre-Lenten carnival since 1898 and have persevered in their "traditional" form despite regulation and prohibition, their music retains a significant degree of oppositionality.

This chapter focuses on the gradual acceptance of Afrocuban *comparsa* music as Cuban national expression between 1902 and 1937 and describes some of the debates over such groups in the popular press of the period. Discourse surrounding *comparsas* shifted significantly, beginning with a position of almost total antagonism that resulted in their prohibition in Havana in the 1910s. After the mid-1930s, however, most civic leaders supported them and lobbied for their reauthorization. I argue that an open disdain for African-derived cultural forms among white middle-class Cubans often served as a means of justifying a racial bias against Afrocubans themselves, and that discourse about *comparsas* served as a reasonably accurate gauge of overall racial tensions.

Afrocubans, ostensibly full citizens of the Republic after the Wars of Independence, found that three decades of revolutionary conflict had left them in nearly the same economic condition as before the 1860s. The frustration of many over their continued social marginalization after 1902 has an artistic corollary in the history of the *comparsa* ensembles. A striking similarity exists between controversies over Afrocuban representation in the established political parties and white-collar professions, among other areas, and over the inclusion of *comparsas* in carnival. By the same token, the gradual policy shift by Havana's municipal government, resulting in the reauthorization of *comparsa* groups, can be linked to a number of political and other extramusical influences. These include the international popularization of jazz and other African-influenced arts in Europe and the United States after the mid-1920s and attempts to expand the Cuban tourist industry.

Origins of the *Comparsa* Controversy

The term *comparsa* has been used in this century to refer to Afrocuban carnival street bands organized by barrio or city district. In addition to including percussive music and elaborate dance routines, contemporary *comparsa* festivities generally involve decorative homemade costumes, large colored lanterns and banners carried by group members, and original songs. The city districts with the most famous *comparsas* in Havana are typically the most socially and economically marginalized, such as Belén, Jesús María, and Cayo Hueso, whose residents have long been predominantly black and mulatto. Modern *comparsas* derive from centuries-old traditions of slave celebrations permitted by colonial authorities on January 6, Epiphany or Kings' Day (in honor of the three kings' arrival in Bethlehem). Such groups in the nineteenth century, and occasionally in the twentieth century, were also referred to as *congas* (Orovio 1981, 99).

Various instruments are played by *comparsa* troupes, often made at home or improvised from inexpensive materials, including stave drums of various shapes and sizes, bells, frying pans, tire rims, trumpets and other brass instruments, and the *corneta china*.[1] *Comparsas* remain a vibrant form of working-class expression throughout Cuba to the present day, although they were suspended in Havana along with other carnival-related festivities from 1990 to 1995 due to economic difficulties.[2] Many examples of modern Cuban *comparsa* music have been recorded commercially; see for instance the recordings *Carnival in Cuba, Congas por barrio,* and the Harry Belafonte compilation *Routes of Rhythm*.[3]

Although their early history is uncertain, *comparsas* may have existed even in the late sixteenth century (Antelo Martínez 1984, 54), becoming an established part of colonial life soon after the formation of the *cabildos de nación* by colonial authorities. The Afrocuban carnival groups of past centuries were often organized by social or ethnic group rather than by neighborhood. Each *cabildo* typically elected a "king" of their African nation as the ritual head of the King's Day *comparsa* troupe. Famous groups of the mid-nineteenth century included La Culebra (The snake), El Pájaro Lindo (The beautiful bird), El

Gavilán (The sparrow hawk), El Sapo (The frog), and El Alacrán (The scorpion) (Urfé 1984, 184). *Diablitos,* male masked dancers in full body raffia costumes, often accompanied nineteenth-century *comparsas,* leading the ensemble in their procession to the city's central square (La Plaza de Armas in the case of Havana), where they would jointly perform for the *Ayuntamiento* or local governing body. *Diablitos* were a favorite subject of *costumbrista* visual artists of the nineteenth century such as Miahle, Puente, and Landaluze, and for that reason their costumes and dances are better documented than those of other Afrocuban performers. The fact that members of *abakuá* sects frequently performed as masked dancers alongside *comparsa* groups tended to make these events controversial, reinforcing the notion among middle-class Cubans that such practices should be abolished.

Slaves and free blacks received money from Cuba's middle classes for their performances on Kings' Day; both government officials and wealthy citizens threw coins at the feet of performers from windows and balconies. Many ensembles competed with the larger *comparsas* for the money and attention of white patrons, including small groups of percussionists and singers called *tangos,* clowning groups dressed as North American minstrels, and ensembles of elegantly dressed black and mulatto female singers.[4] By all accounts, the Día de Reyes celebrations were very loud and nearly uncontrollable at times, in this respect more nearly the "symbolic violations" theorized by Hebdige than *comparsas* of later generations. The following is an account by a contemporary (white) author from 1866:

> Innumerable groups of *comparsas* of African blacks proceed through all the streets in the capital. The rabble is immense, its aspect horrifying. . . . The noise created by all of the drums, the horns, and whistles stuns the ears of the passerby on all sides; on one side one sees a Yoruba king surrounded by his black falange, there a Gangá, over there another of the Carabali nation . . . all of them sovereign for a day, singing monotonously and disagreeably in their African languages.[5]

This account of Kings' Day is typical in characterizing Afrocuban music and dance as "savage" or "repugnant." *Costumbrista* writers before the twentieth century described the festivities either from this perspective or as childlike behavior, amusing but of little artistic value. Many authors, influenced by notions of cultural evolutionism, considered African-derived traditions to be a vestige of a bygone age, representing an earlier level of cultural development that Western society had transcended. Their interest in *comparseros* derived in no small part from a perceived need to document the existence of such expressive forms before they disappeared with the gradual "advancement" of Afrocubans.[6]

There is much disagreement over when the Día de Reyes was finally abolished. Antelo Martínez suggests (1984, 54) that in the early 1870s colonial authorities passed a series of decrees restricting such activities and that in 1874 they were banned entirely. Guanche states (1983, 250) that the prohibition took effect even earlier, in 1862. Most authors, however, maintain that Kings' Day celebrations continued until the mid-1880s. Several reliable sources (e.g., Beruff Mendieta 1937, 18) cite the decree *(bando)* of 19 December 1884 as the first to officially prohibit groups of *cabildo* members from forming *comparsas* and taking to the streets. *Cabildos* themselves were soon prohibited as well in 1888, apparently because they had served as centers of revolutionary activity in Cuba during the Ten Years' War (1868–1878) and "Little War" (1879–1880) and were considered a threat to the Spanish administration. From this period until the end of the Wars of Independence in 1898, few carnivalesque celebrations of any sort took place in Cuba, and Afrocuban *comparsas* had no part in them.

In contrast to the Día de Reyes festivities, most of which derive from African cultural traditions, pre-Lenten carnival celebrations in Cuba have European origins. Spanish general Dionisio Vives, who governed Cuba from 1823 to 1832, is said to have authorized the first publicly subsidized carnivals on the western half of the island in the early nineteenth century (Callejas 1965, 5). These were intended primarily for the white population and were held in February and March.[7] Early carnivals featured a wide variety of music. Some of the period's most popular dance genres were incorporated into the festivities, including the waltz, the rigadoon, and the *contradanza,* with black and mulatto orchestras such as that of Raimundo Valenzuela among the most celebrated groups of the period (Vázquez Millares 1964, 19).

Beginning in the late 1860s, with the abolition of slavery and the eventual closing of the *cabildos de nación,* authorities allowed some black participation in pre-Lenten carnival celebrations. Musical participation, however, was restricted to small *tercio* or *tahona* groups, formed by free blacks who typically sang and/or performed on European-derived string instruments. *Comparsa* ensembles and other similar groups associated with the Día de Reyes could not participate. This period of nineteenth-century "integrated" carnival activity lasted only until the onset of the final War of Independence (1895), at which time colonial leaders suspended all carnival activity indefinitely. The prohibition remained in effect until the first years of the twentieth century and the end of revolutionary hostilities.

An interesting aspect of nineteenth-century pre-Lenten carnival is that some *comparsas* apparently participated that were formed by white Cubans in blackface loosely imitating the groups associated with Afrocuban *cabildos.* Blackface *comparsas* have been documented both in Havana and in other regions, such as Santiago (Galán 1983, 325). Many small ensembles, taking their name from existing slave *comparsas,* such as La Culebra, El Alacrán, El Gavilán, and El Gato Prieto, were formed in this way, as Hispanocuban parodies of Afrocuban artistry. (The groups as recreated after 1898, however, consisted entirely of Afrocuban performers.) Argeliers León, one of the few authors to investigate the role of blackface ensembles in Cuban carnival, mentions that they performed both in exclusive white Spanish clubs during the Christmas holidays (ending with Kings' Day), and in street events associated with spring carnival:

> In the world of the [Cuban] bourgeois salon, *comparsas* of white youths were organized which dressed in some type of . . . representative outfit. There existed many *comparsas* of whites dressed up as blacks, usually with ridiculous ornaments marketed as "black" in commercial venues, or copying the manner of black dress from the southern United States. This same phenomenon can be found in the carnival of Montevideo, Uruguay.[8]

Blackface carnival troupes may have been a pan–Latin American phenomenon; others have recorded instances of such entertainment in the British Caribbean as well.[9] Despite their ostensible imitation of "African tangos" and similar expression, the music and dance performed by blackface *comparsas* bore little relation to that of Afrocuban groups of the same name. The instruments typically employed in the former included the clarinet, trombone, bassoon, and similar instruments of Western origin, in addition to the *güiro* and other hand-held Afrocuban percussion. Dance movements tended to be derived from the *contradanza* or the waltz, with some limited influence from Afrocuban-influenced genres in the form of accentuated hip and shoulder movement (Galán 1983, 325).

The nature of carnival celebrations changed significantly with the defeat of Spanish troops by Cuban and U.S. soldiers in 1898. Although some unofficial celebrations took place during the first years of the North American occupation of Havana (1898–1902), Mayor Carlos de la Torre did not officially reinstate carnival until 1902 (Robreño 1981, 115). As a result of their prominent role as *mambises* or independence fighters, Afrocubans had hoped for greater social and economic integration into society after the war. The inclusion of *comparsas de cabildo* in pre-Lenten carnival seems to have been considered one of their newly won "rights" as citizens of Cuba libre. Similarly, a number of *coros de guaguancó*[10] demanded the right to participate in carnival, creating songs accompanied by boisterous Afrocuban percussion batteries with lyrics alluding to love for their country and eulogizing black and mulatto war heroes such as Antonio Maceo and Quintín Banderas (León n.d., 25).

As a result of the war, more Afrocubans than ever before participated in carnival during the early years of the Republic, and for the first time were able to perform strongly African-influenced music and dance alongside both (white) blackface *comparsas* such as El Alacrán and the flower-covered model-T Fords and *carrozas* (parade floats) of the white middle classes. José Franco recounts that in the carnivals of 1899 and 1900 black *comparseros* dressed in the uniforms of the Cuerpos de Voluntarios and Batallones de Orden Público—armed brigades that had harassed the residents of poor barrios in Havana for years— inspired laughter from onlookers with their comical reenactments of police behavior (León 1985, 61).

Public Controversy and Prohibition of the *Comparsas*

Debates over the cultural legitimacy of *comparsas* and other Afrocuban arts had existed since the earliest days of the colony, but they reached new levels of intensity in national discourse in the early 1900s. With the abolition of slavery in 1886, the institution of universal male suffrage in 1902, and the unavoidable fact that black and mulatto soldiers were largely responsible for the emancipation of the country, questions about the "place" of Afrocubans and their cultural expression within national culture became more urgent. The white middle classes may have accepted the notion of Afrocuban social integration in principle, but they were seldom willing to share white-collar job opportunities, earmark federal funds for badly needed social reform programs, or in any other tangible way strive to overcome the countless disadvantages of blacks and mulattos in postrevolutionary society.

Increasingly, cultural forms came to play a central role in the commentary of those opposing the Afrocuban presence. While municipal authorities were loath to state openly their disdain for Cubans of color, or admit the extent of de facto segregation, they had no reservations about attacking Afrocuban cultural expression as "lewd," "diabolical," or "disgusting." Even the more liberal intellectuals and writers of the early Republic, such as Fernando Ortiz, Israel Castellanos, and *(mulato)* Ramón Vasconcelos, saw no contradiction in accepting blacks rhetorically as Cuban citizens while simultaneously calling for the elimination of all "atavistic" African-derived cultural forms. Vociferous condemnation of *comparsas,* street rumba, *santería* ceremony, and *abakuá* dancers served as one of the primary justifications for racist social policy in Cuba, a means of perpetuating more overt practices of discrimination without admitting to or confronting them directly.

Opposition to the inclusion of *comparsas* in turn-of-the-century celebrations can be found even before carnival was officially reinstated in 1902, suggesting that with the end of the war Afrocubans did not wait for municipal sanction but took to the streets on their own to celebrate victory with drums and other instruments. Attempts to regulate and suppress these activities began as early as 1900 during the U.S. occupation. The mayor of Havana, Dr. Nicasio Estrada Mora, signed an ordinance in April 1900 forbidding the use of all "drums of African origin, in all types of public meetings" involving public streets or private residences. He also specifically forbade the performance of *comparsas, tangos, cabildos, claves,* and other Afrocuban musical ensembles that were believed to "affront the refinement and seriousness" of other residents in Havana (see appendix 1).

Ordinances such as this one seem to have been enforced only sporadically. It is clear that after 1900 *comparsas* were able in many instances to take to the streets, although others were undoubtedly jailed, fined, or denied permission. From 1902 on, however, municipal authorities strictly regulated the organization of carnival processions, with preference given to decorated cars, floats, military bands, and presentations of the (invariably) white king and queen of the carnival at the expense of Afrocubans (León n.d., 25).

The magazines *El Fígaro* and *Cuba y América* provide some of the best visual documentation of early twentieth-century parade events, depicting the idealized "white carnival" image promoted by the middle classes, but also including the occasional Afrocuban ensemble. Newspapers provide plentiful examples of the constant verbal attacks on *comparsas* at that time.[11] Ironically, the few university-trained black professionals who served as spokesmen for the Afrocuban community were often at the forefront of the drive to prohibit any sort of working-class Afrocuban music or ensemble from participating in carnival and to outlaw cultural institutions that perpetuated such expression (Kutzinski 1993, 140).

This state of uneasy pluralism continued for over a decade, with condemnation of *comparsas* and other Afrocuban groups appearing frequently in newspapers, and government ordinances officially outlawing them, yet an unofficial policy of toleration allowing at least some to perform. The reluctance of government authorities to eliminate *comparsas* from carnival undoubtedly reflected the tremendous popularity of such groups among Cuba's urban working classes and the appeal of the carnival spectacle in its many forms to tourists and other foreign visitors. In an emerging nation-state such as Cuba, Afrocuban artistic expression served as an important symbol of *cubanidad,* both domestically and internationally. While abhorrent to some, *comparsas* were highly visible musical groups that played music and created dances unique to the *isleño* experience and provided a source of national identity distinct from that of colonial Spain.

In the spring of 1912, a few months before the onset of the Guerrita del Doce, a fight broke out in Havana between two *comparsas* at the conclusion of a street parade. The dispute, which involved the groups El Gavilán and El Alacrán, took place in Trillo Park near what is now Ameijeiras Hospital. It was initiated by the theft of a parade standard belonging to El Alacrán (León n.d., 22), which had won the day's *comparsa* competition. Envious members of El Gavilán (who had received third prize) stole the standard out of spite. Alacrán performers, most of whom were members of the *abakuá potencia* Ekerewá, attacked their rivals to reclaim the emblem, leaving a number of Gavilanes dead or injured. While this was far from the only violent incident in a large capital city engaged in weeks of heavy drinking and revelry, it was tragic and received a tremendous amount of negative press coverage. These stories served eventually to tip the balance of opinion against the inclusion of *comparsa* groups in carnival for decades. A number of newspaper articles and editorials soon appeared calling for an end to "repugnant African spectacles" detracting from the "civility" of the nation. The following is an example from *Cuba y América*:

> Every year during carnival, we witness scenes that detract from our culture and make one think that our population is still influenced by atavism, an affront to civilization. The spectacle is . . . repugnant: men and women, all sense of propriety lost, go stampeding through the streets to the sound of African music and singing monotonous refrains, reproducing in their movements gestures that might be logical in savage Africa, but are idiocy in civilized Cuba; . . . those *comparsas* which under pretext of carnival celebrations recreate savage scenes in our streets should be banned because of their tendency to lead to criminal acts against civilization, against culture, and against the good name of Cuba.[12]

The parade standard event was followed four years later by a similar incident involving unspecified *comparsa* members and a dispute over a colored lantern. In 1916, mulatto Ramón Vasconcelos denounced all *comparsas* as creating "the most embarrassing, colonial [i.e., slave-associated] spectacle imaginable"; curiously, along with Emilio Roig de Leuchsenring and Fernando Ortiz, Vasconcelos was a prominent figure in the campaign to reauthorize *comparsas* twenty years later.

As mentioned, discourse surrounding the incidents of violence involving Afrocuban *comparsas* in the 1910s polarized existing sentiment and led to an increasingly strict enforcement of legislation prohibiting their involvement in carnival parades. Commentary in the press was closely linked to concurrent public sentiment against practitioners of *santería* and *ñáñigo* initiates, in addition to other forms of Afrocuban music and dance expression such as the nineteenth century–derived *baile de maní* (peanut dance).[13]

Attitudes among the white majority in Cuba had reached a general consensus by the mid-1910s: whatever concessions would eventually be made to integrate Afrocubans more fully into the nation would entail as a prerequisite the elimination of "degenerate" West African–derived (and slavery-associated) cultural forms. As military officer Castillo Boloy put it, blacks in Cuba who "yesterday knew how to prove victorious in the battlefields of the revolution, raise their view to the heavens and say 'I am a human being, I am not a thing'" must learn how to be "civilized" if they desired equality: "Rights are not achieved in rumbas nor in *comparsas,*" he suggested, "but rather in becoming cultured."[14] Journalist and educator Miguel Angel de la Torre mirrored this sentiment, expressing his disbelief that the same slaves and free blacks who proved so valiant during the Wars of Independence could interest themselves in the "lascivious" forms of expression "that made their ancestors spin around in the jungles of Africa to frighten away wild beasts."[15]

The campaign against *comparsas* in the 1910s can be understood as part of a larger movement to modify Cuba culturally and to permit the dissemination of only those images of the nation that conformed to a middle-class European norm. An overt policy of cultural "whitening," prevalent at the time (Carbonell 1961, 12), can be detected in various social policies of the early Republic such as the encouragement of white immigration to the island and the formation of the Liga Blanca de Cuba, dedicated to the total eradication of the Afrocuban population (Pérez 1986, 76; Urrutia 1935b, 20). Artistic modalities such as *comparsa* represented markers of Africanness, and for this reason became targets of intense criticism. These proved to be of such magnitude that Havana's mayor, Dr. Fernando Freyre de Andrade, finally issued new municipal guidelines (published in the *Diario de la Marina,* 25 January 1913), calling for the total prohibition of *comparsas* and any dances associated with them or with *abakuá* groups. In that year, *comparsas* were allowed to participate in street parades only if they agreed to leave their "African" instruments at home and refrained from dancing "lewdly."

> In 1913 all *comparsas* were required to perform accompanied by an official from the police department with a group of vigilantes at his command. In some cases [these individuals] forbade the ensembles from walking along the Paseo de Martí and prohibited them from using African instruments or those of a similar nature such as drums, *güiros,* and maracas. . . . [Groups were] also forbidden to "dance or make movements with the body to the rhythm of the music."[16]

Afrocuban performers managed in some instances to circumvent these prohibitions by substituting their traditional stave drums, pans, and bells with "white drums," the percussion instruments employed by Spanish military bands and other Hispanic groups (Rey 1994). This move proved effective in the short term, as Freyre de Andrade's ordinances specifically targeted overt symbols of "Africanness" rather than percussive music making generally. But by 1916, the suppression of the *comparsa* ensembles in Havana was nearly total.[17] Following a second incident of *comparsa* rivalry and bloodshed in March of that year, again highly profiled in the press,[18] authorities believed they had sufficient justification for their complete prohibition, despite continuing public support among the working classes. Though these regulations applied only to the Havana area, opposition to *comparsas* in other parts of the country later led President Gerardo Machado to sign national legislation banning not only *comparsas* and related carnival activities, including *diablito* dancing, but also traditional rumba performance. His ordinance outlawed any sort of activity in public streets employing "drums or analogous musical instruments of African nature" or involving "bodily contortions that offend morality" (*Gaceta Oficial*, 22 October 1925; see appendix 1). Machado declared the official decree necessary after repeated requests by officials, primarily in Oriente, who desired to forcibly "better" the cultural expression of Afrocubans and to rid the country of "public perversion."

While my study is mostly limited to Havana, the history of carnival in other cities would likely reveal similar controversies over the legitimacy of African-derived culture and their prominence as forms of national expression. The history of *comparsas* in Santiago de Cuba, although unique in many respects, reflects the controversial nature of black street music groups there as well. Some scholars consider cities in Oriente Province to have been generally more tolerant toward Afrocuban expression (primarily because legislation prohibiting *comparsas* in carnival was never effectively enforced there), but I have found few major political and legislative differences relative to Havana. The frequent condemnations of Afrocuban carnival music and dance cited in Pérez Rodríguez's two-volume compendium on carnival in Santiago continue into the early 1930s, as do numerous examples of repressive legislation. Pérez Rodríguez reproduces a municipal ordinance from 1902 outlawing African instruments and signed by the mayor, Emilio Bacardí (owner of the rum company); a similar ordinance signed by Mayor Enrique de Messa in 1907; another by Arsenio Ortiz, chief of police in Santiago, in 1917; and yet another by Mayor José Camacho Padro in 1919 (Pérez Rodríguez 1988, 1:164, 1:170, 1:230, 1:246). One of the more ironic sections in the book contains denunciations of *congas* and *comparsas* by Dr. Desidero Arnaz, mayor of Santiago in the mid-1920s and father of Desi Arnaz Jr. The latter was to become famous as "Mr. Babalú" in the United States, single-handedly contributing to the mass popularization of stylized congas on the *I Love Lucy* show (ibid., 1:338). Less well known than Arnaz's success as a commercial entertainer are the political events surrounding his rapid departure from Santiago de Cuba in the wake of the 1933 revolution, with his father's house in flames and a lynch mob at his heels (Arnaz 1976, 23–32).

Appropriation of the *Comparsas* by the Cuban Theater

As noted in chapter 2, the *teatro vernáculo* was the first commercial venue to incorporate stylized versions of Afrocuban carnival music as part of its entertainment. Theatrical parodies of carnival in the twentieth century have their roots in the similar appropriation of *tango-congos,* associated with Kings' Day, by nineteenth-century playwrights. Stylized *tango-congos* and other music inspired by the *cabildos de nación* first appeared in the theater in the 1880s, ironically the same period in which carnival was being suspended by Spanish authorities.

Some of the earliest theatrical *tango-congos* can be found in stage plays such as *La trichina* by José María de Quintana and *Mefistófeles brujo* by Ignacio Sarachaga (Leal 1982, 264). Interestingly, *comparsa* music and dance in twentieth-century stage productions also first appeared during a time—the 1910s—when the genre was prohibited in Havana, as it was fifty years earlier. This suggests that, in both instances, heated public debate over the prohibition may have been largely responsible for popularization of such music in the theater, with comedians capitalizing on the high public profile of the genre in order to attract larger audiences.

Parodied *tango-congos* continued to be written sporadically in the early twentieth century. One recorded example is the sketch "Los congos de Luvine" by Sergio Acebal, the name Luvine apparently referring to a *cabildo* (Acebal n.d., 3). In many cases, compositions of this sort bore virtually no musical relation to those traditionally associated with Kings' Day, while in others composers used a slow, two-pitched rhythmic pattern to mimic the cadences of *cabildo* drummers, which was usually performed as presented in figure 2. This "*tango-congo* rhythm" can be found in many songs from the 1930s and 1940s and was used in later decades as the basis for *afro* compositions during the heyday of *afrocubanismo* nationalism. Two well-known works incorporating the *tango-congo* pattern—indicating that both Hispanic and Afrocuban composers found inspiration in the same rhythmic cell—are Margarita Lecuona's "Babalú" and Arsenio Rodríguez's "Bruca manigua."[19]

Theatrical presentations of *comparsas* in the 1910s appeared frequently at the Teatro Alhambra, known for rapidly incorporating topical events into its shows. One early example is "Siembra la caña," by Jorge Anckermann, a song

FIGURE 2

featured in the 1912 *sainete La casita criolla* (Díaz Ayala 1981, 100). "Siembra la caña" is an adaptation of the political song "Tumba la caña" (discussed later), written by Santos Ramírez, an Afrocuban musician and leader for many years of the *comparsa* El Alacrán.[20] As in most *teatro vernáculo* music, early stylized *comparsas* replaced the complex polyphonic percussion of Afrocuban street *comparsas* with a rhythmically simplified piano accompaniment, frequently in *danzón* style. Other examples of staged *comparsa* music from this period include "El negro Pancho" and "Conga mandinga," the latter from the *sainete El superhombre* (Anckermann n.d., 6, 3). The primary links between these pieces and Afrocuban carnival expression are provided by references in the lyrics rather than the music itself. Texts are often written in *catedrático* speech or with an exaggerated street dialect, using phrases such as *"vamo' a arrolla'"* (let's go dance down the street) or alluding to costumes, lanterns, and other items associated with carnival.

Roughly at the same time that theater *comparsa* gained popularity, another form of appropriation began: that of hiring traditional Afrocuban *comparsas* to promote white candidates in local and national political campaigns. Ortiz and Vasconcelos point out that many of the same middle-class and elite groups who were harshest in their criticism of the "barbaric" antics of *comparsas* during carnival saw no contradiction in hiring the same performers a few months later to further their political agendas (1946, 139). This habit of incorporating the music of marginal Afrocubans into mainstream politics undoubtedly derives from the parties' desire to generate support among black men, who had only recently been authorized to vote under the new constitution.

Political *comparsa* groups continued to perform through the forties and fifties; Batista, for instance, is said to have had a conga written by composer Armando Valdespí for his campaign in 1940. Presidential candidate Carlos Prío had a similar piece written by Osvaldo Farrés in 1948 for the Partido Auténtico Revolucionario (Díaz Ayala 1988, 173; Linares 1993; Robreño 1994). These authors fail to mention whether the political *comparsas* set new lyrics to existing melodies—a typical practice—but they do reproduce some of the short lyrical phrases or slogans incorporated into both. The Batista tune is said to have stated simply, "All the people love him, the nation loves him / Batista will triumph without any argument," while the piece written for Prío repeated, "Here comes the steamroller, here comes the steamroller / With Prío in front and the people behind him."[21] Interestingly, such forms of radically altered Afrocuban music (at least in functional and semantic terms, if not musically) received harsh criticism beginning in the 1910s from intellectuals Fernando Ortiz and Roig de Leuchsenring (e.g., Beruff Mendieta 1937, 18), who considered them "adulterated." However, they simultaneously encouraged the less overtly political "bastardization" of Afrocuban street music, such as the incorporation of rhythmic and melodic elements from street *comparsa* and other genres into the academic music of *afrocubanismo* composers.[22]

Two of the most famous examples of political *comparsa* song are "La chambelona," associated with the Liberal Party, and "Tumba la caña," associated with the Conservatives. These pieces were used repeatedly in countless political campaigns, with performers merely changing the lyrics to accommodate new candidates and new issues. Selling and promoting political lyrics and entire songs used in election campaigns became an important source of income for Afrocuban performers. A number of musical figures of the early twentieth century either wrote compositions specifically for politicians—as in the case of Ignacio Piñeiro (Herrera 1993)—or recorded adaptations of political *comparsa* music on major North American music labels—as in the case of the Septeto Habanero.[23] In addition to soliciting and promoting their own political songs, each major party frequently paid musicians to parade through the streets playing parodies of the rival party's songs, poking fun at their lyrics as well as their leaders and campaign issues.[24]

The author of "La chambelona," the campaign song of the Liberales and in all likelihood the first piece of political *comparsa* music ever written, was Rafael Hurtado Blanco, a mulatto musician from Santa Clara. (As less information is available about the Conservatives' "Tumba la caña," I will use "La chambelona" as the primary example of appropriation of Afrocuban *comparsas* by politicians.) The term *chambelona* derives from Chamba, a small town near the border between the provinces of Camagüey and Santa Clara; the composition was initially intended to accompany part of a circus show. Although the dates of composition and its first incorporation into political campaigns are in dispute (Guirao 1938, 191; Díaz Ayala 1981, 100; Linares 1993), "La chambelona" may date from the presidential election campaign of 1908, when Liberal José Miguel Gómez ran against Mario Menocal, former chief of police under interim American governor Leonard Wood. Many years later, Hurtado Blanco described in an interview the early history of the song.

> I created this [piece] to use in a circus band where I was playing, out near
> Santiago de Cuba, in the year 1912. The circus was called "Kentucky." . . . From
> Santiago I brought the music to Las Villas. In the year 1916, with Menocal
> President of the Republic, the Liberal Party presented the presidential ticket of
> Dr. Alfredo Zayas and Col. Carlos Mendieta. In the middle of the campaign, my
> music started playing; with the band that I directed [the Liberals] started
> making the political street events more fun to participate in using the music of
> "La chambelona." . . . The first [political] lyrics of "La chambelona" said: "Long
> live Gómez and long live Zayas, and that valiant coronel [Mendieta] / Long live
> Sánchez de Portal and that loud trumpet Rafael [politicians from Las Villas]."

> . . . My boss and friend José Miguel Gómez understood that "La chambelona"
> was destined to have an important place in politics. For that reason he had me
> bring my group to Havana.[25]

The dates given by Hurtado Blanco are somewhat doubtful, given that the
Conservatives' "Tumba la caña" (generally assumed to have been written after
"La chambelona"), was satirized in Havana as early as 1910 in the stage play
Caballería chulesca (Soloni 1963). Conservatives paid *comparsero* Santos Ramírez
(director of El Alacrán) to write "Tumba la caña" as a political theme song for
them, probably as a musical response to Hurtado Blanco's popular tune. This
would imply that "La chambelona" was first used in the campaign of 1908,
following the August Revolution and U.S. intervention under Charles Magoon.
Despite the notoriety of his composition, Hurtado Blanco received little compensation for "La chambelona" and died in poverty in Las Villas.

"La chambelona" and "Tumba la caña" continue to be performed occasionally today, both by state-supported folklore ensembles and in altered form as
popular dance music (e.g., López 1977). The fame of "La chambelona" was
eventually such that its name became synonymous with all political music of
the Liberales, and also the February Revolution of 1917 led by José Miguel Gómez
and the Liberal Party (Fornet 1967, 123). The melodies of the two pieces are
reproduced in Grenet (1939, xlv–xlvi). Their lyrics incorporate a surprising
number of metaphors, many more than in North American and European
campaign songs. One almost never hears politicians' names spoken outright
in *conga*[26] or *chambelona* lyrics; instead, each is assigned a nickname. José Miguel
Gómez, for instance, is referred to as "El Tiburón," the shark, a reference to the
ruthless manner in which he used the presidency to his own financial advantage (Díaz Ayala 1994, 162), while Alfredo Zayas appears as "El Chino," the
Chinaman, owing to his Asian facial features. Cubans similarly referred to Mario
Menocal as "El Mayoral," the overseer, because he ran the Chaparra sugar plantation before entering politics (Linares 1993).

The use of metaphorical references in political song has been noted among
African-American groups in other parts of the Caribbean and South America,
and may have African origins (e.g., Averill 1994, 241). Although no concerted
attempt to collect the lyrics written for political *comparsas* has ever been un-
dertaken, and many are permanently lost, a few fragments have been recorded
or notated (e.g., Grenet 1939, xlvi; Urfé 1955) and others remain in the memories of older Cubans. The version of "La chambelona" used in the disputed
1916 electoral campaign between Menocal and Gómez alternates trumpet solos and the refrain ("Aé, aé, aé la chambelona") with short verses such as "The
king of Spain sent a message telling Menocal, 'Give me back my horse because
you don't know how to ride it.'"[27] The excerpt refers to the gift of a horse made

by the king of Spain to Menocal while he was president. In this context, the horse metaphorically represents the country, while jokes about Menocal's inability to ride allude to his decreasing popularity and assumed failure in the reelection campaign. Menocal often had himself depicted riding a horse, an image with strong aristocratic connotations. Populist candidate Gerardo Machado used the elitist horseman image to poke fun at Conservative candidates during his successful bid for the presidency in 1924, paying *comparsa* bands to sing lyrics in the streets such as: "On your feet, on your feet, on your feet, the horse-riding days are over / On your feet, on your feet, on your feet, not even my corns hurt anymore."[28] Díaz Ayala discusses additional lyric fragments associated with "La chambelona" that attest to the common practice of candidates buying the votes of the working classes with the promise of *botellas* or government jobs under their administration. The excerpt he cites refers to Eugenio Leopoldo Azpiazu and Manuel Varona Suárez—local candidates from the Conservative and Liberal Parties, respectively, who were running for mayor in 1916: "Azpiazu gave me the *botella* and I voted for Varona / *Aé, aé, aé, la chambelona.*"[29]

Stylized salon and cabaret conga compositions have a long and distinguished history in Cuba, beginning at least as early as 1912 with the popularization of Ernesto Lecuona's "La comparsa" for solo piano. The overwhelming appeal of this particular Afrocuban-inspired composition (written by a white adolescent) is ironic, given that its appearance coincided both with the racist violence of the Guerrita del Doce and the prohibition of traditional *comparsas* in carnival during the same period. "La comparsa" is a relatively slow piece for solo piano in a minor key, evoking images more closely associated with the Kings' Day processions of the past century than with modern Afrocuban carnival bands. Stylistically, "La comparsa" is written in the European musical vocabulary of the late nineteenth century with a clear tonal center; the *tango-congo* rhythm appears prominently as an ostinato bass motive (Lecuona 1955). Musicians continue to be influenced by Lecuona's work and by similar compositions from this period.[30]

One effect of the political and economic turbulence in Cuba of the late 1920s and early 1930s was the constant exodus of artistic talent from the country in search of more stable and lucrative environments in which to perform. The Cuban economy, already adversely affected by the abrupt collapse of global sugar prices in 1920, entered into extreme crisis with the onset of the Great Depression of 1929. Hundreds of thousands of Cubans lost their jobs, and living conditions, especially for the country's poor, became desperate.[31] Compounding these difficulties, Gerardo Machado decided in 1928 to force through congressional approval for a six-year extension of his original four-year presidential term, an anticonstitutional act that did much to polarize sentiment

against him. Strikes, violent labor demonstrations, and brutal government repression became commonplace in Havana and elsewhere after this period. In
this volatile context, significant numbers of celebrated performers left to seek
work in the United States and Europe, leading to the internationalization of
several genres of Cuban music, including the rumba (discussed in chapter 6)
and the salon conga based loosely on the music and dance of *comparsa* ensembles.

The most central figure in the history of the resulting "conga craze" of the
mid-1930s was white composer and pianist Eliseo Grenet (1893–1950). Born in
Havana, Grenet studied music from an early age with Raimundo and Pablo
Valenzuela and began his professional career as a young teenager writing the
popular *danzones* "La mora" and "Te lo doy" (*Homenaje a Eliseo Grenet,* 5). At
age sixteen he was asked to direct the orchestra of the Politeama Habanero
Theater, where he wrote countless Afrocuban-inspired works for the stage.[32]
In 1926 he became musical director of the blackface troupe of Arquímedes
Pous, which performed in the Teatro Cubano (later renamed the Regina). Following Pous's death in that same year, he served as director of the house orchestra of the Casino Nacional and organized a troupe of Afrocuban performers called Cubanacán (ibid., 7).

Unlike many of his artistic contemporaries, Grenet had no desire to leave
Cuba during the *machadato,* but was forced to flee in 1932 when his song
"Lamento cubano" (Cuban lament) was judged to be subversive by government authorities. The composer first went to Madrid, where he continued to
perform and write *zarzuela*-like theater productions such as *La virgen morena*
(The dark Virgin, a reference to the Caridad del Cobre, the patron saint of
Cuba) with much critical and financial success (Grenet 1942a). Having begun
his professional career in the *teatro vernáculo,* Grenet had ample experience
composing stylized versions of Afrocuban musical material. He wrote his first
stage conga for an international audience in the 1932 musical *La comparsa de
los Congos* (The *comparsa* of the Congolese), in addition to presenting other
Afrocuban-inspired genres such as the *afro* composition "Lamento esclavo"
(Slave lament) and musical adaptations of Nicolás Guillén's poems "Negro
bembón," "Quirino con su tres," "Yambambó," and "Tú no sabe' inglé.'" The
production's title song, "La *comparsa* de los Congos" is noteworthy for the
inclusion of interlocking bell patterns actually played by *comparsa* performers
on frying pans, and in that sense it may have portrayed black carnival music
more realistically than had ever been done in the Cuban theater (Grenet 1932).
Grenet's productions from this period are said to have been the first to adopt
conga drums into stage entertainment. This practice became popular less than
a decade later in performances by Miguelito Valdés, Desi Arnaz, Chano Pozo,
and others, but in 1932 it remained controversial. Ortiz mentions that the sa-

lon conga of this period, however distinct from its folkloric counterpart, does represent the first popular Cuban dance music to incorporate African-style drumming (1952, 264) with the hands.

Encouraged by his success in Spain, in 1934 Grenet moved to Paris, which with the recent popularization of jazz and "primitivism" was the undisputed European center of African-influenced artistic production. As one might expect, the music and dance presentations written by Grenet fitted easily into the Parisian milieu and were received enthusiastically by French and foreign audiences. The composer first found employment in the newly opened cabaret "La Cueva" (The Cave, 9 rue Mansart), playing keyboard in the orchestra of *(mulato)* bandleader Julio Cueva (Cañizares 1991, 14). Within a year, as a result of clever promotional techniques, Grenet had become the talk of the city by consciously reinventing *comparsa* music for the French ballroom. The rhythms of the piano accompaniment he composed, as well as those of other instruments, are based loosely on the same Afrocuban bell patterns found in *La comparsa de los congos*. Similarly, the "one, two, three—kick" choreography of the accompanying dance derives from rhythmic figures associated with the *tumbadora* (conga drum) figures played by Afrocuban street bands.

Grenet clearly simplified and formalized the choreography associated with *comparsa* in order to make his version more accessible to European audiences. Always the savvy businessman, he invited dozens of Parisian dance teachers to La Cueva cabaret for the public debut of the "new" genre, including many from the influential Union des Professeurs de Danse et d'Education Physique de France. He served a lavish meal, presented a stage show featuring performances of salon conga, and then taught them the steps on the spot (Grenet 1942a, 17). This event resulted in extensive media coverage of both Grenet and the new dance in the press and the popularization of ballroom conga throughout Paris in a matter of days. The widespread appeal of salon conga in that city lasted only a few years, however, owing in part to the outbreak of World War II and the invasion of France by Germany.[33]

On tour in the 1930s, Grenet employed similar tactics that resulted in conga crazes in both England and the United States.[34] In a musical sense, the commercialization of *comparsa* music by Grenet and others resulted in a fusion of rhythmic patterns employed by Afrocuban groups with harmonic and melodic arrangements similar to those written for contemporary jazz bands. Harmonically, the pieces tend to be more complex than those of Afrocuban *comparseros*, and the melodies are extended to 16- or 32-bar phrases so that they become less cyclic, less patterned by short improvisatory call-and-response alternation, and thus correspond more nearly to the form of tin pan alley compositions of the day. Rhythmically and choreographically, the music represents a degree of standardization rarely seen in Afrocuban street traditions.

Salon conga lyrics most often refer to Afrocuban dance events and are written in neo-*bozal* speech emphasizing black working-class pronunciations of Spanish.[35]

Interestingly, most traditional *comparsa* lyrics written by Afrocubans themselves do not incorporate such subject matter, but instead center on nonracial themes derived from the names of the groups in question. The *comparsa* song of Las Jardineras (The gardeners), from the barrio of Jesús María, discuss tending their flower beds, for instance, while those of Los Marqueses (The marquises), from Atarés, make reference to their "aristocratic" status (Pello el Afrokan 1988). In Grenet's "Camina pa' 'lante" (Grenet n.d., 3), by contrast, one black man chides another for not joining the *comparsa* revelers passing by: The lyrics begin: "There goes the sonorous conga felling everything in its path / Why don't you get exited, black man, at the sound of the drumbeat?"[36] Similarly, Ernesto Lecuona's composition "La conga se va" emphasizes the perceived carefree nature of Afrocuban culture as well as the sensuality of the *mulata:*

> Play those maracas, black man,
> Because I want to dance until the light of dawn.
> With crazy abandon, with ardor we will dance, oh my love,
> I know that you want to dance with your fiery dark-skinned woman
> And that with her lips she will deliver vehement passion to you.
> The conga is passing and me, I'm going with it.[37]

It is fascinating to note the heavy emphasis on Afrocuban imagery in salon congas written almost exclusively for white audiences by white middle-class Cuban performers who had probably never seriously considered dancing behind the Afrocuban groups that were their source of inspiration.

Reauthorization of the *Comparsas*

Although significant opposition to the inclusion of *comparsas* in Havana's carnival continued into the 1930s, a number of factors combined to pressure municipal authorities to lift the twenty-five-year-old ban and reauthorize their participation in 1937. Some were purely economic. With the global depression and extremely low international demand for sugar, Cuba needed every peso it could muster, and one of the primary sources of potential income aside from agriculture was tourism.[38] In the 1900s and 1910s, Cuban carnival had brought thousands of foreign visitors to the capital each spring, with *comparsa* groups always one of the central attractions. As a result, business leaders and merchants supported the lifting of the *comparsa* prohibition to promote tourism.

Other factors leading to reauthorization involved the international artistic trends mentioned earlier and the vogue of African-influenced music and dance genres abroad, including several from Cuba itself. With the popularization of commercial rumba, *son,* and especially conga in Europe and the United States, Cuban national culture became increasingly identified abroad with Afrocuban music and dance. Foreigners chose to vacation in Havana with the expectation of viewing the *comparsas* so colorfully described in the lyrics of composers such as Grenet, Lecuona, and Oréfiche, only to find to their amazement that such groups had been prohibited for decades in their country of origin. Consequently, middle-class Cuban artists and intellectuals were confronted with contradictions surrounding their attitudes toward Afrocuban arts and were forced to reconcile their biases against such expression with the growing international interest that they themselves had helped create.

Finally, in the wake of the successful revolution against Gerardo Machado in August and September 1933, and the abrogation of the hated Platt Amendment soon thereafter, nationalist sentiment in Cuba achieved a degree of intensity that had not existed since the Wars of Independence against Spain.[39] Under the brief socialist-inclined administration of Ramón Grau San Martín (1933–1934) and in the early years under Fulgencio Batista (1934–1944), a new sense of populism and pride pervaded the nation; Cuban citizens sought to express these sentiments through existing cultural forms such as *comparsa.* Restrictions on all types of carnival celebrations had become closely associated with Machado, who banned carnival entirely from the late 1920s through 1933 in an attempt to prevent antigovernment violence. The liberation of Cuba from Machado thus coincided with attempts within Havana to liberate carnival from unnecessary military ordinances and to let the *comparsas* participate in festivities as national symbols.

Some Cuban intellectuals of the 1930s responded to public sentiment by voicing tentative support for the reincorporation of *comparsas* into carnival. Figures such as Fernando Ortiz, Ramón Vasconcelos, and Emilio Roig de Leuchsenring, who in the 1900s and 1910s had expressed open disdain for the *comparsas,* now began to view them in a new light and to call for a more tolerant view of the music and dance with which they were associated. Ortiz, while still fearful of the potential violence that might result from their reauthorization, by the mid-1930s had come to refer to them as part of the "spiritual heritage" *(acervo espiritual)* of the nation (Beruff Mendieta 1937, 16). While not unequivocally in favor of their perpetuation in their current form, he nevertheless supported the incorporation of some of the more "picturesque" elements associated with *comparsas*—i.e., the costumes, colored lanterns, and characteristic musical instruments—into public celebrations.

Ramón Vasconcelos, an Afrocuban, also began to promote the acceptance of "regulated" *comparsa* ensembles that would "parade down the street with decency, without a lewd gesture" ("que arrollen con decencia, sin nota lúbrica") and in a musical and choreographic sense conform more nearly to European standards (ibid., 36). Black street arts seem to have been viewed by intellectuals during this period as mildly offensive traditions that nevertheless represented unique forms of Cuban expression. To the individuals mentioned above, these forms of music and dance needed only to "evolve," with the help of middle-class artistic guidance, to be transformed into "decent" and "proper" forms of national culture.

One social group that remained adamantly opposed to the reauthorization of *comparsas* was the black middle class. They expressed themselves publicly through editorials in newspapers and magazines and in the pronouncements of the Comité Conjunto de Sociedades de Color. In their view, *comparsas* did not constitute cultural traditions worthy of perpetuation, but instead reflected the "backwardness" and "lack of culture" of repressed slaves under Spanish colonial rule. To blacks and mulattos who had achieved some measure of economic success and social integration under the Republic, *comparsas* served only as a marker of "otherness" and racial division. Fearing that they would perpetuate stereotypes and impede the process of racial integration in Cuba, black professionals condemned *comparsas* as a degrading spectacle (Roig de Leuchsenring 1946, 154; unsigned article in *Adelante,* March 1936, 1).

Alberto Arredondo, one of the more outspoken Afrocuban critics, denounced the institution of carnival in general as another means by which white businesses exploited Afrocubans. Rather than arguing for their right to parade behind a *comparsa* band on the street, Arredondo suggested that blacks instead fight for their right to march "together with the white man on the road of economic possibility."[40] To Arredondo and many of his Afrocuban contemporaries, *comparsas* were an artistic opiate obscuring more important issues in the clamor of bells and drumbeats, and representing an obstacle to racial equality rather than a valorization of working-class expression. They similarly viewed the political *comparsas* of the day as yet another example of white exploitation of Cubans of color (in this case, of composers and performers) to achieve their own ends. To Arredondo, it was imperative that the Cuban nation not "forget its genesis, and the ethnic legacies contributing to its development." But it should also not "march backwards into history to return to stages [of evolution] which have been left behind."[41] To the majority of black intellectuals of the day, *comparsas* constituted an embarrassment, a lower level of cultural expression whose merit derived more from its value as a historical document than as an artistic modality in its own right (e.g., Acuña Lazcano 1938, 8).

Beginning in 1934, the opposing ideological positions of open disdain for *comparsas* and qualified support for them as unique forms of national expression began to resolve themselves in highly regimented *comparsa* "demonstrations" for tourist audiences in Old Havana. These frequently incorporated musical and choreographic elements from the Afrocuban *comparsas* of earlier decades but presented them in public shows that bore little resemblance to earlier processions. Argeliers León describes an event in 1935 where groups of drummers with colored lanterns performed in the Plaza de Armas, "taking as a central theme the novel 'Cecilia Valdés'; . . . scenes from the book were recreated using common people of the city, predominantly blacks, who also performed the old *comparsa* dances" (n.d., 26). The newly formed National Tourist Commission, created in the mid-1930s with an annual budget of about $40,000, designed these and other events (Beruff Mendieta 1937, 14). It organized entire *comparsa* ensembles but did not initially allow them to parade in the streets, only to perform in fixed locations for judges and a seated audience (Roig de Leuchsenring 1946, 167).

Local authorities in Havana also promoted related forms of entertainment that were considered less threatening than traditional *comparsas*, such as the stylized Afrocuban music for orchestra by (white) stage and film composer Gilberto Valdés.[42] The music of Valdés, according to Mayor Beruff Mendieta, "purified," "elevated," and "perfected" Afrocuban street music, and in that sense was believed to serve the interests of city officials, the tourist commission, and the general public (1937, 5). This sort of "state-sanctioned folklore" was performed in the Anfiteatro de la Habana and generated large amounts of money for Valdés, as well as for Jorge Anckermann and others (García Agüero 1937, 57). At least one of the concerts was free to the public, following the policy of the municipal government to disseminate "decent" cultural forms in order "to put the masses in contact with correct interpretations of their own music" (Beruff Mendieta 1937, 28).

Finally in 1937, after considerable debate, city officials made the decision to reauthorize *comparsas* in the carnival street parades as well, a decision publicized in the *Diario de la Marina* (7 February, 3). To prevent disorder of any type, however, the parade route was much more strictly prescribed than before, and *comparsa* groups who wished to participate were required to register in advance with authorities. Upon reaching O'Reilly Street and the Avenida del Puerto (the end of the parade route), groups were ordered to disband. The police force mobilized a tremendous presence for the 1937 parades, with armed men forming a solid line along the entire route. They had the desired effect in that no violence or "disorderly" behavior was noted during the celebrations; this led one contemporary observer to sum up public sentiment of the day, noting that "it is not necessary to deprive the population of certain lawful desires [to see and perform in *comparsas*], only to bring [carnival participants] to a level of civility and decency compatible with that of our [national] culture."[43]

Apparently the well-publicized carnival celebrations of 1937 generated significant interest among foreign visitors; six steam liners are said to have arrived, bringing more than 16,000 tourists from the United States and Europe. Many of the Afrocuban ensembles that had been prohibited for decades from taking part in carnival again joined in the processions, as well as newly formed groups; these included Los Moros Rosados (The Ruddy Moors), Las Bolleras (a name given to women selling fried food in the streets), Los Componedores (The Composers), Los Colombianos Modernos (The Modern Colombians), Los Marqueses (The Marquises), and Los Guaracheros (The Guaracha Players).[44] As mentioned, the National Tourist Commission took an active role in the creation of "typical *comparsas*" for the event, spending $3,000–4,000 for costumes, parade floats, and hiring musical directors and performers for the groups they created, Los Guajiros (The Peasants) and El Barracón (The Slave Barracks). Well-known *son* and rumba performer Ignacio Piñeiro became musical director of El Barracón, while trumpeter Lázaro Herrera of the Septeto Nacional directed Los Guajiros. For the first time in the history of Cuban carnival, Havana's city government offered cash prizes for the best *comparsas,* as well as others for established categories such as best café orchestra, *son* dancer, parade float, and decorated car.[45] Many of Havana's middle-class and elite Cubans who had little interest in watching or participating in street parades that included Afrocuban *comparsas* and who did not condone their reauthorization nevertheless continued to create their own blackface groups safe within the walls of exclusive social clubs (see illustrations).

Conclusion

Afrocuban *comparsas* played an increasingly central role in integrated carnival celebrations after 1937. Debate over whether *comparsas* should be considered a cultural blight or a national treasure continued for many years, but the ensembles were never again entirely banned from public performance. From the perspective of the 1990s, we can see that the late 1930s represents an important change in attitudes toward carnival on a national level and that decisions made by Mayor Beruff Mendieta set precedents for other city officials throughout the country.

Carnival continued to be used as a political tool, as it is today. For instance, as early as 1959 Che Guevara proclaimed the new socialist government a "revolution with *pachanga*" (festive spirit), discursively linking forthcoming carnival events with populist politics and the rise to power of the Castro government (Leonardo Acosto, personal communication). Somewhat later, revolutionary authorities announced that carnival would no longer be held in February and March, but rather on 26 July. They initially made the change so as not to interrupt the sugarcane harvest of 1970, but later kept it on that date to celebrate the "triumph of socialism." Infrequent *comparsa* performances during the official suspension of Havana's carnival between 1990 and 1995 were also linked to political events. These included groups taking to the streets in November 1993 to celebrate the founding of the CDRs, local Committees in Defense of the Revolution.[46] Finally, in an attempt to attract more tourists, as of 1996 the government has again authorized a modest carnival celebration preceding the Lenten season rather than in July.

As to whether *comparsas* more clearly demonstrate Bakhtinian resistance or social control, I would suggest that both paradigms are overessentialized and obscure a fuller understanding of carnival's social relevance in Cuba by drawing attention away from the fluid and multiple meanings inevitably associated with popular art forms. Carnival as a dialogic modality cannot be understood apart from the context in which it is performed; its meanings and associations can change radically from one month or year to the next or from one decade to the next in response to the agendas of diverse ethnic, class, government, and other social factions. Perhaps, as Hebdige suggests (1988, 83), it is better not to think of *comparsas* as a single cultural phenomenon or object, but rather as "many objects at different 'moments' . . . at different (real and mythical) times (in different conjunctures in relation to imagined pasts and futures) seen from different perspectives for different purposes," and in shifting frames of contextually derived meaning.

Cuban *comparsas* are caught in the ongoing struggles over the meanings of social experience, the social order, and the texts and commodities of that order that perpetuate social inequality (Fiske 1989, 28); more simply stated, they are linked to ideological conflict in the Gramscian sense and to controversy over cultural representations of the nation. As Averill observes, carnival itself wears many masks (1994, 243). It represents a text that can be "read" in many ways and assigned (disputed) meanings according to the desires and aspirations of various listeners. In Cuba, *comparseros* and other Afrocuban carnival participants used music and dance as a form of resistance in the nineteenth century and the first years of the Republic, but this symbolic opposition was recognized and effectively suppressed by 1916. Carnival celebrations from 1916 through the mid-1930s took on new and more coercive significance as a sphere of activity in which African-influenced culture had no place. Finally, beginning in 1937, carnival has represented a more complex and contradictory form of national expression in which policies of overt social control and cooptation have been used in tandem by municipal authorities to diffuse or subvert the inherent oppositional potential of *comparsas*. It is this multifaceted cultural text, in which the seeds of subaltern discontent and the constraints of dominant authority achieve an uneasy equilibrium, that continues to be an important institution in present-day Cuba.

4 ECHALE SALSITA

Sones and Musical Revolution

The "modern," the truly "contemporary" art of this
century developed unexpectedly, overlooked by the
guardians of cultural values, and with the speed to be
expected of a genuine cultural revolution.
—Eric Hobsbawm, *The Age of Empire 1875–1914*

I'm not a Rodríguez, *no* . . . I'm not a Herrera, *no,* I'm
not a Fernández, *no* . . . perhaps my real name is
Lumumba, perhaps it's Kasabubu, *perhaps.* I was born
from Africa, *yes,* that is my land, Africa, my lovely country,
yes, I'm from the Congo, *yes,* I'm from Africa.
—Arsenio Rodríguez, "Yo nací de Africa."[1]

Recent studies of cultural change emphasize the constructed and tran-
sient nature of all artistic expression. They suggest that culture is not
passively or statically "passed down," but actively recreated with each generation in conformity with particular beliefs and values. The reasons for the emergence, perpetuation, and decline of cultural practices are complex and reflect
diverse factors including socioeconomic trends, political events, technological
developments, and resulting changes in how individuals conceive of themselves and their relations to others. Linnekin suggests conceiving of culture as
a "contested narrative field" containing symbolically charged elements that
are continually reevaluated in terms of their ideological significance (1992, 251).

Cultural change in this sense involves an ongoing dialogue with existing
modes of behavior, and ideas about such behavior, and a perpetuation, rejection, or alteration of traditions in light of their perceived meanings in the
present. In urban, postcolonial societies, the reshaping and resignifying of subaltern culture frequently involves a reaction by oppressed groups to the influence of aesthetic systems imposed from "above." Their creative reconciliation
of dominant cultural expression with their own beliefs and customs typically
results in the emergence of a new synthesis and a form for expressing it. It is

this interpenetration of aesthetic spheres which Erlmann describes as "the articulation of heterogeneous worlds," the simultaneous disintegration and reformation of culture in a conflictive environment (1991, 2).

Controversies over minority culture in ethnically and racially divided societies often reflect judgments as to whether such practices conform to established notions of collective identity. The expression of minorities can be perceived (and function) as a form of symbolic resistance, a challenge to the imposed culture of the majority. Alternatively—and this is especially true in the case of syncretic forms—subaltern culture can be accepted and appropriated by others in an attempt to play down social differences and to symbolically reintegrate the disenfranchised into the region or nation. Cultural hegemony on a national level entails a constant reformulation of the norms of group behavior so as to include and thereby neutralize at least some oppositional forms of expression associated with minorities. To regulate subordinate groups, the dominant classes are thus forced to accept the cultural markers of those they repress. "The ruling faction reduces the oppositional potential of a sign . . . by attempting to construct a national consensus of meaning and feeling about it [while] subordinate groups arrest it to mark their identity as separate from that of the ruling faction" (Hall 1979, 337).

This chapter discusses the history of urban *son* dance music in Havana in terms of its early performance within the working-class Afrocuban community, its gradually increasing popularity, and its eventual transformation into "national culture." The chapter focuses primarily on the period from 1920 through 1935, considered by most historians to be the heyday of the genre in its initial commercial form (Reyes 1994). It describes the cultural milieu of the first *conjuntos* (bands) and middle-class attitudes toward them. It then analyzes the performance of *sones* in *academias de baile*, beer gardens, and private parties, and their gradual penetration of and dissemination through the mass media. Finally, the chapter documents the changing attitudes of Cuba's elite and middle classes toward *son* music and dance beginning about 1925. It discusses a shift from policies of police repression and open condemnation of the genre to its general acceptance within the space of only a few years. *Son* is analyzed as mediating stylistically and ideologically between the cultural practices of working-class Afrocubans and the white and black middle classes.

Contextualizing the Modern Urban *Son*

For many years an insignificant regional folk genre, *son* in its urban form has become the most influential Cuban music of the twentieth century. It is described by prominent critics as the "Cuban genre *par excellence*," the "sonorous exponent most representative of national culture" (León 1991a, 21; Urfé in

Blanco 1992, 4), and it continues to be a central part of music making in the Hispanic Caribbean today. *Son* as it existed prior to commercialization has a history dating back over a century, but one initially confined to the rural eastern provinces. Incorporation into the repertories of urban dance bands in Havana, however, resulted in its dissemination and nationwide popularization in the late 1920s (Alvarez 1994).

Given the importance ascribed to the *son* by Cuban musicologists, it is striking that so little information has been collected about its history in the early twentieth century.[2] The emergence of urban *son* in the western provinces as a distinct musical form in the 1910s, for instance, and the manner in which it eventually gained national acclaim have yet to be adequately investigated. This may be partially explained by the fact that *son* first developed as a marginal genre, composed and performed exclusively by blacks and mulattos in the poorest districts of Havana. In its precommercial years, *conjuntos de son* (*son* bands) did not enjoy broad popularity. Instead, they provided an alternative form of entertainment for those Afrocubans either unable or unwilling to participate in publicly condoned musical practices. In this sense, the genre shares a history with other Afrocuban music of roughly the same period and differs only in that it was eventually legitimized by the white majority.

Perhaps the most significant fact about *son* music from today's perspective is the fact that it represents a number of significant "firsts" in Cuban history. It was the first black street genre to gain national acceptance and to be performed commercially without excessive stylistic alteration or transformation.[3] Together with *música guajira* (the music of Hispanic *campesinos*), it was among the first working-class genres to be disseminated on recordings and in radio broadcasts. It was the first to prominently feature musical and vocal improvisation and to incorporate an Afrocuban drum (the *bongó*) performed with the bare hands. For all these reasons, as well as its centrality to the development of musical forms in later years such as *danzonete,* mambo, and salsa, the nationalization of *son* represents a significant turning point in Cuban popular culture. From the late 1920s on, working-class musics influenced by this genre increasingly predominated in the media. The mass popularization of *son* as an instrumental, vocal, and dance form represents an intensification of what Hobsbawm describes as artistic "revolution from below."

Defining the *Son*

Precise definitions of the *son* are difficult to provide, as numerous subclassifications exist (e.g., *changüí, sucu-sucu*) as well as hybrid forms that fuse *son*-derived characteristics with other musics (*son-guajira, son-pregón, guaracha-son, afro-son*). More stylistic cohesion is evident in terms of *sones* composed during the "classic" period prior to about 1940 by the Trío Matamoros, Ñico Saquito, the Cuarteto Machín, the Septeto Nacional, and Septeto Habanero, among others.[4] Structurally, this early *son* music tends to be in duple meter, based on simple European-derived harmonic patterns (I-V, I-IV-V), and to alternate between verse and chorus sections. Short instrumental segments performed on the *tres* (folk guitar) or trumpet are also frequently included between strophic repetitions. The final section of most *son* compositions, called the *montuno,* is performed at a faster tempo and involves relatively rapid alterations between the chorus and an improvising vocal or instrumental soloist. Phrases in this section are generally referred to as *inspiraciones.* The cyclical, antiphonal, and highly improvisatory nature of the *montuno* bears a striking similarity to the formal organization of many traditional West African musics; initial strophic sections, by contrast, more closely resemble Iberian musics.

Son lyrics are most often in Spanish and employ European-derived poetic forms such as *coplas, cuartetas,* and *décimas,* although some African terminology can be found as well (to be discussed later). Lyrical references, which often include bawdy sexual innuendo, may refer to current social themes and political issues, or invoke regional nationalism (Avalos 1992, 4; León 1984, 128). Among the most distinctive musical characteristics of the *son* genre are its prominent *clave* pattern (see figure 3): a tendency for the guitar and *bongó* to emphasize the fourth beat of the (4/4) measure more strongly than the first; and a unique bass rhythm, emphasizing the "and-of-2" (the upbeat falling between beats 2 and 3) and "4," which is generally described as an "anticipated bass."[5] The syncopated bass pattern derived from *son* and its fourth beat–first beat ambivalence are fundamental to the creation of modern salsa dance music.

No one agrees on the exact origins of the *son.* Written references to *sones* in Cuba date from the late sixteenth century; the well-known singer Teodora Ginés, for instance, is mentioned as having performed them in Santiago at that time while accompanying herself on the *vigüela* and *bandola* (Grenet 1939, xxxvi). The musical relationship between this early colonial genre and twentieth-century *son* is unclear, however. León (1984, 119) states that the modern variety developed in the eighteenth century, while Orovio (1981, 392) suggests a later date. Regardless, historians agree that residents in rural Oriente on the outskirts of cities such as Baracoa, Guantánamo, and Santiago were among the first to perform modern precommercial *son.* From the mid-nineteenth century on, *estudiantina* ensembles (strolling bands of student musicians) performed variations of the genre in the towns and cities of Oriente. Rural *soneros* employed various instruments including the *tres,* guitar, maracas, *bongó,* *botijuela* or *botija* (jug bass), *marímbula,*[6] and *güiro* (gourd rasp). *Estudiantinas*

FIGURE 3

often incorporated these instruments, but added others associated with ball-room traditions as well, such as the cello, flute, violin, and *timbal*.[7]

Son instrumentation in the first commercial recordings was quite flexible, with musicians freely altering their ensembles to conform to various contexts. Some artists of the 1920s and 1930s (e.g., the Trío Matamoros, Sindo Garay, María Teresa Vera) recorded *sones* performed solely on guitar and *tres*. Most, however, influenced by *sexteto* and *septeto* bands (sextets and septets) from Havana, created larger ensembles consisting of guitar, *tres*, acoustic bass, maracas, *claves*, *bongó*, and trumpet. These latter groups especially demonstrate a high degree of cultural fusion, with Hispanic contributions such as the string instruments performing alongside those of Afrocuban origin such as the *güiro, clave*, and *bongó* (León 1984, 128). Structurally, lyrically, and in instrumentation, *son* of the 1920s epitomizes the "symbolic reordering" discussed by Erlmann through its fusion of diverse influences (1991, 5).

Genres Antecedent to the *Son*

Afrocubans engaged in many kinds of musical activity during the first decades of the Republic. I have mentioned some of these practices, such as the sacred songs and drumming of *santería* and *abakuá* ceremony and noncommercial rumba events, to underscore the strength and extent of African-derived traditions in Cuba. The significant numbers of blacks and mulattos involved in the performance of classical music, conversely, attest to the strong influence of European music on Afrocubans and to its attractiveness as a marker of cultural distinction and a source of employment. *Danzón* orchestra leaders Enrique Peña and José Urfé, composer Aniceto Díaz, opera singer Zoila Gálvez, and symphonic musician Virgilio Diago, among others, all established themselves as successful artists performing middle-class music.[8] To this list might be added the many *trovadores* (troubadours, balladeers) of the period who wrote and performed songs strongly influenced by light classical music and art song.[9] Well-known Afrocuban *trovadores* included Pepe Sánchez, Sindo Garay, and Manuel Corona. These artists too performed in styles well within the confines of "acceptable entertainment music" as defined by the dominant society.

Straddling the boundary between "legitimate" musical practice and the clandestine sphere of African-influenced traditions performed in the home was a third sort of music making performed by the *coros de clave* and *guaguancó* (Afrocuban choral groups). These ensembles, associated primarily with the western provinces, represent an important precursor to and stylistic influence on early *son* bands in Havana. Surprisingly little is known about them. Urfé suggests that both began as Afrocuban imitations of the recreational choral societies established in Havana by the *sociedades españolas* (1984, 183).

Coros de clave, the more European-influenced of the two groups, developed in the late nineteenth century and remained popular through the 1910s. Famous *coros de clave* from their initial period of popularity (1880s–1890s) include El Arpa de Oro, El Botón de Oro, La Moralidad, and La Juventud (León 1961). Some *coro* ensembles contained as many as 150 members (Reyes 1994; Urfé 1984, 183). They were comprised primarily of male and female vocalists who sang two- or three-part songs in 6/8 time with simple European harmonies, accompanied by instrumentalists playing the *"viola"* (a banjo with the strings taken off that was played as a percussion instrument), guitar, *clave*, and occasionally the *botija*, harp, or other instruments (Orovio 1981, 103). A *clarina* (lead female singer) would typically begin with a solo, followed by responses from the chorus. Ten-line *décima* poetry served most often as the lyrical form of the text. By 1902 there were fifty or sixty *coros de clave* in black working-class barrios, and at least two groups in Havana—La Yaya and El Jiqui—were comprised entirely of white members who publicly denied any African influence in the music they performed (León 1985, 61).

Coros de guaguancó (also called *agrupaciones de guaguancó*), by contrast, seem to have been a slightly more percussive, African-influenced variation performed largely by men. Their instrumentation often incorporated the drums and other percussion instruments associated with traditional rumba (see chapter 6), yet were also known to include European instruments. Songs of the *coros de guaguancó* tended to be in 2/4 time and are said to have first become widely popular in the early twentieth century, somewhat later than those of *clave* groups. Among the earliest *coros de guaguancó* were the Azules Amalianos from the barrio of Jesús María, which formed in 1862. Most of its members worked as stevedores on the docks of Havana (Ramírez n.d.). Famous *coros de guaguancó* of the twentieth century include Los Roncos, Los Apaches, and El Paso Franco (Hernández Cuesta 1994). Los Roncos are especially noteworthy for their leader, Ignacio Piñeiro, who became one of the best-known *son* composers of the 1920s.[10]

The years following the Wars of Independence witnessed a great deal of demographic movement in Cuba. Many rural families whose assets had been devastated as a result of military conflict moved to urban areas after 1898. Others were forced to leave their homes when the lands they farmed and lived on were sold to foreign investors. Unemployed agricultural workers frequently had to move to new provinces in search of work. The creati[on?] [ejército?] *permanente* (permanent army) by the provisional U.S. gove[rnment] also resulted in the displacement of large numbers of Cuban[s. The au-]thorities during the 1906 military intervention, and later offici[al U.S.] administration (1909–1912), deliberately stationed new Cuban s[oldiers far from] their homes and families, so that they would be less likely to question orders if led into combat against the population (Blanco 1992, 9). All of these factors combined to bring *son* musicians from Oriente to Havana and other cities in the 1900s and 1910s, where the genre grew in popularity among the Afrocuban working classes.

In contrast to the musically literate Afrocubans who played in *danzón* orchestras, military bands, and symphony orchestras, the emerging body of celebrated *son* musicians of the 1910s and 1920s had little formal education. Expertise among *soneros* derived for the most part from an active involvement with music making in homes, on street corners, and in local bars. *Son* became popular in poor neighborhoods of Havana at a time when nearly half of all Cubans were still illiterate. It is not surprising, therefore, that its first performers had little schooling. Lorenzo Hierrezuelo, for example, a *son* composer from Oriente Province, was born into a family of agricultural workers in 1907 (Orovio 1981, 209). The efforts of the entire family were needed in the fields during most of the year, leaving little time for formal education. Hierrezuelo learned how to sign his name, but little more; all musical instruction came informally from his father and other relatives (Hierrezuelo 1994). María Teresa Vera, a popular singer of the 1910s and 1920s, had little schooling and could barely write down the lyrics of her own compositions (Linares 1993). Other Afrocuban performers of the period such as Arsenio Rodríguez and Carlos Embale never learned to read or write, let alone master musical notation. Chano Pozo has similarly been described as "un hombre sin escuela" (ibid.), an illiterate who lived from hand to mouth selling newspapers before establishing his popularity as a percussion soloist in nightclubs. The only member of early *son* bands with any formal musical education tended to be the trumpet player, who was added to many ensembles in the late 1920s. Lázaro Herrera, for instance, learned to read music in the military band of Güines, his hometown, before joining the Septeto Nacional in 1927 (Herrera 1993). Félix Chappotín learned to read music by chance as a result of being sent to reform school as an adolescent, as did his counterpart in the United States, Louis Armstrong.

The *Son* as Cultural Bridge

Son can be viewed as a stylistically pivotal genre linking the culture of the Afrocuban underclasses with that of mainstream society. Musicians who performed *sones* publicly in the 1920s, for instance, also performed more markedly African-influenced genres in private. *Soneros* in the Septeto Habanero played traditional rumba, joined in *comparsas,* and knew many of the songs, dances, and *toques* (drum patterns) of *santería* ceremony (Suárez 1994). Almost all members of the Sexteto Munamar from Regla were *abakuás* and *santeros* (J. Valdés 1994). *Tres* player Arsenio Rodríguez came from a family heavily involved in *santería*; he and his entire family were *santería* initiates and incorporated African terminology into many *son* compositions.

Singer Miguelito Valdés was also a *santería* initiate and a "son of Ochún" (ibid.). *Sonero* Antonio Machín included Yoruba ritual greetings to Ifá and Yemayá in his 1932 recording of the song "Una rosa de Francia" by Rodrigo Prats (Bolívar 1996). Carlos Embale established his reputation as a *rumbero* long before he began to collaborate as vocalist with the Septeto Nacional. Ignacio Piñeiro sang rumba as well as *son* and let his involvement with *santería* influence the lyrics of compositions such as "No jueges con los santos" (Don't play with the saints), "Papá Oggún" (Father Oggún), and "Canto lucumí" (Yoruba chant).[11]

Son musicians of the 1940s and 1950s also performed noncommercial Afrocuban musics, with singers such as Beny Moré and René Alvarez singing rumbas and *santería* songs as children before they became commercially successful dance band entertainers (Alvarez 1994). The emergence of *son* in the 1910s significantly widened the syncretic sphere mediating between realms of African- and Iberian-derived culture. It represented an important source of income and form of public recognition for many black musicians otherwise excluded from commercial performance.

Relative to other genres such as rumba and *comparsa, son* might be viewed as a concession by Afrocubans to dominant aesthetic norms. This assertion is contestable, however, given the frequent lyrical and stylistic allusions to African culture in such music. African words and phrases used by the Afrocuban community (then and now) appear constantly in *son* compositions. Terms such as *asere* and *monina,* which are of Carabali origin and mean "friend," "dude," or "buddy";[12] *ekobio,* a greeting used by members of *abakuá* sects; *chévere,* an internationally popular Carabali expression meaning "great" or "cool"; and *mokongo* and *iyamba,* used to refer to the leaders of *abakuás,* appear constantly in *sones* as well as in other forms of more overtly "African" musical expression.[13]

Son-influenced compositions by Ignacio Piñeiro such as "Iyamba Bero"[14] contain extended lyrical sections in Congolese languages and make direct reference to the *bonkó,* a sacred drum of the *abakuá.*[15] Piñeiro's "Viva el bongó" additionally contains friction drum sounds reminiscent of the *ecué,* another *abakuá* instrument. *Sones* by the Sexteto Habanero such as "Carmela mía" and

"Danza carabalí" include final sections in which the tempo switches from 4/4 to 6/8 time, recalling sacred Afrocuban rhythms and dances (Bacallao 1994). Many of the so-called *afro-sones* written by the Sexteto Munamar such as "Acuérdate bien, chaleco" and "Lucumí" were intended to be performed at *bembés* (informal Afrocuban religious gatherings) rather than as secular entertainment (Strachwitz and Avalos 1991).

Many other examples of connections between *son* and noncommercial Afrocuban music can be found. *Son* compositions from the 1910s on frequently refer to the rumba, as is the case with the Piñeiro compositions "Sobre una tumba una rumba," "En la alta sociedad," and "Lindo yambú." They also emphasize the African rather than the Hispanic heritage of *son* performers and listeners, as in Felipe Neri Cabrera's composition "Africana" (Strachwitz n.d.). Even the more European-influenced *danzones* of the period contain overt references to Afrocuban street culture. These include fragments of sacred *santería* melodies in praise of San Lázaro and Oggún written by Joseito Valdés (Valdés 1994).

The fascinating and somewhat ambiguous recording of "Ay Mamá Inés" by the Septeto Nacional is a further example of the interpenetrated musical influences in early *sones* (see Piñeiro 1992). "Ay, Mamá Inés" was originally composed by plantation slaves, but composer Eliseo Grenet converted it into *teatro bufo* dance music in the 1920s. The Septeto Nacional re-recorded "Ay Mamá Inés" about 1930, choosing to sing it in the exaggerated *bozal* dialect employed in the Grenet version (Grenet n.d., 1) but also adding new lyrics in both Spanish and Yoruba to the second chorus. The most striking phrase in the latter section is "Mulé y bibí, casa de mi omó," meaning "Blacks and whites [implicitly: are drinking coffee] in my godmother's house."[16] This piece demonstrates the complexity of *sones* as a sign vehicle. While heavily influenced by Hispanic traditions, they nevertheless reflect the marginal status of the Afrocuban working classes by incorporating cultural forms unknown and/or unacceptable to dominant society. In contrast, those *sones* popularized nationally during the 1930s and 1940s more often play down such references.

In Cuba of the 1910s, African cultural retentions of any sort were considered "barbaric" or vulgar (Martínez Furé 1994). At a time in which even progressive intellectuals still ascribed to notions of white superiority and cultural evolution, African-influenced music represented little more to the majority than the senseless pounding of children. The growing popularity of *sones* among the black and eventually white working classes thus caused considerable anxiety among those devoted to European music. Conservatory-trained composers and critics characterized the period that gave rise to commercial *son* as one of "degeneracy" in which middle-class traditions were increasingly "tainted" by those of the street. As late as 1928, figures such as Eduardo Sánchez de Fuentes denounced urban *son* as a genre of African rather than Cuban origin, one representing "un salto atrás" (a leap backward) for the nation (1928b, 189). He and others called for the suppression of musical activity by black street bands, claiming that their efforts were contributing to an overall decline in the quality of Cuban culture.

Spokesmen of the black middle classes also openly condemned the *son*. Members of the exclusive Club Atenas and the Unión Fraternal refused to allow *son* dancing as part of their recreational gatherings through the mid-1940s, longer than their white counterparts. Trumpeter Lázaro Herrera (1994) mentions that despite their international acclaim, top *son* groups such as the Septeto Nacional were never asked to play in these locations. Atenas and Unión Fraternal members continued to prefer genres such as the waltz, the fox-trot, and the *danzón* long after they had lost popularity among other sectors of the population.

Under the administration of Mario Menocal (1913–1920), ongoing condemnation of *son* by the middle classes resulted in a campaign against it by local authorities.[17] This was the same period that witnessed heated controversy over *comparsa* ensembles and the outbreak of the Guerrita del Doce in Oriente. Blanco cites an incident in 1913 in which residents of a *solar* in the Habana Vieja began playing *sones* in their central courtyard (1992, 15). Shortly after 10 P.M. a dozen policemen arrived and began to beat those taking part in the celebration with truncheons. The following day the same residents were fined for "immoral behavior" and the use of "illegal African instruments." Blanco describes a similar incident in 1919 involving the arrest of ten individuals in Guanabacoa for "dancing the immoral *son*" (ibid., 23). Even members of the relatively well-known Sexteto Habanero were thrown in jail on various occasions for playing *sones* at public gatherings.[18]

Throughout the 1910s, police routinely confiscated or destroyed instruments associated with *son* music such as the *bongó*, maracas, and the *marímbula* or *botija* (Martínez Furé 1994). Occasionally, they also shipped them to the Museum of Anthropology, at the University of Havana, as material evidence of the "inferior" behavior of "primitive" peoples.[19] Perhaps the instrument that aroused the most antagonism was the *bongó*. Because it was played with the hands and in that sense resembled instruments used in *santería* and *abakuá* ceremony, police officials considered the *bongó* especially offensive. Carpentier and others note that municipalities including Havana eventually passed legislation specifically prohibiting its use (1946, 245). *Sonero* Antonio Bacallao remembers his father telling him that in the late 1910s, "You could usually play a little *son*, but you couldn't play it with the *bongó*" (1994).

Although the jailing and harassment of *son* musicians tapered off in the

early 1920s, discrimination against them continued within the music establishment. Musicians' unions refused to accept *son* players as members until
about 1935. Representatives of organizations such as Solidaridad Musical,
formed in 1916, and the Unión Sindicato de Músicos de Cuba (USMC), created in 1923, maintained that only those performers with formal training and
who could read music had a right to membership.[20] This position was apparently used to justify long-standing prejudices against black street culture and
to maintain distinctions between condoned and "nonlegitimate" music making.

Marginalization from music unions meant the loss of employment opportunities for *son* groups and lower wages for their performances, among other
problems. Angry at such treatment, Afrocubans Fernando Collazo and communist labor activist José María Arriete eventually formed their own union in
1932, the Asociación Cubana de Conjuntos Típicos e Instrumentistas, or the
ACCTI (Herrera 1994; Collazo 1987, 164). Arriete could not afford to rent office
space, and instead used his home as an informal headquarters for several years
(Arcaño 1992). How long the union lasted, and at what point the USMC eventually accepted *soneros* as members, remains unclear. In any case, the debate
over whether to include *soneros* in existing unions largely resolved itself in the
1940s; with the declining national popularity of "classic" *son,* fewer *conjuntos*
performed in commercial establishments, and fewer attempted to establish a
relationship with organized labor.[21]

Commercialization of the *Son*

The period between 1920 and 1940 is generally considered the heyday of "classic" *son,* with over four dozen *conjuntos* playing regularly in Havana (Hernández
Cuesta 1994). In contrast to the *coros de clave,* almost all were organized by
men and constituted an important form of socializing for their members. Most
of what has been recorded about early *conjunto* history sheds light only on the
most famous high-profile ensembles lucky enough to make lucrative record
contracts.

The Septeto Habanero, for instance, one of the earliest commercially successful groups, formed in 1918. All of its members came from the barrio of
Pueblo Nuevo on the outskirts of Havana. Several of them had played together
beginning in the mid-1910s, calling themselves the Cuarteto Oriental. This name
later changed to Quarteto Meta Fiña after the group accepted a small cash
payment to promote a soft drink of the same name (Bacallao 1994). All of the
musicians of the Septeto Habanero came from working-class backgrounds.
Antonio Bacallao, the group's first *botija* player, owned a wood shop and worked

primarily as a carpenter, as did guitarist Guillermo Castillo. The band also included a bricklayer for many years, Gerardo Martínez *(clave)*; a soldier of the *ejército permanente,* Carlos Godínez *(tres)*; house painter Oscar Sotolongo *(bongó)*; and others for whom music represented their only form of steady employment (Bacallao 1994).

By the mid-1920s the Habanero began to perform widely at working-class celebrations, on local radio shows, and also occasionally in private parties of the rich. National popularity came as a result of recording contracts with the Victor Talking Machine Company negotiated through the firm of Humara and Lastra. The group's first '78 recordings—among the first to be made by any *conjunto de son*—were made in 1920 in New York City, where the band was invited by Victor.[22] During the same trip they performed live in clubs for North American audiences (Reyes 1994).

Said to have been the first ensemble to "put *son* in a tuxedo" ("vistió de frac el son"), to make it "sophisticated" and "classy," the Habanero enjoyed phenomenal popularity for decades. From the early 1930s, they booked engagements in exclusive Havana nightclubs and resorts and appeared in Mexican and North American feature films. The history of their primary rival, the Septeto Nacional, differs only in that the latter rose to prominence slightly later as a result of performances in the *academia* Habana Sport (Tellería 1977). The Septeto Nacional made recordings for the Columbia label beginning in 1926 and performed in the Hotel Plaza at the invitation of composer Moisés Simons (Herrera 1993). During their peak popularity in the following decade, the band accompanied exhibition rumba dancers in the cabarets Sans Souci and La Campana, toured in Spain, and played at the 1933 Chicago World's Fair (ibid.).

Despite their importance as institutions contributing to the popularization of *son* music, little has been written about the many *academias de baile* (ballroom dancing schools) that once existed in Havana. María Linares (1993) states that they originated in the late nineteenth century and in many respects resembled the *casas de cuna* described by Cirilio Villaverde and others from the 1830s. Whereas *casas de cuna* had traditionally been small dance halls managed by mulatto prostitutes *(mulatas de rumbo)* or madams, *academias de baile* tended to be owned and managed by white male entrepreneurs.

In theory, *academias de baile* were locations where young men could come to dance, or learn to dance. In addition to featuring a small orchestra or *conjunto* frequently comprised of Afrocuban performers, the establishments employed a number of female employees as instructors. Male patrons bought tickets from a cashier (costing a real, the equivalent of a dime, each) entitling them to dance a single number (Arango 1995). After choosing partners, the men would give them a ticket and proceed onto the dance floor. In practice, *academias de baile* functioned as centers of prostitution, as almost all of the "instructors" were willing to offer other services to clients, given adequate compensation. Women selected for work in such establishments were white or mulatto; black women were not hired (Rey 1994).

Music provided by *academia* orchestras at the turn of the century consisted of *danzones*, waltzes, and two-steps, but by the mid-1920s *son* had become the genre of preference. Martínez Furé considers *academias* crucial to the early dissemination of *sones* outside the Afrocuban community, noting that virtually all of the well-known *conjuntos* first established their reputations in such locations (1994). The Havana Sport (earlier called the Benito Vega) on the corner of Galiano and San José streets was perhaps the best known. It was also one of the largest, employing over a hundred women daily (Herrera 1993). Others included the Marte y Belona on the corner of Monte and Amistad; the Rialto at Prado and Neptuno (Rey 1994); the Galatea above the Café Central at Zululeta and Neptuno (Arcaño 1992); and the Carioca and Pompillo in Marianao.[23]

Dance choreography in the *academias* frequently emphasized fancy *vueltas* (turns) as well as exaggerated hip movement and close physical contact deemed unacceptable in more "respectable" locations.[24] Because of the controversial nature of music and dance in these establishments, as well as the fact that they were the scene of frequent stabbings and other violence, police routinely raided *academias* and closed them down for extended periods (Arcaño 1992). Dancer Carmen Curbelo suggests that even the most popular *academias* remained in a constant state of antagonism with authorities (Padura Fuentes 1988). As in the case of early jazz, the close associations between *son* music, "low-life" entertainment, violence, and prostitution first brought this genre to public attention in a decidedly unfavorable light. Lingering negative associations continued to limit the acceptance of *son* among more conservative sectors of the population—especially the middle classes—through the early 1940s.

Two other performance locations contributed to the early popularization of the *son*. First, representatives of the several large *cervecerías* or beer factories in Havana quickly recognized the popularity of *sones* among the Afrocuban working classes and attempted to profit by it. Shortly after the establishment of *son* as entertainment in brothels and *academias de baile* within the city, owners began to contract *conjuntos* to play for crowds in the gardens surrounding factories such as La Tropical (on what is today the calle 41 in Playa), La Polar (at the Finca San Antonio e Imperial in Cerro), and the *maltina* Tívoli (a malt factory, also in the municipality of Cerro).[25] All of the *cervecerías* were privately owned and located some distance from the center of Havana, and thus had more liberty to offer what was still controversial entertainment. Be-

fore the mid-1920s, Afrocubans constituted the overwhelming majority of patrons at beer garden dance events, but beginning about 1927 white working-
class patrons came as well.

Second, wealthy white politicians and business leaders began to contract
conjuntos de son to play in exclusive parties in private residences. These events,
called *"encerronas"* (lock-ins), became popular during the *"vaca gorda"* years
of national economic expansion (1914–1920). A host would buy exorbitant
amounts of food and alcohol, contract prostitutes, hire a dance band, invite a
few select guests, and then "lock" everyone into a rented house or other private
location to celebrate for several days at a time. The tradition flourished at least
through the late 1950s (Herrera 1993). Musicians at such gatherings earned
hundreds of pesos, wages in sharp contrast to the eighty centavos typically
earned per performer at working-class events (Hernández Cuesta 1994). María
Teresa Linares describes the *encerronas* organized by Gerardo Machado:

> Machado, the president, [generally] brought *son* groups to a couple of mineral
> water gardens in San Francisco de Paula [in the district of La Cotorra]; . . . he
> brought his girlfriends, his lovers, his "worldly women," and his political allies,
> to dance the *son*. And the Mendoza family went to parties like that, Paul
> Mendoza and the bankers and the really rich folks of the aristocracy.[26]

Officials of the Zayas administration (1920–1924), among the most corrupt in
Cuban history, were also well known for such "libertine diversions" (Linares
1993). Many popular *soneros* of the 1920s performed at *encerronas*. Miguel
Matamoros, for example, played at private gatherings organized by Federico
Fernández Casas, a politician and wealthy landowner in Oriente. Fernández
Casas was instrumental in inviting Matamoros to the capital and in popularizing his compositions there (Matamoros n.d.). Trumpeter Lázaro Herrera notes
that after the Septeto Habanero became established in the 1920s and began to
receive invitations to play at *encerronas*, the group often declined to perform
for working-class audiences and devoted themselves more exclusively to the
rich (1993).

Paradoxically, the very fact that middle-class society as a whole continued
to condemn *son* music and to discourage its performance in public areas seems
if anything to have increased its appeal for many of Cuba's elite. A perception
of the *son* as an overtly sexual dance attracted them, as did the prostitutes who
taught them new steps. Daring to organize an *encerrona* party with *son* musicians was an indication of one's political authority, suggesting that the host
was especially powerful and had the right to engage in any sort of activity
without facing prosecution. As Martínez Furé describes it (1994), political elites
reveled in the controversy surrounding the *son*, maintaining an attitude that

suggested, "This is forbidden; let's do it. This is savage; let's become savages for a few hours."

The Impact of Technological Change

In Cuba, as elsewhere (e.g., Anderson 1983; Löfgren 1989), the creation of new forms of communication led to the spread of nationalist cultural forms and ideologies. New media such as phonograph records and radio played a central role in both the mass dissemination of cultural forms and their appropriation by dominant groups. In Third World countries with high rates of illiteracy, radio has proved especially effective as a means of creating an extended sense of community and commonality. Hobsbawm argues that technological change, combined with a desire to tap the burgeoning working-class consumer market, led to a gradual "democratization" of cultural forms internationally in the early twentieth century (1989). The eventual acceptance of working-class music as that of the nation may thus derive in part from the nature of capitalism itself, suggesting that economic change can drive ideological change.[27] This section provides a brief overview of the history of radio and recordings in Cuba and their impact on the popularization of *son* music as the country's national dance form. Chapter 5 provides a complementary perspective by examining nationalist ideologies in 1920s Cuba and their impact on attitudes toward *son* and other popular musics.

Although Cubans lacked the equipment to make sound recordings until 1936, foreign record companies had been sending representatives to contract artists in Havana from the 1890s on (Reyes 1994). The earliest firms, such as Edison, Pathé, and Bertini, made cylinder recordings. About 1904, with the advent of discs, Victor and Columbia Records began biannual field excursions to Cuba to search for promising artists, greatly augmenting the number of releases available (Quintana 1954, 65). During these years and into the 1930s, technicians would rent rooms in large hotels such as the Inglaterra and convert them into makeshift recording studios for weeks or months at a time. Victor sales representatives worked closely with the owners of Humara y Lastra on Muralla Street, a major outlet for records, phonographs, and later radios. Agents relied on suggestions from owner Miguel Humara and his employees in deciding which artists to promote. Contracting decisions for Columbia were made in most cases by white Spanish-speaking musicians such as P. J. Ramírez and José M. Lacalle, who worked as independent contractors. The company hired these individuals in New York and sent them to Havana along with several sound engineers (Abril 1916, 26).

Ramírez, Lacalle, and others established the first Cuban offices of Columbia Records in the Palacio de Villalba on Egido Street. Recordings made before 1920 by Victor and Columbia featured classically trained stage artists such as Adolfo Colombo and Regino López of the Alhambra, opera stars Hipólito Lázaro and María Ross, military bands, and middle-class dance orchestras such as those of Enrique Peña and José María Romeu. Better-known performers were invited to New York to record, apparently to take advantage of higher fidelity studio equipment. The intended market for '78 recordings made during these decades included Cuba itself, the United States, Spain, Mexico, and to a lesser extent South America (Reyes 1994). Contemporary advertisements indicate that most records by Latin American artists were distributed throughout the region and that they considered Cuban consumers to be as potentially interested in Argentine tangos and *zambas* and Colombian *pasillos* as in uniquely national genres.[28]

The Brunswick label deserves mention as a pioneer in Afrocuban recordings and among the first to become interested in *sones* and *conjuntos de son*. Representatives from this company began contracting Cuban musicians in the mid-1910s, some years after Victor and Columbia had established a working relationship with preeminent performers (Reyes 1994). Brunswick spent its first years recording *trovadores* such as Juan de la Cruz Hermida, Alberto Villalón, and Mariano Meléndez, but before long expressed a desire to solicit new talent and new musical repertories. In addition to promoting alternative domestic styles within Cuba that had been overlooked by larger firms, they may have also intended to sell some of the records abroad as novelty items (Salazar 1938, 9).

Between 1916 and 1918, Brunswick marketed its first *sones* performed by Afrocuban Alfredo Boloña and a special ensemble created for the recording session. These early "pseudo-*sones*" seem to have been influenced by Europeanized versions of *coro de clave* songs adapted for the comic theater (Reyes 1994). As in the case of noncommercial *coros de clave*, the *sones* of Alfredo Boloña's ensemble featured a female lead singer, in this case light-skinned *mulata* and *teatro bufo* performer Hortensia Valerón. It is unclear exactly how many recordings of this type Brunswick made, or for how long. By the early 1920s, however, the firm had contracted several "classic" *conjuntos de son*, including the Sexteto Munamar and the Sexteto Azul. In later years, the Brunswick catalogue continued to offer a larger proportion of *sones* than other labels. The success of Brunswick at marketing *sones* domestically and internationally appears to have led Columbia and Victor to take the genre more seriously and to contract more *conjuntos*.

Owing in part to its proximity and close economic ties to the United States, Cuba was among the first countries to develop radio broadcasting, preceded only by the United States, England, and France (López 1994). In 1933, Cuba ranked among the developed nations in this respect, having established sixty-two stations, more than any other Latin American country (Acosta 1993, 36). The first powerful station capable of national broadcasts, PWX (which received financial backing from North American investors), began transmitting in 1922; numerous local, low-power broadcasting stations created by middle-class aficionados had been established a year or two earlier.[29]

President Zayas delivered the inaugural speech on PWX, which was held on 10 October to commemorate the onset of the Wars of Independence in 1868. Oddly, PWX's theme song was "La paloma," a piece by Spanish composer Sebastian Yradier, though based on the Cuban habanera. Like most early radio stations, PWX played predominantly classical music. Typical selections included compositions by Beethoven and other romantic composers, French and Italian opera, middle-class Cuban genres such as the habanera, *canción cubana*, and *criolla*. The many live broadcasts on PWX featured outstanding soloists of the Orquesta Sinfónica and the Orquesta Filarmónica, including violinist Joaquín Molina, as well as ballroom dance orchestras (López 1981, 32–33, 57–58). During the early years, little regulatory legislation existed to limit the strength of AM signals, and many U.S. stations could be easily received in Cuba as well.

By the late 1920s, radio had established itself as the primary medium of mass cultural dissemination in Cuba. Radio receivers, always cheaper than phonographs, became even less expensive with the development of new models and installment payment plans (ibid., 79). Radios became a common feature in homes, corner stores, barbershops, cafés, and nightclubs. They offered Cubans access to musical entertainment that would otherwise not have been heard in their immediate community. For the poor and uneducated, radio meant that styles of music that had earlier been performed only in concert halls or on '78 recordings were suddenly available to everyone. For the rich, radio (and records) provided the opportunity to listen to Afrocuban popular song without interacting with Afrocubans themselves. Black and mulatto singers who would never have been allowed to enter elite homes and clubs first gained admission over the airwaves. If not exactly "breaking down racial barriers" or transforming *son* into a "music without color," as suggested by Díaz Ayala (1981, 151), radio greatly facilitated the consumption of such music by mainstream Cuban society. By 1928, a growing interest in working-class musics was reflected in dramatic changes in the programming of even larger stations, with genres such as *son, guajira,* and *guaracha* increasingly dominating the airwaves (López 1981, 79).

Small, independent Cuban radio stations that flourished during the 1920s played a major role in the dissemination of *sones* beyond the confines of the Afrocuban community. Much as in the case of jazz and rhythm and blues in the United States, the programming of younger disk jockeys, who worked for independent stations such as 2DW, 2AB, and 20K (ibid., 52) and who were attracted to genres not yet accepted as mainstream entertainment, more than compensated for *son*'s initial exclusion from major station play lists. Younger disk jockeys had generally been raised in middle-class homes with access to record players and had acquired an appreciation for such music through that medium. Phonographs facilitated the promotion of *sones* on the air by circumventing the need for relatively costly live performances.

National Acceptance of *Son*

The period from 1925 to 1928 constitutes a turning point in the history of *son*, one in which it was transformed from a marginal genre of dubious origins into the epitome of national expression. One of the first indications of changing attitudes came in May 1925 when president Machado publicly asked the Sonora Matancera, at that time a septet-style ensemble, to play at his birthday party (Blanco 1992, 33). As mentioned, such invitations had been common for years but had typically been made in secret as part of semiclandestine *encerrona* gatherings. At roughly the same time, the first public *son* festival took place, and the Machado administration issued a public statement in support of *son* music.[30] Machado's Secretario de Gobernación announced on 23 October that *son* music and dance would henceforth be permitted in hotels, cabarets, and restaurants as long as it was not "scandalous or immoral" (ibid., 34). Attitudes toward the *son* on the part of the Cuban middle classes remained decidedly ambivalent through at least 1927,[31] but even the most outspoken critics could not deny its increasing popularity. The mid-1920s was also the first time that stylized *son* compositions for piano such as those used in the *teatro bufo* began to appear in middle-class leisure publications such as *Carteles* and *Bohemia*.

Popularization of the *son* in Cuba cannot be separated from international artistic currents in Western Europe and the United States. Recordings that facilitated the spread of *sones* in Cuba also spread them and other African-American musics throughout Latin America and to many other parts of the world. Moreover, this dissemination of Afrocuban culture had its corollary in other art forms. In visual art, dance, poetry, and literature as well as music, the late 1920s witnessed an explosion of a rather superficial interest in African and African-American culture among the Western middle classes as demonstrated by the celebrated figures of bohemian Paris and the Harlem Renaissance.

Cuban intellectuals and critics shaping public opinion during this period were highly aware of such international trends, having lived and studied abroad themselves. The international fashionableness of Africanisms undoubtedly contributed to a more tolerant stance on the part of many Cubans toward *son* music. Economic and political circumstances played a role as well. Increasingly violent protest against the pro-U.S. Machado administration and anger at the United States itself led to a strong nationalist campaign on the part of intellectuals. Changing attitudes toward *son* are in part due to their attempts to valorize and promote cultural forms viewed as uniquely Cuban. In the context of the barrage of North American merchandise, films, literature, sports events, and music that entered Cuba during these years, *son* represented an important symbol of national identity and a "weapon against [American] jazz" (Galán 1983, 346).

As a result of their own efforts and promotion by the North American music industry, Cuban *soneros,* black and white, gained large followings in Spain, France, and the United States beginning about 1928. Most chose to tour abroad at this time because political and economic troubles at home made performance careers difficult. In general, Cuban musicians popularizing *son* internationally fall into two categories: (1) the predominantly black and mulatto members of trios, quartets, and "classic" *conjuntos de son,* and (2) predominantly white musicians who performed stylized *sones* influenced by jazz and music of the *teatro bufo.* The former category includes the Septeto Habanero, the Septeto Nacional, and the Quarteto Machín, who often increased their popularity among Cuban audiences as a result of critical acclaim in other countries. Given the high regard for European culture expressed by middle-class Cubans and their disdain for Afrocuban genres, such listeners often proved more willing to admit the artistic legitimacy of *sones* after they had been accepted by Europeans. The 1929 prize-winning performance of the Septeto Nacional at the Exposición Ibero-Americano in Seville, Spain, for instance, represented a significant turning point in the career of that group and led to lucrative invitations to entertain guests in Havana's *sociedades españolas* from which they had previously been excluded (Linares 1992; Tellería 1977). As Emilio Grenet commented in 1939,

> When the primitive [i.e., "classic"] *son* seemed on the verge of opening the door to a negro conquest, it was rejected by our [middle-class] ballrooms as something of bad taste which came from the very low strata of society. The Parisian and American [record] labels became necessary before we could look with favor on a [genre which], ironically enough, now exhibited qualities . . . we had previously been unable to discover. (1939, xliii)

Singers and dancers such as Carmita Quintana, Julio Richards, and Rita Montaner were received enthusiastically while touring abroad in the late 1920s, exposing Parisian audiences to stylized parodies of traditional *sones,* rumbas, congas, *guarachas, pregones,* and other genres of the comic theater. These are the artists and the music, also promoted by the likes of Justo "Don" Azpiazu and Eliseo Grenet, that initiated what became known as the rumba craze of the 1930s. Their repertory fused stylistic components derived from Afrocuban traditions with ragtime, vaudeville music, and early jazz to create "respectable" or "universalized" versions of "typical Cuban music." Songs disseminated by stars of the comic theater and the *conjuntos de son* affected not only how citizens of other nations viewed Cuba, but how Cubans viewed themselves. Faced with the international popularity of Afrocuban genres they had once been ashamed of, middle-class Cubans were forced to reevaluate their biases against *son* and related musics and to accept them as legitimate national expression.

By 1930, *conjuntos de son* had achieved widespread popularity in Cuba, and government-funded organizations such as the Comisión de Turismo Nacional actively promoted musical events that featured them (Blanco 1992, 55). If not yet unanimously heralded as "the Cuban music *par excellence,*" *son* was recognized as the most influential new genre of the day. The early poetic works of mulatto Nicolás Guillén appeared in the conservative *Diario de la Marina* at this time, based in part on the formal structure of *son* music. In his collections such as *Motivos de son, Sóngoro cosongo,* and *West Indies, Ltd.,* Guillén fused themes of *son* music and dance, as well as lyrical segments based on the call-and-response structure of the *montuno* section, with images of everyday street life. His work represents one of the first attempts to incorporate Afrocuban musical themes into Cuban literature.

Liberal intellectuals such as Alejo Carpentier saw in the *son* a powerful symbol of the new Cuba he and others envisioned, one in which African-derived traditions would more directly affect, or at least inspire, national artistic production. *Son,* Carpentier wrote,

> is a product unique to us, as authentically Cuban as any *danza* or bolero. . . .
> What is more, in terms of pure lyrical expression, *son* . . . has created by means
> of its *lyrics* a style of popular poetry as genuinely creole as peasant *décimas*
> could ever be. . . . A whole Antillian mythology . . . lives in those couplets.[32]

Carpentier defends *son* to his contemporaries by comparing its structure to that of an "embryonic symphony" and suggesting that although "crude," it could provide the inspiration for great works of "high" art (1930, 153).

Members of the Septeto Habanero may have been among the first to have "dressed *son* in a tuxedo," but they were not the only musicians experimenting with ways of making *son* music "classier." Afrocuban performers were aware of the fact that large segments of the population considered the music they played primitive and unsophisticated. Several of the earliest celebrity *soneros* chose as a result to blend the *son* style with that of other, more "acceptable" musics. María Teresa Vera and Rafael Zequeira, for instance, achieved early popularity on independent Cuban radio stations and on '78 records because of their unique blend of *sones* with traditional *trova* repertory. The same can be said of groups such as the Trío Luna, organized in the late 1920s by Miguel Luna. Luna sang and played guitar, accompanied by vocalist and *clave* player Antonio Machín, and Eduardo Peláez on *tres*. The sound of this group deemphasized Afrocuban percussion and African-derived lyrical references, while carefully cultivating multipart vocal harmonies and melodic fills on the *tres*.

Perhaps the most successful Afrocuban group of the mid-1920s in bridging the gap between *trova* and *son* was the Trío Matamoros from Santiago. Miguel Matamoros, the leader and author of a majority of the ensemble's original compositions, experimented early on with musical fusion and first popularized such hybrid genres as the *bolero-son* (Hierrezuelo 1994). "Lágrimas negras" (Black tears) is one of his better-known *bolero-sones*, shifting from an initial section in a moderate tempo to a brisk *montuno* call-and-response. Matamoros also wrote songs in styles more popular at the turn of the century than in 1930s such as the *criolla* and habanera. An example of the latter is his "Mariposita de primavera" (Butterfly of springtime), part of the standard repertory of *trovadores* even today.

Finally, the *danzonete*, first introduced by Aniceto Díaz in 1929, serves as an example of *son*'s fusion with the *danzón*. Early *son-danzón* hybrids tended to be little more than *danzones* (typically an instrumental form) with added lyrics and possibly a repeated chorus. Later hybrids demonstrate more direct *son* influence through the inclusion of a *cencerro* or cowbell, the addition of a final *montuno* section, and an emphasis on vocal and instrumental improvisation. Predominantly Afrocuban *charanga* ensembles such as Arcaño y sus Maravillas and La Orquesta Aragón became exponents of music of this type. They were among the first to perform upbeat *son*-like music on violin, flute, and other European instruments not initially associated with the genre.

The mass popularization of *son* music led to an increasing valorization of Afrocuban street culture and of the artists who created it. Unfortunately, in many cases it also led to the exploitation of such artistry on the part of the music industry and other professionals. Afrocuban street musicians generally had little contact with the world of publication, record contracts, and copyright. For that reason they proved easy targets for those interested in profiting financially at their expense. As Bacallao (1994) explains, *soneros* had little protection from plagiarism in a country where song ownership could be established only on the basis of notation. In extreme cases, conservatory-trained composers actually followed street musicians as they performed, memorizing their songs by ear and later transcribing and publishing them as their own. Such was the case in an incident involving white composer Rudy Fanneity and Afrocuban singer/*pregonero* Filiberto Hurtado in Santa Clara (Díaz Ayala 1988,

160). The song that was eventually copyrighted under Fanneity's name and based on Hurtado's music was "Mantecadito," a *chachachá* of the 1940s.

A less overt but equally effective method of financial exploitation involved contractual procedures for recordings and the publication of sheet music. Typically, *soneros* were poor and needed ready cash. As a result, those who negotiated with publishers and record companies often accepted one-time payments in exchange for the exclusive rights to their works, unaware of the significantly larger profits they stood to lose in ceding song ownership to the company. Members of the Trío Matamoros, for instance, are said to have never received a penny in royalty payments from their recordings with Victor.[33] *Son* music also inspired many art music compositions within Cuba and abroad that "borrowed" melodies without compensation. Examples include "The Cuban Overture" by George Gershwin, which incorporates melodic material from Ignacio Piñeiro's *son-pregón* "Echale salsita" and Simons's "El manicero" (Grenet 1939, xxxviii). The "Poema de ambiente cubano" and "Concierto de Violín" by Alejandro García Caturla similarly take melodies from the popular *sones* "Que malas son las mujeres" and "Papá Montero," respectively, as material for their central themes (H. González 1994).

The songs of Eliseo Grenet further illustrate how *sones* and related genres tended to profit established white composers after the 1930s to a greater extent than Afrocubans. As mentioned, Grenet is credited with the composition of "Ay, Mamá Inés," a stylized *tango-congo/son* first performed commercially in the *zarzuela Niña Rita o La Habana en 1830*. The song was (and continues to be) tremendously popular, earning Grenet thousands of dollars. In actuality, the melody and lyrics of "Ay, Mamá Inés" were first performed by the Afrocuban *comparsa* ensemble El Ingenio de Pepilla under the direction of José María Ramírez ("El Colorado") (García Garáfolo 1930, 160). Members of this group from Santa Clara are said to have written the song in 1868 to celebrate the election of Mayor Mariano Mora (ibid.). Grenet's version is not identical to the original, but clearly derives from it. He is credited with sole legal ownership of his version and all those subsequently published.

The history of "Papá Montero" is similar. The piece is named for a well-known Afrocuban musician from Santiago in the early twentieth century (Robreño 1994), and was probably written by friends at the time of his death in the early 1910s (Carpentier 1930, 152). In 1917, *teatro vernáculo* playwright Gustavo Robreño created a *sainete* based on the life of the same individual for *negrito* Arquímedes Pous, which included a stylized version of the original song arranged and copyrighted under Grenet's name. Later recordings of "Papá Montero" by Afrocuban performers María Teresa Vera, Rafael Zequeira, and the Septeto Nacional all credit Grenet with ownership of the piece.

Finally, "Felipe Blanco" represents yet another example of the same phenomenon. This song, a *sucu-sucu/son* (a subgenre originating on the Isle of Pines) written during the War of Independence, tells the story of a Cuban traitor who led Spanish soldiers to a hidden *mambi* (revolutionary) camp. Grenet appropriated most of the song and later added lyrics of his own. Grenet's lyrics are humorous, consisting of puns and sexual double entendre, and are unrelated to those of the original (Linares 1993). The composition, first published under Grenet's name in the 1950s, became the subject of considerable controversy because in the eyes of many it slighted the revolutionary struggle. Public outcry and the eventual banning of the song from the radio are said to have contributed to Grenet's heart attack and death (Cristóbal Sosa, personal communication).

By the late 1930s, the heyday of "classic *son*" had largely ended. With important exceptions, especially ensembles performing in other countries such as the Cuarteto Machín in Spain, the *sextetos* and *septetos* that had enjoyed wide commercial popularity increasingly lost ground to jazz bands and amplified *conjuntos*. Street-corner *son* bands of past years found themselves unable to compete successfully for jobs in a market demanding full horn sections, sophisticated arrangements, and musicians who could read music. Members of El Septeto Munamar, La Sonora de Piñón, El Sexteto Liborio, and a host of other Afrocuban *conjuntos* that had enjoyed brief commercial success found themselves disbanding or performing solely in the Afrocuban community once again.

The relatively few *son* bands that managed to maintain their popularity did so by conforming to new trends and altering their sound accordingly. They tended to eliminate the "unsophisticated" *marímbula, botija,* and *tres* and to replace them with acoustic bass and piano. The Sexteto Gloria Cubana was influential in this sense, having incorporated the piano as early as 1925 (Blanco 1992, 34). The formation of the Sonora Matancera during the same period similarly presaged changes in the instrumentation of other bands. Valentín Cané, the group's leader, played *timbal,* an instrument that before the popularization of the "Sonora sound" had been used primarily in *charangas* and *teatro vernáculo* orchestras.[34] Cané performed in his ensemble in lieu of a *bongosero.* The Sonora arrived in Havana in 1927 and first played at the *academia* Marte y Belona (Collazo 1987, 74). In all, the 1930s represents a period of change in which the repertory of *conjuntos de son* blended with jazz, music of the comic theater, traditional *trova,* and Cuban ballroom dance musics.

In many ways, Arsenio Rodríguez's career exemplifies that of Afrocuban *soneros* who survived the waning popularity of the "classic" *conjunto* and created a new, more enduring commercial sound. Rodríguez was born in 1911 into a poor rural family in Güira de Macurijes, Matanzas Province (Díaz Ayala 1981, 174). As a child he was kicked in the head by a farm animal, resulting in blindness. Choosing one of the few career options available to him, he began playing the *tres* and moved to Havana in search of work as a musician. In the mid-1920s, Rodríguez performed in the Sexteto Munamar[35] and in 1926 organized a similar group under his own direction called the Septeto Boston (Alvarez 1994; Collazo 1987, 68). This group performed beginning in 1929 in the newly opened cabaret La Verbena and on broadcasts of Radio Salas (Collazo 1987, 86). Faced with declining interest in traditional *son*, in the mid-1930s Rodríguez altered the sound of his band by amplifying the bass and adding *tumbadoras* (*conga* drums), piano, and two more horns (Martínez Rodríguez 1993). The new format effectively reconciled the appeal of jazz music broadcast from the United States with that of traditional *son*.

Rodríguez, a dark-skinned black man, developed a heightened racial consciousness at this time, apparently as a result of discrimination by owners and managers of public music venues. Directors of the radio station CMQ, for instance, and other high-prestige establishments refused to allow his *conjunto* to perform (López 1994). Anger at such treatment contributed to Rodríguez's practice of employing exclusively black musicians through the 1950s, an attitude described as "racist" by some (Martínez Rodríguez 1993). It may have also led to his conscious "re-Africanizing" of urban *son* by constantly including African-derived terminology, and in some cases African lyrical themes. Examples include "Soy de Africa" (quoted in the epigraph to this chapter), a song emphasizing the author's African heritage and renouncing his Hispanic surname.

The famous "Bruca manigua" from 1936 demonstrates a similar tendency (Blanco 1992, 74). This piece is in a slow *tango-congo* rhythm. Its lyrics are written from the perspective of a slave who sings of his hatred for his master and his desire for freedom. Rodríguez freely alternates between Congolese and Spanish terminology to such an extent that the piece is virtually unintelligible to those unfamiliar with Afrocuban slang. One prominent line is "Mundele acaba con mi corazón, tanto maltratá cuerpo dan fuirí." *Mundele* in this case means white man, and *fuirí* physical punishment (Cristóbal Sosa, personal communication). The sentence translates roughly as: "White man has broken my heart, so much mistreatment, body beaten." "Bruca manigua" became popular through performances by Rodríguez himself, as well as in later cover versions by the Orquesta Casino de la Playa, Xavier Cugat, and others.[36]

Other groups such as La Orquesta Anacaona performed in a somewhat less oppositional style.[37] La Anacaona was comprised entirely of female musicians of mixed Asian and Afrocuban descent. It is especially significant as one of the most popular "girl groups" in the history of Cuban music, and because it provides an early example of performers from a lower-middle-class background who became involved in *son* performance. La Anacaona was one of over a dozen (predominantly white) female ensembles that formed in the 1930s, including the Orquesta Ensueño and the Orquesta Orbe. Only La Anacaona played *sones,* however; all the rest played only *charanga*-style ballroom dance music or jazz. This is true even of the *charangas* performed by *timbalera* Doña Irene and pianist Dora Herrera, leaders of entirely Afrocuban "girl groups" who performed in *sociedades de color.*

Initially, the Castro sisters, who formed La Anacaona in 1932, played in a traditional *septeto* style.[38] Concepción, the oldest, played guitar, Ada the *tres,* Olga the maracas, Flora the *clave,* "Millo" the *bongó,* and Ondina the trumpet, while Caridad sang lead vocals. Concepción convinced the others to form the band after her hopes of studying medicine were thwarted by Machado's closure of the University of Havana. Two sisters, Alicia and Olga, had studied music privately and were able to score arrangements for the group. They also received performance instruction from Lázaro Herrera of the Septeto Nacional (ibid.).

La Orquesta Anacaona made its musical debut playing in the open-air cafés on the Prado near the capitol building such as the El Dorado, the Saratoga, and the café of the Hotel Pasaje. Though they were well received, the group eventually changed its format and repertory in order to become more marketable. Beginning in 1934, they played *danzón, danzonete,* and related ballroom music as a *charanga,* and in the later 1930s they changed again to form a jazz band. This final format, retained through the 1950s, brought them greatest success.

The repertory of the Orquesta Anacaona included a surprising diversity of genres, including North American fox-trots and swing tunes, Spanish *paso dobles,* tangos, waltzes, and *son*-influenced dance music. Because of its versatility, the group was able to perform in virtually any venue in Havana, from popular beer gardens to exclusive gatherings in the Casino Español. Beginning in 1935, they also toured abroad regularly in Puerto Rico, Mexico, and other Latin American countries. Perhaps to an even greater extent than famous male *soneros,* the light-skinned Anacaona performers crossed color and class boundaries with relative ease, a process facilitated by their gender. Only the addition of a darker-skinned singer, Graciela Pérez, occasionally jeopardized their acceptance in establishments with elite white clientele (ibid.).

Conclusion

Changing attitudes toward the *son* in the 1920s derive ultimately from the increasing significance of all Afrocuban culture to Cuban society. *Son* music, as in the case of many other genres, has functioned historically as an ideological battlefield, a stylistic space mediating African, European, and other cultural influences. Ignored for centuries as an insignificant regional folk genre of the eastern provinces, *son* increasingly threatened the urban middle classes in the 1910s as a result of its popularization on street corners, in brothels, and *academias de baile*. Conservatory-trained musicians, city officials, and other self-appointed guardians of an idealized Cuba free of "atavistic" Africanisms condemned *son* music and dance, and actively suppressed its performance with the help of police. By the late 1920s, however, *son* had become so popular even among the white/Hispanic population that its acceptance as national culture could no longer be avoided. The appropriation of *son* by critics and government officials, and its rhetorical transformation into "the essence of Cubanness," functioned to diffuse its symbolic oppositionality. Unlike noncommercial rumba, *toques de santo,* and other forms of expression that continued to be excluded from dominant definitions of Cuban music, the relatively subdued African influences in *sones* came to be overlooked or even praised. This triagelike ideological shift effectively redefined distinctions between "us" and "them," African and Cuban. Such distinctions remained necessary in order to justify the biases still prevalent in the minds of the white majority toward blacks and black culture.

Various external influences contributed to the popularization of *son* music and its mass acceptance. Technological change in the form of phonograph recordings and radio broadcasts disseminated regional Cuban genres throughout the country at an accelerating pace. It brought *son* music to audiences in the United States and Europe, creating a new international market. New social groups and classes gained an appreciation for the recordings of Cuban *septetos* with little knowledge of or interaction with the Afrocuban culture that gave rise to it. International artistic trends also helped to legitimize the *son*. Representatives of the Harlem Renaissance and "bohemian" Paris, as well as the international jazz craze itself, helped create a body of critics, musicians, and spectators willing to accept expressive forms from Africa and the African diaspora as valid. Finally, the nationalistic fervor pervading Cuba from the late 1920s through the mid-1930s also influenced attitudes toward *son* and other Afrocuban expression. Polarization of public sentiment against the Machado administration and growing criticism of the United States resulted in a new movement to valorize Cuban culture.

By the late 1940s, *son* had lost its controversiality even among conservative Cubans and provided the basis for most dance music repertory on radio and records. In the process of mainstream appropriation, however, *sones* increasingly demonstrated the influence of jazz and ballroom dance music. Many successful *soneros* of later years maintained their popularity only by substituting the acoustic bass and piano for "folk" instruments such as the *botija,* replacing the *bongó* with the *timbal,* composing "sophisticated" arrangements with extended horn sections for their *conjunto,* and diversifying their performance repertoire to include genres other than *son. Charanga* orchestras popular in the 1940s developed dance music heavily influenced by *son* but performed on violin, flute, and other European instruments. Genres of the later 1940s such as mambo manifest many characteristics derived from *son* yet reflect the even stronger influence of North American big bands. *Son* was and continues to be a form of musical and stylistic bricolage, demonstrating the creative fusion of distinct traditions, national and international. It contains oppositional elements potentially liberating to the Afrocuban working-class community, as well as the constraints of middle-class influence, and thus illustrates the contradictions so prevalent in popular culture. It is a metaphor for the social order within which it developed, embodying and perpetuating emerging conceptions of Cubanness.

5 NATIONALIZING BLACKNESS

The Vogue of *Afrocubanismo*

We are experiencing, in effect, as a result of the natural
dictates of historical maturation and in instinctive defense
of the economic vassalage that the United States is
imposing on us, a period of intense affirmation of
cubanidad.
—Juan Marinello, "Vértice del gusto nuevo"[1]

Discovered by Columbus in the fifteenth century, by the
English in the eighteenth, by Humboldt and the creole
intelligentsia in the nineteenth, it remained only for Cuba
to discover itself in the twentieth century, and that is what
occurred [in the 1920s]. . . . What the period 1923–32
brought politically, socially, and culturally was the spirit of
the epoch, and with it the urgent necessity of a change.
—Ambrosio Fornet, *En blanco y negro*[2]

Issues of nationalism apply to many disciplines and scholarly concerns, including topics of long-standing interest to musicologists—the development
of artistic movements, "schools" of composition, and genres. Yet musicologists tend to discuss nationalism as if patriotic inspiration were the exclusive
concern of conservatory-trained composers, failing to acknowledge the central role of the state, international affairs, and local populations in such movements (e.g., Plantinga 1984, 342). Their work often demonstrates an elitist bias
as well, analyzing the phenomenon only in terms of classical music and excluding popular genres (e.g., Randel 1986).

Nationalism affects all forms of cultural expression. It affects how individuals conceive of their relations to others, how they think of themselves as
members of the same group, and how they justify such views. A successful
nationalist movement redefines commonly held notions of self and society
and constructs a new epistemological *us* vis-à-vis others. It enables certain
groups to effectively represent their interests as those of the entire nation and
to exclude alternate representations.

Theorists influenced by Gramsci stress the importance of ideology to politics, suggesting that dominance cannot generally be achieved through physical
control alone, but entails the creation of a sense of moral legitimacy, the "right"
of authorities to rule. Parodoxically, dominant constructs of nation must be
specific enough to distinguish the citizens of one country from others, yet
flexible enough to incorporate all of the ethnic subgroups and classes represented among the population. Hegemonic discourse attempts to generate an
illusion of national commonality and equality, and to promote its acceptance
even among the poorest and most disenfranchised members of society. Ultimately, the study of nationalism is not of race, class, ethnicity, or culture, but
instead of "the ideological structures of domination constructed out of these
distinctions" (Williams 1988, 33). Nationalist discourse is inevitably contested
and thus must constantly change, accommodating itself to new criticisms and
new social realities.

Culture is central to nationalism because conceptions of *us* can be convinc-
ingly justified on the basis of common experiences and customs. Shared language, geographic region, and religious faith can all serve as powerful symbolic markers of a nation. Music often plays a role in political discourse as
well, contributing to a sense of unity among diverse groups by means of mass
dissemination and/or collective ritual. Working-class musics can serve the interests of nationalists and others by functioning as iconic sign vehicles that
conflate the popular memory of expressive genres with a political agenda
(Buchanan 1991). Compositions of the middle classes that incorporate "folk"
genres transform these musics discursively and stylistically, presenting them
in new contexts. They refashion the past of subaltern expression so that it appears to share historical ties to the "legitimate" musics of the majority. The
meanings of nationalist music thus exist not in the sound itself, nor necessarily in the expressed intentions of the composer, but "extratextually, in the myths,
countermyths, and ideology" of the society in which it develops (Fiske 1989b,
97).

This chapter discusses the social conditions in Cuba in 1920–1933 that gave
rise to the sudden vogue of *afrocubanismo*. It discusses the political and economic crises of that period and a realization by many intellectuals of the extent to which U.S. foreign policy had contributed to them. It describes the
history of armed revolutionary struggle against the Machado administration,
the *machadato*, beginning in 1928, and its effect on artistic production. Finally,
the chapter provides an overview of the search by predominantly white middle-
class intellectuals for an effective means of representing the nation through
music.

Because of the current international vogue of *son* music, jazz, and commercial rumba, Afrocuban themes eventually emerged as the most effective sym-

bolic representation of *"lo cubano."* Somewhat paradoxically, however, the Afrocuban-inspired compositions of this period owe as much in a stylistic sense to music of the *teatro vernáculo* and European art song as to black street culture. And despite their heavily "Europeanized" sound, the compositions of white musicians Ernesto Lecuona, Gonzalo Roig, Moisés Simons, and others achieved mass popularity only after having withstood public criticism. Many still did not wish to accept Afrocuban-inspired expressive culture as Cuban and proposed instead images of the Cuban *guajiro* (the Hispanic peasant) and the Indian as alternate national symbols.

The Development of Modern Cuban Nationalism

Argeliers León's essay "Of the Axis and the Hinge" describes the history of artistic nationalism in Cuba as comprised essentially of two periods (1991b). The first stage (or position of the "hinge") begins in the mid-nineteenth century and extends into the early twentieth century. It is characterized as a predominantly "white nationalist" phase in which Afrocubans, though accepted grudgingly as members of society, were excluded from representation in cultural expression. Afrocuban themes only rarely appeared in painting and literature from this period, and the music industry excluded virtually all adaptations of working-class street genres from commercial recordings and printed scores. The second position of the "hinge" corresponds to the late 1920s and continues to the present day. In this phase Afrocuban musics grew increasingly central to national culture, at least as a somewhat abstract source of inspiration. The period extending roughly from 1923 to 1933 thus represents León's "axis," the sociohistorical moment linking distinct epochs of "white" and "black" nationalism.

Although this metaphor may overstate differences between the two stages, which share many common characteristics, León is justified in calling attention to the decade of the *machadato* as pivotal. In addition to witnessing the popularization of previously controversial genres such as *son* and *comparsa,* as we have seen, the era also gave rise to a profusion of popular salon compositions, *zarzuela* libretti, and jazz-influenced dance band arrangements that drew inspiration in some way from nineteenth-century slave celebrations, rumbas, *guarachas,* and other Afrocuban music. By the late 1920s, long-standing biases against Afrocuban street culture among representatives of the middle class had been aggressively challenged by a younger generation seeking new modes of nationalist expression.

Most historians link Cuban nationalist movements of the nineteenth century to economic factors, observing that separatist discourses first appeared when Cuban-born sugar planters began to dominate the island's economy. No longer in need of financial support from Spain by the 1830s, and feeling exploited rather than aided by colonial administrators, planters gradually developed a separate class consciousness (Portuondo 1972, 52), increasingly referring to themselves as Cubans or *isleños* (islanders) rather than *peninsulares* (from the Iberian peninsula).

Political discourse in turn affected musical production. Early nationalist forms such as the *teatro vernáculo* appeared in the mid-nineteenth century, as well as the contradanzas and other compositions of Manuel Saumell (1817–1870), considered the country's first musical nationalist (Carpentier 1946, 179–95). Genres such as those promoted by Saumell represent a break with Spanish and European culture, but a subtle one. He and his ideological descendants had been raised in a musical world of *jotas, paso dobles,* and a host of other Euro-Iberian musics and refused to valorize overtly Afrocuban expression. As might be expected, works written by Saumell and other nineteenth-century composers—Ignacio Cervantes, Gaspar Villate y Montes, Nicolás Ruiz Espadero, for example—are essentially European in terms of their overall sound, though they contain occasional melodic, rhythmic, and lyrical references to popular culture.[3]

Contemporary works in other media, such as painting and poetry, demonstrate a similar preference for European stylistic models (see López Segrera 1989, 38–69). The "founding fathers" of the Cuban independence movement, such as José Antonio Saco (1797–1879) and José de la Luz y Caballero (1800–1862), expressed their distaste for the Afrocuban presence on the island and in no way considered blacks equal citizens in the country they hoped to create (Carbonell 1961). The artistic production of their friends and colleagues naturally did not incorporate "degenerate retentions" from Africa.

Heavily demarcated divisions between *la alta sociedad* (elite society) and *las clases dirigidas* (the masses) through the early twentieth century, as well as between whites and blacks, problematized attempts to create a pan-national culture. The fact that distinct social groups and classes existed in relative isolation meant that they also shared little in terms of cultural expression and could not easily reconcile such differences within a single genre or style. The central dilemma facing the overwhelmingly white middle-class artists in the nineteenth and early twentieth centuries was how to create a "Cuban" culture while simultaneously distancing it from black and working-class expression, of which they did not approve. Class consciousness and cultural orientation in this case conflicted directly with nationalist aspirations. Ironically, the genres that served best as "primordial" symbols of Cubanness to Spain and the international community were the syncretic musics of working-class blacks, consistently denounced by nationalist leaders. The period of the *machadato* was the first in which, heavily pressured by political and economic circumstances, middle-class intellectuals tentatively accepted Afrocuban culture as their own.

The Twentieth-Century Context: Neocolonialism and Revolution

Cuba at the turn of the century was still dominated by colonialism, in particular the United States' Monroe Doctrine and notions of Manifest Destiny. Because of Cuba's proximity to Florida, and because of U.S. military involvement in the final months of the War of Independence (1895–1898), some North American leaders felt they had earned the right to annex Cuba and convert it into a colony. They suggested (falsely) that the Cuban revolution had been successful only because of U.S. involvement, and that Cubans owed America a debt of gratitude for their "liberation." A minority in Congress who had insisted on passage of the Teller Amendment prior to military involvement in Cuba, however, argued that Cubans should be free to govern their own country without foreign interference.[4]

During the postwar military occupation (1898–1902), McKinley administration officials excluded Cubans from peace negotiations with Spain and later supported puppet officials subservient to U.S. authority as leaders in the new Cuban government (Benjamin 1990, 61, 74). Cuba was finally granted ostensible independence in 1902 but remained subject to the constraints of the Platt Amendment (1901). This document authorized U.S. troops to invade Cuba at any time in order to "protect national interests," limited Cuba's right to engage in international relations or to accrue foreign debt, and assured the United States considerable political leverage in Cuba's domestic affairs. The imposed "agreement," combined with a number of reciprocal trade pacts between the two countries, essentially transformed "the substance of Cuban sovereignty into an extension of the United States national system" (Pérez 1988, 186). Without having to defend its actions against those who lobbied for the country's full independence, the McKinley administration effectively converted Cuba into an American protectorate.

United States businesses invested heavily in Cuba in the early twentieth century. The Cuban economy, devastated in the wake of decades of revolution, sorely needed external capital to rebuild and eagerly accepted the presence of U.S. enterprises. The Hershey Company, the American Sugar Refining Company, and United Fruit were among the largest investors. Free from most international competition and unrestrained by legal limits to land acquisition by foreign interests, U.S. landholdings expanded rapidly and by the 1920s dominated the Cuban economy. In 1927, during the peak period of U.S. investment,

North American mills accounted for over 80 percent of all sugar production in Cuba (Kutzinski 1993, 136).

By the 1930s, North Americans had invested $800 million in the sugar industry, $110 million in loans to the Cuban government, $110 million in the formation of a public utility infrastructure, $50 million in factories, $50 million in tobacco production, $40 million in retail firms, and $35 million in mining ventures (Arredondo 1939, 100). The total value of U.S. investment at this time surpassed that of its holdings in any other nation (Benjamin 1977, 19). Historians point out that the proliferation of U.S. industry led to a paradoxical situation in which some Cuban nationals accrued wealth and wielded significant political authority but did not control the means of production in their own country. The true oligarchs were North American investors who owned over half of all farmland, in addition to virtually all railroads, utilities, construction companies, and other key interests.[5]

During the *"vaca gorda"* years of the 1910s, international demand remained high for sugar and other products. The onset of World War I disrupted European agricultural production and contributed to the consistently high price of sugar through the decade. Experiencing relative financial prosperity, most Cubans tended to be unconcerned that their economy had been monopolized by foreign investment. Close relations with the prosperous and industrially developed United States seemed to offer potential benefits to all. Modest taxation of North American businesses generated tremendous revenues for federal coffers, so that even the notorious misuse of public funds by elected officials drew little attention.

Zafra (sugar harvest) revenues from 1919 to 1920, the peak of this lucrative "dance of the millions," amounted to $1.22 billion, more than had all harvests from 1900 to 1914 combined (Aguilar 1972, 43). In the early 1920s, however, rapidly falling demand for sugar and resulting economic hardship began to change the Cuban political climate. By December 1920, prices had fallen almost 400 percent from a high of 22.5 cents per pound to 5.51 cents (ibid.). Cuban farmers and landowners who had established their businesses on credit found their earnings devastated and many were forced into bankruptcy. They forfeited their lands outright through foreclosure or sold them at low prices to North Americans, thereby increasing the Cuban territory owned by foreigners.

Economic difficulties continued through the decade, leading to reflection about the causes of the country's continued unemployment and poverty. Workers and intellectuals who had never before criticized unrestrained U.S. investment began to do so for the first time. Revolutions in Russia and Mexico, and Augusto Sandino's anti-interventionist campaigns in Nicaragua during the same period also affected Cuban attitudes toward the American presence, bringing issues of economic dominance to public attention. Early manifestations of political tension with the United States in the mid-1920s included renewed public debate over the Platt Amendment, harsh criticism of U.S. political and military intervention throughout Latin America, and the creation of tariff legislation by Gerardo Machado designed to protect Cuban business against excessive U.S. competition (Aguilar 1972, 47).

Unions began to organize workers and to agitate for a national minimum wage, an eight-hour workday, and laws requiring foreign businesses to hire Cubans. The Cuban Communist Party was also founded during this period. Even conservative newspapers such as the *Diario de la Marina* began to publish strongly worded anti-imperialist articles beginning in 1927, as did the generally apolitical *Carteles* magazine.[6] Many Cuban popular songs appeared during the 1920s criticizing North American imperialism or referring to other political issues.[7]

Early twentieth-century economic dominance had its corollary in the cultural realm. Because of the size, proximity, and relative affluence of the United States, North American popular culture had been widely disseminated in Cuba since the late nineteenth century. During the early Republic, Cuban newspapers, magazines, radio programs, and movie theaters foregrounded American culture at least as prominently as that of Cuba. Middle-class leisure publications of the 1920s such as *Carteles* and *Bohemia* featured stories on celebrities such as Norma Talmadge, Ethyl Clayton, Rudolph Valentino, Charles Lindbergh, Jack Dempsey, Josephine Baker, and Al Jolson. U.S. beauty contests, sports events, dances, political controversies, and related subjects dominated the headlines of popular literature.

Even feature stories of domestic interest contained advertisements for Nestlé chocolate, Orange Crush soda, Palmolive soap, Goodyear tires, and Listerine mouthwash. North American music was played constantly on Cuban radio, with some stations such as CMOX later devoting themselves entirely to this repertory (Collazo 1987, 134). Martínez Furé (1994) notes that Cubans, regardless of their views on U.S. politics, have long been (and continue to be) strongly attracted to North American culture. Wealthier Cubans in past decades sent their sons and daughters to high school and college in the United States, reinforcing their exposure to the "American way of life." Educated Cubans read Faulkner, Fitzgerald, and Hemingway, vacationed in Miami or New York, and danced the charleston. In general, they considered American culture a part of their own.

However, in the context of nationwide depression and outcry over the extent of U.S. investment in Cuba, North American culture came to be viewed with suspicion. Anti-U.S. sentiment that initially had focused on economic and political issues extended to include all "Americanisms." Cuban journalists and critics considered for the first time that the ubiquity of North American culture might be detrimental, an insidious counterpart to economic control. Everything from the north suddenly implied "contamination" (Sánchez de Fuentes 1928c, 6), imposition, an obstacle to independence and prosperity. Alberto Arredondo, writing after the *machadato*, expressed sentiments typical of the period:

> Our first constitution was a copy of the American constitution; our educational reforms . . . were instigated by North Americans during the first years of the Republic and later under Machado. . . . Our electoral laws [were] created by North Americans, our journalism has always followed North American models; the fox-trot took hold throughout the island; movie theaters, cables, and radios continued to impose day after day the rhythms of commercialized North American culture; our social clubs and organizations imitated the United States and Europe, ignoring Cuba and transforming our most intimate and fecund national traditions; . . . our architecture followed the American path, our young people chewed chiclets and smoked [American-style] cigarettes; our children played with American toys; our chauffeurs drove only Yankee cars, our national sport was baseball.[8]

Musical publications from the late twenties and thirties encouraged Cubans to promote national musical genres such as *son* and *danzón* rather than jazz (Linares 1970, 106). Eduardo Sánchez de Fuentes, elected president of the Academia de Artes y Letras, railed against the "subversive" influences of jazz in speeches and articles.[9] Although North American music attracted the most criticism, composer Emilio Grenet also denounced the "imposition" of European opera, Argentine tango, and the Spanish *couplet*, which he describes as having been "'shoved between the sticks of our *claves*' with the most scandalous irreverence" (1939, xxxii).

Many social and technological factors contributed to growing interest in and awareness of national forms of expression. Railroad construction by British and North American firms accelerated the movement of migrant workers from isolated rural areas to other parts of the island and helped disseminate regional cultures throughout Cuba. The creation of the *carretera central* (central highway), begun in the 1920s, also did much to "unite the nation" figuratively and literally. Other forms of transportation such as bus and sea travel expanded by the 1930s and added to the concentration of the population in urban areas (Schwartz 1977, 31). Radio and record distribution contributed fundamentally to the mass popularization of *sones* and other recently "nationalized" musics of the period.

Liberal presidential candidate Gerardo Machado, elected in 1924, initially enjoyed popularity among a majority of the electorate. As late as 1926, his initiatives to stabilize sugar prices and to diversify the economy, as well as his relatively generous spending on public works projects, were met with enthusiasm by voters (Aguilar 1972, 73). His decision to illegally extend his term in 1928 generated considerably less enthusiasm, however, but even this might have been tolerated were it not for the onset of global economic crisis. Cubans had become accustomed to corruption and authoritarianism, but needed a full stomach to do so. The stock market crash on Wall Street devastated what remained of the Cuban economy and caused standards of living to plummet. International sugar prices fell from already low levels to an absolute low of a half cent per pound in 1930 (ibid., 98). *Zafra* harvests in 1930 generated only about a quarter of the revenues they had the previous year. Tobacco, rum, coffee, and other exports usually less susceptible to price variation could no longer be sold in quantity to the United States as a result of the Hawley-Smoot Tariff Act (1930) and the Chadbourne Plan (1931), which restricted trade for the benefit of domestic producers. By the early 1930s, as many as 250,000 heads of families—about a third of the population—were without employment (Pérez 1986, 280).

Economic desperation created widespread political unrest throughout the island, heightened anger over United States foreign policy, and galvanized opposition to Machado. An increasingly violent series of protests and strikes aimed at toppling the government began among farmers, urban workers, and unpaid white-collar government officials. Beginning in 1930, in a desperate attempt to remain in power, Machado outlawed rival political parties, closed down the university, suspended constitutional guarantees, censored or banned the sale of major newspapers, and waged open warfare against opposition leaders, including those of the Communist Party, the Directorio Estudiantil Universitario, and ABC revolutionaries.[10] The infamous death squads of the *porra,* or secret police, assassinated many labor leaders and student activists, and exiled or imprisoned countless others. Even entertainment publications such as *Bohemia* eventually denounced Machado as the "Mussolini of the Caribbean" and called for his resignation.[11] Finally, a general strike in August 1933 by transportation workers expanded to include virtually all unionized labor and brought the economy to a standstill. This event resulted in the exile of Machado to the United States, a country that had supported him until the final months of the conflict.

The Emergence of *Afrocubanismo*

Music and dance remained exceedingly popular throughout the worst years of *machadato* violence and economic upheaval. For many, popular music provided a form of escapism, a means of temporarily forgetting the realities of the moment and focusing only on the romantic sentiments that proliferated in contemporary song lyrics. Roig de Leuchsenring wrote in 1932 that the public "delivered themselves up to dancing" in especially large numbers during the bloodiest periods of the *machadato:* "It seems that Cubans endeavor to exhaust themselves physically and morally with dance and gaming in a suicidal fit of collective lunacy, in order to anesthetize their maladies and misfortunes."[12]

Although relatively rare, some political protest songs became popular as well. Examples include pieces criticizing the *"prórroga de poderes,"* Machado's extension of his term beyond 1928 (Blanco 1992, 47); "Bomba lacrimosa" (Tear gas bomb) by Miguel Matamoros which mixes references to government-instigated street violence with sexual double entendre;[13] Ignacio Piñeiro's "Incitadora región" from 1930 (Strachwitz and Avalos 1991); unspecified works by *trovador* Rosendo Ruiz, for which he was forced into exile (de León 1990, 139); and compositions by Sindo Garay, including "Los tabaqueros" (The cigar makers) and "Oración por todos" (Prayer for all). The former describes the murder of striking factory workers by government forces, while the latter was inspired by the assassination of student activist Julio Antonio Mella in Mexico (Rodríguez Domínguez 1978, 62, 126).

More than providing an avenue of escapism or a forum for political commentary, however, the 1920s and 1930s inspired tremendous quantities of nationalistic music and other art. Antecedents of this trend can be found in earlier decades, with the establishment of national music institutes, performance ensembles, cultural organizations, and in the writings of the Cuba Contemporánea group (Wright 1988). Early centers of state-sanctioned musical activity include the Conservatorio Nacional de Música, founded in 1885 by Hubert de Blanck; the Academia Municipal de Música de la Habana, created in 1903 through the efforts of Guillermo Tomás (later renamed the Conservatorio Muni-cipal); and the Escuela Municipal de Música and Academia Nacional de Artes y Letras, both of which date from 1910 (Calero Martín 1929, 36; Díaz Ayala 1981, 82). All of these institutions promoted European classical repertory, although the works of Cuban art music composers did receive some attention.

The first philanthropic society with an openly nationalist musical agenda was Pro-Arte Musical, created by María Teresa García Montes de Gilberga in June 1919 (Orovio 1981, 312). As one might expect, members of Pro-Arte ascribed to conservative nationalist goals tempered by elitism, promoting both the performance of Cuban music as well as the "elevation" of public taste. Antagonistic to most working-class expression, and especially that of Afrocubans, Pro-Arte members were dismayed that the public desired "to hear the [stage] rumbas [of the comic theater] by [Jorge] Anckermann" rather than "quality music" (Giralt 1920, 12). Pro-Arte established a fund used to subsidize the performance of notable foreign concert musicians in Havana, including Fritz Kreisler, Pablo Casals, and Jascha Heifetz, and it sponsored frequent public events in the Teatro-Auditorium del Vedado at Calzada and D Streets (Rosell 1992 2:184). Pro-Arte was a driving force in 1922 behind the formation of the first symphony orchestra in Cuba, the Orquesta Sinfónica de la Habana. This ensemble promoted the work of Cuban "white nationalist" composers Guillermo Tomás, Eduardo Sánchez de Fuentes, Ignacio Cervantes, and José Mauri.[14]

Members of the Cuba Contemporánea group, formed in 1913, represented the more liberal and patriotic thinkers of their day.[15] Their most important goal was the regeneration of a sense of national self-worth among the population. Years of government scandal and violence requiring U.S. military intervention had caused leaders to doubt the ability of Cubans to effectively govern themselves. Discourse about the "decadent" nature of the Cuban psyche, and of Cuban culture, reached its peak during this decade.

Intellectuals associated with Cuba Contemporánea did not blame political instability on the United States, as coming generations would do, but rather on a lack of familiarity with history and the ideals of nineteenth-century revolutionaries. They endeavored to teach Cubans about the writings of José Martí, Máximo Gómez, Carlos Manuel de Céspedes, and Antonio Maceo through lectures and the dissemination of literature. Their journal, *Cuba Contemporánea,* began publication in 1913 and contained many articles of a similar nature. The group also created the Siglo XX Press in 1917, which printed numerous biographies as well as cultural works such as *El folk-lor en la música cubana* by Sánchez de Fuentes (1923)[16] and the monumental eighteen-volume *La evolución de la cultura cubana 1608–1927* (1928). Members of Cuba Contemporanea were instrumental in reprinting essays by José Antonio Saco, developing the Cuadernos de Cultura series under the auspices of the Education Ministry and the Colección de Libros Cubanos edited by Fernando Ortiz (Beruff Mendieta 1937, 40).

In conjunction with the Academia Nacional de Artes y Letras and the Academia Nacional de Arte y Historia, Cuba Contemporánea activists sponsored regular *tertulias* (informal gatherings) on issues related to the arts. However, as with Pro-Arte Musical, their impact was limited as a result of an elitist orientation. Viewing themselves as leaders, not partners, in cultural change, members had little contact with public officials, leftist intellectuals, or representatives of the working classes. The *Cuba Contemporánea* journal failed to interest even the literate middle classes because of its dry, pedantic tone (Wright

1988). With increasing criticism of U.S. foreign policy beginning in the mid-1920s, the group lost all appeal because of its pro-American bias. Hopelessly behind the vanguard of intellectual thought by that time, the association disbanded in 1927.

The early 1920s witnessed an escalation of nationalist rhetoric and intensified cultural production. Essays by Emilio Roig de Leuchsenring first appeared in the magazines *Social* and *Carteles* at this time, condemning the United States' interventionist policies and questioning its role in Cuban affairs (Roig de Leuchsenring 1919, 1920, 1923). Under the leadership of Roig, Enrique Gay-Calvó, Manuel Márquez Sterling, and others, controversy over the Platt Amendment and its infringement on Cuban sovereignty entered public discourse more forcefully than ever (Wright 1988, 117). Organizations such as Rubén Martínez Villena's Falange de Acción Cubana, Fernando Ortiz's Junta de Renovación Cubana, and the Veterans and Patriots movement all formed around 1923 to fight government corruption and promote pride in the nation. Artists and literary figures broke their political silence and began to take a more aggressive stand on a number of issues. The most famous instance of early political activism among artists, the so-called Protest of the Thirteen, took place in March 1923 and involved figures of the emerging Minorista vanguard such as Alejo Carpentier.

At the same time, artists' promotion of national cultural forms became more aggressive. Sánchez de Fuentes organized the first Festivals of Cuban Song beginning in 1922, initially in Cienfuegos and later in Havana.[17] Performers included Rita Montaner, Tomasita Núñez, and Néstor de la Torre (Sánchez de Fuentes 1928c, 143). Popular genres remained largely excluded from the festival, however, which featured works by middle-class composers Tomás Buelta y Flores and Manuel Jiménez (both mulattos), Laureano Fuentes Matons, Gaspar Villate, and Nicolás Ruiz Espadero. Participants maintained a conscious distinction between the carefully selected "Cuban music" promoted by the festival and "popular music," of which they did not approve. Some expressed the hope that genres like the *canción cubana* would eventually supplant others such as *son*, resulting in the "aristocratization" of national traditions (ibid.). Another significant event of this period was the publication of Fernando Ortiz's *Catuaro de cubanismos* (1923) and *Glosario de afronegrismos* (1924), perhaps the first scholarly studies of Afrocuban popular culture that did not view it as a "social pathology" but as a potential source of national pride.

One other landmark of 1923 was the creation of the Sociedad de Folklore Cubano, with Enrique José Varona as its first president (del Morro 1923). Founded on 6 January (to coincide with the anniversary of the nineteenth-century Kings' Day celebrations), the group's first meeting took place at the

Sociedad Económica de Amigos del País at Dragones 62 in Habana Vieja (Cairo Ballester 1988, 3). The membership roster reads like a list of key white intellectuals of the decade, including lawyer and writer José Chacón y Calvo, Fernando Ortiz, Israel Castellanos, Emilio Roig de Leuchsenring, Rubén Martínez Villena, Alberto Lamar Schweyer, Jorge Mañach, Jose Antonio Fernández de Castro, and Juan Marinello.

The central goal of the Folklore Society, like the others mentioned, was the "national reconstruction" of Cuba through the valorization of its arts and culture. Ostensibly designed to study all types of folklore, members concentrated almost exclusively on Hispanicisms during the first five years. Those present at the initial meetings voiced their intention to study and classify genres of popular song derived from Spanish traditions including *romances, décimas,* and boleros, but avoided discussion of Afrocuban arts. To the extent that such forms interested members, they were to serve as the object of "descriptive study oriented toward the goal of social therapy." Academic studies of Afrocuban music, it was hoped, would curb "certain morbid practices such as acts of witchcraft and *ñáñiguismo* in which . . . low cultural life manifests itself."[18] "Picturesque" *(pintorescas)* Afrocuban traditions of the past such as slave dances of the colonial period seem to have been accepted as "national patrimony," but most contemporary genres continued to be viewed as an embarrassment to civilization.

By the late 1920s, the representations of pan-Cuban expression promoted by middle-class artists and institutions had largely been overshadowed by the national and international popularization of *son* and cabaret rumba, discussed in chapters 4 and 6. The rural expressive forms studied by Cuban folklorists and the art song compositions promoted by the Academia Nacional de Artes y Letras proved much less appealing commercially than works by Miguel Matamoros, Ignacio Piñeiro, Ernesto Lecuona, and others. Intellectuals and critics could see that their conception of artistic nationalism needed revision and that any future construct would have to situate urban working-class expression more centrally. Some such as Roig de Leuchsenring viewed the international interest in jazz, *son,* and other African-American musics as a positive occurrence. He considered the vogue of diaspora culture a powerful force that could further nationalist agendas within Cuba. A promotion of "whitened" Afrocuban music (such as that of the *teatro vernáculo*) would reinforce images of the nation already accepted by many at home and abroad. It would help ensure that Cuban culture remained vital rather than succumbing to North American influences. Roig de Leuchsenring commented,

> For some time, and in many ways, there has been a call among us for . . . a
> unique form of [Cuban] creole art. . . . If as a result of well-known geographic,

economic, and political circumstances we must, in order not to perish as a sovereign State and even as a people, maintain our own language, land, and economy, we also must have our own artistic forms. . . . [These will contribute], along with [other factors], to national vitalization and greatness.[19]

To Roig and like-minded individuals, syncretic Afrocuban forms had the potential to serve as a barrier to national disintegration and the possibility of cultural subsumption by the United States. While Juan Marinello argued against the promotion of *costumbrista* nationalism on the grounds that it created aesthetic limitations for artists (1929, 137), most contemporaries did not share his convictions. The question for most musicians, poets, and visual artists during this period was not whether or not to create nationalist art, but what form it should take.

Symbolic Alternatives: *Indigenismo* and *Guajirismo* Nationalism

Although the music of *afrocubanismo* artists ultimately proved most effective in symbolizing Cubanness during the *machadato,* it was not the only form of nationalist composition. Pervasive biases against Afrocuban street culture among middle-class musicians problematized the acceptance even of salon rumbas, congas, and related musics as national expression. Many patriotic songs of the period avoided racial references altogether, as in the case of Jorge Anckermann's "A mi Cuba" (Anckermann 1942), Sánchez de Fuentes's habanera "Tú," or Moisés Simons's "Así es mi patria" (Pathé 06640-b). These works invoked the common struggles of the revolutionary war, the writings of José Martí, or depictions of the countryside in order to inspire nationalist sentiment.

Another means of representing the nation symbolically through music— rather unsuccessful in the long term relative to *afrocubanismo*—might be described as indigenous nationalism. Images of the Siboney and Arawak Indians who lived in the Caribbean before the conquest provided an alternative basis for constructing Cuban cultural heritage. They were especially appealing to those uncomfortable with privileging the nation's African heritage yet desirous of establishing racial primordials as contributing factors to *cubanidad*. The movement has its roots in the mid-nineteenth-century literary works of authors such as Ramón de Palma (1812–1860), Cristóbal Napolés Fajardo, known as "El Cucalambé" (ca. 1829–1862), and José Fornaris (1827–1890).

Early *indigenismo* literature offered an outlet for nationalist expression during a period of intense censorship by colonial authorities, one in which patriotic sentiment could be expressed only through metaphor or indirect allusion (Fornaris 1967, 15; Cruz 1974, 8). Musical works from the nineteenth century also incorporated references to the Indian, as in "La piragua" (The canoe), "La indiana," and other *contradanzas* cited by Lapique Becali (1979, 26). The fact that forms of Siboney music such as the *areíto* had been prohibited by colonial authorities as early as the sixteenth century (Ortiz 1965, 73), and that the brutal oppression of native peoples had resulted in their virtual extinction during the same period, did not dissuade many artists from depicting *el indio* as the progenitor of the nation.[20]

Reimagining the past and their relationship to it, advocates of musical *indigenismo* generated a considerable body of work inspired by historical figures such as Hatuey, Anacaona, and Yumurí. Neighboring Latin American countries like Mexico, with large Indian populations and strong nationalist movements of their own, undoubtedly contributed to the perpetuation of *indigenismo* art in Cuba during the twentieth century. The public parks in Havana named after Indian leaders during the Republic (Collazo 1987, 147), the marble statue of "La india" constructed near the capitol building, and other public references discursively linked Cubans to their ostensible Siboney heritage and the brave and independent spirit with which it was associated. The profile of the militant war chief Hatuey, whom Spaniards burned at the stake because of his refusal to submit to their authority, became (and remains today) a common sight on bottles manufactured by a beer company of the same name.

The first musicologist to assert that the unique qualities of Cuban music derived from indigenous rather than Afrocuban sources was Antonio Bachiller y Morales (1812–1889). In *Cuba primitiva* (1880), he included an extended discussion of Siboney song and dance, noting that "the music of our Indians has been incorporated into [Cuban folk song] to a greater extent than we had earlier imagined" (Simons 1927b). Bachiller y Morales notated a number of what are described as Indian melodies and published them in the same book. These include "Canto de guerra" (War chant), "Canto a la tarde" (Afternoon song), and "Canto a la aurora" (Song to the dawn), in addition to the famous "Areíto de Anacaona."[21]

Bachiller y Morales influenced later musical figures like Sánchez de Fuentes and Moisés Simons, who used his writings in the 1920s to justify their own beliefs about the centrality of Siboney expression to Cuban music. Extending the hypotheses presented in *Cuba primitiva,* they ascribed indigenous origins to numerous instruments and musical forms developed by Afrocubans and Hispanics. These included the *marímbula* used in early *sones,* the *tres* and other folkloric string instruments, the *clave,* and many drums used in rumba and *santería* ceremony (Sánchez de Fuentes 1928b, 157; Simons 1927b).

Similarly, such critics believed that indigenous melodies had heavily affected the song repertory of *guajiro* (peasant) musicians in rural areas. They suggested that stylistic characteristics of the *punto cubano, zapateo,* and *guajira,* such as melodic leaps of fourths and fifths as well as unspecified rhythmic patterns, demonstrated the influence of the *siboneyes* on traditions derived from Spain (Simons 1927b). Sánchez de Fuentes described the music and dance of (predominantly black and mulatto) Oriente Province, particularly the region around Mayarí, as markedly "Indian-sounding" (1928c, 14). He further maintained that even the *contradanza, danza, danzón,* habanera, and other middle-class salon genres contain indigenous influences.[22] By contrast, he categorically denied the presence of characteristics derived from the black community. "*La raza cubana*" and its culture, as conceived by Sánchez de Fuentes and many of his contemporaries, remained free of "contamination" by "the African factor" (1928b, 170).

In the early Republic, much Cuban music was written that incorporated indigenous subject matter. Sánchez de Fuentes himself wrote two of the best-known early examples, the *indigenismo* operas *Yumurí* and *Doreya.* The former, based on a libretto by Rafael Fernández de Castro—then governor of Havana Province—premiered in the Teatro Albisu on 26 October 1898 (González 1986, 316). The plot of this *ópera seria* is primarily fictional. It revolves around the Indian princess Yumurí who is betrothed to a warrior of her tribe, Cunabaco, yet has fallen in love with the Spanish conquistador Alonso de Pineda. Pineda eventually kills his Indian rival and makes off with Yumurí into the hills, but both later die in a sudden earthquake.

The second opera, *Doreya,* with a libretto by Hilarión Cabrisas, debuted on 7 February 1918 (ibid., 418). Its plot is quite similar to Sánchez de Fuentes's earlier work. Princess Doreya is the daughter of a Siboney cacique who has fallen in love with a Spaniard. She wants to run away with him, but the tribe won't allow her to, as her father hates white men. Desperate, she and the Spaniard eventually elope together, only to be pursued and killed by members of the tribe. Some Cuban historians (e.g., Lapique Becali 1974, 222) describe these works as "*indigenismo de fantasía*" because they are identical stylistically to Italian opera and do not incorporate a single indigenous instrument or other influence into the musical accompaniment.

Various compositions by Ernesto Lecuona from the *machadato* incorporate themes similar to those of *Yumurí* and *Doreya,* conflating imagery of the Indian with that of the Cuban nation. His famous "Canto Siboney," for instance, written as part of the *zarzuela La tierra de Venus,* dates from 1927 (Orlando Martínez 1988, 87). Rita Montaner and Margarita Cueto popularized the song by recording it a short time later for Columbia and RCA Victor, respectively, as did the Victor orchestra itself (arranging the melody as a jazz foxtrot) and even unlikely figures such as Bing Crosby.[23] As with most other *indigenismo* compositions, the lyrics of "Canto Siboney" constitute virtually its only reference to native culture; it otherwise sounds much like any other commercial tune from the same period, although the major-minor sectional modulations suggest the influence of the habanera. Lecuona presents "Siboney" as the object of empassioned love. Performed in light operatic style by Montaner, Cueto, and others, the song contains the following refrain:

> Siboney, I love you, I'm dying for your love,
> Siboney, in your honeyed mouth you have placed your sweetness,
> Come here, I love you, you are my ultimate treasure,
> Siboney, in the rustle of your palm tree I think of you . . .
> Listen to the echo of my song of crystal,
> Don't lose yourself out in the wild countryside.[24]

Lecuona's "Canto indio," a similar piece, dates from 1929 and was originally written as part of the *zarzuela La flor del sitio* (Orlando Martínez 1988, 87). The *tango-congo* ostinato rhythm employed in this composition seems somewhat incongruous but is apparently used to create an ambience of "generic primitivism" rather than to bring slave dances to mind (Lecuona 1929b). As in the case of "Siboney," the lyrics of "Canto indio" romanticize indigenous life and culture, while the music accompanying them is in the style of European parlor song and excludes indigenous characteristics.

Other middle-class works of the 1920s and 1930s could be cited as examples of *indigenismo*, including the parlor song "Hatuey" by Eliseo Grenet (see illustrations). As with proponents of *afrocubanismo*, many of the same individuals who championed the creation of middle-class music with Indian themes frequently held ambivalent views of truly indigenous music. Sánchez de Fuentes, for instance, in one essay describes sixteenth-century *areítos* as "rudimentary" and Siboney dance as "primitive" (1938a, 9). Similarly, Emilio Grenet refers to the "roughness and lack of culture of the [Cuban] Indian" (1939, xix), and Calero Martín to the "extreme monotony of indigenous music" (1929, 21). These authors were well aware that the stylized works they promoted bore little relation to the Siboney traditions heard by the conquistadors and happily maintained the distinction.

Finally, many working-class Afrocuban musicians also found indigenous imagery attractive. Like North American blacks who participate in Mardi Gras Indian celebrations in New Orleans (Lipsitz 1990, 233–56), Cuban blacks were drawn to Siboney imagery as a symbol of independence, bravery, and perhaps also of nonwhite resistance to white authority. Slaves and free blacks in Cuba dressed as Indians in Kings' Day celebrations of the nineteenth century (e.g., Ortiz 1984, 31), donned feather headdresses in *comparsa* bands of the early 1900s, and named their *conjuntos de son* after Indian leaders. Examples of the latter include the Sexteto Guarina, formed in 1927, and the Sexteto "Los

Siboneyes," created in 1929 (Blanco 1992, 41, 49). Mulatto troubadour Sindo Garay is similarly remembered for having given his three children indigenous names because from an early age he "felt like an Indian" (de León 1990). Compositions inspired by indigenous groups remain common today among white and black musicians. Salsa tunes such as "Anacaona" by Puerto Rican C. Curet Alonso have become standard dance repertory for many club bands,[25] while the recently re-formed "Orquesta Anacaona" in Havana continues discursive traditions established by the earlier female orchestra of the same name, and by the "Orquesta Siboney" jazz band of Alfredo Brito from the 1930s.

"*Guajiro* nationalism" was a related if slightly less widespread alternative to the *afrocubanismo* movement that also affected the arts in the early 1900s. Promoting the culture of the *guajiro,* or rural Hispanic peasant, as that of the nation appealed to conservative elements of Cuban society just as indigenous imagery had. It provided an alternative to the increasing prominence of Afrocuban influences in the media, by which many felt threatened. The origins of *guajirismo* can be traced to similar developments in Western Europe such as the emergence of Biedermeier art, depictions of peasants in ballets and operas, and other forms of middle-class romanticization of "the folk." Probably its most prominent symbol during the early Republic was Liborio, the ubiquitous cartoon character in Cuban newspapers that represented the nation.

León notes that *guajirismo*-inspired music first appeared in Cuba during the Wars of Independence, serving "as a refuge for whites who sought a genre that was at once distinctively Cuban and yet devoid of African-derived elements" (1991, 16). In light of the "intense racism" manifested by white youths in Havana at the turn of the century (ibid.), salon and theater music inspired by the *punto, décima, zapateo,* and other genres provided one of the few acceptable means of expressing pride in the nation. This is not to suggest, however, that rural white Cubans themselves escaped ridicule or prejudice exhibited by the urban middle classes; they were often subject to the same biases that confronted Afrocubans (María Teresa Linares, personal communication).

Examples of *guajirismo* musical nationalism from the early Republic include the *punto cubano* "El arroyo que murmura" (The stream that ripples) by Jorge Anckermann, written in 1899 for piano and voice (Robreño 1943). This piece is in 6/8 time and concludes with a rapid *zapateo* section, imitating the formal and melodic structure of many Iberian dance genres popular in rural areas. Similar compositions by the same author include "La choza" (The hut) and "Tengo una famosa vega" (I have a famous tobacco plantation).[26] Another example is the *capricho* "Me siento cubana" (I feel Cuban) by Moisés Simons, probably from the 1910s, first popularized by Andalucian artist Amalia Molina (Simons n.d. 2). The Simons piece is also in 6/8 time, with lyrics that discuss emigration from Spain to the West Indies. "¡Cuba! you are a prodigy of the invincible Hispanic race / My Spain boasts of you . . ."[27]

The *machadato* represents the final period in which composers wrote significant numbers of popular song with *guajirismo*-inspired imagery. *Afrocubanismo* in its early years produced an artistic backlash of sorts among conservatives. Themes of the Hispanic peasant, which had diminished in popularity during the late 1910s, figured prominently once again. In Carpentier's words,

> The movement initiated by a few composers in favor of Afrocuban music provoked a violent reaction on the part of adversaries of everything black. To Afrocuban subject matter they opposed [*guajiro* symbolism] as representative of a white musical tradition, nobler, more melodic, "cleaner."[28]

Guajirismo compositions from this later period include Gonzalo Roig's parlor song "Guajira" from 1932, music from his *zarzuela El jibarito* (1932), and the *punto guajiro* in his *zarzuela El clarín* from 1933 (Orovio 1981, 340–44). Ernesto Lecuona's "Canto del guajiro" and "Zapateo y guajira" and Sánchez de Fuentes's "Punto carretero" and "Guajira" represent similar works by other authors (Orlando Martínez 1989, 90–91; Sánchez de Fuentes 1974).

Members of the avant-garde also wrote *guajirismo* art music at roughly the same time, such as Amadeo Roldán's "Guajira vueltabajera" for cello and piano from 1928, which incorporated traditional *campesino* melodies (González 1994). Though many supported this trend, it generated considerable controversy. For Alejandro García Caturla, one of the most prominent composers, music written in a quasi-operatic style about Hispanic peasants seemed ridiculous. To the advocates of *guajirismo,* he wrote, what is "essentially 'creole' within Cuban folklore is music coming from a white farmer's peasant hut, set in the faded picture frame of a tearful aria . . . in the style of Donizetti."[29] Roig de Leuchsenring voiced similar criticisms, attacking the representation of the *guajiro* in Cuban song as sterile and lacking in realism. He underscored the irony of attempts to embody the national experience in compositions employing the names of Cuban genres but in the style of the European salon (1927, 18). While justified in many respects, Roig's commentary applies nearly as well to the nationalized forms of Afrocuban expression that he and others promoted.

The Nationalization of Blackness

One finds a fascinating interpenetration of conflicting racist, nationalist, and artistic discourses in Havana of the early 1930s. Anti-black sentiment remained relatively strong among most commentators, yet it was increasingly challenged by anti-imperialists who supported all forms of Cuban expression. Ideological reactions to foreign dominance thus proved central to the valorization of Afrocuban musical expression. Rumbas, congas, *pregones,* and *guarachas* of the comic theater provided a powerful model for artists who desired to reaffirm themselves and their cultural heritage symbolically. The "jazz craze" and the popularity abroad of other forms of working-class expression (e.g., tango, *son*) also added impetus to the *afrocubanismo* movement. Composers who received criticism for their African-inspired works at home had only to point to international artistic celebrities such as George Gershwin or Katherine Dunham as justification.

The very meaning of the term *race,* as with so many other aspects of Cuban thought, underwent scrutiny for the first time during this period. Fernando Ortiz and his colleagues realized that contemporary notions of *"la raza cubana"* invoked by political figures tended to exclude blacks, Chinese, and other minorities rather than incorporating them into nationalist discourse. Ortiz began to question the validity of racial constructs and to propose that Cubans define themselves in terms of shared cultural heritage rather than shared ancestry (del Morro 1929, 716). Even Juan Marinello, the communist activist who a year earlier had reacted tepidly to the promotion of Afrocuban nationalist expression, accepted the idea wholeheartedly by 1930. He argued that blacks had "special significance in Cuba" as a result of their participation in the revolutions against Spain and the unjust social practices to which they were still subjected in the Republic. For these reasons, he suggested, Afrocuban themes were "especially rich" and deserved a more prominent place in the arts despite occasionally "crude" or "regressive" stylistic characteristics.

> The physical characteristics of blacks, enriched and multiplied through intermarriage with whites and [Chinese], and their dances of a maligned and enchanting primitiveness inspire the finest plastic arts. Their music may someday come to be that which defines our presence on the world map of new aesthetics. Progressive musical works [inspired by] Afrocuban rituals have demarcated a path toward the essentially vernacular, toward universally renowned expression.[30]

In this way, musics such as rumba and *toques de santo,* which even ten years earlier had been prohibited by presidential decree, gradually attained tentative acceptance in the public sphere. The new status of such music was far from unambiguous, however. As the above passage suggests, artists and political activists did not condone the acceptance of Afrocuban street culture as it existed, but rather imagery derived from such expression as the basis for European-style composition. Given that self-proclaimed leftists such as Roig de Leuchsenring and Marinello qualified their support of Afrocuban expression to such an extent, it is not surprising that more conservative individuals refused to accept even the discursive privileging of "blackness" advocated by them.

Sánchez de Fuentes, for instance, never ceased to combat the popularization of *afrocubanista* art, referring to it until his death in the 1940s as "a lamentable regression of our traditions" (Lapique Becali 1974, 219). He and other critics found the "traces of slavery" in such compositions an affront to civility (Sánchez de Fuentes 1928b, 200). Citing the more famous middle-class composers of the nineteenth century, Sánchez de Fuentes argued that none had incorporated "Africanisms" into their music, and that by doing so now the *afrocubanistas* were bastardizing a national tradition stretching back nearly a hundred years. The music that to him best represented Cuba "developed completely free of African influences" and should remain so (ibid., 195):

> None of our creative artists, born and trained on our soil, chose to [take inspiration from] African themes. . . . The most learned of our maestros, Ignacio Cervantes, never did so. . . . [José] White never did so, [José Manuel] Jiménez never did so.[31]

Sánchez de Fuentes condemned the popularity of compositions employing Afrocuban themes as consigning "conscientious composers" to a marginal status in their own country (ibid.). It is interesting to note that he never criticizes the inclusion of black performers in the Orquesta Sinfónica de la Habana or other "high art" institutions, however. He also makes a point in the quote above of mentioning Afrocubans (White and Jiménez) among those who have contributed to Cuba's "true" musical heritage. This commentary serves as further evidence that cultural norms often prove more central to "racial" discourses than skin color itself.

By 1932, Roig de Leuchsenring could announce triumphantly that Afrocuban themes had been generally recognized as the most "essential and characteristic" element of Cuban popular dance music, as well as many other forms of entertainment (1932, 80). They had been repositioned virtually at the center of a new conception of Cuban culture. This period is one of intense artistic production, one that gave rise to many of the "classic" works that remain popular and have defined national artistic production since that time. Even Sánchez de Fuentes by the 1930s grudgingly recognized the stage rumba and the *son* as "characteristic dances" of Cuba, despite his personal preference for other genres (1932, 102).

But long-standing biases against black street culture did not simply disappear in the heat of revolutionary conflict, as some have suggested. Rather, the conflicting tendencies of racism and cultural nationalism were resolved through a process of stylization. In the countless *pregones, afros, claves, lamentos,* rumbas, congas, *sones, guarachas,* and *tango-congos* written during this period, one notices a marked difference between Afrocuban music as represented commercially—primarily by white, middle-class *afrocubanistas*—and as played by Afrocubans themselves. This distinction was a conscious one, recognized by all in the music establishment. Composers used many terms to describe the process of transforming Afrocuban expression commercially including "purify" *(depurar)*, "make sophisticated" *(sofisticar)*, "dress with elegance" *(vestir con elegancia)*, and "universalize" *(universalizar)*. They accepted as given the idea that street music did not constitute valid expression in its own right and needed to be altered in order to increase its mass appeal.[32]

Emilio Grenet expressed these sentiments succinctly when he noted that "the music of the black which becomes popular is always an interpretation by a white musician who poses as a dilettante of [Afrocuban] music, a spectator or commentator at most but never a protagonist" (1939, xlii). The popularity of Afrocuban *son* bands in the 1930s suggests that street music did not always require stylization prior to mass acceptance; this does not detract, however, from the fact that *afrocubanista* works received more national and international promotion than the contemporary music and dance of Afrocubans themselves. In a society heavily divided by race and class, only "universalized" arts generated enough popular support to (temporarily) overcome such barriers. I do not mean to suggest, however, that stylized music was created solely by white Hispanics; Afrocubans themselves often wrote such pieces as well, especially middle-class performers.[33]

Afrocubanista Composition

The works discussed in this section are characteristic of the "artistic revolution" associated with the *machadato*. Tremendous amounts of Afrocuban-inspired popular music date from these years, and an exhaustive overview cannot be provided here. Instead, I will discuss musical *afrocubanismo* in three representative categories: salon music, *zarzuela* stage productions, and music for dance bands. Taken together, they provide some insight into the diversity of thematically related compositions written in the early 1930s and the performers and contexts associated with them. They are not intended to be all-inclusive or to cover all forms of nationalist music making at that time, but only to underscore notable tendencies in popular entertainment.

Salon Music

Musical themes related to black working-class culture are largely absent from sheet music published before the 1920s. From about 1925 through the thirties, by contrast, many—perhaps even most—well-known popular songs allude to them in some way. The compositions of Ernesto Lecuona (1896–1963) illustrate this phenomenon nicely. Lecuona, born into a middle-class white home in Guanabacoa, began to study the piano as a child with his older sister Ernestina and later continued in the Conservatorio Carlos Alfredo de Peyrellade (Orlando Martínez 1989, 11–12). After the premature death of his father, Lecuona performed and wrote primarily commercial music to help support his family. Beginning in the 1910s, he played piano in silent film theaters such as the Parisién, Fedora, and Turín and collaborated with Arquímedes Pous as musical director of the Santos y Artigas Circus (González and Enríquez 1995, 14–15). In later years, his compositions for piano, especially the more European-influenced works such as "Andalusian Suite," became well known internationally, and as a result Lecuona spent much of his time touring the United States and Europe. The author's salon compositions represent a sophisticated fusion of classical and popular styles. It was this ability to incorporate diverse musical influences into the same composition that contributed greatly to his success as an artist.

"La bella durmiente" (The sleeping beauty) and "Vals de la mariposa" (Waltz of the butterfly) from 1919 are characteristic of Lecuona's early works in that they sound like European salon music and contain no Afrocuban musical or lyrical referents. Beginning in 1923,[34] however, and continuing for over a decade, he began to publish an increasing number of Afrocuban-inspired works. "La mulata" (1923), "La danza negra" (1925), "La conga se va" (1927), "Negrita" (1928), "Lamento africano" (1929), "Danza de los ñáñigos" (1930), "La mulata chancletera" (1930), and "La negra lucumí" (1931) represent only a handful of the well-known compositions written by Lecuona that helped popularize Afrocuban themes among the middle classes (Barral 1932a, 38). Mulatto singer and pianist Rita Montaner worked closely with Lecuona beginning in the 1920s and contributed greatly to the success of his Afrocuban vocal works, as well as those by Moisés Simons and others (Collazo 1987, 62).

Lecuona's "Los enamorados" (The couple in love) is another example of salon music influenced by *afrocubanismo*. This piece, from 1930, is a piano reduction of a *serenata* by the same name in the *zarzuela María la O*. It is typical in that works published as sheet music by Lecuona and his contemporaries often derive from theatrical productions of various sorts. "Los enamorados" is written as a European-style waltz in 3/4 time with lyrics that discuss the exciting atmosphere of nineteenth-century Kings' Day celebrations: "Today is the fiesta of the Kings, fiesta of crazy happiness, night of beautiful poetry, sweet hopefulness and blue fantasy . . ."[35] While legislation still prohibited *comparsas* from performing in Havana because of the "affront to morality" they represented, Lecuona was able in this work to discursively transform the nineteenth-century carnival dances of Kings' Day into a celebration appealing to all Cubans. Afrocuban street parades are described as setting a festive tone for more "refined" entertainment to be enjoyed by the middle classes in the privacy of their homes. Countless other works could be cited to emphasize the extent and impact of *afrocubanismo* on salon music. Moisés Simons, Eliseo Grenet, Margarita Lecuona, and Gilberto Valdés figure prominently among white artists whose popularity increased within Cuba and internationally during the *machadato* as a result of writing Afrocuban-inspired popular song.[36]

Although most *afrocubanista* salon composition represents the perspective of white, middle-class composers, some of the best-known interpreters of the period were in fact Afrocuban. In general, middle-class Afrocuban musicians with sufficient formal training to perform salon works expressed little interest in *afrocubanismo;* indeed, many considered the movement offensive (see chapters 3 and 7). Yet it was primarily black and mulatto performers such as Eusebia Cosme[37] (an interpreter of the poetry of Emilio Ballagas, Nicolás Guillén, and others), Rita Montaner (discussed in chapter 6), and Ignacio Villa who came to symbolize the *afrocubanismo* period for the Cuban public.

Ignacio Villa (commonly referred to as "Bola de Nieve" or "Snowball") stands out as the only dark-skinned Afrocuban to achieve recognition as a performer of *afrocubanista* salon repertory, and the only one to compose a number of such works himself.[38] Villa is in many respects a counterpart to Louis Armstrong in the United States, an early black crossover figure accused by some of being an "Uncle Tom." This classically trained pianist appeared on stage in elegant dress and seemed invariably to have an enormous grin on his face. Born in Guanabacoa in 1902, Villa began to pursue musical studies from an early age, first privately with Gerardo Guanche, and later in the Conservatorio de José Mateu. He studied flute and mandolin in addition to the piano (Guirao 1938, 182). Villa's grandfather, Estanislao Bertemetti, was a practicing *mayombero* and *abakuá;* his parents seem to have been involved in African-derived religious worship as well (Martínez Rodríguez 1986). Inés, his mother, is said to have organized frequent social events in their home at which street rumba was performed (González 1994). The artist thus grew up in an environment saturated with traditional Afrocuban culture. His decision to study European art music represents a significant shift away from this orientation.

Villa's professional career began in silent movie theaters, but he continued to study the piano intensely and by the 1930s had established a strong reputation as a classical accompanist. In 1933 Rita Montaner contracted him for a tour of Mexico. During this period, he began to sing himself on occasion, interpreting the Grenet-Guillén compositions for which he became most famous. In later years he spent much time abroad and befriended African Americans Lena Horne, Paul Robeson, and Teddy Wilson (Martínez Rodríguez 1986).

Villa's performance repertory, including his own songs, tended in a musical sense to resemble those of tin pan alley contemporaries Jerome Kern and Cole Porter. Lyrically they emphasized *bozal* parodies of Afrocuban speech.[39] Armando Oréfiche's "Messier Julián," a song frequently played by Villa, is typical. The singer in this case portrays a comic version of the *negro catedrático*. He boasts of his cultural sophistication and his accomplishments as an international entertainer while his unrefined accent and mispronunciations of foreign terms suggest that he is in fact a fool.

Villa's penchant for gaudy dress and lifelong familiarity with Afrocuban street slang enabled him to personify the *catedrático* with ease. Interviews later in life suggest that he may have actually internalized some of the stereotypes about Afrocubans that he perpetuated on stage. Villa frequently mocked himself, telling an interviewer that he had "the voice of a peach vendor," for instance, and describing his early performance career as follows: "I debuted [in Cuba after the tour in Mexico] and luckily no one threw orange peels at me, or rocks or anything. They tolerated me. I continued abusing people [with my performances], and today I'm still doing the same."[40] As an Afrocuban classical musician who became famous for interpreting songs of the white middle classes that depicted black street culture, Ignacio Villa personifies all of the complexities and ironies of *afrocubanismo*. His performances overtly reflect the tensions between racism, populism, and elitism so prevalent in Cuban works of this period.

Zarzuelas

The *afrocubanismo* movement affected the *zarzuela* repertory as much as it did the publication of salon music for piano and voice. Though the *zarzuela* is a Spanish-derived operatic genre, Cuban composers of the *machadato* made concerted attempts to nationalize it by incorporating *costumbrista* imagery and emphasizing domestic historical events. In this sense, their approach was similar to that of nineteenth-century authors who developed the blackface theater by incorporating local imagery into the Spanish *tonadilla* (González and Enríquez 1995, 15). Most *zarzuelas* written during the *machadato* are set in the mid-1800s and adopt Afrocuban themes from the colonial period rather than from the twentieth century. The songs and dances of slaves including *tango-congos, lamentos,* and Kings' Day processions are especially prominent, appearing in virtually all productions.

Afrocuban imagery from the past seems to have been viewed both as more picturesque and as less controversial than contemporary expression. It could be freely reinvented on the stage with little or no regard for sociohistorical authenticity since it had never been carefully documented in its day. It had the additional advantage of avoiding sensitive issues such as contemporary racial conflict, discrimination, and black urban poverty that otherwise might have surfaced in the dialogue of the libretto. With the abolition of slavery in the 1880s, depictions of the suffering of Afrocubans under colonial authorities became a relatively noncontroversial means of incorporating "serious" themes into the *zarzuela*. Issues pertaining to Afrocuban oppression could be alluded to in slave songs without implying that they still existed or needed to be addressed in the present.

The *mulata* consistently figures among the most prominent characters in *zarzuelas* written during the *machadato*. Even in light of the long-standing fascination with this character type demonstrated in novels and the comic theater, the sheer number of musical works featuring *mulatas* as central characters from 1925 to 1940 is remarkable. The prominence of the *mulata* is even more noteworthy when one considers that before that date she appears in few if any *zarzuelas*, with the (debatable) exception of José Maurí's *La esclava* from 1921. Maurí (1855–1937), a violinist and composer, was actually born in Spain, as were other Cuban nationalist figures of the day (e.g., Amadeo Roldán, Pedro Sanjuan). His *zarzuela*, with a text by Tomás Juliá, debuted in the Teatro Nacional in June 1921 (Díaz Ayala 1981, 47). Actually, the plot has little to do with Afrocubans. It concerns a white-looking aristocratic woman of the past century who learns that her mother was a *mulata* slave and that she too is legally the property of a local plantation owner. This information causes her untold anguish until a rich admirer eventually buys her freedom as well as that of her father's other slaves. Despite his aid, the heroine eventually kills herself, apparently too shamed by the knowledge of her heritage to continue living (González 1986, 487).

One of the most famous *zarzuelas* after *La esclava* that featured *mulatas* and nineteenth-century slave imagery was Gonzalo Roig's *Cecilia Valdés*, an extremely popular adaptation of the Villaverde novel first performed in the Teatro Martí in 1931.[41] Productions with similar themes by Ernesto Lecuona include *Niña Rita o La Habana en 1830* (1927), *El cafetal* and *El batey* (both from 1929), *María la O*—perhaps his best-known *zarzuela*—*El maizal*, and *El calesero* (all from 1930), *Rosa la china* (1932), and *Lola Cruz* (1935). *María Belén Chacón* (1934) and *Amalia Batista* (1936) by Rodrigo Prats are yet other examples. As in much nineteenth-century literature, these works use interracial love triangles as a central theme (Linares 1993). The *mulata* represents a focal point between two rival suitors, one black or *mulato* and one white. In many instances, the black suitor is depicted as honest and sincere in his love for the heroine, and the white suitor as somewhat more fickle. The white man desires an ongoing sexual relationship with the *mulata*, yet would never dare marry her or make official his relationship for fear of condemnation from his family. The *mulata* for her part prefers the attentions of the white suitor and rejects the more sincere advances of his darker rival. Trapped in this context of conflicting desire and constraining social convention, the affair inevitably ends in tragedy.

So common is the love triangle in *zarzuelas* and other forms of artistic expression (including that of the comic theater) that it deserves recognition as one of the most pervasive tropes of Cuban culture. The complexities of interracial love metaphorically allude to Cuban social relations more generally by referencing the simultaneous attraction and repulsion to Afrocubans and their artistic expression that characterize mainstream attitudes. *Mulatas* depicted in *zarzuelas* tend to be light-skinned *"blanconazas"* who pass for whites, not those of obvious Afrocuban heritage. In most cases the role of the *mulata* is taken by a white actress on stage. Works such as *María la O* and *Cecilia Valdés* are based loosely on historical figures, while others are entirely fictional.[42]

A number of female performers who rose to prominence as *mulatas* of the *teatro vernáculo* later found work in more "serious" *zarzuela* productions. Examples include Candita Quintana, Hortensia Coalla, Conchita Bañuls, Mimi Cal, and Caridad Suárez (Orlando Martínez 1989, 87). The *zarzuelas* mentioned above all represented critical and financial successes, and were performed constantly through the 1930s by new companies and lead actors (Collazo 1987, 95–192). In later decades, their plots were adapted for motion pictures and remain popular today in that form.

The biography and musical works of Gonzalo Roig (1890–1970) exemplify those of many *zarzuela* composers. Born into a white family of tobacco growers, Roig received formal musical instruction on the violin and piano from an early age (Cañizares 1978, 40). Beginning about 1912 he worked as a theater orchestra leader, first in the well-known Alhambra and later in the Molino Rojo and Campoamor. During the same period, he also supplemented his income by playing for tourists in a string quartet at the exclusive Hotel Miramar Garden. By the 1920s, Roig's reputation as a composer and conductor had been firmly established. In 1922 he was chosen to direct the newly formed Orquesta Sinfónica de la Habana, and in 1927 he assumed the additional responsibility of directing the Escuela Municipal de Música and Banda Nacional (Orovio 1981, 333).

Like Ernesto Lecuona's music, Roig's compositions before the mid-1920s incorporate few Afrocuban themes; by contrast, many from the *machadato* period do so. One example of his *afrocubanismo*-inspired *zarzuela* works is "Canto de la esclava" (Slave song) from *Cecilia Valdés*.[43] This piece is highly elaborate, employing full orchestral accompaniment, a large mixed chorus, bells, and a battery of tom-toms playing a rhythm reminiscent of the *tango-congo* as the lead soprano sings the main melody. String players maintain a brusque ostinato figure consisting of open intervals that strongly emphasizes the "2" and "4" of the 4/4 measure; it is similar in some respects to techniques heard in Stravinsky's "Rite of Spring" and brings to mind images of tribal violence. "Canto de la esclava" is in a minor key with a pentatonic melody, chosen in all likelihood because of its associations with the melodies of "primitive" Indian and African cultures. The lyrics are written from the perspective of a slave laboring on a rural plantation and dreaming of freedom: "I am the black Gangá woman who longs night and day / For my old country which now I will never see again." Elisa Altamirano, a white performer, sang the piece in blackface at its premiere. Many supporting characters, such as light-skinned (Afrocuban) Carmita Quintana, similarly darkened their complexions to portray other slave characters. As mentioned, even blacks with classical training were rarely accepted as singers and actors in Cuba and did not perform in *zarzuelas* such as this one.

"Canto de la esclava" represents only one of countless *afrocubanista* compositions by Roig from the same period. Others include "Po Po Po," a *tango-congo* also from Cecilia Valdés (Roig n.d. 2); the conga "Sevilla-Habana" from a *zarzuela* of the same name (1933); "Son oriental" and the *pregón* "El tamalero" from *La hija del sol* (1933); the *son-rumba* "Cincuenta pesos" from *La Habana de noche* (1936); as well as all of the music from the lesser known *zarzuelas La mulata* (1931) and *El cimarrón* (The runaway slave, 1936).[44]

Dance Band Repertory

Given the extent of racial tension in the 1930s and the increasing popularity of Afrocuban-influenced music, it was perhaps inevitable that ensembles of white musicians would emerge to perform it in segregated establishments. All-white groups of the early 1920s typically performed jazz and other dance musics uninfluenced by Afrocuban genres. They played regularly in elite hotels such as the Nacional and Sevilla Biltmore, in gambling houses catering to wealthy tourists such as the Casino Nacional, as house bands in the more prestigious radio stations, at events organized by the *sociedades españolas,* and at private resorts including the Havana Yacht Club. Some of the musicians came from relatively wealthy families, as is the case with Justo "Don" Azpiazu, and had studied abroad in the United States or elsewhere. These bands often developed out of theater orchestras, providing a less expensive alternative to the North American jazz groups that toured Cuba beginning in the late 1910s.

With the growing national interest in Afrocuban genres beginning about 1928, white Cuban jazz band repertory began to more prominently feature stylized *sones,* rumbas, and congas. Because of their many recordings, one might think that these white ensembles—which included the jazz band Los Hermanos Castro, La Orquesta Hermanos Lebatard, La Orquesta Casino de la Playa, La Orquesta Siboney, and the jazz band Los Hermanos Palau, as well as the Havana Casino orchestra of Justo Azpiazu—effectively overshadowed those catering to black and working-class audiences (such as the *conjunto* of Arsenio

Rodríguez, the *charanga* of Antonio Arcaño, and the Sonora Matancera). In actuality, jazz bands dominated musical recording and international touring by virtue of a more marketable image and influential business connections, but never achieved widespread popularity among Cuban listeners as a whole (Martínez Furé 1994; Bacallao 1994). They generally appealed only to a small segment of the population, while most listened to the *septetos, conjuntos,* and other groups mentioned in chapter 4.

The jazz band Los Hermanos Lebatard is typical of many white groups. In the 1920s, the band consisted of brothers Gonzalo, Germán, Luís, and Julio Lebatard, as well as Armando Oréfiche on piano and Gilberto Valdés on saxophone and flute (Collazo 1987, 18). They performed for many years in the Teatro Encanto accompanying stage acts of the blackface theater (Acosta 1993, 31), in addition to soliciting work in the more exclusive venues listed above. The experience of band members with *teatro vernáculo* repertory proved beneficial in the early 1930s during the heyday of *afrocubanismo.* Oréfiche reorganized the group under his direction in 1932 and renamed it the Lecuona Cuban Boys, to capitalize on the popularity of Ernesto Lecuona's works at home and abroad. The new band, whose repertory consisted predominantly of stylized Afrocuban material, toured in various parts of Europe the same year and then returned in 1933 to accompany stage acts in the cabaret Montmartre (Collazo 1987, 131). During the remainder of the 1930s the Lecuona Cuban Boys made frequent international tours, returning to Cuba only at the end of the decade when forced to do so by the onset of World War II.

The repertory of the Lecuona Cuban Boys in the 1930s represents a unique synthesis of jazz and European popular genres with a diversity of Cuban styles. They played *indigenismo* tunes such as Lecuona's "Canto indio," fox-trots with titles in Spanish ("Antillana"), waltzes ("Ti-pi-tin"), *tango-congo*-influenced exotica ("Hindú"), cabaret rumbas ("Rumba blanca," "Rumba tambah"), boleros, *zarzuela* arias arranged for dance band ("María la O," "María Belén Chacón"), and salon congas ("Cafunga-conga," "Panamá"). "Rumba blanca" (White rumba), written by Oréfiche himself, is essentially an up-tempo jazz-*son* hybrid with maraca, *clave,* and other percussion instruments featured prominently. The lyrics indicate the extent of the appropriation of Afrocuban culture by middle-class listeners: "You don't have to be a Yoruban African, nor a slave / To want to enjoy yourself when the *bongó* sounds. . . . Bring on the delicious rhythm, everybody listen to the bewitching white rumba."[45] "Rumba tambah" is also interesting, a piece reminiscent of comic theater *guarachas* but highly arranged with complex harmonies and horn lines. Its lyrics are written in *bozal* style with intentional grammatical irregularities.

The jazz band Los Hermanos Castro offers another example of the popularization of Afrocuban musics by predominantly white performers.[46] Director and saxophonist Manolo Castro formed the group in 1928, which included his brothers Andrés (trumpet), Antonio (trombone), and Juanito (piano), as well as singer Miguelito Valdés. It was one of the first Cuban big bands patterned after those of the United States to achieve commercial success (Acosta 1993, 24, 52). In its early years, Los Hermanos Castro played in the Campoamor and Encanto theaters and accompanied a diversity of stage acts. In 1932 they accepted a contract to perform on the excursion liner *Belgelan* (Collazo 1987, 118). Shortly thereafter they toured briefly in Venezuela and the United States, where Warner Brothers hired them to record music for the feature film *Havana Cocktail*.

In 1937 the original Los Hermanos Castro split up. Pianist Anselmo Sacasas and trumpet player Wilfredo de los Reyes left the group to form another, and under the leadership of violinist Guillermo Portela they began calling themselves the Orquesta Casino de la Playa. This new band performed the same year in the exclusive Casino Nacional, accompanying both North American exhibition dancers and the *pareja de rumba* Yolanda y Pablito.[47] They also recorded a number of Afrocuban-inspired compositions sung by Miguelito Valdés, including Arsenio Rodríguez's "Bruca manigua," Rafael Hernández's "Cachita," and Margarita Lecuona's "Babalú."[48]

A very light-skinned *mulato* himself born in the predominantly Afrocuban barrio of Cayo Hueso, Miguelito Valdés (1916–1978) had considerable exposure to commercially marginal forms of Afrocuban culture as an adolescent (Rosell 1992 2:214; Díaz Ayala 1981, 165). He knew much of the vocabulary used by *abakuás* and *santeros* and could incorporate it into extemporized *inspiraciones* during performances. Valdés's vocals added an extra degree of *cubanidad* to the group's otherwise standard jazz-influenced repertory. The extent of racial tension among musicians in the 1930s is exemplified by the fact that (the otherwise white) Orquesta Casino de la Playa always employed black *bongosero* Ramón Castro to perform during their recording sessions, but substituted him with a white percussionist whenever they performed live in segregated venues. In the same way, they employed *tresero* Arsenio Rodríguez on at least one of their albums but never shared the stage with him (Cristóbal Díaz Ayala, personal communication).

Conclusion

The revolution against Machado in 1933 represented in many respects the culmination of widespread discontent among Cubans that had been growing for at least a decade. Their anger focused primarily on Cuban political corruption and economic decline, and on the extent of U.S. control over domestic affairs that many felt had contributed to the crises of the 1920s. In a political and cultural sense, the changes brought about as a result of the *machadato* have heavily affected conceptions of *cubanidad* developing since that time. The in-tellectual legacy of authors such as Rubén Martínez Villena, Juan Marinello, and Emilio Roig de Leuchsenring proved decisive in contributing to the edu-cation of young social leaders (including Fidel Castro) who in turn organized mid-century labor activism, expanded ranks of the Cuban Communist Party, called for political reform, and eventually led the socialist revolution of the 1950s.

In a similar way, the appropriation of Afrocuban culture by middle-class artists as that of the nation, its promotion in national festivals, its (tentative) valorization by scholarly societies, and its representation in *zarzuelas* and other forms of popular song has set the tone for commercial composition to the present day. The works of Lecuona, Roig, Oréfiche, and countless others con-tinue to be performed by Cuban music students and to provide the dominant model for the mediation of African and Hispanic stylistic influences. Living in a period still largely antagonistic toward Afrocuban street music, these com-posers nevertheless realized that national expression would have to incorpo-rate "blackness" in at least a rhetorical sense. Rejecting symbolic representa-tions of Cuba that foregrounded the Indian or *guajiro,* leading composers of the *machadato* chose instead to stylistically fuse genres such as *son* and street rumba with Italian opera, music of the comic theater, and jazz dance reper-tory. In this way they were able to create songs with a uniquely "popular" and "Cuban" sound that were also viewed as "sophisticated," clearly distinguish-able from working-class expression.

Cuban society remained in turmoil for some time after Machado's depar-ture in August 1933. Indiscriminate mob violence against known or suspected government sympathizers continued for months, resulting in murders, lootings, and the destruction of property. In September, the Sargent's Rebellion of Fulgencio Batista led to the replacement of the provisional Céspedes govern-ment with the administration of Ramón Grau San Martín. Grau was the first Cuban leader in the twentieth century to come to power against the wishes of the United States. Riding a wave of anti-imperialist sentiment, he quickly passed legislation annulling the Platt Amendment, declaring immigrant labor illegal, protecting Cuban workers against foreign competition, reducing the rates of U.S.-owned utility companies, and in other ways asserting the sovereignty of the nation (Aguilar 1972, 174). He also chose to suspend loan payments to North American creditors, a decision that led to the U.S.-condoned military coup forcing him from power in 1934. Under the Batista military dictatorship that followed, government soldiers arrested or killed a majority of opposition lead-ers, violently suppressed labor activism, and gradually established "order" (Benjamin 1990, 95, 103). By 1937, the University of Havana had reopened and revolutionary activity had largely ceased.

Nationalist sentiment remained strong under Batista, however, and the Afrocuban presence in national culture became if anything more apparent in the late 1930s than at the beginning of the decade. Festive ceremonies sponsored by municipalities and the federal government commemorated the deaths of Antonio Maceo and other Afrocuban leaders of the War of Independence (Beruff Mendieta 1937, 39). In 1933, the first national music festival to include a presentation by an Afrocuban *comparsa* was held in Cienfuegos (Urfé 1982, 158). In 1935, the Sensemayá radio show went on the air on CMCF, a program devoted solely to *afrocubanista* composition. It featured artists such as Ignacio Villa, Rita Montaner, and Gilberto Valdés (González Torres 1935, 13).

In 1936, Fernando Ortiz founded the Sociedad de Estudios Afrocubanos, the first organization of its kind devoted solely to the scholarly investigation of Afrocuban subject matter. Initial members included art music composers Amadeo Roldán, Alejandro García Caturla, and Gonzalo Roig, political activists Marinello and Roig de Leuchsenring, and black middle-class artists Nicolás Guillén, Eusebia Cosme, Regino Pedroso, and Marcelino Arozarena. In 1938 Ortiz together with percussionists Pablo Roche, Jesús Pérez and Aguedo Morales organized the first public concerts of *santería* music and dance (Ortiz 1965, 175; Herrera-Sixto and Pedroso 1992), and in 1939 the first Congreso Cubano del Arte in Santiago prominently represented Afrocuban genres. The national secretary of education, Dr. Aurelio Fernández Concheso, participated in this event, as did the mayor of Santiago, Juan F. Castellvi.[49]

It is important to reiterate the "objective conditions" of Afrocubans living at this time in order to interpret the significance of the *afrocubanismo* movement. The race war of 1912 remained a vivid memory in the minds of many. The blackface theater, with its largely racist depictions of the *negrito* and *mulata*, continued to be one of the most popular forms of Cuban entertainment. Performing publicly in *comparsa* bands was still a criminal offense in Havana through the late 1930s, as were other forms of Afrocuban music and dance banned nationally by the presidential decrees of 1922 and 1925. Blacks did not have the right to form political parties of their own, and were subject to job discrimination and policies of segregation enforced by many clubs and businesses.

In the context of such cultural and racial antagonism, the meanings of *afrocubanismo* are decidedly ambivalent. The predominantly white/Hispanic proponents of stylized *afrocubanista* art can be viewed both as advocates of a more progressive modality of expression, and as coopting the resistant expression of the subaltern. In the shifting discourses associated with the *machadato*, artistic leaders managed to define a new and more inclusive representation of the Cuban community with their compositions. They disseminated musical works that depicted Afrocubans as an important part of the nation, even as social reality continued to demonstrate their subjugation and exploitation. *Afrocubanista* composition foregrounds the commonalities of Cuban citizens and obscures hierarchies of internal difference. While in some senses representing a more tolerant position toward Afrocuban culture, it simultaneously demonstrates intolerance to anything but "universalized folklore." Stylistically, its emergence constitutes a new period of hegemonic concession in which black street culture is accepted, but only on European or middle-class terms. The two nationalist phases "hinged" to León's axis in this sense are more similar to one another than they might first appear.

Víctor Patricio
Landaluze, "Día de
Reyes," oil painting,
1881 *(top)*.
Museo de Bellas Artes,
Havana.

Víctor Patricio
Landaluze, "Escena
galante," oil painting,
1881, depicting a
calesero figure
courting a *mulata*
(bottom).
Museo de Bellas Artes,
Havana.

Police chief Estanislao Mansip. "Attributes taken by surprise in the cuarto Fambá [an *abakuá* shrine] in the fiesta that was celebrated in Pogolotti barrio on 20 May 1914. The excellent services of the present Chief of Police of Marianao, captain Estanislao Mansip, contributed [to their seizure]" (Roche Monteagudo 1925). Biblioteca Nacional José Martí.

Negrito, probably Paquito Rodríguez. Centro Odilio Urfé.

Arquímedes Pous, in blackface, with Margot González, in the *sainete Habana-Barcelona-Habana* (1924) *(right)*. *Bohemia* archives.

Blackface troupe of Arquímedes Pous depicted in a scene from *¡Oh, La Habana!* (1924) *(below)*. *Bohemia* archives.

Blanca Becerra, comic
actress, 1920s.
Biblioteca Nacional José
Martí.

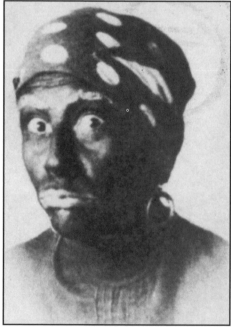

Blanca Becerra in costume
depicting a *negra conga*
(Congolese woman).
Reprinted in *Carteles*
(Ramírez 1943b) .
Biblioteca Nacional José
Martí.

Cover for sheet music of "¡Ay! Mamá Inés" by Eliseo Grenet (late 1920s), showing an unidentified actress, probably Rita Montaner, dressed as a *negro calesero* in the *zarzuela Niña Rita*. Museo Nacional de la Música.

Negrito comedy sketch seen by the author in the Cortijo bar of the Hotel Vedado, 5 July 1992.

Automobile entry that won first prize in the carnival competitions of 1908. The participants featured here epitomize the "white" carnival image favored by civic leaders.
Photo from *El Fígaro*, 8 March 1908, 113. Biblioteca del Historiador de la Ciudad, Plaza de Armas.

"Los Moros Rosados," a prize-winning group in the *comparsa* competitions of 1908. Photo from *El Fígaro*, 22 March 1908, 145.

Musicians from the
comparsa "Los
Colombianos
Modernos"
performing in the
highly regulated
carnival celebrations
of 1935 *(above)*.
Biblioteca del
Historiador de la
Ciudad, Plaza de Armas.

A *comparsa* of "high
society" whites
masquerading in
Afrocuban costumes
as part of segregated
carnival celebrations
in the Casino
Español, 1943 *(right)*.
(Roig de Leuchsenring
1946.)

Earliest known photo of a *conjunto de son*, the Sexteto Habanero, 1919. Back row: Guillermo Castillo (guitar), Carlos Godines *(tres)*, Gerardo Martínez *(clave)*. Front row: Antonio Bacallao *(botija)*, Oscar Sotolongo *(bongó)*, Felipe Neri Cabrera (maraca). Child unidentified. Note the squared shape of the tack-head *bongó*. Francisco Bacallao collection.

The Orquesta Anacaona from the mid-1930s, here making the instrumental transition from *sexteto* to jazz band. Hermanas Castro collection.

Typical *son* group from the 1920s: "Los Melodiosos" from Cienfuegos,
"Ramitos," the older white performer, is standing second to the left at back.
Other performers are unidentified. Centro Odilio Urfé.

The nine-member Sexteto Gloria Cubana, the first *conjunto de son* to
incorporate the piano (Blanco 1992, 34). Keyboardist and director María
Teresa Ovando is seated in the center with her husband Feliciano standing at
her side. Other members are unidentified. Centro Odilio Urfé.

"Sexteto Liborio," 1926. Centro Odilio Urfé, Havana.

The dance band of Moisés Simons at the Hotel Plaza, 1920s. Simons is standing at back left next to the keyboard. Museo Nacional de la Música.

Cover for sheet music of "Tata
Cuñengue," a *tango-congo* by
Eliseo Grenet and Teofilo
Radillo (1931). Tata Cuñengue
is a figure from Congolese
folklore, a magician with
strong powers over evil (Urfé
1984, 184).
Museo Nacional de la Música.

Cover for sheet music of
"Hatuey," a *capricho indígena*
by Eliseo Grenet.
Museo Nacional de la Música.

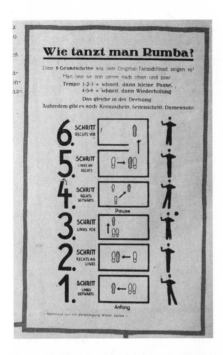

How-to guide for German-speaking rumba dancers created by instructor Walter Carlos. Photo from *Wintergarten*, October 1931 (see Roquelosabe 1931).
Biblioteca Nacional José Martí.

Cover for sheet music of "Flan y merengue," a rumba–fox-trot by Moisés Simons (early 1930s).
Museo Nacional de la Música.

Cover for sheet music of an English language version of "El manisero" by Moisés Simons, (early 1930s). Printed in the United States and promoted by Eusebio Azpiazu's wife, Marion Sunshine.
Museo Nacional de la Música.

Conservatory-trained pianist and *afro* interpreter Ignacio Villa ("Bola de Nieve"), 1936.
Museo Nacional de la Música.

Stage rumba dancers René (Rivero) and Estela (Ramona Ajón) performing with the Septeto Nacional, 1933 *(above)*. Lázaro Herrera collection.

René Rivero in *guarachero* costume sliding across the floor while balancing a glass of water on his head, 1930s *(opposite, top)*. Rivero family collection.

Carmita Ortiz and Julio Richards on their first trip to Paris in 1927 *(left)*. Photo from *Social,* January 1928. Biblioteca Nacional José Martí.

Dance band of the Marianao
cabaret de tercera "El Rumba
Palace," early 1930s *(above)*.
The renowned *timbalero* "El
Chori" (Silvano Shueg
Hechavarría) is featured at
front center, with dancer
Carmen Curbelo at far right
(see Padura Fuentes 1988).
Juventud Rebelde archives.

Carmen Curbelo, *academia de
baile* instructor and Marianao
rumbera, early 1930s (see
Padura Fuentes 1988)*(left)*.
Juventud Rebelde archives.

Marcelo Pogolotti, "Fordismo" (Fordism), anti-imperialist/surrealist pen and pencil sketch, 1931. Museo de Bellas Artes.

Marcelo Pogolotti, "Los negocios marchan" (The business deals continue), pen and pencil sketch depicting *machadato* violence, 1931. Museo de Bellas Artes.

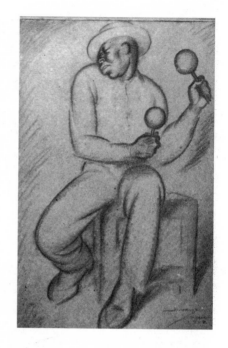

Jaime Valls,
advertisement for "La
Llave" soap, 1910s
(top, left).
Museo de Bellas Artes.

Jaime Valls,
"Maraquero" (Maraca
player), pencil sketch,
1927 *(top, right)*.
Museo de Bellas Artes.

Jaime Valls, "La mulata,"
oil painting, late 1920s
(bottom).
Avelina Alcalde Valls
collection.

Eduardo Abela, "El triunfo de la rumba" (The triumph of the rumba), oil painting, 1928. Museo de Bellas Artes.

THE RUMBA CRAZE

Afrocuban Arts as International Popular Culture

This is the "century of the rumba." ... It is danced in the
haughtiest salons; the most select shows have chosen it as
one of their choreographic numbers of highest esteem and
best taste ... in New York, Paris, London, and Vienna [the
rumba] is the queen and tyrant of the most sophisticated
cabarets; and in its native country it has learned with cruel
and tenacious despotism to fend off, in retaliation, the
rebukes and disdains of which they made it a propitiatory
victim when it was innocent and unknown.
—Federico Villoch, "La rumba de Lina Frutos"[1]

The 1930s gave rise to a brief but influential rumba craze in Europe, the
United States, Latin America, and other countries. The history of commercial rumba, like that of other Latin American genres, demonstrates that
the early twentieth century was a period of expanding international cultural
influence (see Roberts 1979). Cuban genres such as the habanera and *danzón*
anticipated the rumba craze by decades, achieving considerable popularity
abroad as early as 1900. Interest in rumba peaked about fifteen years after international dissemination of the Argentine tango and occurred more or less
concurrently with the vogue of "exotic" genres in other countries including
the United States (jazz, "hillbilly," and Hawaiian music), Trinidad (calypso),
Martinique (the *beguine*), and Brazil (samba, *maxixe*).

In the wake of colonial dominance in the Third World and the expansion
of the urban working class in industrialized countries, cultural forms that had
developed in relative isolation gradually became part of the "global cultural
ecumene" (Foster 1991). New recording technologies, the development of radio, and rapid forms of transportation brought sounds associated with particular geographic regions to new audiences and reproduced them in entirely
different contexts. These trends also led to the vogue of primitivism, with artists such as Mondrian, Picasso, Matisse, Klee, and others using artifacts dis-

played in colonial museums as the inspiration for a
garde aesthetic (Torgovnick 1990).

Despite rumba's prominent role in what might be cai
of marginal culture, little has been written about it. Th
dissemination of commercial rumba, although mentioned b
works, has never been the subject of serious study; within Cu
cabaret music has not yet gained recognition as a potential foc
research. This omission is especially significant given the many ⌐nces to
transculturation in the writings of Cuban social scientists. The term
transculturation, developed by Fernando Ortiz about 1940 after reading the
works of R. C. Thurnwald (*Blacks and Whites in East Africa,* 1935) and Melville
Herskovits (*Acculturation: The Study of Culture Contact,* 1938), refers to the
transfer of cultural forms between distinct social groups over time.[2] Presented
as a theory, Ortiz's writings on the subject provide more of a description of
various kinds of syncretism than an explanation of why and how syncretic
forms develop. Authors since the 1940s refer constantly to transculturation
(e.g., Guanche 1983), yet they do not expand on Ortiz's work by further analyzing processes of cultural change and exchange. Commercial rumba would
seem to provide the perfect case study for them, since the alterations of the
genre initiated in the comic theater and among *afrocubanista* composers before 1930 became even more extreme after its appropriation by musicians in
other countries.

Musical change has been of great interest to North American and European
scholars of popular culture. Much can be learned about the repression of ethnic minorities by examining the formation of stylistically mediated culture
and the ways in which aesthetic alterations further the agendas of dominant
groups. Stuart Hall recognizes that musical transformation can provide insights into the conflicts between industry and/or the state and the diversified
cultural formations of the people. He defines transformation as

> the active reworking [of existing traditions and activities] so that they come out
> a different way: they appear to "persist"—yet from one period to another, they
> come to stand in a different relation to the ways working people live and the
> ways they define their relations to each other, to "the others" and to the
> conditions of life. (1981, 228)

A similar concept of transformation is developed even more specifically by
Richard Bauman and Charles Briggs in their article on the "decentering,"
"decontextualization," and "recontextualization" of expressive culture (1990,
75). They discuss various types of transformation such as changes in "fram-
ing," or how a work is linked to the past by references to place, time, location,

ticular social groups, or other artistic genres; changes in the style or structure of the artistic "text"; changes in social funtion; and changes in performative context. In this chapter I examine some of the transformations associated with Cuban rumba musically and discursively as it gained international acclaim. I briefly describe the noncommercial genre performed by Afrocubans since the late nineteenth century and the attitudes of municipal authorities toward it before the 1920s. I then examine how middle-class Cuban artists began to tour abroad beginning about 1927, bringing "universalized" rumba to audiences in Paris, New York, and elsewhere. Finally, I will show how North American and European artists began writing rumbas of their own after exposure to these presentations, and how the genre's popularity abroad eventually led to the proliferation of new rumba stage acts in Havana. The latter event enabled many Afrocubans to penetrate the world of commercial entertainment for the first time and to add their own interpretations of rumba to the many already in existence.

The Noncommercial Genre

Unlike commercial rumba, much has been written about its folkloric counterpart.[3] Rumba first developed in the black urban slums of Havana and Matanzas in the mid-nineteenth century (Urfé 1982, 153). Performed solely by percussion instruments and voice, it is distinctly more "African-sounding" than most stage or ballroom compositions of the same name. The music's cyclic, repetitive rhythms create a complex interlocking textural base over which the *quintero* or solo drummer improvises. His performance (drumming is typically a male activity) is highly sensitive to the actions of others, based on cues from other instrumentalists, the spontaneous interjections of singers and the movements of dancer(s). Rumba has long functioned as a "social chronicle of the dispossessed," providing a means of public expression for those without representation in the media (Acosta 1991, 54). Lyrics (almost always included in rumba) refer to many subjects and can be political, for example, criticizing the subjugation or mistreatment of blacks and Cubans in general by authorities in the United States, the Cuban government, and others (ibid.).

Rumba *guaguancó,* the subgenre of traditional rumba most influential on cabaret acts since the 1930s, involves couple interaction in what is essentially a ritualized enactment of sexual conquest. The male dancer remains close beside his partner and at an appropriate moment thrusts out his pelvis, a movement referred to as the *vacunao.* He attempts to surprise her with the action and to make physical contact. The female avoids him by quickly turning and/ or covering herself at appropriate moments, an action known as *botao.* Because of the strongly African-influenced musical form of the *guaguancó*, the sexual nature of its choreography, and its close associations with the poorest and most socially marginal Afrocubans in western areas, middle-class and elite Cuban society condemned the genre for many years. Primarily for this reason, rumba music was rarely recorded commercially in its traditional form through the late 1960s.

Traditional rumba remains a controversial form even in socialist Cuba. Rogelio Martínez Furé, one of the cofounders of the Conjunto Folklórico Nacional, told me that in the 1960s and 1970s his attempts to establish "Sábado de la rumba" events in El Vedado (a primarily white, affluent district of Havana) were met by considerable opposition from neighbors who did not want such activity taking place near their homes. Once they were established, residents grudgingly accepted the gatherings. Even so, critics suggested that their primary benefit to the community was not cultural, but rather that they "kept all the [black] delinquents off the street for a while," and in a single location where their actions could be monitored (Martínez Furé 1994).

The definition of rumba given by Alejo Carpentier, a literary figure and well-known critic of Caribbean and Latin American music, emphasizes the gamut of associations linked both to the noncommercial genre and to the term as used in everyday Cuban discourse. From his description we recognize that the term *rumba* is associated with a diversity of music and dance styles, and that it has taken on many new meanings since the nineteenth century.

> Everything can be labeled [a rumba]; all of the rhythms constituting Cuban music . . . everything which can be performed in 2/4 time can fuse with this genre which, more than a genre, represents an "atmosphere" or feeling; . . . in Cuba there is no single "rumba," but various "rumbas" . . . the word "rumba" has passed into the parlance of the Cuban as a synonym for revelry, lascivious dance, carousing with loose women of the street.[4]

This commentary, as well as the diversity of commercial musics published as rumbas, suggest that the genre cannot be adequately covered by a single definition. Many compositions since the mid-nineteenth century use the term in titles or lyrics to evoke images of revelry while demonstrating few of the musical characteristics of noncommercial rumba. Others written for cabaret shows clearly manifest some musical and choreographic resemblance to traditional *guaguancó* or *columbia* subgenres. *Rumba* is perhaps best understood as comprised of both specific associations with music and dance styles and broad, historically derived associations with Cuba's black underclasses, their life styles, attitudes, and culture. References to rumba in popular song can reflect racist attitudes of the early twentieth century by mimicking or ridiculing blacks. Alternately, they can serve as an oppositional voice among marginalized Afrocubans themselves by alluding to forms of expression excluded from the commercial realm.

The campaign against "atavisms" in colonial Cuba led to legislation designed to suppress Afrocuban musical activity, including rumba. As early as the 1880s, municipal authorities in Havana began to regulate its performance. An ordinance dated 30 October 1888 reads:

> [The rumba] dances known as "El papalote" and "El yambú" are hereby prohibited, in addition to similar dances known by other names that in their rhythms, characteristics, or unbecoming costumes demonstrate obscenity or infringe upon this directive in other respects. All chiefs of police are to advise themselves of the intent of the present announcement.[5]

Documents from the 1890s similarly attest to the prosecution of Cuban blacks for having played "box-drums and danced *ñáñigo* rumbas in the street" (Martínez Rodríguez 1977, 2). Suppression of rumba performance did not slacken in the early Republic. The *"rumba de cajón"* tradition, that of performing on packing crates instead of barrel-stave drums, developed at the turn of the century in response to the decree of 6 April 1900 by Havana's Mayor Nicasio Estrada Mora forbidding all performance on "African instruments" (Sánchez de Fuentes 1928b, 199). Other ordinances banning street music by *coros de clave* and *coros de guaguancó* circulated about 1913 (Martínez Furé 1994). During the *machadato,* rumba continued to be denounced by representatives of European musical institutions as "monotonous," "lascivious," "rudimentary," or worse. This period, which gave rise to widespread international interest in stylized African-American musics, also witnessed a strong counter-reaction among white supremacists. Cuban critics used the fact that jazz had been banned on German radio in 1933 to justify their own campaigns against Afrocuban genres (e.g., Sánchez de Fuentes 1938b, 173).

Tellingly, police regulation directed against rumba in the early twentieth century applied solely to working-class music making and not to adaptations of the same music in the theater or cabaret (Leaf 1948, 8). Through a combination of overt dominance, public ridicule, censorship of the mass media, and dissemination of stylistically altered versions of musical expression that conformed more closely to the European "norm," the state and its cultural representatives effectively "reinvented" the rumba in forms more to their liking. The result was to perpetuate a contested but highly effective "white cultural supremacy" on the island for decades (ibid.). Whatever its tentative concessions to subaltern tastes, the rumba craze of the 1930s was thus accompanied by a similarly widespread suppression of noncommercial Afrocuban arts and promoted by an entertainment industry most hospitable only to forms of Afrocuban expression derived from the middle-class imagination.

International Rumba and the Jazz Age

Paris of the 1920s had established itself as the center of a Western artistic movement embracing "blackness" and "primitivist" art as fashionable entertainment. This "curious colonialism" (Arredondo 1938, 5) of the arts first developed among the French literary and visual avant-garde of the 1910s (Moore 1990). War statuettes of the Dahomey, bronze coins of the Lodi, Congolese wood sculptures, and other *l'art nègre* objects became the subject of intense interest among an artistic circle that included Braque, Derain, Vlaminck, Modigliani, and Renato Maran.[6] By the following decade, partially as a result of having been legitimized "from above," Africanism began to influence middle- and working-class art as well. In music halls, theaters, cinemas, and on the radio, discussions and images of "the Negro" captivated mass audiences.

Josephine Baker featured prominently among African-American artists in Paris at that time. The *"danses sauvages"* she performed as part of the Revue Nègre inspired both praise and considerable controversy, due in no small part to sketches in which she appeared on stage wearing only a feathered headdress and banana skirt. French producers choreographing her acts knew next to nothing of African or African-American culture. The versions of "blackness" they promoted can only be described as a racist and exoticized fantasy, replete with giant watermelon backdrops, cotton pickers, cannibal scenes, grotesque clowning, and blackface comedy. The Ballets Russes, reflecting Japanese and Balinese influences, echoed these acts in the high art realm. Darius Milhaud, Jean Cocteau, Guillaume Apollinaire, and other influential French intellectuals frequented such presentations, as did North Americans of the "lost generation" living in Paris (Rose 1989, 20).

Jazz musicians, singers, and entertainers abounded in Paris in the 1920s, and the charleston and black bottom achieved tremendous popularity.[7] Conservatives attacked what they viewed as the "decadence" of the epoch, and the interest in "crude," "unsophisticated" art forms that threatened established bourgeois canons. To them it seemed as if the "masterworks of the human spirit" were being "thrown into a great bonfire around which savages will dance naked" (Rose 1989, 36). Baker and other celebrities thus inspired discourse about race throughout Europe and contributed to the publication of antiblack diatribes such as Emile Fournier-Fabre's *Le Choc suprême, ou la mêlée des races* (1921) and Maurice Muret's *Le crépuscule des nations blanches* (1925). Ideologues of the emerging Nazi party such as Oswald Spengler articulated the views of many when he wrote in *The Decline of the West,* "France has betrayed European culture. In the name of her own impotence she has awakened the African continent. The black horde is not an apparition. The blood of Europe has been poisoned by the perverse miscegenation of France."[8]

Black artists of the Harlem Renaissance and the vogue of jazz music generated similar controversy in the United States and in Cuba. Critics in Havana, for instance, described jazz as "an infernal and diabolical creation, sent by the devil to destroy humanity," and *afrocubanismo* composition as "an art of barbarians, useful only for exciting the fatigued and lugubrious senses of a corrupt and decadent public."[9] Others belittled *negrismo* art generally as "blatant [cultural] retrocession" *(franco retroceso)* and as inspired by works "whose location on the ladder of culture hardly occupies the modest neolithic rung."[10] Yet far from representing polar extremes, 1920s primitivism and Aryan supremacist discourse can be viewed as related phenomena (Rose 1989, 36). Both derive from exaggerated and stereotypical constructs of racial difference, the former glorifying them and the latter condemning them.

In an ideological sense, the "jazz age" had a profound impact on cultural life in Cuba. As in most colonized nations, Cuba's leaders looked to Europe and the United States for artistic inspiration. Many had studied or toured abroad and could not help being influenced by international trends. Also, North American music had long been a significant influence in Cuba. Families returning from exile after the War of Independence popularized ragtime music in Havana around 1900 (Acosta 1992, 2). Beginning in the late 1910s, North American orchestras began to perform regularly on the island, resulting in competition between jazz and national genres such as the *danzón* (Castillo Faílde 1964, 169). Well-known entertainment troupes and artists from Europe came to Cuba during the 1920s, including the Folies Bergère and Josephine Baker herself.[11] North American celebrity acts also performed there; the Original Dixieland Jazz Band and the orchestras of Jimmy Holmes, Max Dolin, Fred Waring, Rudy Vallee, and Earl Carpenter all played extended engagements in Havana (Acosta 1993, 38).

With substantial numbers of American tourists visiting Cuba each year, jazz ensembles provided Cuban musicians with badly needed income. Eliseo and Emilio Grenet, Jaime Prats, Alejandro García Caturla, Moisés Simons, and many others played jazz early in their careers (Acosta 1993, 5; Martínez Rodríguez 1993). The increasing popularity of black entertainment in France and the United States thus coincided with the emergence of the *afrocubanismo* movement. It also contributed to the decision by many Cuban artists to take their *zarzuela* troupes, comic theater shows, *conjuntos de son,* and cabaret acts abroad in an attempt to capitalize on the vogue of African-American art. In addition, widespread unemployment and violence under the Machado administration accelerated the exodus of performers to Europe and the United States.

Early international rumba stars were predominantly white, relatively wealthy, and in most cases had been conservatory-trained as instrumentalists and/or vocalists. The first artists to establish successful careers in Europe had already made names for themselves at home in theatrical productions or nightclubs. These included actress Tessi Moreno, the *pareja de baile* (cabaret dance team) Carmita Ortiz and Julio Richards, jazz band leader Filiberto Rico, and mulata singer Rita Montaner. The "Afrocuban" music they first performed abroad consisted of song and dance from the blackface theater and stylized *sones, guarachas,* and rumbas written by Simons, Grenet, Lecuona, and others. This was the repertory—for example, "Negrita" and "El calesero" by Lecuona, "Vacúnala" and "Lamento negro" by Simons, "Quirino con su tres" and "Ay, Mamá Inés" by Eliseo Grenet—that Cuban and foreign critics alike hailed as contributing to the "triumph of the rumba." International rumba thus bore little stylistic relation to the traditional genre, but it by no means constituted a "foreign bastardization" of Cuban music as many suggest (see Carpentier 1946, 360). On the contrary, the first international stars were themselves Cuban and sang songs by Cuban composers that had already been popularized at home. Only in later years would foreign artists compose and perform "bastardized" rumbas of their own.

The biography of Carmita Ortiz, a white performer, closely resembles that of many early commercial *rumberas.* Carmen María Hortensia was born in Havana in 1909, the daughter of an engineer and a professional actress (Meluzá Otero 1945a, 23). The relative affluence of the family enabled them to vacation in New York during most summers. Ortiz made her first stage appearances in a children's chorus, and at age sixteen began reciting poetry at the Teatro Actualidades (Ramírez 1943a, 6). Apparently she received voice training, because she later found work in the Teatro Martí as a second soprano. Ortiz first captured public attention in 1925 with a dance act that she developed with juggler Julio Richards (Julio Pons). From this period through the 1930s, the pair featured a variety of international folk genres in their stage acts (Barral 1932b). On 12 August 1927, they performed some of the first rumbas seen by Parisian audiences as part of the "Quatour Cubain," which included actors Josefina Ruiz and Rafaelito Betancourt. Ortiz wore the fancy, ruffled *guarachera* outfits of the *teatro vernáculo.* She and Richards eventually separated from the others, signed their own contracts, and began touring extensively in Germany, Switzerland, Italy, and later Central and South America. Ortiz returned to Havana, married *negrito* actor Alberto Garrido, and became a major *farándula* celebrity. Her career ended abruptly in her mid-thirties when she died as a result of complications after surgery.[12]

Pianist and singer Rita Montaner y Facenda (1900–1958) also figures prominently in the national and international popularization of Cuban stage rumba. She was born in Guanabacoa to a white father—a pharmacist and former captain in the Liberation Army—and a mulatto mother, Mercedes Facenda. Having begun piano lessons at home as a child, at age ten Montaner enrolled in the Conservatorio Eduardo Peyrellade to study voice, solfège, music theory, and keyboard (Martínez Malo 1988, 19). She first achieved recognition as a pianist, then as a vocalist interpreting European art music. Montaner took part in the first concerts of *"música típica cubana"* organized by Sánchez de Fuentes in 1922, performing works by Mauri, Anckermann, and Simons, and over the next several years became one of Havana's best-known salon artists (ibid., 136). She made the decision to perform Afrocuban-inspired works beginning in 1927, making her debut in blackface on 29 September as the (male) *negro calesero* José Rosario in Lecuona's *Niña Rita*. In the same year, she appeared with Josephine Baker in Paris and began to include jazz pieces popularized by Baker in her own repertory (Pérez Perazzo 1988, 67). Her early stage act in Paris included the *afrocubanismo* works "Carabalí" by Félix Caignet, and "Negrita" and "La mulata" by Lecuona, in addition to various *pregones,* tangos, fox-trots, *criollas,* and *canciones cubanas* (Martínez Malo 1988, 144). In the early 1930s, Montaner performed in New York with Al Jolson and eventually became a film star in her own right, featuring in such productions as *La noche del pecado* (1934), *Romance del palmar* (1938), *Sucedió en la Habana* (1938), *Romance Musical* (1941), *María la O* (1947), and *Angelitos negros* (1948).

Rita Montaner's repertory, which from the late 1920s included both European-style art song and stage rumbas, reflects the stylistic tensions inherent in early twentieth-century popular music, as does her biography. As a relatively wealthy classical musician, Montaner had little to do professionally with music of the *teatro vernáculo* before her late twenties; in this respect she is an unlikely *rumbera* figure. On the other hand, she was also mulatto and a practitioner of *santería* who grew up in a barrio famous for its strong Afrocuban traditions. Black and mulatto entertainers such as Montaner and Ignacio Villa served as cultural mediators, performing rumbas and other genres in a "sophisticated" manner yet with an "aura of authenticity." They translated working-class musical expression into a form acceptable to the middle-class public, yet legitimized its associations with Afrocubans through their very presence. These artists adopted multiple personae in song and crossed social boundaries of race, class, gender to an unprecedented degree.

Montaner's interpretation of "Negrita" deserves mention as an example of such "boundary-crossing."[13] She begins the piece singing in a refined, operatic style. The lyrics of the first section are those of a white male suitor courting his *"negrita."* Abruptly, Montaner lowers her vocal register to sing the response of the female, apparently a "*mulata del rumbo*" (a "worldly" *mulata,* an "easy lay"). As the *mulata,* she adopts a brusque, untrained sound and uses *bozal* speech to indicate the woman's lack of education. Later, Montaner shifts back to the original vocal modality and concludes the song in the persona of the white male.

Documentation on the performance of rumba and other *afrocubanista* repertory abroad is difficult to obtain. Most available information comes from articles published in Cuban magazines in the late 1920s by Alejo Carpentier and others living in Paris. Carpentier, an early advocate of *afrocubanismo,* began to promote the movement in 1925 following an exposure to modern classical music inspired by jazz. He moved to Paris in 1928, after serving a brief jail term for "subversion" under the Machado administration, and he personally observed the enthusiasm with which Quintana, Montaner, and others were received.

> Rita Montaner . . . shouts at us, at the top of her lungs and with a formidable
> sense of rhythm, songs of the urban slum written by a Simons or Grenet,
> evoking (according to the song) the ambience of a *solar*'s central courtyard, the
> cane field of a sugar plantation, a Chinese food stand, a *ñáñigo* fiesta, the tasty
> caramel candy [of a street hawker]. "Why invoke these [cultural] defects,
> vulgarities?" some will ask. Defects? Why call the notes of color that constitute a
> rich and vibrant folkloric contribution "defects"? Woe to those lackluster and
> insipid countries that lack defects such as these!"[14]

Carpentier's commentary acknowledges that stylized Afrocuban expression seemed demeaning to many middle-class Cubans, who did not wish to see it disseminated abroad. Even he demonstrated ambivalence toward black working-class expression on more than one occasion. Writing in *Carteles* in December 1929, for instance, Carpentier struck a more conciliatory tone with opponents of the rumba craze. He admitted that "vulgar" expression could be a source of national embarrassment, but suggested that this was true only in undeveloped countries. Cubans, he argued, lived in an industrially advanced society and should not fear that foreigners would think of them as "uncivilized" merely because their national songs were influenced by Africa. "Crude" genres from bygone days, he implied, added "color" and vitality to an otherwise austere modern environment.

> I agree that certain primitive customs, certain habits of the rabble developing
> either in the city or the countryside, can prove to be a danger for the civility of a
> country, when the country finds itself still living in its Middle Ages, without
> decent highways, without streetcars, and drinking from crude earthenware jugs.
> But when it possesses one of the most beautiful capitals in the world, when it

has incredible quantities of trains and automobiles . . . a nation like Cuba should proudly conserve a few elements of local color. Let us protect our *guajira* music, our Afrocuban music! Let us defend it against its detractors! Let us praise the *son,* the noisy *solar,* the *güiro,* the *décima,* the lithography on cigar boxes, *santería* drumming, the picturesque *pregón,* the *mulata* with rings of gold, the light sandals of the *rumbero.* . . . Blessed be the lineage of Papá Montero and María la O! . . . When one sees things from abroad, the value of these popular treasures is understood as never before!"[15]

Two of the earliest establishments that contributed to the popularization of commercial rumba abroad were Melody's Bar and the Cabaña Bambú in the Montmartre district of Paris (ibid., 105). Melody's had existed before 1931 as one of countless low-profile cabarets in the area, but this quickly changed when its owners, capitalizing on the vogue of Cuban music in the city, hired the orchestra of Filiberto Rico and began to promote rumba stage acts. The exact composition of the orchestra is unknown, but like many Cuban jazz bands it included maraca, *clave, cencerro,* and *timbal,* in addition to horns and rhythm instruments. Moisés Simons is said to have frequented Melody's, playing his own compositions for solo piano such as "Marta" and "La negra Quirina" (ibid., 106). The rhythmic novelty of these acts attracted large audiences, many of whom had earlier frequented nearby tango bars. Melody's success led to the opening of the Cabaña Bambú on the same block and eventually to a proliferation of similar venues. For a short time in the early 1930s, Carpentier notes, the entire Montmartre district was dominated by shows featuring Cuban music and dance.

The Club du Faubourg, another Paris cabaret, promoted a diversity of events not restricted to music and dance. Politicians, religious leaders, literary celebrities, feminist activists, philosophers, and many others received invitations to give presentations or to stage debates before the public at the Faubourg. In the spring of 1932, managers of the club asked Simons, Carpentier, and others to organize a presentation to discuss and demonstrate Cuban music.[16] Turnout for the event was high, with perhaps as many as 2,000 spectators (ibid., 98–99). Singer Maricusa Cuadrado and the dancer "Rhana" performed to live instrumental accompaniment, together with other artists engaged at the Casino de Paris and the Palace and Empire Theaters. The audience enthusiastically applauded Simons's *pregón* "El manicero" (The peanut vendor) and other songs. Local newspapers covered the event heavily, contributing to an increasing awareness of cabaret rumba among the French public.

Moisés Simons remained in Paris longer than virtually any other Cuban artist and contributed perhaps more than any other—with the possible exception of Eliseo Grenet—to the dissemination of stylized Afrocuban music there.

Simons was born in Havana in 1889 to a family of Jewish immigrants from the Basque region of Spain (Muñoz Albuquere 1989). Leandro Simón Guergué, a music professor, initiated his son's studies of theory and solfège at home. By age nineteen, Simons had distinguished himself as a composer and pianist and found work as the musical director of the Martí Theater, and later of the Payret. In the 1920s he formed and led the jazz house orchestra of the Hotel Plaza, owned in part by his brother Faustino.[17] During these years, Simons distinguished himself by writing dance music that fused elements of the *danzón* with North American jazz repertoire, not *afrocubanismo* works.[18] His move to Paris in 1928 and recognition of the popularity of African-American music there, however, led to an abrupt shift in compositional style. Drawing on his theater experience, Simons established contacts in Paris and Madrid and eventually premiered a series of original *sainete*-like comedies incorporating Afrocuban themes, all of which were well received.

One of Simons's earliest international works was *Niña Mercé,* a comedy performed in 1930 both in the Teatro Calderón of Madrid and in Paris. Others from the period include *Toi c'est moi,* which opened on 18 October 1934 at the Théâtre Bouffes Parisiens and ran for more than 400 nights before closing, and *Le chant des tropiques* (1936), which debuted in the Théâtre Paris featuring Antonio Machín and rumba dancers "Ofelia" and "Pimienta." Theater shows created by Simons proved influential on French pop singers Raquel Meller and Tino Rossi, among others, who performed many of his songs. Simons reluctantly returned to Havana in the early 1940s after the onset of World War II. He had already been forced to change his name from Simón to conceal his Jewish heritage and later began to fear for his life. The composer continued to write new stage works and produced a few in Madrid during the war, but died suddenly in June 1945 at age fifty-six.

Internationalized *afrocubanismo* works by Simons are similar to salon compositions in the same style by Lecuona and Grenet discussed in chapter 5. Musically, most of them resemble *sones* of the comic theater because of their emphasis on beat "4" of the 4/4 accompaniment, imitating the anticipated bass pattern of *son.* This feature is evident regardless of whether the songs are subtitled "*guaracha,*" "rumba," "*son,*" or "*pregón.*" The *Album Simons* (1929) provides a number of examples of Afrocuban-inspired songs from the author's first years in Paris, including "Vacúnala" (subtitled *rumba hampona*), "La negra Quirina" *(rumba culinaria),* "Patica y mondonguito" *(pregón arrabalero),* and "Con picante y sin picante" *(sonsonete).* Lyrically, they mix discourse about overtly sexual behavior with metaphors of food, a time-tested device in Cuba and much of Latin America. Again, Simons wrote most of this material for white artists, with the exception of Rita Montaner.

The title of Simons's stage rumba "Vacúnala" comes from *vacunar,* the verb describing the pelvic thrust of traditional *guaguancó* performance. It is a fast piece in 2/4 time that incorporates an ostinato *tresillo* figure in the bass: "If you see some meat going by, *vacúnala* / If you want to make her yours, *vacúnala* / ... Because that vacunao stuff is what gets results."[19] Another song, "Con picante y sin picante," popularized by Rita Montaner, evokes a sensuous *mulata* proclaiming in street dialect how plump and juicy her "tamales" are. "La negra Quirina" consists of a male-female dialogue in which black sexuality is emphasized. It too incorporates food symbolism. [She:] "I want to eat, I want to eat so much, jerked beef with uncooked garlic sauce, yuca root and okra, and in the woods after lunch, on the shores of the [River] Almendares, navigate together. . . . [He:] I also want to eat, ground beef and rice with fried eggs. . . . I'm going to take you, I'm going to take you to the shores of the Almendares, *china,* to have lunch."[20]

Certainly Xavier Cugat (1900–1990) stands out as one of the most commercially successful and famous band leaders associated with the rumba craze. Born in Catalonia, Spain, like a surprising number of international *rumberos,*[21] Cugat moved with his family at an early age to Havana. Uninterested in popular music as an adolescent and largely unfamiliar with Afrocuban genres, the young Cugat dedicated himself to the violin. He moved to New York in the hopes of furthering his career, but critical success eluded him. Only after admitting failure as a classical artist and supporting himself for years as a cartoonist at the *Los Angeles Times* did he consider organizing a dance band. Despite his personal opinion that all popular songs were "simple, repetitious, and stifling," Cugat recognized the increasing popularity of Latin American music in the United States and after the early 1930s devoted himself exclusively to the world of entertainment (Cugat 1948, 76).

In 1932 the managers of the Waldorf Astoria Hotel contracted Cugat as their house orchestra leader (Perazzo 1988, 70). His live coast-to-coast radio broadcasts that began later that decade from New York, the "Dinner and the Waldorf Show," generated tremendous demand for stylized Latin musics in the United States, as did his frequent film appearances (see Roberts 1979, 85). The Waldorf orchestra served as a forum for introducing new singers and dancers to the North American public; Machito (Francisco Grillo), Miguelito Valdés, Tito Rodríguez, and others first established themselves as international Latin celebrities in the ensemble.

While criticized as "inauthentic" (e.g., Carpentier 1944, 360), Cugat did not claim to play in a traditional style and freely admitted that his renditions of Afrocuban music had little to do with street culture in Havana or elsewhere (Roberts 1979, 87). Despite an elitist bias, therefore, he can hardly be criticized for his "inappropriate" repertoire. Cugat merely continued a centuries-old process of musical transformation, parody, and "whitening" of African-American art, one that continued into the twentieth century in the works of Lecuona, Roig, Simons, Grenet, Gershwin, Jerome Kern, W. C. Handy, and countless others. Criticism of Cugat by Cubans undoubtedly derived in part from his close association with "rumba" among American audiences, even though he was not Cuban-born and played music from a diversity of countries in addition to those of the Hispanic Caribbean. The repertory of Cugat's orchestra included arrangements of Spanish, Mexican, Argentine, Venezuelan, and Brazilian folk songs, in addition to those from English- and French-speaking Latin America. The band also played North American jazz standards, quasi–Middle Eastern "exotic" numbers, and even the Chiquita Banana song, a commercial advertising jingle (Cugat 1948, 168). The North American music industry referred to almost all of these pieces as "rumbas," angering those who perceived a clear distinction between stylized Afrocuban genres from Cuba and stylized genres from elsewhere.

So many other orchestras performed Cuban music abroad in the 1930s that only a few can be mentioned here. Most were groups of white performers, although some Afrocubans also achieved international recognition. Among Afrocuban artists touring abroad at this time, Fernando Collazo (1909–1939) and Julio Cueva (1897–1975) stand out as important figures. One of the most popular interpreters of Cuban music in Paris of the 1930s, Collazo sang regularly at La Cabaña Cubana (Carpentier 1976, 122). He began his career in the late 1920s by founding the Orquesta Gris, a *charanga,* and later in 1930 the *son* band Septeto Cuba. Collazo is said to have been featured in the first musical film made in Cuba, *Maracas y bongó,* from 1932. Julio Cueva's performances in Europe, by contrast, consisted primarily of work with jazz bands. A light-skinned pianist and trumpet player, Cueva grew up in the city of Trinidad; Simons and Azpiazu invited him to tour abroad in the late 1920s. He remained in Paris after the tour and with the financial help of Cuban Víctor Jalkh opened the club "La Cueva" in Paris in June 1934 (Cañizares 1991).

Other Afrocubans living in Spain in the 1930s include mulatto *sonero* Antonio Machín and dancer María Morales. Born in Sagua la Grande, Machín was one of the first Afrocubans of the thirties to perform with a white jazz orchestra and also the first to play at the exclusive Casino Nacional as part of the orchestra of Justo Azpiazu in the late 1920s (Díaz Ayala 1992). In 1935 Machín went to Europe on tour with his own group, the Cuarteto Machín. He performed in France and Spain, eventually settling in the latter to avoid the Nazi occupation of Paris. He remained in Spain until his death in 1977.

María Morales, known internationally as "La Perla Negra," achieved widespread recognition in Spain, France, and Italy. Born to Afrocuban parents living in Spain, Morales studied classical dance from an early age. Appearances in primitivist stage productions patterned after works of the Ballets Russes first brought her national attention. Critics in Madrid hailed Morales as "the celebrated Ethiopian dancer" of the decade and enthusiastically reviewed a number of productions featuring her, including *El asombro de Damasco, La danza macabra,* and *Gitana mora,* from the mid-1920s (Acosta 1950).

Countless white ensembles performed abroad in the twenties and thirties. The Havana Casino Orchestra of Justo Angel "Don" Azpiazu (1893–1943) received much acclaim for its performances of jazz-influenced rumba in the United States as well as in Europe.[22] Enrique Madriguera's ensemble played at the Embassy Club and Pierre's in New York (Roberts 1979, 60); Desi Arnaz began his musical career in 1937 in what would become the Conga Bar at Broadway and 57th Street (Collazo 1987, 165); Nilo Menéndez and (Puerto Rican) Augusto Coen had their own ensembles in New York; Arturo Santirzo and his group frequented the Miami area (Kevin Mooney, personal communication); Panchito Riset performed regularly in Los Angeles; the Lecuona Cuban Boys toured with Josephine Baker in 1938 in France, Belgium, Greece, and Turkey, among other countries, before heading back to Havana (Collazo 1987, 168, 179, 183); Eliseo Grenet flew to New York in 1936 with Carmita Ortiz and Julio Richards, performing salon rumbas and congas for journalists Walter Winchell and Danton Walker in the Steinway Building (*Homenaje a Eliseo Grenet,* 5). Grenet also wrote a series of Afrocuban-inspired compositions for films in Mexico, Argentina, and the United States in the 1930s, including *La princesa tin-tan* (with Josephine Baker), *Escándalo de estrellas, Conga Bar* (with Miguelito Valdés), *Milonga de arrabal* (with Libertad Lamarque), and *Estampas coloniales.*

At about the same time, publishers and performers in the United States and Europe began to appropriate the term *rumba* (or *rhumba*), using it as a generic label for Latin American–influenced composition. Largely unaware of traditional rumba and unclear as to its differences from commercial rumba, they applied the term indiscriminately. The earlier semiotic expansion of the term *rumba* within Cuba—that is, its gradual association with all Afrocuban dance music rather than with specific genres—soon paled in comparison with the diversity of music and dances later called rumba on the international market. Any song or composition drawing even the most tangential inspiration from Latin America was suddenly a potential rumba.

The E. B. Marks Music Corporation printed a version of Grenet's *tango-congo* "Ay Mamá Inés" in English and labeled it "the greatest of all Cuban rumbas" (Grenet 1932). Paul Whiteman distinguished himself early on as a high-profile "gringo *rumbero,*" arranging and popularizing countless "sweet jazz" versions of similar pieces. Cab Calloway wrote "Doin' the Rhumba" and other Cuban-inspired jazz pieces (e.g., Calloway 1982). Cole Porter included the "biguine-rumba" "The Gypsy in Me" in his 1934 musical *Anything Goes* (ibid. 1979, 83). George Raft, Carole Lombard, and Ann Sheridan starred in a Paramount film entitled *Rumba* in 1935, which also featured Cuban *rumbera* Carmen Curbelo (to be discussed later). The Henry King Orchestra released a five-album set of "rumbas" in 1938 including (the *canción*) "Siboney," (the "rumba-fox-trot") "Havana Is Calling Me," (the *pregón*) "The Peanut Vendor," and (the *afro*) "Tabú."[23]

The Havana Novelty Orchestra, an invention of RCA Victor, recorded jazz two-step versions of "Ay Mamá Inés," and other Cuban songs with prominent banjo and clarinet solos and a strong Dixieland flavor.[24] Dinah Shore sang "Jungle Drums," "Cuban Episode," and "Rhumba-cardi" with the Cugat orchestra in 1939 and 1940, while the Andrew Sisters recorded their own "Rhumbaboogie" with a swing band at roughly the same time (Roberts 1979, 91, 107). In the Middle East, the Balkans, Manchuria, and Japan, "rumba" music of all kinds achieved fleeting popularity (Avilés Ramírez 1932, 28; Hokosawa 1994). Ballroom dancers first demonstrated an interest in rumba at this time. The international dance music known as rumba represents a fusion of elements taken from the fox-trot and the *son*. This conflation of *son* and jazz music with lyrical references to rumba appeared originally in the Cuban blackface theater. The dance as popularized in the United States and elsewhere thus has virtually nothing in common with traditional rumba. Nevertheless, it became tremendously popular for years as high-society entertainment. In Berlin's Wintergarten, for instance, Walter Carlos and his wife created a sensation as rumba performers as early as 1931 (Roquelosabe 1931, 55; see illustrations).

This profusion of "decentered" and "recentered" rumbas at first gratified but later irritated Cuban critics. They welcomed the popularity of Cuban music abroad, yet expressed dissatisfaction over the superficial and stereotyped images of their country perpetuated by the entertainment industry. Carpentier's enthusiasm over the "triumph of the rumba" in Paris before 1930 changed dramatically in later years. He wrote to readers of *Carteles* that Cuban songs had been appropriated by French entertainers and altered so drastically that they were barely recognizable. In particular he mentions the composition "La rumba d'amour," an adaptation of "El manisero" with French lyrics by singer Henri Varna. Tunes such as this, which proliferated in the Paris theater, Carpentier argued, had nothing to do with Cuba. He felt that Varna and others set the music of Moisés Simons and others "in an almost absurd context" by using it to accompany seminude dancers, can-can lines, and silent film shorts of Mickey Mouse and Felix the Cat, and by playing it in conjunction with jazz dance arrangements of Wagner's *Tannhäuser* and women in *Madame Butterfly* costumes dancing the black bottom. To Carpentier, it suddenly seemed as if rumba music performed in Paris "had nothing in common with the [genre] except its name" (1931, 18). Journalist Avilés Ramírez expressed similar concerns about rumba elsewhere in Europe. "How many types of fantastically interpreted rumba are there [in Europe's capitals]? The rumba has been converted into a musical postulate, from which a hundred more have been born."[25]

Cuban authors criticized the proliferation of rumba in the United States as well. Emilio Grenet, in the introduction to *Cuban Popular Music*, denounced rumbas written in the United States as "adulterated" (1939, lxii). Carpentier railed against what he viewed as the intentional appropriation of Cuban songs by North American businesses, suggesting that it represented yet another example of imperialist meddling in his nation's affairs:

> And with dull imitations like [the films] *Sweet Rosita* or *Speak Easy,* the Yankees demonstrate that they have already begun to satisfy their imperialist appetites in the realm of our music as they have done in so many other ways, and that they are quite willing to play an arbitrating role in the global invasion of Cuban songs in order to adorn themselves again, according to established practice, with borrowed feathers.[26]

Ernesto Lecuona expressed a similar opinion after having been invited to Hollywood in 1931 to perform in the MGM musical *Cuban Love Song.* The production starred Lawrence Tibbett and Mexican Actress Lupe Vélez and featured compositions by Simons, Lecuona, and the jazz band Hermanos Palau (Collazo 1987, 117). Lecuona described it as "yet another Americanized [stereotype], making us play a ridiculous role."[27]

The Rumba Craze Returns Home: Tourist Cabarets in Havana

As with salon conga, the rumba stage acts popularized in Europe and the United States had a strong influence on the expectations of tourists arriving in Cuba. Foreigners who had been led to believe that this "typical music" was the epitome of national expression found that most middle-class and elite entertainment venues *(cabarets de primera y segunda)* preferred not to hire Afrocuban performers, nor rumba dancers of any sort. Instead, managers promoted either blackface comedy—at the Hotel Nacional, for instance—or stage shows featuring tangos, jazz dance, and other genres performed by white Cubans (Rey 1992). Rumba dance, even stylized *"rumba de fantasía,"* did not become acceptable in any cabaret before about 1929 (ibid.). As late as the 1940s owners of the Tropicana and other up-scale venues presented stage rumba grudgingly and only during the winter, at the height of the tourist season (Leaf 1948, 35). The attraction of foreigners to Afrocuban expression became a subject of much discussion in Havana after the onset of the *afrocubanismo* movement. The cover of *Bohemia* magazine of 17 July 1938, for instance, depicts a topless *mulata* dancing for a smiling male tourist and his disapproving wife. Demand from abroad dramatically changed the nature of Havana's nightlife, leading to the increasing prominence of Afrocuban expression in existing clubs and the establishment of entirely new ones such as those built on the beaches in Marianao.

North American tourists, who began to visit Cuba with the expansion of U.S. investment in the early 1900s, later came to Cuba because of travel restrictions imposed during the first World War. Wealthy families and businessmen who once vacationed in London or Paris began to travel instead to Latin America. The enactment of the Eighteenth Amendment in January 1920 that forbade the sale and consumption of alcohol in the United States also expanded the ranks of Cuban tourists (Avalos 1992, 6). Rum smuggling developed into a major industry during Prohibition (1920–1933), with many Americans buying large quantities of liquor for personal use or to sell clandestinely upon their return (Acosta 1992, 4). This was especially true of those arriving in their own boats at Barlovento (today the Marina Hemingway) west of Havana (Herrera 1994b).

Between 1926 and 1937, an average of 120,000 tourists visited Cuba each year, except for a brief slump during the worst periods of *machadato* violence.[28] In 1936 over 150,000 tourists came to Cuba, and in the following year over 170,000. Tourists in the winter months consisted largely of families avoiding northern temperatures, while in the off-season more single men arrived interested in gambling, drinking, and prostitution (Quiñones 1992). A sharp distinction existed between elite tourism, generally confined to the Siboney and Miramar districts (associated with the Sans Souci, Casino Nacional, and Jockey Club), and that of more modest establishments (Herrera 1994b).

Afrocubans, generally without access to higher education and denied white-collar employment, were heavily overrepresented in Cuba's expanding tourist economy (Pérez 1986, 306). Unlike the international rumba stars of the 1920s, those who performed Afrocuban music and dance in 1930s Havana tended more often to be blacks or mulattos themselves. In the dozens of new *cabarets de tercera* (third-class cabarets) in Habana Vieja and Marianao, especially, Afrocubans predominated as musicians and dancers. They came from poorer backgrounds, had little formal education, and—in the case of many arriving from provinces other than Havana and Matanzas—often had little familiarity with traditional rumba. Small clubs such as El Pampillo, Los Tres Hermanos, El Paraíso, El Pennsylvania, and El Rumba Palace, which opened around 1929 in Marianao, showcased black working-class artists who happily challenged the social stigma surrounding (both traditional and stylized) rumba and created the stage acts tourists wanted to see. This area also served as a center of prostitution, featuring two *academias de baile* (La Carioca and El Pompillo) as well as a conveniently located *posada* flophouse, La Gran China.[29]

Rumba music in the cabarets of Havana tended to be played by small *conjuntos de son* or jazz bands. No single format predominated, but instruments such as the piano, acoustic bass, trumpet, *bongó,* and *timbal* were the most common (Rey 1994). Often during an extended dance segment, percussionists would "trade fours" with the rest of the ensemble, playing "hot" rhythmic breaks to the accompaniment of the remainder of the group. Larger cabarets often employed both a *conjunto* and a string orchestra or jazz band and alternated performances by the two groups during the evening (Herrera 1994b). The Sexteto Oriente, for instance, performed regularly in the cabaret Montmartre beginning in 1927 as a complement to its dance band (Avalos 1992, 6). Many *academias de baile* similarly alternated between house orchestras performing primarily jazz- and *danzón*-based repertory and acoustic *son* bands.

Perhaps the most famous instrumentalist of 1930s and 1940s rumba shows was a *timbalero* called "El Chori," Silvano Shueg Hechavarría (1900–1974), a *santería* devotee from Santiago de Cuba who arrived in Havana in 1927 (Campoamor 1966, 26). Shueg first found employment in the *academia de baile* Marte y Belona, but within a few years established himself in cabarets such as Los Tres Hermanos, El Ranchito, El Rumba Palace, and La Taverna de Pedro. His diverse act included solo numbers in which he sang and used beer and wine bottles or metal pans as percussion instruments; he also played *timbal* as part of a dance band. Shueg's dance ensemble consisted of other musicians on the *bongó* or conga, *tres,* guitar, and bass (Padura Fuentes 1987, 7). At the height of his fame he received visits and artistic recognition from celebrities Agustín Lara, Cab Calloway, Marlon Brando, and Toña la Negra. As with so many performers from this period, no substantial documentation exists on his life or career.[30]

Cabaret entertainment of the 1930s is difficult to describe in general terms. Female cabaret costumes often consisted of fishnet stockings, bikinis with sequins, stiletto heels, feather boas, and other regalia inspired by international stage shows. Dancers also wore full-length white dresses, colorful head scarves, and vestments associated with *santería* deities (Mora 1995). The same show might feature boleros, European-style songs such as Gonzalo Roig's "Quiéreme mucho," popular *sones* of the day, tangos, rumba sketches influenced by the blackface theater, and mock *santería* drumming involving percussion solos (Mora 1995). Cabaret acts tended to end the evening with an extended rumba dance featuring all of the evening's performers, apparently adopting this tradition from the *teatro vernáculo* (ibid.).

Cabarets incorporated many dance styles in addition to those associated with the rumba. *Sones, danzones,* salon congas, and Spanish *pasodobles* often served as the basis for choreographic sketches within the same act. *Rumberos/*

rumberas learned to incorporate all of these influences and to match the evening's repertory to the expectations of club owners and the requests of patrons. In dance as well as music, they synthesized diverse traditions, some derived from noncommercial rumba and others entirely unrelated. Pirouettes, lifts, and other movements from classical ballet appeared together with techniques such as *vasos en la cabeza,* dancing with a glass of water on one's head, and *rumba de cuchillo,* dancing while rapidly passing sharp knives over one's body and face (Herrera 1994). The latter variations derive from the *columbia,* a form of rumba performed by *abakuá* initiates.[31]

The extent of Afrocuban cultural influences on stage varied greatly according to the background of the entertainers and their performance context, but tended to be strongest in smaller, working-class locales. Exhibition rumba in these venues, though clearly transformed to emphasize its sexual content and influenced by contemporary popular musics, nevertheless resembled noncommercial rumba to a greater extent than shows in the major casinos. Leaf describes a *guaguancó*-like presentation he witnessed in the Kursaal that seems to have been typical:

> The exhibition rumba dancers perform separately for most of the dance,
> alternately taking the spotlight and stepping into the background while the
> other performs. Much of the girl's dance is done with her back to the audience,
> her body shimmying and quivering from head to foot, arching her body
> backward to pick up a handkerchief from the floor with her teeth and perform-
> ing similar thematic movements. (1948, 16)

Other rumba choreography included a variation known as "shoeing the mule" (*herrar la mula*), in which the female dancer performed much of the act on her hands and knees (Lekis 1960, 60). This may have been developed by Luís Correa and Carmen Curbelo in Marianao (Padura Fuentes 1988, 8). "The screw" (*El tornillo*) was yet another variation in which a dancer begins a series of rapid turns on one foot, gradually bends the knees, then rises again, all the while maintaining the spin (Herrera 1994b). Moves of this kind are found in classical ballet and probably have European origins.

Conga dance routines also incorporated a diversity of movements and variations. Among the most typical were "trains" (*trenes*) or "tails" (*colas*), the infamous conga lines in which dancers proceed in single file, each holding the hips of the dancer in front; turns performed alternately to the right and left while slowly moving forward; and overtly erotic movements in which a male dancer walks closely behind his partner, rotating his hips and occasionally presses his pelvis into her buttocks (Fernández Robaina 1994).

Dark-skinned musicians such as El Chori played in smaller cabarets, but with few exceptions did not perform as dancers.[32] The vast majority of Afrocuban dance artists were mulattos, such as Rubén Zaldívar and Lola Díaz, Los Hermanos Barranco, Claribel Gasulla, Alfredo Valdés and Aida (Herrera 1994). Afrocubans René and Estela (René Rivero Guillén and Ramona Ajón) also deserve mention as one of the first *parejas de baile* (cabaret dance team) to achieve international acclaim.[33]

René Rivero (1909–1941), from Matanzas, first danced publicly as a young boy in the Edén Concert and the Molino Rojo with his sister Hilda. His father, a clarinetist, encouraged his children to be performers. Later Rivero found a new partner, Ramona Ajón (who took the stage name of Estela), after his parents began to object to Hilda's involvement with the "semilegitimate" world of low-budget cabarets. Talent scouts from the United States who saw René and Estela dance in Mariano offered them movie contracts and arranged international tours. In 1933 they performed as part of a dance troupe for five months at the Chicago World's Fair, together with the Septeto Nacional and Septeto Montmartre, and later appeared in the film *Una reunión de acusados* with William Powell. They also danced in numerous Mexican films such as *Tierra brava, Cielito lindo, México canta,* and *María.* The World's Fair engagement did much to stimulate interest in Cuban entertainers among U.S. audiences, although the act was far from "traditional." Among other sketches, female artists appeared on stage in a *"danza del abanico"* entirely nude except for two large fans held between themselves and the public (Herrera 1993).

Mulatto dancer Carmen Curbelo was born in 1909 in Cienfuegos, the eighth of twenty children.[34] In 1929, desperate for employment, she left her own family of four and headed for Havana, hoping to send money home. Initially, Curbelo washed clothes and kept house for musicians from the provinces. Attractive and light-skinned, she secured work at an *academia de baile* on the corner of Zanja and Galiano, despite a total lack of dance experience. In the *academia,* Curbelo learned the steps of the *danzón, son,* and *paso doble.* Within a year, city police closed the establishment, as well as another in Marianao that hired her—probably the result of a prostitution crackdown—and she began to look for work in cabarets instead. In the early 1930s, Curbelo debuted as a *rumbera* in Los Tres Hermanos with Luís Correa, whom she describes as a small, fat Puerto Rican with no teeth who danced exceptionally well. By 1933 she had established herself as a stage celebrity (see illustrations). The pace was intense: one often had to "dance a *son,* a rumba, and a conga, then rest for ten minutes and start the same set again for six consecutive hours" (Padura Fuentes 1988). For her services, Curbelo received as much as five pesos a night in the larger cabarets such as the Sans Souci and Montmartre. In *cabarets de tercera,* by contrast, entertainers did not receive a fixed salary but instead split tips with the musicians accompanying them and received a percentage of the profits from sales of alcohol. Occasionally a rich patron might give each dancer twenty or thirty pesos to take home, but more often their nightly earnings did not even cover bus fare.

As in the case of *son* and *comparsa* music, one must address issues of ownership and financial exploitation when considering the popularization of commercial rumba. Trained composers regularly used existing street rumba melodies as the basis for stage acts and commercial publications. Rarely did they attempt to locate or legally recognize the original author, copyrighting the songs instead under their own names.

> As for plagiarism, the rumba proved to be quite favorable as a victim, since [traditional] *rumberos* . . . had little to do with the mass media and commercial mechanisms in general; their compositions spread spontaneously from house to house, street to street, and barrio to barrio, sometimes falling into the hands of "professional" musicians who registered the "anonymous" compositions as their own. . . . Many rumberos were *deprived* of the fruits of their work by such practices. (Acosta 1991, 69–70)

Appropriated rumbas cited by Acosta include "Sepárate mujer" by Peñita, as well as "Veinte le doy a mi gallo pinto" and "Siento que me regaña el corazón" by Gonzalo Asencio (Tío Tom). Afrocuban jazz band leader Julio Cueva also arranged and copyrighted arrangements of street rumba under his own name (Linares 1993).

The myth of the cabaret *rumbera,* derived from *costumbrista* literature, *zarzuelas,* and the *mulata* of the blackface theater, inspired hundreds of films from the 1930s through the 1950s. Mayra Martínez describes the protagonists as variations on the *femme fatale,* a "sensual and sinful" Caribbean woman whose misfortune derives from "the transgression, sometimes against her own wishes, of established moral canons."[35] Like the *zarzuela* heroines of Roig and Lecuona, the *rumbera* is typically a sex toy for white men who "discover" her on the streets and initiate a relationship with her. They either renounce her eventually or bring misfortune on themselves if they cannot. In the former case, the woman is stigmatized and abandoned, often turning to prostitution to survive, hopelessly caught in a destructive chain of events. The *rumbera* is the locus of attraction and repulsion. She is "safe to lust after," the incarnation of sexuality, but also a threat, a destabilizing presence.

> [The *rumbera* is] the ideal woman to compliment the erotic repressions and the secret desires of the average man and his authorized machismo. She is the image of treacherous beauty, presented in a common, everyday form and yet rejected. She is the perfect lover, but not the perfect wife.[36]

Compared with the objective conditions of countless women "leading a miserable existence" and subject to sexist dominance, the cabaret *mulata* construct represents "a pallid reflection of the ordinary unhappiness" of female working-class life (M. Martínez 1989, 40). Films such as *Tin-tan o la origen de la rumba* (1932), *Bella la salvaje* from the late 1930s,[37] and countless others produced later in Mexico such as *Piel canela, Carita de cielo,* and *Perdida* brought the *rumbera* to new Spanish-speaking audiences throughout Europe and Latin America. Stars of these productions included Cuban actresses Rosa Carmina, Ninón Sevilla, María Antonieta Pons, Rosita Fornés, Amalia Aguilar, and Mexican Meche Barba.

Rumbera film actresses, who were overwhelmingly white/Hispanic, rarely grew up performing Afrocuban dances. In some cases, movie directors first exposed them to the commercial rumba and taught them to imitate it, as in the case of Rosa Carmina (ibid.). In others the women themselves expressed an interest in Afrocuban dance as young adults and began to participate in *comparsa* parades and other activities despite the strong objections of their families. Ninón Sevilla mentions that her family did all they could to keep her from pursuing a career as a dancer, exclaiming at one point "better to die than be an artist like that!" (ibid.).

Conclusion

Beginning as early as the 1830s in the writings of Spanish *costumbristas* and continuing at an accelerating pace, the Afrocuban rumba has been continuously appropriated and transformed by others. This process of transculturation or recentering is poorly understood but clearly occurs within a framework of racial inequality and class struggle. Mainstream Cuban artists of the late 1920s— predominantly white performers of *zarzuelas* and the blackface theater—first disseminated depictions of rumba internationally in European and North American dance halls. Soon thereafter, recording artists from other countries with ties to big business produced new rumba adaptations. Finally, Afrocubans themselves of diverse backgrounds also performed commercial rumba within Cuba and for the international community, although their interpretations were limited in many respects to conventions established by the dominant society. Yet despite the ideological impact of the rumba craze in Cuba and the gradually increasing prominence of percussion-only accompaniment in mainstream Latin dance repertory, traditional rumba remains a marginal genre. In Cuba and elsewhere, a widespread bias against African-derived drumming and dance limit the attention devoted to such expression in the mass media. To the extent that it does affect television and radio programming, commercial rumba tends still to be transculturated, reconciled in a musical sense with traditions derived from Europe, the United States, and elsewhere.

The peak popularity of stage rumba came in the 1950s with the mass proliferation of clubs and cabarets throughout Cuba accommodating an even larger tourist presence; the wholesale production of feature-length *rumbera* films; and magazines such as *Gente* and *Show* devoted to following Havana's nightlife. Domestic television series from the same decade—for example, "Jueves de Partagás," sponsored by the famous cigar manufacturer, and "El Cabaret Regalías"—brought stage rumba into the homes and lives of hundreds of thousands of Cubans on a regular basis. Chelo Alonso, Alicia Alvarez, Ana Gloria, Celeste Mendoza, and countless others distinguished themselves as *rumbera-vedettes* on such programs.[38] More recently in socialist Cuba, and especially since the "special period" of the 1990s, rumba shows represent one of the central attractions with which the state tempts foreign visitors. The "joyously kitsch" presentations of the Tropicana, for instance—$65 a ticket plus dinner—featuring jungle scenes, interpreters of *afros,* stylized *santería* songs, conga lines, and other sketches perpetuate the dissemination of transformed folkloric imagery (Manuel 1991b, 302).

Musicians and dancers since the 1930s have continued to use the term *rumba* in various ways. Just as commercial rumba earlier defied monolithic definition, so its more recent forms and meanings remain difficult to categorize. From Obdulio Morales's "Rumbantela" to Gilberto Valdés's "Que vengan los rumberos," Beny Moré's "De la rumba al chachachá," the Orquesta Aragón's "Gua-cha-rumba," Eddie Palmieri's "Mi primera rumba," and Tite Curet Alonso's "La esencia del guaguancó," discourse about rumba remains central to Afrohispanic dance music (Grillo 1989; Moré n.d.; Aragón 1992; Palmieri 1992; Manuel 1994, 273). Middle-class and foreign artists unfamiliar with noncommercial rumba as well as Afrocuban working-class performers themselves apply the term to compositions that have only the most tangential relation to the genre as it developed in the slums of Havana and Matanzas.

Given these facts, we must reevaluate notions of rumba and its relation to Cuban national expression. Such is the diversity of the repertory referred to as rumba, and the musical influences that have contributed to it, that to speak of particular compositions as authentic and others as inauthentic seems ridiculous. As Ruth Glasser notes, it is not only ethnic "outsiders" who have been prone to the free recreation and stereotyping of the traditional genre; ethnic "insiders" divided by class and race are also consistently involved in the same processes (1995, 183). Why should Moisés Simons, for instance, be praised without reservation as "an exalted representative" of Cuban culture and "one of the purest stylizers . . . of Afrocuban rhythms" while Cugat and Cole Porter receive criticism?[39] Further analysis of the works of Cuban orchestras with an overtly jazz-influenced sound, such as those of Armando Oréfiche or Justo Azpiazu, will refute the notion that a clear distinction exists between "pure" adaptations and "adulteration." Even more important, any study attempting to assess the significance of commercial rumba must begin by considering racial and class tensions within Cuba and abroad, and the relationship of all such factors to musical change. Who outside the Afrocuban community is involved in the performance of rumba, for instance; how do they choose to alter traditional rumba on the stage, and why? Who is exploited and who benefits as a result of the commercialization of this marginal culture? A more racially critical, self-reflective, and pan-national perspective is required of musicologists before the full relevance of rumba, past and present, can be appreciated.

7 THE MINORISTA VANGUARD

Modernism and *Afrocubanismo*

The young Latin American composer has realized now
that . . . [certain] ethnic contributions, certain creole
processes, certain historical and social imperatives . . . have
profoundly affected the formation of his sensibilities. In
search of his own roots, our musician takes hold,
therefore, of that which offers the most solutions: folklore.
It is a rich material . . . collected in its brute state, where it
existed in the public domain. The tradition is excellent.
But now, what to do with it? Stylize it! Elevate popular
expression to that of a universal character by means of
knowledge, of science. . . . [In this way] two results are
achieved at the same time: being "modern" and being
"national." What a tremendous relief!
—Alejo Carpentier, *Ese músico que llevo adentro*[1]

The term *afrocubanismo* has been used to refer to a wide variety of cultural
expression since the late 1920s. Many artists associated with this movement, such as those discussed in chapters 5 and 6, achieved tremendous national and international recognition during their lifetimes; their works continue to be reinterpreted and performed today. The avant-garde artistic production of the Minoristas, however, has not been as widely disseminated. Composers, visual artists, and poets of this group represented the elite of the 1920s
Cuban art world. They came from relatively wealthy backgrounds, were white,
well educated, and often prominent social and political leaders. Minorista artists kept abreast of progressive intellectual currents in Europe and the United
States and created unique works that demonstrate both the influence of
afrocubanismo nationalism and of modern aesthetics in the form of cubism,
serialism, atonality, and other styles. Surprisingly, music written by the
vanguardia—for instance, that of Alejandro García Caturla and Amadeo
Roldán—is not well known even in Cuba. Their collected works have never

been published in score form, and before the recent anthology releases by EGREM in the early 1990s, recordings of their compositions were virtually impossible to find.[2]

I use the terms *Minoristas* (the artistic minority or elite) and *vanguardia* (the artistic vanguard) synonymously, as did members of the movements themselves, to distinguish them from those involved primarily with commercial entertainment. Rather than generating profit, the Minoristas endeavored to create sophisticated and socially relevant art of enduring value. They represented the progressive thinkers of Cuban music conservatories, literary journals, and art academies. This chapter explores the paradox of the Minoristas: the "cruel indifference" to their work demonstrated by most of the population, despite their ideological importance in promoting and guiding the *afrocubanismo* movement (Henríquez 1978, 6). It describes the formation of the group in the early 1920s, their initial goals, and their adoption of Afrocuban themes beginning about 1925. After presenting an overview of the musical imagery found in the visual art and writings by prominent *vanguardista* activists, I survey the work of representative composers from the group and note their contradictory attitudes toward Afrocuban culture, as well as the critiques leveled against them by the middle-class black community.

Minorismo and Political Activism

The "critical decade" of the 1920s witnessed a profusion of new and polemical artistic activity closely linked to political events.[3] Minorista artists first promoted much of it, even though they existed as a cohesive entity for only five years (approximately 1923–1928). After that time, most members remained active in politics and art but increasingly acted in smaller groups. The escalation of *machadato* violence accelerated the disintegration of the *minorismo* movement. Antagonisms arose between moderates pursuing "purely cultural" goals and those devoted to revolution; moreover, the arrest and imprisonment of some members for alleged subversion beginning in 1928 also disrupted the organization and contributed to its demise.

Virtually all Minoristas lived in Havana. They were younger men born at the turn of the century who began their professional careers in an epoch of disillusionment following the "dance of the millions." The economic turbulence of the 1920s thus directly contributed to the rise of a new intelligentsia concerned with both political and cultural change. In their "Declaration" of 1923, members assailed government corruption and "Yankee imperialism" and promoted "new vernacular art" (Cairo Ballester 1988, 7). Culture played a central role in the goals of the Minoristas, who initially sought not revolution but social renovation. In the context of widespread corruption and economic instability, academic arts seemed to offer Cuban society a "higher" source of inspiration (Wright 1988, 16). Jorge Mañach explained some of his reasons for involvement in cultural publications during the 1920s: "We thought that public life could be divided into two components: one [consisting] of culture and the other of [social, political?] devastation. And we thought that by expanding the first of these little by little, endeavoring to educate—by means of articles, lectures, books, and verse—we would nullify [the other]."[4]

Artists of all types joined the Minoristas. They initially included journalists and authors such as José Antonio Fernández de Castro, Alejo Carpentier, and Emilio Roig de Leuchsenring, poets like José Tallet and Agustín Acosta, and painters Eduardo Abela and Jaime Valls. The movement developed out of regular Sunday *tertulias* in the Café Martí. Early meetings took place during a period of crisis; falling sugar prices in 1919 and the collapse of the national banking system left the Cuban treasury with insufficient funds to pay government employees and continue loan payments to the United States.

The "Protest of the Thirteen," the first public action of the Minoristas, brought them national attention virtually overnight. This event followed one of many questionable financial transactions of the Zayas administration, the purchase of a convent in Havana for approximately two and a half times its real value. It is unclear who owned the convent or profited most from the sale, although Zayas himself was reputed to have made several hundred thousand pesos (Cairo Ballester 1978, 39). Given the financial difficulties of the moment and the fact that the purchase had not been authorized by Congress, it prompted widespread criticism. On an impulse, Minoristas led by Rubén Martínez Villena disrupted a meeting in the Academia de Ciencias to accuse Zayas appointee Erasmo Regüeiferos of misconduct in signing the appropriation (ibid., 309). Martínez Villena later sent letters to the *Heraldo de Cuba* and other major newspapers in which he apologized for the interruption but reasserted his accusations. The event resulted in a lawsuit against Martínez Villena and his companions brought by Regüeiferos, which kept the issue alive in the press for months.

Minorismo and Culture

In Europe, the United States, and elsewhere, the 1910s and 1920s witnessed the development of academic artistry more directly inspired by popular cultural trends than in most decades before or since. The vogue of U.S. ragtime and jazz music, especially, is evident in art music compositions such as Debussy's "Golliwog's Cake Walk" (1918); Stravinsky's "Ragtime" (1918); Paul Hindemith's "Suite for Piano" (1922); Ravel's "La tasse de thé" from the opera *L'Enfant et les sortilèges* (1925); the Ernst Krenek opera *Johnny Spielt Auf* (1926); and the *Ne-*

gro Folk Symphony No. 1 by an African American, William Dawson (1934). Others incorporating influences from jazz into their compositions included Darius Milhaud, Erik Satie, Kurt Weill, Francis Poulenc, John Alden Carpenter, Cyril Scott, Georges Auric, and Arthur Honegger (Arredondo 1939, 127). To a lesser extent, the popularity of Cuban music abroad resulted in similar compositions, as in Gershwin's "Cuban Overture" from 1932 and Harl McDonald's symphony no. 2, "The Rhumba," from 1934 (Grenet 1939, xlix).

Prominent artists of the *minorismo* generation lived abroad in the 1920s and received direct exposure to the influence of the international avant-garde. Painters Andrés Nogueira, Carlos Enríquez, Amelia Peláez, and Eduardo Abela all traveled to Paris during this period. Composers Carlo Borbolla and Alejandro García Caturla also went to Paris, the former to study with Louis Auvert and the latter with Nadia Boulanger; Amadeo Roldán studied under Professor Conrado del Campo in Madrid. Early *afrocubanista* poets, including Nicolás Guillén, avidly read the works of Harlem Renaissance poet Langston Hughes and playwright Eugene O'Neill and drew inspiration from them in their own early attempts to incorporate Afrocuban subject matter (Guirao 1938, xv).

As in the case of *son* and commercial rumba, the acceptance of Afrocuban-inspired compositions abroad significantly boosted the reputations of classical artists at home. Performances of Amadeo Roldán's orchestral poems "Oriental" and "Fiesta negra" by the Cleveland Symphony in 1928, for instance, forced many critics in Havana to reassess their opinions of him.[5] The Festivals of American Music in Paris beginning in 1929 also helped legitimize Afrocuban symphonic composition.[6]

International trends thus contributed heavily to the emergence of the *afrocubanista* avant-garde, as white Cuban intellectuals recognized. Poet Ramón Guirao emphasized in the introduction to his 1938 collection of Afrocuban-inspired poetry that Cubans had "acquired the dark merchandise in other aesthetic markets," noting that many embraced the movement without comprehending the "black reality" of their own country.[7] As in the United States and Europe, a majority of elite white artists in 1920s Havana who embraced *afrocubanismo* had little personal understanding of Afrocuban culture. The model of artistic appropriation established by Picasso, Stravinsky, and others a decade earlier required no familiarity with the original contexts and meanings of non-Western expression. To the avant-garde, African culture represented a stylistic system that could be used to diversify existing Western traditions; they never intended their work to be a celebration of "otherness."

In an era dominated by cultural evolutionism, these views seemed natural to the middle classes of Havana. Journalist José Antonio Fernández de Castro described the attitude of many when he stated that his interest in Afrocuban subject matter was limited to the "musical, artistic, or literary contribution of the black race to universal [i.e., European bourgeois] culture" (Fernández de Castro 1935, 10). Poet Emilio Ballagas, attempting to clarify misunderstandings among readers of his *Cuaderno de poesía negra* (1934), stressed that the so-called black poetry that had become became fashionable in many Latin American countries was written almost exclusively by whites such as himself in a style derived from Western Europe. It could only be honestly described, he argued, as Hispanic poetry with Africanist subject matter: "The black poetry that is cultivated in the Hispanic Antilles, in Colombia, in Venezuela, or in Ecuador is in origin nothing else than Spanish poetry. It is not only the language that pours forth the Africanist emotion, but also the very creative impulse that has come from Spain."[8]

Adolfo Salazar made similar comments about music, contending that *vanguardista* composers knew little of Afrocuban traditions but that such ignorance was not considered an obstacle to effective composition (1938, 16–17). On the contrary, individuals who wrote music more directly influenced by street genres tended to be criticized for their "crude" or "primitive" works rather than praised for their "authenticity." To (white) art music composers of the 1920s, Afrocuban- and jazz-inspired composition represented the fusion of "civilization" and "barbarity," the interpenetration of cultural forms created by "a virgin and still infantile race," the Negro, with that of "their older brothers," the Caucasians.[9] African-influenced arts both attracted and repelled the intelligentsia, who perceived them as rudimentary yet vital, a potentially beneficial influence on overly restrictive and codified Western traditions (Martínez Furé 1994). These attitudes dominated discourse among Cuban musicologists during their early exposure to the works of the international avant-garde and their subsequent attempts to reach consensus regarding the place of Afrocuban street music in classical composition.

Alejo Carpentier, an early advocate of *afrocubanismo* modernism, decided to support the movement after listening to jazz-influenced compositions by Darius Milhaud. He noted the impression these pieces made on him in an article for *El País* in 1925:

> This marked interest on the part of modern artists in [jazz rhythms], which forcefully brings with it a rough, frank sonorous discourse, . . . has made me think more than once about the immense treasure that we squander in not utilizing the richest resources of our national music. If the gentle and tender *guajira,* bolero, and *clave* . . . produce after a while an irresistible sensation of monotony because of the uniformity of all their accents and the tenuous shade of their melodies, then the brutish and as of yet unexploited elements of our popular dances contain a . . . formidable rhythmic power. . . . [Afrocuban

musics] could be stylized, conserving their instruments and their strong flavor, utilizing that original and robust "polyrhythm" in symbolic creations of high aesthetic value, inspired directly in our "folklore."[10]

Minoristas used the term *vanguardismo* from the mid-1920s on to refer to the artistic movement of their creation. They promoted their works in magazines and newspapers from about 1924 through the early 1930s. Two of the earliest magazines in which creations of the Minoristas appeared were *Social* and *Carteles*. *Social* began publication in 1916 as an entertainment magazine for wealthier Cubans. The owners' decision in 1923 to put control of day-to-day management in the hands of Emilio Roig de Leuchsenring, however, significantly altered its content. By regulating submissions and by contributing constantly to the magazine himself, Roig created one of the first organs for the dissemination of Minorista thought. He increased the size of each issue and extended its readership base. While continuing to feature topics such as feminine fashion and film reviews, Roig also began to discuss more sensitive political issues and to showcase *vanguardista* drawings and poetry. Examples include the early sketches "Cabeza de mulata achinada" (Head of the Chinese-mulatto woman) and "La rumba" by Jaime Valls.[11] Under Roig's direction, *Social* also reprinted essays by intellectuals from a number of Spanish-speaking nations and gradually formed a relationship with other literary magazines to promote international dialogue.

Carteles, also an important magazine of the 1920s, began publication in 1919 under the direction of Alfredo Quílez. In 1924 Alejo Carpentier became its editor-in-chief, with assistance from Conrado Massaguer, Roig de Leuchsenring, and others who similarly shifted its focus to cultural issues (Cairo Ballester 1978, 126). A number of important Minorista publications first appeared in *Carteles,* including their "Declaration" of May 1927. Although less aggressive in promoting modern art than *Social, Carteles* proved important to the overall valorization of Afrocuban music and dance within Cuba. First in Havana, and later while living in exile abroad, Carpentier followed prominent artists of the "jazz craze" in his contributions to *Carteles* and described the success of Cuban entertainers in Paris and New York.

Several other publications helped disseminate and create support for *vanguardista* art in Cuba. *Musicalia,* a magazine devoted almost exclusively to modern, experimental composition, first appeared in 1928 under the direction of Antonio and María Quevedo (Orovio 1981, 324). The Quevedos, who founded a social organization promoting contemporary music in Havana at roughly the same time, were close friends of García Caturla and Roldán and did much to support their work. The contents of *Musicalia* included score facsimile reproductions of short compositions for piano, interviews with Latin and North American composers, and concert reviews.

In terms of prose and visual art, the Sunday literary supplement of the *Diario de la Marina*—directed by José Antonio Fernández de Castro from 1927 to 1929—afforded Minoristas crucial representation in a widely read national paper.[12] Poems, essays, and drawings by Rubén Martínez Villena, José Tallet, Juan Marinello, Agustín Acosta, Eduardo Abela, Ramón Guirao, and Alfonso Hernández Catá, as well as by Puerto Rican poet Luís Palés Matos, predominate in the pages of the supplement in the later 1920s.[13] The "Ideales de una Raza" column, written by mulatto Gustavo Urrutia, debuted the early Afrocuban-inspired poetry of Nicolás Guillén on 20 April 1930 (Guillén 1980). These poems, later published in *Motivos de son* ("Negro bembón," "Mulata," "Búcate plata," etc.) appeared together with a futurist drawing of a black musician by Fernández de Castro. In following years, Guillén's work inspired musical settings by numerous composers.

Perhaps the most aggressively avant-garde publications of the Minoristas were *Atuei* and *La Revista de Avance*.[14] Minorista artists designed and wrote exclusively for these magazines from the outset. Editors Enrique de la Osa and Francisco Masiques of the short-lived *Atuei* announced three primary objectives: the promotion of cultural nationalism; the criticism of political wrongdoings in the United States and Cuba; and the dissemination of avant-garde art (Cairo Ballester 1978, 146). *Atuei* has the distinction of publishing the first Afrocuban-inspired poem in Cuba, José Tallet's "La rumba" (August 1928).

La Revista de Avance, by contrast, represents a less political and more unequivocally cultural publication. The five initial editors—Martín Casanovas, Francisco Ichaso, Jorge Mañach, Juan Marinello, and José Tallet—demonstrated their *"inquietud renovadora"* (Mañach 1927, 18) by promoting experimental works, Afrocuban-inspired and otherwise, as well as interviews with internationally recognized artists such as Diego Rivera, Paul Valéry, Carlos Chávez, and Bernard Shaw. Poetry and visual art inspired by Afrocuban music appeared frequently in *La Revista de Avance,* including the poem "La Habana" by Argentine writer José María Delgado (30 June 1927), Guirao's "Bailadora de rumba" (15 September 1928), and a reproduction of Eduardo Abela's oil painting "El triunfo de la rumba" (15 January 1930). Beginning in January 1929, essays on race and culture appeared in the magazine defending Afrocuban expression against the prejudice of middle-class Cuban society. In the same year, editorials denouncing the extension of Machado's presidential term resulted in the imprisonment of Juan Marinello (also accused of fomenting antigovernment protests among university students) and the cessation of publication of *La Revista de Avance* soon thereafter.

The profusion of cultural publications by Minoristas did not mean they abstained from political involvement. On the contrary, academic artists became even more active immediately preceding and during the *machadato*. *Revista de Avance* editors Casanovas, Marinello, and Mañach, for example, wrote constantly about politics. Casanovas, a Spaniard, took part in the "Protest of the Thirteen" and spoke out against U.S. imperialism. Marinello helped found the Cuban Communist Party in 1925 and challenged the authority of Machado in later years, while Mañach played a pivotal role in forming the ABC Revolutionaries. Poet José Tallet followed his tenure in the Falange de Acción Cubana in the early 1920s by helping to organize the Universidad Popular José Martí, an institution dedicated to educating the Cuban working classes about socialist principles. Tallet, Martínez Villena, and others also offered instruction there beginning in 1925 (Guirao 1938, 64). José Fernández de Castro and Francisco Ichaso signed articles denouncing interventionist foreign policy.[15]

By 1929, *La Revista de Avance,* which began as a self-consciously apolitical publication, had become a forum for critiques of national and international affairs.[16] Emilio Roig de Leuchsenring published a constant stream of essays in the popular press between 1919 and the late 1920s supporting Cuban self-determination, denouncing the Platt Amendment, and promoting pan–Latin American solidarity. Painter Marcelo Pogolotti drew politicized visual art beginning about 1930 depicting unemployment and police brutality in Havana.[17] His colleague Carlos Enríquez fled to Europe for fear of repression from the secret police in 1930, as Alejo Carpentier, Raúl Roa, and Rubén Martínez Villena had already done. For three years, he lived primarily in Spain and France, illustrating essays and books incriminating the Machado administration, such as *El terror en Cuba* published by the Comité de Jóvenes Revolucionarios ("Cronología," 3).

Afrocuban Musical Themes in *Vanguardista* Poetry and Visual Art

The Minoristas and their contemporaries produced a vast quantity of poetry and paintings, much of it focused on the music and dance created by Afrocuban artists. Given the concurrent popularity of *conjuntos de son,* salon rumbas, and *comparsa* bands, it is not surprising that imagery of music and dance feature prominently in those works. Poetry anthologies such as *Orbita de la poesía afrocubana 1928-37* (Guirao 1938) or *Antología de la poesía negra hispano-americana* (Ballagas 1935) provide many examples. José Antonio Portuondo's poem "Rumba de la negra Pancha" is typical, including extended descriptions of the lips *(bemba)* and breasts of a black female dancer, both of which are likened to "ripe medlar fruits" (ibid., 134). Like the *mulata* of the comic theater and the cabaret rumbera, this woman is transformed into the embodiment of lust *(lujuria)*, sensuality, and "spice" *(pimienta)*.

Alfonso Hernández Catá's poems "Rumba" and "Son" from 1931, and Guirao's own "Bailadora de rumba" contain similarly stereotyped images of black performers, images bordering at times on racist.[18] "Rumba," for instance, makes reference to "crude beefsteak lips" *(labios de crudo bisté)* and "spattered" noses *(la nariz desparramada)*. A black rumbero "undulating" beside his female companion in the same poem is described metaphorically as "half crime, half kiss." Consciously misspelled words characteristic of *bozal* speech predominate in Minorista poetry from this period. Black performers constitute a spectacle, variously grotesque, sensual, frivolous, or comical. Even in the best *negrista* poetry (with the exception of Guillén), they appear devoid of context, with no concern for the position of Afrocubans within Cuban society, their poverty, their squalid living conditions, or the discrimination affecting their lives.

Emilio Ballagas (1908–1954) is representative in many ways of *vanguardia* poets of the early 1930s. Born into a white middle-class family in Camagüey, Ballagas studied literature in Havana and in 1933 began teaching as a professor in Santa Clara (García 1980, 105). He published the majority of his Afrocuban-inspired works in *Cuaderno de poesía negra* from 1934. References to music and dance appear throughout this publication, as for instance in "Elegía a María Belén Chacón," "Rumba," and "Comparsa habanera." Again, images of revelry, dancing, alcohol, swaying breasts, and buttocks mix with those of animal sacrifice and nonsensical phrases imitating Yoruba and Carabalí languages (for instance, *"bamba uenibamba bó"* from "Comparsa habanera"). From today's perspective, the poetry of Ballagas and his contemporaries differs little from *costumbrista* parodies of the 1830s. It is unique only for having been created by the elite of Cuban society for the first time, and for having been accepted more openly as national expression.

José Zacarías Tallet (1893–198?) was also born into a wealthy white family in Matanzas Province. As an adolescent he lived in New York and studied accounting at the Heffly Institute of Commerce (Le Riverend 1984, 997). Although politically active and a close friend of Rubén Martínez Villena, Tallet's early publications reflect no engagement with Afrocuban subject matter. Biographer Néstor Baguer notes that the poem "La rumba," acclaimed by the Minoristas, is in no way representative of Tallet's overall literary production (1988, 129). Ironically, Tallet did not consider it one of his better works. "La rumba" draws upon many of the same stereotypes to depict black street culture as are found in later poems by Tallet's contemporaries. The author focuses on the "rotund breasts" *(senos rotundos)* and "lascivious gestures *(lacivios gestos)* of the *rumbera* protagonist and likens the movements of her male companion to those of one possessed by the devil (Guirao 1938, 66). In the atmosphere surrounding the event, Tallet suggests, one notices "the smell of jungle," the "odor of rustic slave barracks." Perhaps the most noteworthy aspect of this first nationally recognized *afrocubanista* poem is that the impulse to write came not from Tallet himself but from friends: a colleague gave him the nonsensical phrase "Mambimba, mabomba, mabomo y bombó" and bet that he couldn't incorporate it into a poem. For Tallet, the composition represented no more than "poetic gymnastics"; others, however, were so impressed with it that they submitted it for publication in *Atuei.*[19]

As with poetry, the *afrocubanismo* aesthetic first appeared in the realm of graphic art in the mid-1920s. With few exceptions, visual *vanguardismo* also remained the realm of the white Hispanic middle classes who had little firsthand exposure to black street culture.[20] Early "rebellious" painters who distanced themselves from the conservative Asociación de Pintores y Escultores and distinguished themselves as modernists included Juan José Sicre, Víctor Manuel, Antonio Gattorno, Eduardo Abela, Amelia Peláez, Marcelo Pogolotti, and Carlos Enríquez (Vázquez Díaz 1988, 7). Their innovations were typically aesthetic in nature, but also involved the creation of works based on nationalist themes. For brevity's sake, I will discuss two representative artists, Valls and Abela, who are considered the most influential.

Jaime Valls Díaz (1883–1955) was born in Barcelona and remained there until his late teens.[21] He is yet another foreign national (although after 1927 a naturalized Cuban) who distinguished himself as an innovator of "Cuban" art. Valls worked as a commercial illustrator for many years, designing advertisements for the newspaper *La Discusión* as well as various magazines. Unlike his Cuban contemporaries, Valls began to include images of Afrocubans in his work from the early 1910s. Like Víctor Landaluze, he seems to have been fascinated with blacks as a young man and to have regarded them as a picturesque feature of his surroundings rather than an embarrassment. Advertisements for soap, canned fruits, and other products by Valls include images of black dancers, black children at play, black servants waiting on white patrons, and *mulatas* chatting with *gallego* shopkeepers (see illustrations).

By the early 1920s, Valls had saved enough money to purchase his own studio at Escobar 78 in Centro Habana. There he frequently organized parties, inviting celebrity singers and entertainers from the Alhambra Theater and elsewhere. In 1927 the *Diario de la Marina* documented these gatherings, noting the stylized "music of the peasant hut, of the sugarcane field, of the working-class barrio" performed at the studio by Simons, Lecuona, and others.[22] Valls's interest in Afrocuban music and dance first took serious form about 1926, when he began to produce (lovely) pencil sketches and oil paintings of Afrocuban subjects. Perhaps the most famous of these is the "Rumba" series depicting nude female dancers. Valls achieved widespread recognition for the sketches, prompting Roig de Leuchsenring to describe him as "the first of our [visual] artists who has taken the resolution . . . to dedicate himself completely to making Cuban works."[23] Other compositions by Valls from the late 1920s that depict musical activity include the sketches "El dúo," "Maraquero" (Maraca player), and "Sexteto" from 1927, untitled drawings of *son* dancers from 1928, and "El tocador de clave" (The *clave* player).[24] On 8 April 1928, many of these drawings made the front page of the *Diario de la Marina* together with a biographical article about the author. The Guirao poem "Bailadora de rumba" appears on the same page dedicated to Valls.

Eduardo Abela (1891?–1963) represents a more typical *vanguardia* painter in that his interest in Afrocuban subjects lasted only a short time. Born in San Antonio de los Baños on the outskirts of Havana, Abela began his artistic studies in 1911 in the Academia San Alejandro, Miramar (Seone Gallo 1986, 261). He first created political cartoons and is perhaps best remembered today for the character "El Bobo" (The fool), whose popularity spanned several decades in Cuban newspapers. At the suggestion of Alejo Carpentier, Abela went to Paris in 1928 during the peak of the *afrocubanismo* movement. There, in only three months, he painted all of the Afrocuban-influenced works for which he is remembered.

Before his friendship with Carpentier, Abela knew nothing of Afrocuban arts, yet considered them vulgar and aesthetically inferior (Seone Gallo 1986, 187). After his arrival in Paris, Carpentier took him to see exhibitions of African art in museums, frequently against his will, and lectured him on its importance. Abela resisted, but toward the end of his stay took Carpentier's advice seriously enough to paint a series of surrealist-expressionist oils incorporating Afrocuban themes. These include "Antillas," depicting carnival street musicians; "El gallo místico" (The mystic rooster), inspired by *santería* ritual and dance; "El Alacrán" and "El Gavilán," whose titles derive from two of the famous *comparsa* ensembles banned in the 1910s; "En casa de María de la O," "Percusiones," "Ritmos," "Los funerales de Papá Montero," and the famous "El triunfo de la rumba." When Abela painted these works, he had never seen a *santería* ceremony, nor even a *comparsa*. This fact, if known, did not disturb French or Cuban critics. Carpentier quickly organized an exposition of Abela's paintings in the Galerie Zak on the rue Boétie, which housed works by Picasso, Derain, and Modigliani (Carpentier 1976 1:112). The exposition received favorable coverage in the press and rave reviews from Carpentier himself (Seone Gallo 1986, 243; Carpentier 1976 1, 114). His commentary, published in the January 1929 edition of *Social*, led to the duplication of many of Abela's paintings in Havana and their further impact on Cuban artists.[25]

Abela's later artistic production reverted to styles he had cultivated before

1928. Although by his own account he remained more sympathetic to Afrocuban culture as a source of inspiration, his work failed to demonstrate this attitude. Without employment or a place to live upon returning to Havana, Abela found work again as a caricaturist. As before, he had no contact with Afrocuban street culture and no friends who could introduce him to it. Years later, Abela expressed regret that he did not make more of an attempt to study Afrocuban folklore and to continue to manifest its inspiration in his art:

> I don't want to hide from you that since [the 1920s] I have been left with the disagreeable sensation . . . that, in abandoning [*afrocubanista*] painting, I lost my artistic "spark." . . . In this moment I'm speaking of it and still—more than thirty years have passed!—I feel unease and bitterness. . . . If I had become familiar with *santeros, babalaos, bembés,* black celebrations, and all that Alejo talked about in Paris, perhaps I would have found . . . inspiration. But, leaving aside the lack of time, how could I attend alone and learn about all of this if I didn't even know how to behave in the places where it took place? I say alone because . . . there was not a single person among those that I knew then who would have confessed to me an interest in learning about such things from the "inside." . . . And there was also a fear of everything black, a fear of customs that, perhaps for being almost unknown, or poorly understood, were considered vulgar. . . . I can't fail to mention that there were many—not as few as you, who didn't live the epoch, might think—for whom a black was a delinquent, or at least potential delinquent.[26]

Vanguardista Musicians and Musical Works

Representatives of the musical *vanguardia* expressed a desire to create nationalist music representative of all Cubans.[27] Paradoxically, they gave substance to such sentiment in a highly experimental form unintelligible to the vast majority of the population (López Segrera 1989, 146). With the exception of Gilberto Valdés, *vanguardistas* made no attempt to compose within the confines of functional tonality or in other ways to disseminate "accessible" music. Far from unequivocally valorizing folkloric expression, they wished instead to "become" folklore, as their Brazilian contemporary Heitor Villa Lobos boasted, and to replace "inferior" street musics with new creations of ostensibly greater worth (Carpentier 1980, 261).

As unlikely as it may seem from today's perspective, however, avant-garde *afrocubanismo* composers represented the ultra-liberals of their day and were roundly criticized for their concessions to Afrocuban aesthetics. To the music establishment, the incorporation of *batá* drums, a *bongó,* a *clave,* or even maracas into symphonic works constituted "blasphemy, the worst affront that one [could] inflict on national music,"[28] as did the performance of classical works on the *tres* or other folkloric string instruments. *Vanguardistas* often found that ensembles such as the Orquesta Sinfónica de la Habana refused to perform their pieces. For much of their careers they remained isolated and marginalized, praised by the intelligentsia of Europe and the United States but largely ignored in their own country.[29]

Pianist Carlo Borbolla (1902–198?), a little-known composer active in the 1920s, shared the fate of Pedro Sanjuan Nortes and others whose Afrocuban-inspired creations were almost never heard after the 1940s. Borbolla, an isolated autodidact, lived for many years in Manzanillo, Oriente Province, the son of a designer of hurdy-gurdies (H. González 1994). In 1926 Borbolla went to Paris for four years to study piano with Pierre Lucas and composition with Louis Auvert (Orovio 1981, 56). There he wrote his Afrocuban-inspired works for piano, including the art-*sones* "Allá en Oriente" (Out there in Oriente), "Ma Teodora," "Con un viejo tres" (With an old *tres*), and "Un son entre las palmas" (A *son* among the palms), as well as eighteen rumba-inspired compositions and three keyboard congas (Carpentier 1946, 352; Borbolla n.d.). The *sones*, especially, incorporate many traditional nineteenth-century rhythmic figures. They are highly chromatic and polytonal. Some are written in contrapuntal form with fuguelike expositions, while others bear more formal resemblance to commerical *sones*. Borbolla died in Havana in the mid-1980s, largely unrecognized as a composer and unable to negotiate recordings or additional printed editions of his work (H. González 1994).

Amadeo Roldán (1900–1939), together with Alejo Carpentier, helped initiate the *afrocubanismo* movement in mid-1920s Cuba. Born in France to a Spanish father and Cuban mother (from Santiago), Roldán spent his early years in Europe. He studied composition at the Conservatorio de Madrid and won prizes for his violin performances (H. González 1994). In 1919 he moved to Havana to work as a music professor, performing regularly in both the Orquesta Sinfónica and Orquesta Filarmónica, as well as in cafés and theaters (Orovio 1981, 350). Roldán's interest in Afrocuban subject matter dates from approximately 1923. At this time he began to frequent *santería* and *abakuá* ceremonies with Carpentier, where he hand-transcribed melodic and rhythmic fragments later used in compositions (H. González 1994). Much as in the case of Valls and Fernando Ortiz, Roldán's upbringing and studies abroad seem to have led to a greater willingness to investigate Afrocuban subject matter than was demonstrated by his colleagues. Experience in other countries allowed Roldán to view Cuban social interactions from a new perspective and to address subjects that had rarely been studied or even discussed previously (Moore 1994, 35).

Roldán's "Obertura sobre temas cubanos," which debuted on 29 November

1925 in the Teatro Nacional, was the first Afrocuban-inspired symphonic work written and performed in twentieth-century Cuba. It constitutes a milestone in the history of Cuban music because of its overtly nationalist style and its use of popular melodies (Cairo Ballester 1988, 19). The progressive Orquesta Filarmónica debuted Roldán's "Obertura" under the direction of Pedro Sanjuan. As might be expected of experimental works, it received decidedly mixed reviews. While some received it favorably, others described its harmonies as "excessively tortured" (Carpentier 1976 2:84) and denounced the incorporation of Afrohaitian melodies from the nineteenth century such as "El cocuyé" (H. González 1994). A second major composition with an Afrocuban theme, Roldán's "Tres pequeños poemas" from 1926, provoked even more controversy because of an extended percussion break in the third movement entitled "Fiesta negra."[30] Sánchez de Fuentes spoke out vociferously against these pieces, claiming that they compromised national culture:

> The national work of aggrandizing [Cuban] music should not be sacrificed to illegitimate interest in attracting the rabble—always disposed to vulgarity and regression—to the call of an African drum. . . . The time is right to perfect our musical personality; . . . we need to moralize it and not prostitute it.[31]

Later, more aggressively experimental *afrocubanista* works considered among Roldán's best include the Carpentier dance collaborations "La rebambaramba" (1928) and "El milagro de Anaquillé" (1929); the orchestral score "Rítmicas" (1930); and the song cycle "Motivos de Son" for solo male vocalist and orchestra based on the poetry of Guillén (1934).[32] These latter compositions make overt use of Afrocuban motives and yet—with the exception of "El milagro de Anaquillé"—contain few recognizable popular melodies or rhythms.[33] "Rítmicas," for instance, incorporates small rhythmic fragments taken from black street musics as compositional material, transforming them through superimposition, variation, and harmonization. The result is innovative, even brilliant, but bears little relation to popular expression. As with his contemporaries, Roldán's primary interest remained one of "universalizing" Afrocuban expression, fusing it with classical traditions rather than valorizing it in its existing form (Roldán 1933, 176–77). Tragically, Roldán died at age thirty-nine from an infection (Hilario González, personal communication).

Composer, violinist, and judge Alejandro García Caturla (1906–1940) was born to a prominent family in Remedios, Las Villas, an area where racism is strong and where the Ku Klux Klan organized meetings in the 1930s (see chapter 1). Many white residents did not subscribe to constructs of the "mulatto nation" in a racial or cultural sense and viewed themselves as having exclusively Spanish heritage (H. González 1994). García Caturla began musical study as an adolescent with Fernando Estrems and María Montalván and continued in Havana with Pedro Sanjuan (Orovio 1981, 162). In 1928 he also spent six months in Paris working with Nadia Boulanger. Despite having less formal training than many contemporaries, García Caturla became recognized as a composer of "true genius" and a central figure in the *afrocubanista* vanguard by the late 1920s (Carpentier 1946, 318). His early Afrocuban-influenced compositions include "Danza negra" for piano (1925), "Danza del tambor" for piano and cello (1927), and "Yamba-O" for male chorus and orchestra (1928–1929) with lyrics by Alejo Carpentier.[34] Like Roldán, García Caturla used the poetry of Guillén as the lyrical basis of several art songs, including "Bito Manué" (1930) and "Mulata" (1933).

Unlike Roldán, García Caturla more frequently worked recognizable Afrocuban melodic fragments into his music. "La rumba" from 1933 for soprano and orchestra, for example, incorporated the melody of "Tira si va' a tirá, mata si va' a matá," a contemporary street *comparsa*.[35] Saxophones and horns featured prominently in the score make implicit reference to popular stage rumbas of the day and result in a somewhat more accessible work than was typical of the Minoristas. "Bereceuse campesina" similarly adopts the *son* melody "Cuando yo era chiquito, mamá, tomaba la leche en pomo," though the setting is far from traditional (H. González 1973). Other techniques that evoke Afrocuban street music include imitating the performance style of folkloric instruments with the orchestra or piano. In "Dos poemas afrocubanos" (1929), for instance, the piano accompaniment imitates the sound of a *tres*.[36]

García Caturla stands out among (white) *afrocubanistas* for having maintained relatively open intimate relationships with black women; he had eleven children by them whom he accepted as his own. The object of his first affections was Manuela, a domestic servant in his house. It appears to have been common for members of elite families to have casual sex with Afrocuban servants, even as adolescents. A similar example is provided by Desi Arnaz Jr., who mentions sleeping with the twelve-year-old daughter of the family cook in Santiago as a boy (Arnaz 1976, 14). Elite families permitted such relationships but refused to officially sanction them through marriage. García Caturla's case is unique in that he developed an unusually strong attachment to Manuela and (after her death in the early 1930s) to her sister Catalina. Such was his affection for Manuela and their children that he is said to have cut short his stay in Paris with Nadia Boulanger in order to return home to them (H. González 1994). Ironically, in 1940 a black gunman shot and killed Caturla, apparently hired by defendants in a trial in which he was involved (Lapique Becali 1993a).

Aside from melodic references to particular songs, analysts have identified a number of characteristics in the works of Roldán and García Caturla which they consider Afrocuban-influenced (e.g., Lezcano 1991). These include a preference for (1) polyrhythm or "additive rhythm," especially contrasting time signatures of duple and triple meter played simultaneously in the main melody and accompaniment; (2) *tresillo* and *cinquillo* figures, and other characteristic Afrocuban rhythmic cells as compositional motives; (3) orchestral scoring that incorporates instruments such as the friction drum, *clave*, or *bongó*; (4) an avoidance of strong-beat rhythmic emphasis—typical of most *sones*—and a tendency instead to emphasize "4" of the 4/4 measure (this is described as the "silent downbeat" by Lezcano); and (5) the use of pentatonic melodies found in Afrocuban as opposed to Iberian folkloric traditions, as is the case in García Caturla's "Dos poemas afrocubanos."

While these are important aspects of both composers' works, they are not their only (or even their primary) musical influences. One finds an incredible diversity of sounds in the works of García Caturla and Roldán. Afrocuban-derived elements are used in tandem with canonic imitation, polytonality, quartal harmonies, serial techniques, musical themes taken from nineteenth-century Cuban art music, as well as references to non-Afrocuban folk traditions such as *música guajira*.[37] In some cases, these juxtapositions result in a patchwork or confused musical texture. To me, García Caturla's music, because of its originality, is the more engaging, yet it often lacks stylistic cohesion. An unnamed contemporary of the Minoristas described García Caturla's music in this way:

> One sees in his works the *son* and the minuet; the sonata and the *comparsa*, all encased in a language that unites traditional folk cadences, modalism, the peculiar structure of creole melody in Cuba as well as the aggressive chromaticism of the European vanguard of the day. (Asche 1983, 10)

Undoubtedly, the experimental twentieth-century techniques employed by these composers reflected the influence of association with the Pan American Association of Composers (PAAC), based in New York. The PAAC, led for many years by Henry Cowell, served as an important vehicle for García Caturla and Roldán. Through this group, they met modernist composers and performers from various countries and became close associates of North Americans Nicolas Slonimsky, Charles Ives, Henry Brant, and Martha Graham, in addition to Cowell. They also met composers from Europe and Latin America such as Edgar Varèse, Heitor Villa Lobos, and Carlos Chávez (Root 1972, 52). With the help of PAAC members, García Caturla and Roldán organized a number of performances and recorded broadcasts of their compositions in the United States and participated in a highly publicized European concert tour in 1931–1932 featuring modern art music of the Americas. Unfortunately, European audiences expressed little interest in modernist composition, and even European arts agencies refused to help fund the events (ibid., 54). Unable to sell tickets or generate support, the PAAC was forced to end the tour early. Even so, outstanding debts remained, and financial crisis was averted only when Charles Ives agreed to pay them himself.

The music of Gilberto Valdés (1905–1971) straddles the line between experimental and popular music. Described by Hilario González (1994) as the "Irving Berlin of *afrocubanismo*" and by Carpentier as "a tropical Gershwin," Valdés more effectively than any other reconciled the aspirations of 1930s academic composers with those of the cabaret and motion picture industry. In this sense, his career is similar to that of Arnold Schönberg's colleague Erich Wolfgang Korngold, a well-known composer for Hollywood films (Hobsbawm 1987, 242). Born in Jovellanos, Matanzas Province, Valdés played flute and clarinet professionally as an adolescent, performing in the orchestra of José Raventós in Jovellanos (archive of Radamés Giró). He moved to Havana, where he studied composition with Pedro Sanjuan, Amadeo Roldán, and others while pursuing a degree in accounting ("Autores de la música popular" n.d.). Valdés's professional musical career seems to have begun as a member of the Orquesta Siboney jazz band of Alfredo Brito.

Valdés is noteworthy as the first classically trained Cuban composer to write music with extended lyrical passages in African languages, the first to incorporate entire *cantos* and *toques* from Afrocuban religious repertoire into orchestral works, and the first to allow actual *santería* musicians into his ensemble, which may have occurred around 1930 (H. González 1994; Carpentier 1946, 356). He collaborated with many of the best Afrocuban percussionists of the day, including "Roncona," "Brazo Fuerte," "Silvestre," "Chambas," and "El Niño," acquiring a substantial knowledge of *santería* ritual drumming and song as a result (Demaison 1938, 155). For many years after 1940, Valdés lived outside Cuba, touring with various groups including the dance troupe of Katherine Dunham.[38]

In the late 1930s and 1940s, Valdés composed several classical compositions in the style of García Caturla and Roldán. These include the orchestral works "Danza de los braceros," "Liko Ta Tumbé," and "Guaguancó" (Carpentier 1946, 358) as well as the quasi–art songs "Evocación negra" (Valdés n.d. 1) and "Bembé" for voice and piano. "Evocación negra" is a slow, through-composed piece in the style of *lamentos* and *afros*, but with extended neoimpressionist tonality. "Bembé," described on the cover page as a *"danza lucumí,"* contains shifts from duple meter to 6/8 time, apparently referencing Afrocuban religious repertory in the latter sections. More typical of Valdés's later compositions is "Ilé'nkó = Ilé'nbé," a musical stageplay for voices and orchestra from 1937. It may have been written as part of tourist shows organized during carnival season (see chapter 3). The author states on the score that the title is an intimate greeting between a man and a woman in Yoruba.[39] This work is one of Valdés's first attempts to set an African language text to music. The hypothetical setting of "Ilé'nkó = Ilé'nbé" is a nineteenth-century slave barracks during a Sunday fiesta. The characters include "Evaristo," a slave, a *mulata tiposa* (tall, good-looking *mulata*), drummers, and bemused slaveowners. "Ilé'nkó = Ilé'nbé" is written in a popular tonal style, with only the Yoruba lyrics, the prominent Afrocuban percussion, and perhaps the dance choreography distinguishing it from the works of Lecuona, Roig, and Simons.

Later in his career, Valdés increasingly wrote informal pieces for concert settings and film scores. Works from this period include the Afrocuban lullaby "Ogguere" from 1937 (Fornet 1967, 159); the *pregones* "Mango mangüé" (Valdés 1940b), "Ecó" (Valdés 1941a), and "El botellero"; the *lamento* "Baró," sung by a nineteenth-century *calesero* figure; the salon conga "Vamo a bailá Mercé," first appearing in the film *Mi tía de América* (ca. 1940); and "Rumba abierta," used in *Sucedió en la Habana* from 1938 starring Rita Montaner, Alberto Garrido, and Pablo Duarte ("Autores de la música popular" n.d.). Montaner contributed greatly to the early dissemination of Valdés's compositions by premiering them in a well-publicized concert in the Principal de la Comedia Theater in 1936 (Collazo 1987, 146).

Publications on culture from the 1920s and 1930s reveal that *minorismo* composers not only suffered the criticism of conservatives for their interest in Africanisms, but also were decidedly ambivalent themselves about Afrocuban street arts. Perhaps such attitudes were inevitable in a movement that simultaneously aspired to elitism and nationalism. Nineteenth-century-derived conceptions of culture remained strong among Minoristas, who maintained a clear distinction between their own works and the "crude" expression of the masses. Well into the 1940s, professional composers considered themselves the sole creators of "musical art" in Cuba (e.g., Agüero y Barreras 1946, 128). They spoke of artistic "progress" as something initiated and perpetuated by themselves, suggesting (as did the popular *afrocubanistas*) that the responsibility of the composer was to "elevate" and improve street culture.

Conceptions of cultural evolutionism played a central role in Minorista philosophy. Intellectuals endeavored to accelerate a movement away from "barbarity" and toward "civility" in the arts. In a musical sense, such ideas manifested themselves in assertions that the harmonic complexity of a given piece, the size of the ensemble performing it, the relative technological sophistication of its instruments, and/or the complexity of its scales relative to those used in European musics determined its place on a perceived evolutionary continuum. References to "defective" or "primitive" scales (Salazar 1938, 9), "monotonous" melodies (Agüero y Barreras 1946, 123), and "primitive" percussion instruments and rhythms (Sánchez de Fuentes 1932, 101) appear constantly in musicological essays from the period in reference to both Afrocuban musics and those of indigenous or *guajiro* origin.

Critic Gaspar Agüero y Barreras, for example, conflated social and cultural evolution in his writings, suggesting that tribal societies were incapable of complex artistic expression. In discussing pre-Conquest instruments in Cuba, he commented, "I deduce the inferiority of the music of the Siboneys, even in comparison with that of the black Africans, regardless of the fact that both are in the first stage of their social evolution."[40] Pedro Sanjuan conceived of African-derived musics in Cuba as virtually timeless, dating from the earliest period of human existence. Afrocuban genres, he wrote, have "profound, very profound roots: they date from times in which mankind had not yet measured sound, had not divided its vibrations [into precise octaves and scales]. . . . At that time . . . man did not speak, he spontaneously shouted his inflexions."[41]

Popular composer Moisés Simons echoed these sentiments, describing *guajiro* music of the Vueltabajo region of Pinar del Río as having "a rude uncouth character, like all primitive songs" and deprecating Afrocuban music in a similar manner.[42] Yet Simons encouraged the incorporation of stylized elements of folklore into art music composition: if African and indigenous contributions are crude or rudimentary, he insisted, "it is perfectly natural that it should be that way. All musical contributions are rudimentary, almost embryonic, as art begins [its development]. . . . [Nevertheless,] the melodic, harmonic, and rhythmic characteristics [of such musics can be] beneficial to great composers in forming their masterworks."[43]

Even staunch proponents of *vanguardista* modernism viewed black street culture as primitive. Francisco Ichaso praised the work of Roldán in an article in *La Revista de Avance* precisely because of his ability to glean the "musical subsoil" *(subsuelo musical)* of Cuba and convert what he found into "artistic material" (1928, 244). "In the presence of the savage catechumen," he writes, the missionary [Roldán] adopts a policy of conversion, in the exact sense of the term. He smooths [the savage's] instincts, tunes his sensibilities, educates him, civilizes him."[44]

García Caturla, despite his belief that Afrocuban folklore needed to be "polished" and "divested of crudities," was ironically criticized for not "universalizing" his compositions sufficiently (e.g., 1929, 17; 1933, 173). Adolfo Salazar complained in *Estudios afrocubanos* that the composer's works "totally lack a tonal sense, a harmonic "plan" based on the historic cement of European music . . . like a cathedral to be built on sand. A precarious edifice. The black's own expression is no cathedral, but rather a peasant hut."[45] As might be expected, Salazar had even harsher words for individuals such as Gilberto Valdés, who featured street musicians in his performances and based his works on traditional Afrocuban songs and dances. Rather than "true" composition, Salazar described Valdés's work as "a primitive music, a music that seems to originate in an ancestral stage of art" in which conservatories and compositional treaties did not yet exist; he singled out Valdés's "Rumba abierta" for special criticism and dismissed it as "a better rumba than those which one hears in the city slums, but essentially the same thing."[46]

Black Middle-Class Reactions to *Afrocubanista* Modernism

Criticisms of the *afrocubanista* vanguard raised by the middle-class black community must be viewed in light of their overriding concern for integration into Cuban society. For representatives of this group, the most effective means of acceptance was to "play by the rules," avoid divisive racial issues, and conform to patterns of behavior established by the mainstream. This entailed a distancing from all markers of "Africanness," physical and cultural. The integrationist mind set, which developed throughout the Americas, had a pronounced effect on many facets of black social life. Perhaps most striking was a widespread preference among dark-skinned Afrocubans for marrying those with a lighter skin color. Another was the development of distinct and mutually antagonistic *sociedades de color* for mulattos and darker-skinned blacks, especially in the eastern provinces. Culturally, such attitudes manifested themselves in a condemnation of working-class Afrocuban music and dance. Spokesmen of Havana's prestigious Club Atenas and Club Minerva (open only to wealthy, educated Afrocubans)—clubs whose names, it should be noted, refer to "high" Western civilization—figured prominently in campaigns against *son,* rumba, and *comparsa* music, and in other ways sought to discourage the spread of African-influenced culture (e.g., Martínez 1938, 11). Leonardo Acosta had personal experiences with such attitudes while playing saxophone in orchestras of the 1950s.

> In the Club Atenas things got so absurd that orchestras were obligated by the "Comisión de Orden" to play waltzes, fox-trots, *danzones* or boleros, and were decisively prohibited from including any rumbas, *sones,* or mambos. Meanwhile, the "high-society" whites were going crazy dancing black music, and traditionally ended their fiestas with a street conga.[47]

The Afrocuban middle classes recognized the contributions of Afrocuban artists to Cuban culture, but only those who created works in a European style. *Adelante,* an important Afrocuban publication of the 1930s, prominently featured articles on middle-class black classical artists José White, Claudio Brindis de Salas, Tomás Alarcón, Lico Jiménez, Juan Francisco Manzano, and Zoila

Gálvez, but excluded working-class artists of any period (e.g., Villareal 1935, 13). Contributors to *Adelante* used the term culture to mean elite culture. European arts held special importance for them as a "unifying instrument" (Arredondo 1937, 8), a means by which blacks could demonstrate their education and help break down barriers of prejudice. The same authors either ignored or categorically denied the influence of African-derived culture on the black community. Juan Antonio Martín was one of many to deny that Afrocubans in the twentieth century had been affected in any way by African traditions (Martín 1937, 7). "Vestigial" practices as exemplified by the Día de Reyes and similar celebrations, he argued, had gradually died out as blacks "bettered" themselves following the abolition of slavery.

Franz Fanon discusses black-on-black cultural bias in Martinique, emphasizing the often contradictory and hypocritical views of middle-class social leaders. He suggests that the primary conceptual shortfall of integrationists is their failure to realize that despite their best attempts they will continue to be rebuffed by dominant society. The middle-class black community, much like the *mulata* of the Cuban *zarzuela*, is inevitably caught in a social paradox, rejecting its black cultural heritage and in turn being rejected by the Hispanic elite. Fanon argues that the risk of distancing oneself from such heritage in this way is achieving qualified acceptance at the cost of self-marginalization or condemnation.

> At the age of twenty . . . the Antillean recognizes that he is living an error. Why is that? Quite simply because . . . [he] has recognized himself as a Negro, but, by virtue of an ethical transit, he also feels . . . that one is a Negro to the degree to which one is wicked, sloppy, malicious, instinctual. Everything that is the opposite of these Negro modes of behavior is white. (Fanon 1967, 192)

Like the French petit bourgeois, upwardly mobile blacks tend to express an "undifferentiated reverence" for European arts, a vain striving for integration into an aristocratic culture to which they are essentially alien (Bourdieu 1984, 323). "Uncertain of their classifications, divided between the tastes they incline to and the tastes they aspire to," members of the black community are wary of any cultural forms that draw attention to ethnic difference (ibid., 326).

Most black leaders reacted negatively to *afrocubanista* art from the outset, denouncing its tendency to stereotype blacks and to depict them in a demeaning fashion (Martínez 1938, 11). As individuals who had struggled for decades to overcome discrimination, they were outraged by poetry and songs that described blacks as drunken, lascivious, or worse. Many objected to the very term *afrocubano*, pointing out that the distinction between Cuban and Afrocuban implied that blacks had an identity different from other citizens.[48] They did not view the new vogue of blackness as an attempt to redress the marginal status of Afrocuban culture historically, but rather as a means of further exoticizing and excluding them.

To black intellectual Alberto Arredondo, for instance, Cuban history "created a kind of man that is neither like those of Africa or Spain" (1939, 111). Singling out any group discursively on racial grounds, he reasoned, only weakened the emergent sense of commonality among all Cubans. Even worse, the fantastic nature of *afrocubanista* art took attention away from the objective social needs of the black community:

> The same time period that has given rise to the theory of [black] "self-determination" in Cuba[49] has witnessed the development of *afrocubanismo*. "Black verse" is written, "black art" is created, "black articles" are published. . . . Acts and commemorations referring to blacks or black subject matter are constantly celebrated. . . . And there is nothing more absurd, more obfuscatory, more denaturalizing of the problems of "the black in our nation" and "the black in our social reality" than this unjust label "*afrocubanismo*."[50]

Arredondo attacked what he viewed as the fantastical ideational world of *afrocubanista* poetry, contending that "what pretends to be called '*poesía negra*' treats the Negro badly because it caricatures him, disfigures his outline, and presents him in an ambience that is not his, in a world that blacks don't live in and don't want to live in."[51] *Afrocubanista* poetry written by the few blacks and mulattos involved in the movement such as Nicolás Guillén and Marcelino Arozarena became the subject of even greater controversy. Professional members of the Club Atenas, who made up the core readership of the newspaper column in which Guillén's poetry first appeared, found his works offensive (Kutzinski 1993, 152). They could accept neither the street slang used in his poetry nor his direct references to taboo subjects such as racial shame and black-on-black color hierarchies. They felt that Guillén, rather than contributing to the dissemination of concerns vital to Afrocubans, presented the community as weak, divided, and culturally backward.

To Arredondo and others, not only did an emphasis on African-derived culture factionalize the population and overemphasize racial difference, but also it generated criticism of the black community and thus escalated racial tensions (Arredondo 1939, 132). If studies of the music and dance of nineteenth-century slaves and the Siboneys had a *raison d'être*, he suggested, it was only to document the cultural "progress" of the nation since that time. Incorporating such "rudimentary" musics into present-day compositions seemed ludicrous. The laudable goals of investigating, conserving, and "purifying" the nation's cultural heritage, maintained Arredondo, should not be confused with accepting "savage African rites" as contemporary musical expression (ibid., 136).

Not surprisingly, the greater the degree of stylistic transformation of Afrocuban themes in *vanguardista* compositions, the more easily critics accepted such works. Editors of *Adelante* viewed compositions by García Caturla and Roldán with apprehension, but they reserved their harshest criticisms for those of Gilberto Valdés featuring untrained street musicians. They accused Valdés of attempting to revive musical forms from an earlier stage of development as a means of embarrassing the black community and maintained that his work in no way represented the preferences of Afrocubans of the 1930s. Rhythms and melodies incorporated by Valdés, wrote Arredondo, demonstrated nothing but the extent of cultural impoverishment of black slaves. Through a process of "self-improvement" *(superación)* and synthesis, Cuban music had ostensibly "evolved." Afrocubans no longer spoke the broken *bozal* Spanish of colonial times or sang savage war chants and should not be represented as if they did (Arredondo 1939, 123).

Conclusion

Among the fundamental inconsistencies of the *minorismo* movement can be recognized a desire on the part of members to unite with the international avant-garde of the 1920s and 1930s while simultaneously addressing issues relevant to the Cuban people. With the cosmopolitan aesthetic paradigms of the cubists, fauvists, futurists, primitivists, serialists, et cetera, *vanguardistas* hoped to create Cuban art, a progressive nationalist style based on foreign paradigms (Vázquez Díaz 1988, 5). Their work is self-defeating in this sense. It ascribes to an "absolute" aesthetic model distanced from social reality, yet purports to derive relevance from oblique references to the same reality. It manifests both a disdain for and fascination with popular culture (López Segrera 1989, 150). Conflicting goals of universalism and populism problematized the relevance and the acceptance of Minorista artists; while hailed in Paris, New York, and Madrid as visionary, their work inspired less favorable commentary at home.

Whatever their shortcomings, the Minoristas must be recognized as liberal thinkers who actively promoted the acceptance of Afrocuban expression in a more inclusive sense than most of their contemporaries. In many cases, they continued to produce Afrocuban-inspired art despite severe criticism and professional marginalization. Nevertheless, their interest in Afrocuban street culture had clearly defined limits. They viewed black folklore as an important source of inspiration, yet of little artistic value as performed by blacks themselves.

Advocates of *minorismo* believed that the fundamental problems of their country could be solved through the production and dissemination of modern art. They hoped that their works would eventually be adopted by all, re-

placing less "sophisticated" expression and "raising" cultural standards throughout the island. These hopes proved to be ill-founded. Although inspired by
working-class genres, the complex artistic forms cultivated by *vanguardistas*
appealed "neither to the bourgeois public nor the proletariat," but ultimately
constituted only "an art produced for artists" (López Segrera 1989, 191). Even
in the 1920s and 1930s the influence of *minorismo* remained confined to academic elites, as it continues to be today. Perhaps Jorge Mañach described the
mentality of the Minoristas best when he wrote that the movement seemed "a
kind of flight, an inconsistent exaltation of [a] marginal attitude we thought
should and would be able to sustain us. . . . That which surrounded us in life
was so sordid, so mediocre . . . that we sought our spiritual redemption by
elevating [our thoughts] to ideal planes, or complicating our parlance so that
in any case no one was going to listen to us."[52]

Vanguardista artists have been accused by U.S. critics of disseminating racial images in their works that fail to address substantive issues of the Afrocuban
community. Kutzinski describes them as advocates of "a peculiar form of
multiculturalism," one that "acknowledges, indeed celebrates, racial diversity
while at the same time disavowing divisive social realities." Not unlike nineteenth-century *costumbrismo*, *minorismo* "had all the makings of a folkloric
spectacle whose political effect was to displace and obfuscate actual . . . problems and conflicts, especially racial ones" (Kutzinski 1993, 5, 145). While commentary by past leaders of the Afrocuban community tends to support this
view, most Cuban authors in recent years have had nothing but praise for the
Minoristas. As in the case of Fernando Ortiz, artistic figures of the early twentieth century have been shrouded with an aura of inviability to such an extent
that historians are loathe to speak of their shortcomings. As symbols of a pan-
national ideal of racial integration and harmony they have endured into the
present as a powerful force. One might suggest, however, that they are in danger of becoming "empty symbols," if they are not so already, more important
for what they represent than for the impact their artistic works have actually
had in the lives of Cubans today.

CONCLUSION

> It is only through the struggles of the subordinated that
> the tyranny of social forms and practices, both those
> inherited from capitalism and its past, and those created
> by new forms of social order . . . can be recognized for the
> fetters on the liberation of human capacities that they are.
> It is only in such struggles that emancipatory social
> forms—through which differences can be recognized and
> celebrated, as ingredients of a collectively human future,
> rather than regulated and denied—are discovered.
> —Philip Corrigan and Derek Sayer, *The Great Arch*

Music and Historical Relevance

In many respects, the 1990s is a strange time to conduct research in Havana on popular music. During the current period of economic and political crisis in which so much of consequence is occurring daily, the relevance of sixty-year-old cultural expression seems limited, to say the least. Severe shortages of food, electricity, transportation, housing, and the most basic domestic products (soap, razors, detergent, toothpaste, cooking oil) have caused many Cubans to despair. Middle-aged citizens who devoted the best years of their lives to serving the socialist revolution feel increasingly disillusioned and cheated. After decades of voluntary assistance in rural literacy campaigns, summer sugarcane harvests, housing construction, and a host of related activities, they find themselves in worse living conditions than those of the early 1960s. The youth of today, too young to remember life in presocialist Cuba, are also restless. They have grown into adulthood during a period in which jobs are scarce, the national currency can buy virtually nothing, and prospects for the future are far from promising. This is the situation confronting the researcher in Havana today, a decidedly uncomfortable one in which each academic is forced to justify his or her own presence and interests.

But the past does have important implications for the present. A knowledge of history can help us extend our understanding of Cuba beyond the confines of essentialized dogma of the right or left. In an extremely polarized and antagonistic political environment, historical research can contextualize the ideological differences of various factions and suggest strategies of reconciliation. It can shed light on race relations in Cuba, which have received little attention until recent years. Cuba, like Brazil, has often been described as an oasis of tolerance and harmony in an otherwise racially divided hemisphere; new investigations have forced the international community to revise such views. Studies of expressive culture are also useful in providing information about the shared ethos and identity of social groups. In a world of mass communication and mass manipulation of public opinion, it is imperative that we appreciate how artistic modalities are appropriated and articulated in new contexts, and how they change meaning as a result. Especially in times of crisis—whether in 1930 or 1990—the role of culture in maintaining social cohesion and providing a sense of who "we" are has proven fundamental to discourse in Cuba.

It is disheartening that a country so ostensibly concerned with Marxism and the socioeconomic "base" has not been more critical in evaluating artistic forms. This is especially true of the 1920s and 1930s, the "golden age" of Cuban popular song. Political and cultural retrospectives on the *machadato* have not been reconciled with one another. Books and films addressing economic hardship, North American imperialism, and/or the revolution of the 1930s typically fail to consider the effect of these events on cultural production, while those on the lives of Ernesto Lecuona, Rita Montaner, *son* musicians, and other entertainers do not interpret their popularity in terms of larger social processes.

Commentary on the arts in Cuba reinforces rather than problematizes the accepted notion (or myth) of a monolithic and commonly shared culture.[1] While the best critics recognize the effect of U.S. economic policies on Cuban music (e.g., Acosta 1982; León 1984), even they decline to consider internal divisions in the form of domestic racial conflict and its relation to musical change. Cubans have yet to critically study the *afrocubanismo* movement and to admit that the national acceptance of black street culture is a relatively new phenomenon. Many today have never even heard of *afrocubanismo*. They assume that Afrocuban arts had achieved mass popularity long before 1930. Notions of commonly shared culture have been naturalized to such an extent that at a lecture I presented in Havana in 1993 two professors from the Instituto Superior de Arte (one white, one black) rejected my assertion that traditional rumba of the 1930s was almost exclusively the domain of working-class Afrocubans. They could not believe that such expression had been aggressively suppressed in earlier years and insisted that all Cubans had danced traditional rumba at that time.

Within ethnomusicology, interpretive, or hermeneutic cultural history should be more strongly emphasized. (I refer to studies that not only document the cultural practices of the past but also treat the past as its own "symbolic system." Hermeneutic analysis concerns itself primarily with the context-specific meaning of expressive forms, not only the expression itself.) This book, building on the work of Peña (1985), Erlmann (1990), and others, attempts to demonstrate how such a focus might be applied. Unfortunately, history has become a residual avenue of research for ethnomusicologists, heavily overshadowed by synchronic studies. Given that anthropological theory has influenced ethnomusicology more than any other discipline, such an orientation was perhaps inevitable. My feeling, nevertheless, is that historical analysis is now a blind spot within ethnomusicology. Music and other cultural forms function as a "crucible in which time and memories are collected and preserved" (Neuman 1991, 269). They are modalities closely linked to emotional response, and thus provide a unique window into the beliefs and values of social groups, contemporary or otherwise. Discourse about the arts of the past is a primary means—in some cases the only means—of directly accessing the values of social groups toward one another, especially those infrequently articulated or unconsciously maintained. Studies of history can also effect social change in the present and draw attention to the needs of the disenfranchised. As Raymond Williams writes, "Much of the most accessible and influential work of the counter-hegemony is historical: the recovery of discarded areas, or the redress of selective and reductive interpretations" (1977, 116). A music history concerned in this sense with the meanings of the artistic expression of the past has yet to emerge either in Cuba or the United States.

Shared Histories: Cuba and the United States

Cuban music is especially interesting to me as a North American because its history is also the history of my own country's music. Virtually all the criticisms I have implicitly raised regarding the treatment of blacks and mulattos in Cuba, for instance, could also be leveled at the United States. In a general sense, our countries share a common demographic past. Both once contained indigenous populations that were subjected to brutal treatment at the hands of European colonizers. Both imported hundreds of thousands of West African slaves whose descendants are today the most poorly educated and disadvantaged members of society. Both countries have demonstrated a marked interest in the expressive forms of black subculture for centuries and in recent years have adopted the music and dance of blacks as national expression. White

Cubans and white Americans also share an unfortunate tendency to appropriate black street culture while doing little or nothing to rectify existing social
inequalities between the races. As Cristóbal Díaz Ayala commented to me, "We
buy the product, but abhor the producer. Long live [jazz, rhythm and blues],
the conga, the *mulata,* and fried plantains, but down with the *negro!*"

Despite the mainstreaming of marginal expression, white citizens of Cuba
and the United States continue to express ambivalent attitudes about black
culture. Just as rumba and *toques de santo* are derided by many *habaneros* as
vulgar and/or primitive, so the close associations between rap music and the
inner-city ghetto result in criticism of that genre in this country. In general,
Cuban and North American societies are obsessed with racial distinctions and
the very concept of race. From the O. J. Simpson and Colin Ferguson trials and
feature stories on race in U.S. magazines,[2] to never-ending references to "good"
and "bad" hair, noses, and lips, and derogatory racial jokes in Cuba,[3] racial
discourse in both countries is ubiquitous. As an art form consistently dominated by black innovations and performers, music deserves a special place in
any investigation addressing issues of racial interaction in both nations. The
Cuban case, far from being irrelevant, can provide insights into the history of
prejudice in the United States and can help us better evaluate our own biases.

Robert Farris Thompson has devoted much of his career to underscoring
the common cultural ties between various countries in the Americas, especially African influences. He suggests that, culturally, the United States is also a
"mulatto" nation that has been heavily influenced by West African music and
dance aesthetics, body movement, and linguistic forms.[4] Thompson adds that
the United States fails to recognize such influences because cultural fusion in
our country has not occurred in the context of widespread racial intermarriage and because African-American cultural history continues to be
underrepresented in public education. From his perspective, Cuba and the
United States may have more in common than most realize. However, many
cultural differences are obvious as well, one of the most important being the
extent to which *mulatos* and creole imagery have become central to national
identity in Cuba, as opposed to North America. Despite strong mainstream
interest in blues, rock 'n' roll, rap, and a steady "blackening" and "browning" of
its population base, the United States still largely conceives of itself as a white
country.

Official Cuban discourse on race, to the extent that it exists, focuses more
directly on the centrality of Afrocubans to national culture. Yet this apparently
progressive position often obscures a complex reality in which racial prejudice
continues to exist, in some ways more patently than in North America. In my
experience, one hears derisive racial commentary more frequently in Havana
than in Los Angeles, for instance.[5] And there is a striking lack of self-reflexivity

or self-consciousness about such commentary. Many North Americans have negative views of African Americans, but they are more uncomfortable about expressing them. Perhaps this is a result of national consciousness raising in the wake of the civil rights movement and mass racial conflicts since the 1960s, events that have had no counterpart in socialist Cuba. Some have also questioned whether the more varied racial distinctions recognized in the Hispanic Caribbean (*mulato, trigueño,* etc.) are beneficial to the Afrocuban population as a whole. While allowing for more accurate references to particular physical attributes, such terms often divide the Afrocuban community. Mintz and Price suggest that complex terminology may make broad racial identification more difficult, perpetuating black-on-black prejudice and hampering political organization (1985, 59).

Culture and Nation

One goal of this book is to demonstrate the numerous ways that musical production not only "reflects" social inequalities, but is itself a means by which racial tension, economic exploitation, and dominant political discourses are perpetuated or manifested. It also attempts to demonstrate that working-class music can represent an important site of popular resistance by expressing the cultural difference of the marginal and—perhaps most often—by blending oppositional and subordinating characteristics. Whether one considers the *teatro vernáculo, comparsa* bands, the *zarzuela,* or other genres, *afrocubanista* artistic activity is inevitably implicated in struggles over the meaning of Afrocuban culture within Cuba. These struggles represented tangible aspects of a hegemonic process that, regrettably, tended to exclude Afrocubans from participation in national culture more often than it afforded access. Commercial music and dance of the *machadato* thus contributed to the perpetuation of racial division, providing an ideological complement to more overt practices of discrimination.

Despite this, the *afrocubanismo* period constitutes a relatively progressive moment in Cuba's history, one that began a massive shift toward a greater acceptance of working-class expression. Music, dance, literature, and visual art from this period continue to affect present-day artists strongly and have served as the conceptual foundation of modern Cuban culture. This is the primary importance of *afrocubanismo,* and why it deserves further study. Why did stylized street music and dance have such an influence on national consciousness exactly when they did, and why, especially among classically trained musicians, would the same influences generate little interest a decade later? The answer to the first question can only be that various factors contributed to the onset of *afrocubanismo.* Although dominant society showed some interest in Afrocuban genres in the nineteenth century, the volatile social conditions of the 1920s and 1930s proved necessary to force a broader reexamination of inherited colonial prejudice and a tentative acceptance of black working-class culture. Increasingly antagonistic foreign relations with the United States, frustrated nationalist aspirations, economic crisis, political instability and revolution, artistic influences from abroad, and technological innovations all combined to shape the formation of *afrocubanismo*. Ultimately, a qualified acceptance of black expression was the only recourse of intellectuals and performers desirous of creating ideological unity in a country so heavily influenced by Africa.

As to reasons for the decline of the movement, I believe that conceptual tensions inherent in the attitudes of both the public and many prominent musicians eventually forced them to search for new thematic inspiration. Mainstream Cuban audiences came to accept representations of blackness in popular culture for a time, but only a blackness presented from a certain perspective, using particular stereotypes, and limited to well-defined aesthetic conventions. Listening to a white vocalist in blackface sing *zarzuela*-style slave laments while accompanied by a string orchestra, or to Bola de Nieve as he sat at a grand piano in a tuxedo and jokingly invoked the African god Babalú-Ayé—this kind of entertainment could be tolerated, even enjoyed. But when working-class blacks themselves became increasingly involved in popular entertainment beginning in the mid-1930s (as was inevitable), when they infused their compositions with influences from *abakuá* ceremony and *toques de santo,* when street *rumberos* began to predominate as entertainers in cabaret shows, when Fernando Ortiz arranged to have sacred *batá* drums performed on a concert stage, most turn-of-the-century listeners were horrified. Developments of this sort forced the Cuban intelligentsia to confront the fact that *afrocubanista* composition had little in common with the actual working-class expression of Afrocubans. They realized that their rhetorical acceptance of such music had been premature, and thus they chose for a time to deemphasize black subject matter.

To me, the defining characteristic of the *afrocubanismo* movement was its ambivalence toward African-influenced expression. The *orichas* or African deities, the *negro calesero,* the rumba, and all other perceived Africanisms served as simultaneous sources of pride and embarrassment to the nation. They were both powerful icons to rally behind *and* markers of degeneracy, reminders of a cultural legacy most considered shameful. An ongoing antagonism characterized the *machadato* period, antagonism between an emerging racially and culturally based nationalism incorporating mulatto imagery and a widespread belief in the inherent superiority of whites over those of black or mixed ancestry. *Afrocubanismo* as it initially emerged thus contained fundamental contradictions reflecting the divisiveness of race in the early Republic. Its reinterpretations of Afrocuban street culture represent a fantasy of sorts, a white middle-class projection of an "alternative folklore" that transformed the musical reality of the nation into more palatable form.

The entire history of Cuban popular music since the early nineteenth century can be viewed as a debate over the relative prominence of Afrocuban forms in a country dominated by Eurohispanic culture. Controversy first emerged over the *danza, contradanza,* and *danzón,* all of which were considered to contain undesirable Africanisms. By the twentieth century, these same genres achieved the near total acceptance of conservatives, while *comparsas* and *conjuntos de son* generated new polemics. In the context of such intercultural antagonism, the period from 1920 to 1940 represents a pivotal moment in which Cuba collectively reinvented itself by negotiating a new equilibrium between "black" and "white." Some musicians refused to write or perform in an *afrocubanista* style, of course, and even those who did produced "elevated" works conforming to middle-class tastes. But the *afrocubanismo* craze provided new conceptual maneuvering room for Afrocubans themselves who increasingly entered the field of commercial entertainment. They challenged stereotypical representations of blacks and black culture disseminated in the theater, salon, and cabaret, and developed their own interpretations of popular music. Though heavily constrained by dominant convention, they would slowly expand the parameters of mainstream dance music and of other expressive forms to more accurately reflect the totality of cultural traditions represented in Cuba.

Epilogue: Cuban National Culture Since 1940

By the mid-1940s, the views of middle-class Cuban artists toward the *afrocubanismo* movement had changed significantly. The phenomenal prominence of African themes that had affected their work from about 1925 through the late 1930s vanished as quickly as they had appeared. To many in the 1940s, *afrocubanista* art seemed "excessively radical" and aesthetically limiting. They felt that such art had served its purpose as a source of nationalist pride and a means of disseminating uniquely Cuban sounds to the international community, but no longer represented the spirit of the times. Alejo Carpentier expressed this attitude in a 1944 article from *Conservatorio* magazine.

> By means of those Afrocuban elements we wanted to react against
> oversentimentality, against languidness, against melodies without nerve or
> structure [in existing Cuban repertories]. The reaction was, perhaps, excessively
> radical, as all reactions tend to be. But it was a way of orienting the public

toward new genres, creating in them a new consciousness of the diversity of their folklore and the symphonic possibilities that such folklore offered. Certainly—and I can confess this now—we did not delude ourselves too much about the possibilities of Afrocuban themes. We knew that a [body of] folklore, however rich, cannot eternally nourish [a classical] musician who has to address, sooner or later, the eternal problems of universal music.[6]

To López Segrera, Cuban "high" culture of the 1940s brings to a culmination the experimentalist endeavors initiated by Minorista artists while avoiding the social ideals to which that group had also adhered (1989, 199). No longer did middle-class musicians, poets, and writers search for inspiration in popular culture or themes of national relevance. Instead, they retreated to the ivory tower, choosing modes of expression based exclusively on the paradigms of the international avant-garde. Artistic "rebellion" in the 1940s consisted of formal experimentation, not the conceptual articulation of modern art to marginal groups or classes. The occasional political work, such as Cintio Vitier's poem "Elegía a Jesús Menéndez" (discussing the assassination of a black labor organizer) or the writings of Julio Le Riverend and Mirta Aguirre, was overshadowed by countless others that avoided such subject matter. In the field of literature, the 1940s gave rise to *Orígenes* magazine (1944–1956) featuring the works of poets José Lezama Lima and Octavio Smith, playwright Virgilio Piñeiro, and others, as well as the even more conservative *Revista Cubana de Filosofía* (ibid., 227). Afrocuban themes do not feature prominently in either publication.

The most influential art music institution of the period was undoubtedly the Grupo de Renovación Musical, created in 1942 by Spaniard José Ardévol (Fornet 1967, 168). Well-known composers associated with this group include Julián Orbón, Hilario González, Harold Gramatges, Serafín Pro, and Gisela Hernández. All of these artists rejected the influence of turn-of-the-century neoromantics and impressionists such as early Stravinsky or Debussy in favor of neoclassicists like Hindemith and Britten, and all downplayed Afrocuban themes. Their compositions of the 1940s have been characterized as "extremely formalist and frigid" (López Segrera 1989, 245). To Ardévol and his contemporaries, orchestrational technique and a familiarity with the musical "masterworks" of the past took on a new importance. Members of the Grupo de Renovación often criticized the generation of García Caturla and Borbolla as insufficiently trained in composition. Although they purported to maintain "deep spiritual roots in the nation" (Ardévol 1945, 4), they aspired to do so in a much more oblique manner than the Minoristas had adopted. In Ardévol's words:

A [nationalist] composer can exist that does not work with these [Afrocuban] folkloric elements. . . . If the composer does not pursue vain entelechies nor a universalism without roots, but rather creates in accord with a state of sensibility that is a legitimate product of his Cuban environment . . . his music will be as Cuban as that of others who work directly with our folklore.[7]

Ardévol condemns nationalist musical works based on working-class genres as a "confining prison" (ibid.) rather than potentially liberating. It is unclear how a "universalism without roots" might be distinguished from "grounded universalism," or whether members of the Grupo de Renovación actually created works that more effectively represented Cuba than earlier artists. The relative prominence of Minorista compositions in the repertoire and discourse of today, relative to those of Ardévol and his colleagues, however, suggests that they did not. In any event, the rejection of Afrocuban subject matter by the Grupo de Renovación and others effectively ended the *afrocubanismo* movement. With a few notable exceptions (such as the midcentury paintings of Wifredo Lam), it would be decades before Afrocuban subject matter became a prominent theme in conservatory arts once again. Only after the emergence of (composer and guitarist) Leo Brouwer, (painters) René Portocarrero and Carlos Mendive, and others in the 1960s would a new reconciliation of "universal" and traditional Afrocuban expression be achieved.

But if "high" culture increasingly distanced itself from Afrocuban expression beginning in the late 1930s, mainstream popular culture remained heavily influenced by it. Afrocuban performers and groups continued to dominate the field of dance entertainment, with La Orquesta Aragón, Arcaño y sus Maravillas (a racially mixed band), the *conjunto* of Arsenio Rodríguez, and the Sonora Matancera among the most popular artists of the era. Many of these groups continued to record music of the *afrocubanismo* period and to compose songs in a similar style. (White) *santería* initiate Celina González, together with her husband, Reutilio Domínguez, made commercial recordings for decades that featured Afrocuban religious themes as a central component. Celina and Reutilio, together with (Afrocubans) Celia Cruz, Mercedita Valdés, Obdulio Morales, and others began weekly programs dedicated to *afro* compositions on Radio Cadena Suaritos beginning in the late 1940s (Orovio 1996).

During roughly the same period, Dámazo Pérez Prado, an Afrocuban composer and pianist who had performed for nearly a decade in the cabarets El Kursaal and Pennsylvania (Collazo 1987, 184), distinguished himself by his unique keyboard style and promoted the national and international popularity of the mambo. This genre is noteworthy for being based on small, repetitive motivic fragments and a cyclic, African-influenced formal structure similar to the final *montuno* section of the *son*. The formal qualities of the mambo enabled musically illiterate performers such as Beny Moré (also Afrocuban) to function as band leaders, and to compose and arrange songs by singing the recurrent melodic phrases they wished to have performed to various sections of the band.

Beginning in the early 1950s, Celia Cruz and Mercedita Valdés further increased the prominence of "Africanisms" by recording sacred *santería* chants in Yoruban dialects for the newly formed Panart label.[8] Although initially accompanied by classically trained choruses and/or instrumentalists, the Afrocuban music released by Panart and other Cuban record companies contributed significantly to mainstreaming genres that had previously been unrecorded. Not surprisingly, such trends did not please all critics. In an article about Afrocuban-inspired artistic expression as part of a volume commemorating the fiftieth anniversary of the Republic, Juan Luís Martín showed how controversial it still was. Recalling the views of Eduardo Sánchez de Fuentes thirty years earlier, he denied any significant African contribution to national culture and attacked recordings such as those by Cruz and Valdés as unmusical and "un-Cuban": "The [current] 'Afromania' craze has attempted to revalorize black folkloric elements, or supposedly black elements. And in the resulting genres, true [musical] creations of the land and the nation have been cast aside, forgotten. They are suffering beneath the crudity of the rhythms of percussion instruments."[9]

The influence of noncommercial Afrocuban genres on popular music continued to increase in the 1960s, despite criticism in the press. Demographic trends contributed significantly to such developments; the mass exodus of tens of thousands of primarily white Cubans in the wake of socialist revolution notably "blackened" the island, as did a dramatic decline in infant mortality among Afrocubans following the institution of universal health care. With the popularization of the *mozambique* in the early 1960s, dance steps derived from *santería* (specifically, those associated with *ritmo yesá* and *toques* to Ochún) directly entered the realm of popular entertainment for the first time (Martínez Furé 1994). Other dances popularized soon thereafter, however briefly, such as "El pilón," "El pacá," and "El coyulde" contained similar influences. Furé describes the latter, for instance, as "completely *lucumí*" (ibid.), taken entirely from ritual movements performed to Oyá and Obatalá. The founding of the Conjunto Folklórico Nacional also represents an important milestone, as it was the first government-supported institution to offer instruction in traditional Afrocuban music and dance, albeit in "purified" and secularized form.[10]

Ironically, support for black street culture on stage and in the academy came during a period of official intolerance toward Afrocuban religion practiced at home. During the early years of the revolution, authorities invoked Marxist writings to justify crackdowns on all forms of religious worship, including *santería* ceremony (C. Moore 1988, 299). Conflicts involving music and dance represented only one facet of more widespread racial tension. In contrast to its early policy decisions affecting Cuban women or blue-collar workers, for instance, the government refused to allow Afrocubans to organize politically and still does not allow them to do so. While the Castro leadership banned all forms of racial segregation and offered many new opportunities for poorer citizens (better housing, free education, and medical attention), it did not create any programs specifically designed to help Afrocubans achieve full social equality. Blacks and mulattos began the revolution as an underclass and have tended to remain undereducated and underrepresented in positions of authority. This is especially apparent in university appointments, in higher levels of the military, and in the Central Committee of the Cuban Communist Party. The disproportionately large numbers of blacks and mulattos who have chosen to leave the country in boats and rafts since 1980 seems to attest to their continuing dissatisfaction and disenfranchisement.

Perhaps the most disturbing aspect of the early socialist period was the apparent unwillingness of leaders in the Ministry of Education to promote the study of African-influenced culture in public schools. Carlos Moore notes that even the University of Havana offered virtually no courses on Afrocuban subject matter through the mid-1970s and that students who formed their own study groups to pursue such interests were harassed and even jailed as a result (1988, 315). Moore also singles out the World Cultural Congress of January 1968 as a particularly demeaning moment in Cuban history. Minister of Education José Llanusa Gobels is said to have harassed black and mulatto intellectuals who hoped to attend the conference after learning that they intended to advocate the development of an Afrocuban studies curriculum (ibid.). Those affected by the incident included an impressive array of internationally recognized figures, including filmmaker Sara Gómez, novelist Esteban Cárdenas, historians Walterio Carbonell and Pedro Deschamps Chapeaux, folklorist Rogelio Martínez Furé, poet Nancy Morejón, and ethnologists Alberto Pedro and Serafín "Tato" Quiñones. Officials eventually barred all of these individuals from participation in the Congress and sent Walterio Carbonell, along with two others, to a labor camp prison in Camagüey for protesting the decision (ibid.). Nicolás Guillén was the only Afrocuban allowed on the Cuban delegation to this event, yet his son was denied permission to attend.

Thankfully, policies have changed significantly since the 1970s. Some change resulted from an attempt by the Cuban government to establish better relations with various African nations, as well as its support of UNITA rebels in the Angolan civil war. Some may be due to the influence of African and African-American political activists in other countries and highly publicized visits to Cuba by Miriam Makeba, Stokely Carmichael, Angela Davis, (Black Panther leader) Huey Newton, Sidney Poitier, Harry Belafonte, and others. By the early 1980s, the Castro government had softened its de facto policy of intolerance. Party leaders began to engage in substantive discussions of racial issues, appoint more blacks to prominent party positions—such as the aforementioned Esteban Lazo, appointed to the Politbureau, and Gladys and Juan Robinson Agramonte, placed on the Central Committee—and to promote Afrocuban cultural events more openly. This new period of relative cultural tolerance has resulted in the opening of the Casa de Africa, a museum dedicated to African and African-influenced culture in Habana Vieja; the more intensive international promotion of groups such as the Conjunto Folklórico and the Muñequitos de Matanzas; numerous recording contracts offered to *santería* performers and religious leaders by the state; the first Congress on Yoruba Culture, held in 1988; and yearly academic meetings on African influences in Latin America sponsored by the Casa de las Américas. Since the collapse of the Soviet Union, attracting tourists to Cuba as a means of generating hard currency has become even more critical than before. Capitalizing on the appeal of Afrocuban culture abroad, the Castro government has recently developed "folklore tourism" packages for those interested in learning songs and dances of Afrocuban origin.

In the 1990s, African-derived religious expression has become if anything more widely practiced than in the past. It is not uncommon to see initiates wandering the streets in sacred vestments or to hear popular singers and entertainers openly incorporating sacred melodies and lyrics into otherwise secular stage acts. New groups like Mezcla and Síntesis have emerged that create popular dance tunes by fusing *batá* drum patterns and *santería* chants with synthesizers, electric guitars, and drum machines. Singer Lázaro Ros, especially, has distinguished himself as an important collaborator within this new tendency. Countless pop singles that have been released since about 1992 that contain lyrical references to the *orichas* and the religious practices associated with them—such as Adalberto Alvarez's "¿Qué tú quieres que te de?," NG y la Band's "Santa Palabra"; and Pachito Alonso's "La reina de Ifé"—illustrate the new visibility of *santería*. These same songs had been banned on the radio as recently as six or seven years ago. The Dan Den release "Viejo Lázaro,"[11] is yet another example of the same kind of composition. The lyrics of this piece, dedicated to the god Babalú Ayé, are a tribute to his divine power and suggest that the listener petition his help. "Viejo Lázaro" ends in a *montuno* section with a choral refrain taken from a popular saying: "He that doesn't have a Congo ancestor has one from the Calabar" ("El que no tiene de congo tiene de carabalí"). This gleeful recognition of Cuba's changing demographic and cultural orientation seems to have much in common with releases such as Public Enemy's *Fear of a Black Planet* and its confrontation with racial anxieties in the United States.

If cultural analysis teaches us anything, it is that the socially determined meanings of particular genres and traditions are constantly changing. They change as a result of associations with new contexts, performers, audiences, and media of dissemination, and by virtue of their relation to larger sociohistorical processes. This semiotic mutability of culture (and especially popular culture) is an ongoing process. One change does not preclude another; the initial meanings inherent in an object or event have the potential to reemerge at a later time. Traditional Afrocuban genres, for instance, are far from useless as symbols of oppositionality even if they have been appropriated by the mainstream and stylistically altered. The 1980s re-release by Mercedita Valdés of the *afro* "Lacho"[12] represents a case in point. This song, by Facundo Rivero, is written in a style typical of the *afrocubanismo* period. With a keyboard accompaniment reminiscent of tin pan alley, the singer assumes the role of a working-class black woman, using *bozal* speech as she pretends to lull a young child to sleep. Valdés adds a lengthy introduction to her version in which she speaks in an African-derived dialect. Her incorporation of sacred vocabulary derived from *santería* ceremony, as well as her presence as a major figure in the contemporary Afrocuban religious community (until very recently; she died in 1995), alter the meanings of "Lacho" in significant ways. The 1970s remake of Ernesto Lecuona's "La comparsa" by Irakere is perhaps an even more complex example (Irakere n.d.). Afrocuban Jesús "Chucho" Valdés, the group's leader, took the melody of what was essentially a parody of nineteenth-century *comparsa* bands and used it as the basis for a new Cuban funk/ fusion composition. Rhythms and instruments played in present-day *comparsas*—such as *sartenes* (frying pans) and conga drums—can be heard in this piece, together with a Fender Rhodes piano, drum kit, electric guitar, bass riffs reminiscent of the Commodores or Tower of Power, and of course the original Lecuona melody. Remakes of songs like "La comparsa" offer fascinating insights into processes of stylistic change and ethnic negotiation. They attest to the ways in which conceptions of marginal identity are constructed from reinterpretations of the past, existing subcultural traditions, and symbols of "otherness" appropriated from abroad.

As George Lipsitz says, popular culture "ain't no sideshow" (1990, 3). It is complex and polysemic. It is inevitably political, performed in real social contexts by positioned agents and conceptually aligned with the social concerns of various groups. It represents a marker of individual and collective identity, and as such can prove central to struggles for recognition on the part of re-pressed minorities, or the cooptation of such struggles. Conflicts over the meanings, usages, functions, and appropriateness of popular culture are part of larger social processes of dominance and resistance. As such they offer in-sights not only into the realm of artistic creation, but into the domain of ideo-logical formation and negotiation as well.

APPENDIX 1

Previously Uncollected Legislation Pertaining to Musical Activity in Cuba

Estrada Mora, N., Mayor of Havana

1900   Ordinance, "Ayuntamiento de la Habana." *Gaceta de la Habana: Periódico oficial del gobierno* 62, no. 82, tomo 1 (6 April 1900), 655. [IH]

Ayuntamiento de la Habana

Haciendo uso esta Alcaldía de las facultades que le están conferidas en asuntos de orden público y policía, ha acordado lo siguiente:

1°. Queda absolutamente prohibido el uso de *tambores,* de origen africano, en toda clase de reuniones, ya se celebren éstas en la vía pública, como en el interior de los edificios.

2°. Queda igualmente prohibido que transiten por las calles de esta ciudad las *agrupaciones ó comparsas,* conocidas con el nombre de *Tangos, Cabildos y Claves* cualquieras otras que conduzcan *símbolos, alegorías y objetos* que pugnan con la seriedad y cultura de los habitantes de este país.

La policía y demás agentes de la autoridad quedan encargados de exigir el exacto cumplimiento de estas disposiciones, y los contraventores á las mismas serán castigados con una multa de diez pesos en oro americano, sin perjuicio de cualquier otra responsabilidad que pudiesen incurrir por desobedencia á las órdenes de la autoridad.

Habana, abril 4 de 1900.
El Alcalde Municipal
N Estrada Mora

Lancís, Ricardo R., Secretario de Gobernación

1922   "Resolución." *Gaceta Oficial de la República de Cuba* 20, no. 121, tomo 5 (22 November 1922), 11346–47. [ANC]

Resolución Por cuanto: al amparo de Reglamentos legalizados por los Gobiernos Provinciales, funcionan con carácter de sociedades de Socorro y Recreo, ciertas instituciones, cuyos componentes los integran individuos que dicen [o] profesan distintas religiones africanas; siendo dirigidas sus ceremonias por negros nativos de ambos sexos, al igual que sus concurrentes, que demuestran gran fanatismo con las extrañas reverencias que otorgan a determinados objetos, que se ostentan en el altar que presentan los días destinados al culto.

Por cuanto: una de las ceremonias consiste en bailes *al estilo lucumí,* según ellos que efectúan acompañados de cantos incomprensibles para los profanos, y tocando instrumentos que producen ruído desagradable, muy parecido al del tambor: colocando en el centro del local una vasija que contiene una piedra que llaman *Santa,* que es alimentada con sangre de gallo, paloma o carnero, teniendo precisamente que ser blancos el cuero o las plumas de aquéllos; procedimientos que también emplean *para hacer curas,* esquivando para ello la vigilancia de que son objeto, porque sus atributos usuales están señalados como *de brujería* y con los que se practica a diario la especulación; cultos a los que no es ajena la concurrencia de personas que, a juzgar por su porte y compostura, parecen de posición holgada.

Por cuanto: a los aludidos bailes los ejecutan al son de un tambor o instrumento que iguala su sonido, al mismo tiempo que formando una gritería ensordecedora que molesta a los vecinos; siendo lo más grave, lo escandaloso del baile, por forma en que se efectúa, ya que las figuras que realizan llegan al extremo de que resulta un espectáculo ofensivo a la moral y a las buenas costumbres.

Por cuanto: la experiencia ha enseñado que la celebración de tales fiestas, en las que se toca el tango llamado Bembé, proceden siempre al robo, secuestro o asesinato de algún niño de la raza blanca, cuya sangre pide tras el baile y la invocación a sus santos, uno de aquellos fanáticos, para la supuesta curación de un enfermo.

Por cuanto: la existencia de tales prácticas, han traído consigo la repetición de atentados de idéntica naturaleza, contra la tranquilidad y el sosiego de la vida en los campos, y recientemente el asesinato de una niña en la provincia de Camagüey.

En el uso de las facultades que me confieren las leyes,

Resuelvo: Prohibir en todo el territorio de la República, como perjudiciales a la seguridad pública y contrarios a la moral y las buenas costumbres, los bailes de la naturaleza a que se deja hecha referencia y especialmente el conocido con el nombre de "Bembé," y cualesquiera otras ceremonias que, pugnando con la cultura y civilización de un pueblo, están señaladas como símbolos de barberie y perturbadoras del orden social.

Comuníquese esta Resolución a los Gobernadores Provinciales, para que a su vez lo hagan a los Alcaldes Municipales respectivos; a los Jefes de Policía Secreta y Nacional, y publíquese en la Gaceta Oficial, para que general conocimiento.

Habana, noviembre 21 de 1922.
Ricardo R. Lancís
Secretario de Gobernación

Machado, Gerardo, President of Cuba
1925   Decreto no. 2156. *Gaceta Oficial de la República de Cuba* 23, no. 96, tomo 4
        (22 October 1925), p. 10034.

Por cuanto: la logia Reconciliación de Guantánamo se ha dirigido a esta
Secretaría, solicitando que se dicten medidas para que las autoridades de la República no permitan, en las calles, manifestaciones populares, en las que los
circunstancias realizan contorsiones inmorales con sus cuerpos, incitados por el
tabal africano y conocidas vulgarmente con el nombre de arrolladoras; ejecutando
movimientos lascivios en una inconcebible promiscuidad de sexos, en las que, con
insolento impudor, toman parte niños y ancianos; en ocasiones exitados por la
embriaguez alcohólica y produciéndose siempre, desde hora temprana hasta la muy
avanzada de la madrugada, con esos espectáculos, verdaderamente indignos de una
nación culta y civilizada, lamentables actos que degeneran a las veces en hechos de
sangre, realizados a impulsos de bajas pasiones y venganzas personales.

Por cuanto: Las autoridades municipales están en el deber de atender a todo
cuanto conduzca al mejoramiento de las costumbres y de la moral pública,
impidiendo o remediando su perversión, y de velar estrictamente por la celebración
de reuniones en la vía y lugares públicos, cuidando de la circulación quieta y pacífica
de las mismas y del orden en ellas debe de observarse.

Por cuanto: Según resolución de esta Secretaría del 21 de Noviembre de 1922 . . .
quedaron prohibidos todos los bailes al estilo *lucumí* y, entre ellos, el conocido con
el nombre de *bembé,* así como cualesquiera otras ceremonias contrarias a la moral y
a las buenas costumbres.

Por cuanto: Por análogas consideraciones no debe permitirse en una nación
civilizada como la nuestra, porque la autorización o tolerancia sería atentatorio a su
cultura, que circulen por las calles de nuestras ciudades y pueblos manifestaciones
públicas integradas por individuos que al golpe de tambores o de instrumentos que
producen ruídos semejantes realizan los actos indignos anteriormente aludidos.

Por cuanto: Nuestra legislación vigente sobre la materia dispone que ejecutan
hechos punibles los que con toda clase de actos ofendieran a la moral y a las buenas
costumbres; los que promoviesen o tomaran parte activa en encerradas u otras
reuniones tumultuosas, con quebranto del sosiego público; los que con su
esparcimiento nocturno turbasen el orden, así como los que lo menos cabasen
levemente, usando de medios que de un modo racional puedan producir alarma o
perturbación, de lo que resulta evidente que incurren en responsabilidad tanto las
autoridades como sus agentes si presencian, sin impedirlas, tales reuniones o
manifestaciones.

Por cuanto: en virtud de las razones apuntadas es un deber del Gobierno evitar
todos los actos que tiendan a rebajar el nivel moral de nuestras costumbres públicas
y el respeto que nuestra República merece como nación culta y civilizada.

Por tanto: En uso de las facultades que me confieren las leyes y vistos los artículos
126, incisos 10 y 24 y 165, insisos 2 y 6 de la Ley Orgánica de los Municipios; la
Resolución de esta Secretaría del 21 de Noviembre de 1922 (G.O. del día 22); los
artículos 594, inciso 2 y 597, incisos 1, 2 y 4 del Código Penal,

RESUELVO: Prohibir, en todo el territorio de la República, por ser contrario a la moral y a las buenas costumbres y perturbadoras del orden público, las reuniones o manifestaciones que circulen por las calles de las ciudades y pueblos en la forma que se ha descrito, o sea, las que muestran su regocijo mediante el uso del tambor o instrumentos musicales del sabor africano, u otros análagos y en las que sus componentes ejecuten contorsiones con sus cuerpos que ofendan a la moral y que sus gritos y cantos perturben el sosiego público; quedando vigente en todas partes la Resolución dictado por esta Secretaría el 21 de noviembre de 1922.

El Secretario de Gobernación queda encargado del cumplimiento de este Decreto.

Dado en la Habana, Palacio Presidencial, el 16 de Octubre de 1925.

Gerardo Machado, Presidente

Rogerio Zayas Bazán,

Secretario de Gobernación

APPENDIX 2

List of *Sextetos* in Havana Between 1920 and 1945, by Barrio

This list was compiled from a handwritten sheet given to me by Florencio Hernández Cuesta ("Carusito"). Hernández Cuesta mentions that many of these groups performed only briefly and that most of them never adopted a *septeto* format by incorporating a trumpet. He also notes that the Sonora Matancera and the Gloria Matancera (both from Matanzas) eventually moved to the barrio of Jesús María in Havana. This probably occurred in the late 1920s.

Barrio of Pueblo Nuevo (also called Barrio de los Barracones)

Sexteto Habanero, directed by Guillermo Castillo
Sexteto Nacional, directed by Ignacio Piñeiro
Sexteto Boloña, directed by Alfredo Boloña
Sexteto Cuba, directed by Fernando Collazo
Sexteto Habanero Juvenil, directed by Guillermo Alan
Sexteto Oriente, directed by Román Báez
Sexteto Flores, directed by Flores Díaz
Sexteto Gloria Cubana, directed by "Feliciano"
Sexteto Habana, director unknown
Sexteto Los Marquesitos, directed by Trancerco Abarez

Barrio Los Sitios

Sexteto Occidente, directed by María Teresa Vera
Sexteto Diosa del Amor, directed by Joseíto Fernández
Sexteto Sinsonte de Oro, directed by Angel Duarte
Sexteto Area Triunfar, directed by Guillermo Pérez (Macudo)
Sexteto Típico Cubano, directed by Antonio Vitorino
Sexteto Corsario, directed by Julián Saahecha
Sexteto Hermano Enriso, directed by Nené Enriso
Sexteto Los Angeles, directed by Angel Vardes

Barrio de Cayo Hueso

Sexteto Segundo Boloña, directed by Segundo Boloña
Sexteto Guarina, director unknown
Sexteto Fasenda, director unknown
Sexteto Tanque Mora, director unknown
Sexteto Universo, directed by Alebardo Barroso
Sexteto La Viajera, director unknown
Sexteto Hatuey Camagüeyano, directed by José Marquetti
Sexteto Jóvenes del Cayo, directed by Domingo Vargas
Sexteto Trovadores del Cayo, directed by Isolena Carrillo

Barrio de Belén

Sexteto Carabina de Ases, directed by Félix Chappottín
Sexteto Dandys de Belén, directed by Joseíto Vergeré

Barrio de Luyanó

Sexteto Terry, director unknown
Sexteto Bohemio, director unknown
Sexteto Cubano del 27, directed by Ruíz Noda
Sexteto Columbia, director unknown
Sexteto Favorito, directed by Carlos Anido

Barrio de Marianao

Sexteto Bellamar, directed by Esteban Requeira
Sexteto Lira Redención, director unknown
Sexteto Colón, director unknown
Sexteto Hatuey, director unknown
Sexteto Bayamo, director unknown
Estudiantina Vaquera, director unknown
Estudiantina Invencible, director unknown

Barrio del Cerro

Sexteto Valentino, director unknown
Sexteto Yara, directed by Santos Ramírez

Barrio del Pilar

Sexteto Chimbo, director unknown
Sexteto Jabón Candado, director unknown
Sexteto Jabón La Llave, directed by Gerónimo García
Sexteto Botón de Oro, directed by Luz Plas
Sexteto Fram Tam Sport, director unknown

Barrio de la Víbora

Sexteto Brillante Marinero, director unknown
Sexteto Jóvenes Viboreños, director unknown

Barrio del Vedado

Sexteto Los Siboneyes, directed by Joseíto Núñez

Barrio de Jesús María

Sexteto Jiquani, directed by Carla Rodríguez
Sexteto Minerva, director unknown
Sexteto Lira Habana, director unknown

Barrio San Leopoldo

Sexteto Parreño, director unknown
Sexteto Leopoldo, director unknown

Barrio San Miguel del Padrón

Sexteto Cárdenas, director unknown

Barrio de Guanabacoa

Sexteto Munamar, directed by J. Izquierdo
Sexteto Los Melodiosos, director unknown
Sexteto San Francisco, director unknown
Sexteto Bolero del 35, directed by Tata Gutiérrez
Sexteto Jinasna Habanera, director unknown

Barrio de Regla

Sexteto Cubano del 32, directed by Luís Felipes

Barrio Colón

Sexteto Seis Criollos, directed by "Polo"
Sexteto Las Criolletas, directed by "Elia"

APPENDIX 3

Two Examples of *Afrocubanista* Poetry with Musical Themes

Reproduced from *Orbita de la poesía afrocubana 1928-1937,* edited by Ramón Guirao (Havana: Ucar, García y Cía., 1938). Thanks to Alira Ashvo-Muñoz for her help in clarifying several terms. Note that some of the lyrics are nonsense syllables.

La rumba
José Zacarías Tallet

Zumba mamá, la rumba y tambó
mabimba, mabomba, bomba y bombó.

The rumba and drum are buzzing, mama
mabimba, mabomba, bomba y bombó.

Zumba mamá, la rumba y tambó
mabimba, mabomba, bomba y bombó.

The rumba and drum are buzzing, mama
mabimba, mabomba, bomba y bombó.

Como baila la rumba la negra Tomasa,
como baila la rumba José Encarnación.
Ella mueve una nalga, ella mueve la otra,
él se estira, se encoge, dispara la grupa,
el vientre sobre el uno y el otro talón.

Oh, how Tomasa the black dances rumba,
oh, how José Encarnación dances rumba.
She moves a buttock, she moves the other
he stretches, contracts, tosses the rump,
the belly over one, then the other heel.

Chachi, chaqui, chaqui, charaqui.
Chaqui, chaqui, chaqui, charaqui.

Chachi, chaqui, chaqui, charaqui.
Chaqui, chaqui, chaqui, charaqui.

Las ancas potentes de niña Tomasa
en torno de un eje invisible,
como un reguilete rotan con furor,
desafiando con rítmico, lúbrico disloque
el salaz ataque de Che Encarnación:

The powerful hindquarters of Tomasa
circling an invisible axis,
revolve with fury like a shuttle,
dueling with rhythm, lubric dislocation
the salacious attack of Che Encarnación:

muñeco de cuerda que rígido el cuerpo,
hacia atrás el busto, en arco hacia alante
abdomen y piernas, brazos encogidos,
a saltos iguales, de la inquieta grupa
va en persecución.

Cambia e' paso, Cheché, cambia e' paso.
Cambia e' paso, Cheché, cambia e' paso.
Cambia e' paso, Cheché, cambia e' paso.

La negra Tomasa con lascivo gesto
hurta la cadera, alza la cabeza,
y en alto los brazos, enlaza las manos,
en ellas reposa la ebónica nuca
y procaz ofrece sus senos rotundos
que oscilando de diestra a siniestra
encandilan a Chepe Cachón.

Chachi, chaqui, chaqui, charaqui.
Chachi, chaqui, chaqui, charaqui.

Frenético el negro se lanza al asalto
y, el pañuelo de seda en sus manos,
se dispone a marcar a la negra Tomasa,
que lo reta insolente,
con un buen vacunao.
¡Ahora!, lanzando con rabia el fuetazo,
aulla. (Los ojos son ascuas,
le falta la voz, y hay un diablo
en el cuerpo de Che Encarnación.)

La negra Tomasa esquiva el castigo
y en tono de burla, lanza un insulante
y estridente ¡no!
y valiente se vuelve y menea la grupa
ante el derrotado José Encarnación.

Zumba mamá, la rumba y tambó
mabimba, babomba, bomba y bombó.

Repican los palos,
suena la maraca,
zumba la botija,
se rompe el bongó.

---

rope doll, how rigid the body,
bust toward the back, arching forward
abdomen and legs, arms contracted,
in equal leaps, follow in pursuit
of the restless behind.

Change steps, Cheché, change steps.
Change steps, Cheché, change steps.
Change steps, Cheché, change steps.

Tomasa the black with lascivious gesture
withdraws the hip, raises her head,
and with arms raised, folds her hands,
in them she rests her ebony nape
and boldly offers her rotund breasts
that oscillate from right to left
and dazzle Chepe Cachón.

Chachi, chaqui, chaqui, charaqui.
Chachi, chaqui, chaqui, charaqui.

Frenetic, the Negro hurls himself in assault
and, silk handkerchief in his hands,
gets ready to put his mark on Tomasa,
who challenges him insolently,
with a good *vacunao.*
Now! Flinging the horsewhip with fury,
he howls. (The eyes are red coals,
he loses his voice, and there is a devil
in the body of Che Encarnación.)

Tomasa the black eludes the punishment
and in a mocking tone, hurls an insulting
and strident *no!*
and valiantly turns, swinging her buttocks
in front of the defeated José Encarnación.

The rumba and drum are buzzing, mama
mabimba, babomba, bomba y bombó.

The sticks ring out,
the maraca sounds,
the *botija* jug hums,
the bongo drum breaks.

Hasta el suelo sobre un pie se baja
y da media vuelta, José Encarnación.
Y niña Tomasa se desarticula
y hay olor a selva
y hay olor a grajo
y hay olor a hembra
y hay olor a macho
y hay olor a solar urbano
y olor a rústico barracón.
Y las dos cabezas son dos cocos secos
en que alguno con yeso escribiera
arriba, una diéresis, abajo, un guión.
Y los dos cuerpos de los dos negros
son dos espejos de sudor.

Repican las claves,
suena la maraca,
zumba la botija,
se rompe el bongó.

Chaqui, chaqui, chaqui, charaqui.
Chaqui, chaqui, chaqui, charaqui.

Llega el paroxismo,
tiemblan los danzantes,
y el bembé le baja a Chepe Cachón;
y el bongó se rompe al volverse loco;
a niña Tomasa le baja el changó.

Piquitiquipán, piquitiquipán,
piquitiquipán, piquitiquipán.

Al suelo se viene la niña Tomasa,
al suelo se viene José Encarnación.
Y allí se revuelan con mil contorsiones,
se les sube el santo, se rompió el bongó,
se acabó la rumba, con con, co, mabó.
Paca, paca, paca, paca, paca,
pam, pam, pam.

Over a single foot he drops to the ground
and spins around, José Encarnación.
And the Tomasa girl comes apart
and there is a smell of jungle
and there is a smell of jackdaw
and there is a smell of woman
and there is a smell of man
and there is a smell of urban slum
and a smell of rustic slave barracks
And the two heads are two dry coconuts
on which someone wrote with plaster
above, a dieresis, below, a hyphen.
And the two bodies of the two blacks
are two mirrors of sweat.

The *claves* ring out,
the maraca sounds,
the *botija* jug hums,
the bongo drum breaks.

Chaqui, chaqui, chaqui, charaqui.
Chaqui, chaqui, chaqui, charaqui.

Paroxysm comes,
the dancers tremble,
the *bembé* comes down on Chepe Cachón
and the *bongó*, going crazy, breaks apart;
Changó comes down on the Tomasa girl.

Piquitiquipán, piquitiquipán,
piquitiquipán, piquitiquipán.

To the floor falls the Tomasa girl,
To the floor falls José Encarnación.
And there they writhe in contortions,
the *santo* takes them, the *bongó* breaks,
the rumba ends, *con con, co, mabó.*
Paca, paca, paca, paca, paca,
pam, pam, pam.

Originally published in *Atuei*, August 1928.

Comparsa habanera (ca. 1934)

Emilio Ballagas

La comparsa del farol	The *comparsa* with colored lanterns
(bamba uenibamba bó.)	*(bamba uenibamba bó.)*
Pasa tocando tambor.	Passes by playing the drums.
¡Los diablitos de la sangre	The blood-brother devils
se encienden en ron y sol!	are lit up in rum and sunshine!
A'ora berá como yo no yoro	Now you'll see that I don't cry
(Jálame lá calimbanyé . . .)	*(Jálame lá calimbanyé . . .)*
Y' ora berá como yombondombo.	And now you'll see how *yombondombo*.
(Júlume la cumbumbanyé . . .)	*(Júlume la cumbumbanyé . . .)*
El santo se va subiendo	The *santo* is possessing someone
cabalgando en el clamor.	riding horseback in the clamor.
"Emaforibia yambó.	"*Emaforibia yambó.*
Uenibamba uenigó."	*Uenibamba uenigó.*"
¡En los labios de caimito	In the lips of the little star apple
los dientes blancos de anón!	The white teeth of the *anón* fruit!
La comparsa del farol	The *comparsa* of colored lanterns
ronca que roncando va.	moves hoarsely and raucously
¡Ronca comparsa candonga	Raucous the pitiful *comparsa*,
que ronca en tambor se va!	raucously with drums it heads off!
Y . . . ¡Sube la loma! Y ¡dale al tambor!	And . . . Up the hill! And hit that drum!
Sudando los congos van tras el farol.	The Congolese, sweating behind the lantern.
(Con cantos yorubas alzan el clamor.)	(Raising the clamor with Yoruba chants.)
Resbalando en un patín de jabón	Losing their balance on a cake of soap
sus piernas se mueven al vapor del ron.	their legs move in the vapor of rum.
Con plumas plumero	The mulatto woman Fermina Quintera
de loro parlero	Has adorned herself with dressy feathers
se adorna la parda Fermina Quintero.	of a talking parrot.
Con las verdes plumas	With the green feathers
del loro verdero.	of the greenish parrot
¡Llorando de la muerte	Crying at the death
de Papá Montero!	of Papa Montero!
La comparsa del farol	The *comparsa* of colored lanterns
ronca que roncando va.	moves hoarsely and raucously.
Ronca comparsa condonga	Raucous the pitiful *comparsa*,

bronca de la cañandonga . . .
¡La conga ronca se va!

Se va la comparsa negra bajo el sol
moviendo los hombros, bajando el clamor
Y ¡sube la loma! (Y baja el clamor.
Pasa la comparsa mientras baja el sol.)

Los diablitos de la sangre
se enciende de ron y sol.

Bailan las negras rumberas
con candela en las caderas.
Abren sus anchas narices
ventanas de par en par
a un panorama sensual . . .

La conga ronca se va
al compás del atabal . . .

¡Sube la loma, dale al tambor!
Sudando los negros van tras el farol.
(Los congos dan vueltas y buscan el sol
pero no lo encuentran porque ya bajó.)

La comparsa enciende su rojo farol
con carbón de negros mojados en ron.

La comparsa negra meneándose va
por la oscura plaza de la Catedral.
La comparsa conga va con su clamor
por la calle estrecha de San Juan de Dios.

"Apaga la bela
que'l muelto se va.
Amarra el pañuelo
que lo atajo ya.

Y ¡enciende la bela
que'l muelto salió!
Ensiende dos belas
¡Que tengo el Changó!"

rudely with cheap aguardiente . . .
The raucous *comparsa* heads off!

Beneath the sun the black *comparsa* goes
moving the shoulders, the clamor descends.
Up the hill! (And the clamor dies down.
The *comparsa* passes as the sun goes down.)

The blood-brother devils
are lit up in rum and sunshine.

The black *rumberas* dance
with fire in their hips.
They open their broad noses
windows flung wide
to a sensual panorama . . .

The rowdy *comparsa* heads off
to the rhythm of the drum.

Up the hill, hit that drum!
Sweating the blacks follow behind the lantern
(The Congolese circle and look for the sun
But they don't find it, it has already set.)

The *comparsa* lights its red lantern
with the coal of blacks soaked in rum.

The black *comparsa* moves shaking its hips
through the dark plaza of the Cathedral.
The Congo *comparsa* moves with its clamor
through the narrow street San Juan de Dios.

"Put out the candle
'cause the spirit of the dead man is leaving.
Tie the handkerchief
I've already gotten hold of it.

And light the candle!
now that the spirit's gone!
Light the candles
Cause now I've been possessed by Changó!"

La comparsa conga temblando salió
de la calle estrecha de San Juan de Dios.
¡Clamor en la noche del ronco tambor!

Rembombiando viene
rembombiando va . . .
La conga rembomba
rueda en el tambor.
La conga matonga
sube su clamor
ronda que rondando
¡ronca en el tambor!

Detrás de una iglesia se pierde la ola
de negros que zumban maruga
en la rumba.

Y apaga la vela
Y ¡enciende la vela!
Sube el farol,
Abaja el farol.

Con su larga cola la culebra va.
Con su larga cola muriéndose va
la negra comparsa del guaricandá.

La comparsa ronca perdiéndose va.
¡Que lejos! . . . lejana . . . muriéndose va.
Se apaga la vela: se hunde el tambor.
¡La comparsa conga desapareció!

The Congolese *comparsa* left trembling
through the narrow street San Juan de Dios.
Clamor in the night from the rowdy drum!

Making a racket it comes
making a racket it goes . . .
The carnival group beats away
rolling with the drum.
The *matonga* carnival band
increases the noise
making the rounds, wandering about
Raucous in the sound of the drum!

Behind the church one wing is lost
of blacks that shake rattles
dancing the rumba.

And put out the candle
And light the candle!
Raise the lantern,
Lower the lantern.

With its long tail the snake goes by.
With its long tail, dying
the black *comparsa* of the common folk.

The rowdy *comparsa* is disappearing.
How far off! . . . distant . . . dying away.
The candle is out, the drum sinks down.
The Congolese *comparsa* disappeared!

NOTES

Unless otherwise specified, all translations are by the author.

Introduction

1. Casas Romero, "Estela," n.d.

2. Manuel 1988 notes that antecedents of the *afrocubanismo* craze of the late 1920s lie in the popularization of the *contradanza, danzón,* and other genres in the later nineteenth century. Thus African-influenced musics have played a limited role in Cuban cultural nationalism for over a century (see chapter 1). My primary interest, however, lies in the sweeping, overt interest in Afrocuban culture beginning about 1925, when Afrocuban influences first became a central component of Cuban identity.

3. See Carbonell 1961, 26. Carbonell is an Afrocuban historian and author affiliated with the Bibliotecta Nacional José Martí in Havana.

Chapter 1. Afrocubans and National Culture

1. For an example of this term used in a musical context, see Celia Cruz's rendition of "Bemba colorá" (Big red African lips) on *Celia Cruz: The Best,* Globo Records CD #80587. Miami: Sony, Inc., 1991. The lyrics include rather derogatory commentary such as: "Sing that rumba, sing that *son* of yours, your little *guaracha* and your *danzón* / To me you're nothing, you have big red African lips" ("Canta tu rumba, canta tu son, tu guarachita y tu danzón / Pa' mí tú no eres na', tú tienes la bemba colorá").

2. Alira Ashvo-Muñoz, personal communication. Examples of popular songs that employ *"negra"* in this manner include the Ernesto Lecuona composition "Negra me muero" (1939).

3. Examples of *"chino"* and *"china"* in song lyrics from the nineteenth century can be found in Hallorans 1882; a more recent example is music from Ernesto Lecuona's *zarzuela Rosa la China.*

4. Gilberto Freyre, a Brazilian scholar, did some of the earliest work on conceptions of race in Latin America. See *The Mansions and the Shanties* (1933) and *The Masters and the Slaves* (1936) for information on the linguistic history of the terms *negro* and *negra* in the Americas (Elizabeth Marchant, personal communication).

5. Early verbal and visual portrayals of slave dances by foreign artists include the oil paintings of Federico Miahle and Henry Cleenwerk (Museo de Bellas Artes, Havana) and the travel diary of Walter Goodman (1873); Pérez 1992, a collection of nineteenth-century travel writings on Cuba, contains many insights into cultural practices of the period.

6. See León 1984 on Afrocuban arts in the nineteenth and twentieth centuries, especially Yoruba-, Bantu-, and *abakuá*-related traditions. See also Barnet on slave dances (1966, 29); and Ortiz 1981.

7. "El folklore afrocubano era rechazado como cosa de negros, un elemento extraño a la nacionalidad que nos retrotraía a una prehistoria bárbara" (Fornet 1967, 49).

8. *Náñigos* (also known as *abakuás*) are members of male secret societies in Cuba of West African origin (from the Cameroon area) and at the turn of the century were associated with working-class laborers and dock workers in Havana and Regla. Most were black, but in the later nineteenth century some sects began to allow limited white membership. *Náñigo potencias* or brotherhoods have been described as Afrocuban "cults of masculinity" (Martínez Furé, personal communication). While disseminating some positive values, such as the importance of being a good father, they also tend to perpetuate sexist attitudes and violence if the honor of the group is threatened. The *potencias* were outlawed in the nineteenth century but continue to flourish. Especially in the early twentieth century, *ñáñigos* represented a highly controversial and persecuted group. Critics cited the violence they instigated as an example of the "barbarity" of Afrocubans generally.

9. E.g., Roche Monteagudo 1925, 52–54, 113. See illustrations for a reproduction of the photograph from 1914 (originally printed in ibid., 73) depicting confiscated *ñáñigo* instruments in a Havana police station.

10. Carpentier 1946, 147–49, and Deschamps Chapeaux 1971 provide exhaustive lists of famous Afrocuban musicians of the nineteenth century.

11. "Entre los enormes males que esta raza infeliz ha traído a nuestro suelo, uno de ellos es el haber alejado de las artes a nuestra población blanca . . ." (Saco 1960, 77).

12. See Paquette 1988. Historians remain divided over whether the Escalera conspiracy was a fabrication by antiblack groups. It is remembered as a conspiracy of the Afrocuban middle classes who organized secretly to combat slavery and foment slave rebellion. The event resulted in prolonged Inquisition-like investigations, as well as the torture, murder, imprisonment, and forced exile of thousands of Afrocubans.

13. Ibid., 209–32. Statistics on the number of deaths and imprisonments during La Escalera are uncertain. Cruz puts the number of executions at about 400 (1974, 49). Paquette does not speculate on totals, but states that in Matanzas Province

alone 78 prisoners were killed outright and an additional 1,700 imprisoned or banished from the island in 1844 (1988, 229).

14. Valdés is a very common surname among blacks and mulattos and was frequently given to an orphaned or abandoned child when a parent's name was unknown or could not be revealed (Alira Aschvo-Muñoz, personal communication). Such was the case with Plácido, whose birth resulted from a clandestine relationship between a dancer from a wealthy white family and a mulatto salon owner (Le Riverend 1984, 2:1059).

15. See Díaz Ayala 1988.

16. "Este hombre, que era un enemigo decidido de la independencia del país y de cuanto movimiento progresista . . . fue también el iniciador de una pintura cubana" (Portuondo 1972, 61).

17. Arredondo 1939, 32. Aline Helg's *Our Rightful Share* (1995) represents the most comprehensive study of racial tensions during the Wars of Independence to date.

18. Castillo Faílde 1964, 87; Sánchez de Fuentes 1928a, 77. Several readers have pointed out that the origin of the *danzón* is more typically associated with the late 1870s rather than earlier. Faílde himself disputes the veracity of the source he includes in his study. Although documentation is patchy, a dance of some sort called *danzón* clearly existed decades before the Faílde orchestra popularized the genre in Matanzas and other parts of Cuba.

19. Castillo Faílde 1964 provides a more detailed history of the *danzón*.

20. "Empezamos con la danza, vino el danzón . . . enseguida vendrá la rumba, y como es natural, acabaremos bailando ñáñigo" (Castillo Faílde 1964, 155).

21. Some of the better-known exceptions include *Biografía de un cimarrón* (Barnet 1966); *Tiempo muerto* (García 1969); and *Sindo Garay: Memorias de un trovador* (de León 1990).

22. "La sublime emancipación de los esclavos por sus amos cubanos borró . . . el odio todo de la esclavitud" [1895]; "En los campos de batalla muriendo por Cuba, han subido juntos por los aires, las almas de los blancos y los negros" [1893] (Martí 1959, 14, 27).

23. This practice bears a disturbing resemblance to that of the Castro government after the 1959 revolution. As in earlier decades, the position of officials through the mid-1980s was that racism had been eliminated with the rise of socialism and as a result the topic deserved no further investigation or commentary.

24. Peter Wade notes that policies of subsidized European immigration in an attempt to "whiten" the nation are evident in Colombia and other Latin American countries as well (1993, 13).

25. Arredondo 1939, 66. The Guerrita del Doce left a lasting impression on the residents of Oriente, and many of their sentiments were eventually expressed in popular song. These songs have never been published or analyzed, but folklorist Rogelio Martínez Furé sang one for me (in a 1994 interview) that included the lyrics: "Oh God, José Miguel, why did you kill so many innocent blacks [repeated] / I'm going to call Evaristo, yes, I'm going to call Pedro Ivonet [another leader of the PIC] / Oh God, I'm a warrior, a warrior" ("Ay Dios, José Miguel, ¿por qué mataste a tantos

negros inocentes / Voy a llamar a Evaristo que no, voy a llamar a Pedro Ivonet / Ay, Dios guerrillero soy, guerrillero").

26. Another case is mentioned in the *Diario de la Marina,* 6 July 1927, 12, involving the supposed kidnapping of a four-year-old white girl.

27. My thanks to Díaz Ayala 1981 for citing and partially reproducing this legislation. In addition, several interviewees in Havana told me that a surprising amount of antagonism continues to exist in Cuba toward Afrocuban music of this kind. Tomás Jimeno stated that no Afrocuban percussion instruments or traditional rhythmic patterns of any sort were taught in national conservatories or other music institutions through the late 1960s and that interest in such music as a legitimate form of national expression has developed only since that time (1992). Rogelio Martínez Furé added that ordinances against drumming continued to appear in Cuban police stations through the 1970s.

28. James Brow (personal communication) notes that before the publication of Franz Boas's *The Mind of Primitive Man* (1911) European-derived discourses on race and culture were fundamentally interpenetrated. In general, intellectuals of the period did not distinguish between the two terms. References to the *"atraso"* or backwardness of "la raza cubana" (the Cuban race) in early twentieth-century Cuba thus presuppose the negative cultural and racial effects of intermarriage between African and European descendants. Authors tended to argue that the Cuban people suffered from exposure to "primitive" Africans and had been "retarded" in their own cultural/racial evolutionary development as a result. They viewed miscegenation in the colonial era as leading to a national state of psychosocial "decadence" in the twentieth century. Articles such as Fernando Ortiz's "La decadencia cubana" (1924) reflect this intellectual tradition. See Wade 1993, 15, for similar writings by early twentieth-century Colombian authors.

29. This was sometimes referred to as "moral degeneracy" *(atraso moral).*

30. "Los infelices esclavos danzaban como bárbaros . . . el baile africano de los barracones, por sus selvátios movimientos, que más bien eran saltos de irracionales . . . En cuanto lo oyen pierden . . . el dominio de sí mismo" (Castellanos 1914b, 152).

31. "Hay que elevar el nivel moral, educar la cerebración inculta de los que continúan apegados al bárbaro tronco de la raza secular, cuya influencia hace supervivir las tradiciones tenebrosas. Hay que vencer los organismos incapacitados de adaptarse al molde jurídico de los pueblos civilizados" (Castellanos 1916, 107).

32. "La música de los negros . . . ha sido juzgada, aún por los críticos menos severos, como más estrepitosa que bella: la mayor parte de sus instrumentos tienden a hacer ruido y no a producir sonidos agradables" (Castellanos 1927, 197).

33. It is important to note that the Cuban public initially demonstrated little interest in Ortiz's writings, including his later works (M. Valdés 1993). As a result, Ortiz was forced to finance early publications out of his own pocket, since publishers refused to assume the financial risks involved. For many years, Ortiz chose not to print his larger monographs because of the expense. Finally in the early 1950s, Raúl Roa, minister of culture in the Carlos Prío administration, lobbied for government

funding to aid Ortiz with his publications. This is why the entire five-volume set *Los instrumentos de la música afrocubana* appeared at that time, followed closely by *La africanía de la música folklórica de Cuba* and *El teatro y los bailes de los negros en el folklore de Cuba*.

34. Examples of such advertisements appear in the *Diario de la Marina*, 4 July, 19; and 6 July, 24.

35. "Muchas damas de nuestra sociedad habían exclamado su repulsa a la posibilidad de entrar en contacto con manos negras en las operaciones del cobro de los pasajes" (Arredondo 1939, 158).

36. Similar patterns of favoritism are found in Cuba today. Especially with the advent of the current economic crisis, Cubans in the 1990s have been forced to rely on networks of friends and relatives to procure extra food for their families and find other basic goods unavailable in government shops. For this reason, Cuba is often referred to jokingly as the country of *"socioismo"* (friendship-ism) rather than *"socialismo"* (socialism).

37. Celebrity performers such as Nat "King" Cole, Harry Belafonte, and Josephine Baker suffered humiliating experiences in Cuba. For an account of how Baker was refused a room at the Nacional in the late 1940s, see París 1966, 61.

38. Acosta 1993, 35. An unsigned editorial in *Adelante* magazine (January 1938, 1) contains additional information on racial segregation.

39. "La República no ha podido cumplir con su compromiso de circunstancias sociales y económicas, se ha frustrado aquel bello programa revolucionario ... en la práctica todo conspira a nuestro desaliento y extinción, en un plan deliberado y urgente" (Urrutia 1932, 67).

40. Alvarez 1994; Bacallao 1994; Castro et al. 1994; Rivero 1994; Suárez 1994. *Cabarets de primera* included the Montmartre in Vedado, the Sans Souci and Casino Nacional west of Miramar, the Cabaret Nacional below what is today the García Lorca Theater, the famous Tropicana in Marianao, the Eden Concert on Zululeta street, and the Club Bolero in Habana Vieja.

41. See the *Blue Guide to Cuba* (1938) for a more complete listing of these organizations and their locations.

42. This establishment was located on Zululeta Street near the Capitol building.

43. *Danzonero* Antonio Arcaño (1992) notes that the Unión Fraternal was the black-mulatto social organization with the largest membership in Cuba. It was located on Revillagigedo Street, on the corner of Misión.

44. Early photographs in the archives of the Centro Odilio Urfé suggest that in both ensembles nearly half of all performers were Afrocuban. Relative to overall demographics, blacks and mulattos seem to be significantly overrepresented in the "high" art world of the twentieth century, as in the colonial era.

Chapter 2. Minstrelsy in Havana

1. "Falta aún el teatro cubano de los dilemas blanquinegros, en el cual la personificación oscura no sea sólo la del blanco cómico con careta de negrito

paluchero y truhanero . . . sino la escena en la cual el negro diga lo suyo, 'lo que le salga de adentro,' y lo diga en su lengua, en sus modales, en sus tonos, en sus emociones, hasta en las más dolientes" (Ortiz 1938, xxix).

2. Although generally considered an artistic form of the past, *teatro vernáculo* comedy and song sketches continue to be performed on occasion in Havana even today. I witnessed the performance of a *negrito* act in the Cortijo bar of the Hotel Vedado on 5 July 1992 (see illustrations).

3. Most authors (e.g., Robreño 1961, 23) downplay or fail to mention entirely the influence of North American minstrelsy on the development of the Cuban comic theater, ascribing influence only to Spanish sources and occasionally the *bouffes parisiennes*. While the Spanish *tonadilla* does bear a strong similarity to the *teatro vernáculo*, especially in its presentation of recurring archetypal characters based on gender and race, such as the *gitana* or Gypsy woman, the failure to analyze North American influences seems a significant omission. The fact that minstrelsy developed in the United States during almost exactly the same period as the *teatro vernáculo* in Cuba seems too much of a coincidence to overlook. Díaz Ayala mentions that the minstrel troupes of Campbell, Christie, and Webb from the United States all toured Cuba between 1860 and 1865, seeking work outside the war-torn southern states (1981, 63). In the twentieth century, the influence of minstrelsy on comic theater productions is manifested in many ways, including the use of white gloves and other articles of clothing associated with minstrels by *negritos* and the use of jazz music beginning in the 1910s. See Glasser's commentary (1995, 24).

4. Robreño discusses various *sainete* subgenres in greater detail (1961, 52). His classifications include the *sainete costumbrista,* the *sainete del solar,* the *sainete político,* and the *sainete-revista de la actualidad.*

5. Cruz 1974. This tradition of parodying black speech has its counterpart in the music of other Latin American countries that imported African slaves; Stevenson 1976, 316; and Béhague 1979, 18–54, for instance, discuss the lyrics of *negrillas* and related *villancicos de negros* composed in South American countries such as Peru and Bolivia.

6. Robreño 1961, 52, 69. Most of the *sainetes* of the *teatro vernáculo* mentioned in the literature are not easily obtainable today, in Cuba or elsewhere. One of the few books containing examples of *sainete* texts is the collection *Teatro Alhambra: antología* (Robreño 1979). *La isla de los cotorros* and *La casita criolla* appear in this anthology. Within Cuba, the Centro de Música "Odilio Urfé" at the corner of G and Calzada Streets has the largest extant collection of original *teatro vernáculo* music scores and libretti. On the *sainete* as a forum for political expression, see Leal 1982, 241–67.

7. Leal 1980, 89. Esteban Montejo confirms Leal's figures regarding agricultural pay in *Biografía de un cimarrón* (Barnet 1966, 65).

8. In the 1920s and 1930s, the most prominent theaters in Havana included the Teatro Nacional on the Prado near the Capitol building; the Teatro Regina (earlier called the Molino Rojo and the Teatro Cubano), on the corner of Neptuno and

Galiano; the Principal de la Comedia, on the corner of Animas and Zululeta; the Teatro Martí, at Zululeta and Dragones; the Teatro Encanto on Neptuno, between Industria and Consulado Streets; the Teatro Fausto, at the corner of Prado and Colón; and the Teatro Alhambra, on the corner of Consulado and Virtudes.

9. Rey 1994. While accepted as dancers and musicians, Afrocubans have yet to assume an equal position in theatrical, television, or film productions (ibid.).

10. Peter Manuel points out a striking similarity between stock figures of North American minstrel shows such as "Jim Crow" and "Zip Coon" and those of the Cuban blackface theater (personal communication).

11. "Si las expresiones afrocubanas 'representan' al negro visto con pupila negra ... los autores blancos crearán su antípoda en el negrito, es decir, en el personaje negro representado por actores blancos, para público blanco, actuando en español o en bozal ... y por supuesto, mostrando el punto de vista de la cultura esclavista. Es así que el negrito penetra hondamente en nuestra historia y escamotea la versión del negro para servirse de ella como fuente de burla y escarnio ideológico" (Leal 1980, 30).

12. The Cuban *zarzuela* is derived from the Spanish musical genre of the same name, but was increasingly associated in early twentieth-century Cuba with overtly nationalistic themes. See chapter 5.

13. The song Montaner premiered in 1927, with musical accompaniment that might have come directly from a Rogers and Hart musical, is familiar to most Cubans even today. The version I listened to was recorded by her for Columbia a short time later, '78 #2964-x (96269). The lyrics begin: "When I go out on the Prado [a wide central avenue in Havana] riding in my coach, or in a horse and buggy / All the *mulatas* seeing me there looking so handsome always say: 'Coach driver, you conceited coach driver, I would like to be your lover / If I knew, coach driver, that your love would be true.'" ["Cuando de paseo por el Prado voy con mi volanta o en quitrín / Todas las mulatas al verme tan guapo con zalamería me suelen decir: 'Calesero, pinturero, y quisiera, calesero, ser tu amor / Si supiera, calesero, que sincera también fuera tu pasión.'"]

14. See Rosell 1992 for biographical information on many of these actors. Enrique "Bernabé" Arredondo's autobiography, *La vida de un comediante* (1981), is one of the few books on the life of a *negrito* actor. Except for this volume and passing comments in histories of Cuban theater (e.g., Robreño 1961; Leal 1979, 1980), little research has been conducted on *negrito* performance. Of the actors listed, Sergio Acebal deserves mention as a particularly important figure in the Alhambra Theater, performing there from 1912 until it closed in 1935. Robreño considers Acebal the most influential *negrito* of all time (1961, 59).

15. Of the few extant musical recordings made by the Pous company and other *teatro vernáculo* artists, most can be found in the collection of '78 records at the National Music Museum in La Habana Vieja, Havana.

16. Leal 1982, 235, provides a concise summary of the *mulata* theme in nineteenth-century Cuban theater.

17. Yo soy de azúcar, para querer / Y soy de fuego para el placer / Vengan, vengan a mirar la negrita del Manglar. . . . Es flexible mi cintura, mi corazón un volcán / Por mi preciosa figura cuántos ¡ay! suspirarán" (Hallorans 1882, 79).

18. "La mulata es como el pan; / Se debe comer caliente; / Que en dejándola enfriar / Ni el diablo le mete el diente" (ibid., 64).

19. "Al igual que el negro, [la mulata] tiene un bajo nivel cultural y económico. En ocasiones se le encuentra ligada con el gallego en busca de una posición económica, o lo está con el negro en virtud de una identidad de valores . . . A las características propias de las ideas acerca del papel de la mujer en la sociedad, este género introduce un estereotipo propio de aquella ideología; esto es, la mulata es la representación de la sexualidad . . . es esta función de la mulata, que está acreditando el género, la confirmación de los valores de matrimonio burgués; de una parte, respeto a la 'señora' y de otra, la liberación de los instintos sexuales fuera del matrimonio" (López 1979, 695).

20. Lechuga Hevia 1946, 32. Biographies of early actors and actresses of the *teatro vernáculo* have never been collected. The information I have found often comes from one or two articles encountered after paging through stacks of newspapers and periodicals at the Biblioteca Nacional José Martí and should by no means be considered exhaustive.

21. These observations suggest that the Cuban popular theater may have played a greater role in gradual popularization of *son* than is generally recognized.

22. Alira Ashvo-Muñoz, personal communication. Famous *gallegos* of the Teatro Alhambra included José López Falcó, Francisco "Pancho" Bas, Adolfo Otero, and Regino López (Robreño 1961, 59). Others unassociated with the Alhambra include Federico Piñeiro, Pedro Castany, and Félix Gutiérrez.

23. The dialogue is also disturbingly apropos of the 1990s, given the extremely harsh economic conditions faced by the nation as a result of the collapse of Eastern bloc countries and severely restricted international trade.

24. "Los blancos, a pesar de no poder resistir la sugestión de sus ritmos y bailes, no adoptaron sus tambores. Por sus dificultades y porque no querían 'rebajarse' a tañer 'instrumentos de negros,' es decir (con el criterio de aquel entonces) de gente vil, de bárbaros y salvajes" (Ortiz 1952, 259).

25. "Tenían aquéllas [las guarachas del pasado] un ritmo completamente distinto, y es lo que pudiéramos llamar un diálogo musical, entre las guaracheras y los guaracheros; éstos vestidos con sus camisas alforjadas, pantalón blanco y lustroso botín; ellas con pañuelo a la cabeza y otro que ponían detrás de los hombros y luciendo esas vistosas batas que aún hoy vemos en algunas estampas criollas que nos brinda la televisión" (Robreño 1961, 28). Alira Ashvo-Muñoz tells me that the practice among women of wearing a colorful head scarf is directly African-derived (personal communication).

26. Díaz Ayala suggests that the *guarachera* costume may have also developed in part from the *batas de cola* of Spanish flamenco dancers (personal communication).

27. "Los curros eran agrupaciones que aparecieron en La Habana que trataban de

imitar . . . [a] los negros primeros que vinieron como esclavos directamente de España; . . . hablaban un español muy acentuado y hacían a todos unos parlamentos al estilo del romance . . . y se vestían con un pantalón muy estrecho con pantuflas de piel de venado, con . . . una argolla en la oreja, y un sombrero alón al estilo cordobés y la camisa de seda muy amplia y rizada con pañuelo al cuello. Vestimenta muy parecida a la de los andaluces. En el teatro empiezan a reproducir este traje y a exagerarlo, y ponerle vuelitos en las mangas" (Linares 1992).

28. Recorded examples include Anckermann n.d. 3, Grenet 1932, and Roig n.d. 2.

29. Examples include Anckermann n.d. 1, "Clave a Maceo," a sheet music rendition of what was almost certainly a popular melody of the street in the years after the War of Independence; and Anckermann n.d. 2, "Canción tropical," a *clave* for voice and piano from the zarzuela *El triunfo de la clave.*

30. These pieces were recorded by Pous between 1915 and 1924; see Díaz Ayala 1988, 134–36, on the incorporation of the *pregón cubano* into theatrical performance in the Alhambra and other theaters. See the discography in Díaz Ayala 1995, 212, for the dates of early compositions.

31. Chávez Álvarez 1991, 26–28. Murder suspects in such cases were routinely subjected to imprisonment, torture, and even death. Afrocuban witch trials in Cuba date from the seventeenth century. Chávez Álvarez documents half a dozen well-publicized cases involving multiple defendants between 1904 and 1923 (ibid.).

32. On traditional rumba, see chapter 6.

33. Some would say *stolen* rather than *taken,* as the songs tended to be copy-righted under the name of the professional composer who arranged and notated them, with no attempt to acknowledge or compensate the author of the original melody.

34. Santiago Oquendo deserves mention as a famous *timbalero* of the early twentieth-century theater shows (Soloni 1963).

35. "Zanjadas todas las diferencias, todo queda entre cubanos y alguién propone olvidar las penas con una rumba" (ibid.).

36. "Baile monótono, sencillo, especie de marcha en avance a todo lo largo del salon, cogidos de la mano ambos compañeros, hombre y mujer" (Villoch 1938, 12).

37. "Es un baile que participa de la indolencia criolla y las fogosidades y enardecimientos de los naturales del interior de Africa . . . con toques de bolero andaluz y contoneos en espiral de sugestivo baile flamenco, todo ello envuelto en una atmósfera de intensa voluptuosidad, y revestido de la rumba elegancia que le comunica el rítmico estremecimiento de los hombros, la ondulación lenta y suave de la cintura y las caderas; y el manejo de los brazos, flexibles tentáculos que sostienen y agitan el pañuelo de seda de colores, complemento inseparable de la bailadora" (ibid., 12).

38. "Que dislocaciones y sacudimientos epilépticos los de Pepe Serna. . . . Serna le imprimió a la rumba un raro y nervioso aspecto bailándola con un estremecimiento de todo el cuerpo . . . Y no se engañó el aplaudido popular rumbero de Alhambra; esa es la rumba loca y deslocante, y sacada de quicio, con que hoy triunfan en los

cabarets y en los shows los principales y más renombrados artistas de ambos sexos que la cultivan; Pepe Serna, se le debe, pues, indiscutiblemente, la creación de la rumba moderna" (Villoch 1945, 37).

39. "La rumba no puede ser un texto de arte cubano, porque la rumba es algo que sólo conmueve a aquellas personas carentes en lo absoluto de conocimientos refinados con las bellezas del arte que prodigiosamente supieron manejar Schubert, Chopin" (*La antorcha,* 26 October 1919, 1, 4, quoted in Fernández Robaina 1985, 430). The collection of *La antorcha* at the National Library in Havana is no longer available for examination, apparently having been lost or stolen.

40. "Debe prohibirse porque ese baile que no es típico ni nacional debe desterrarse de las escenarias de los teatros" (*Diario de la Marina,* 26 January 1913, 11).

41. "La rumba," *Diario de la Marina,* 1 February 1913, 3.

42. "Bajo la máscara del negro que ríe, se esconda la mueca de la frustración nacional" (Rine Leal 1980, 83).

Chapter 3. *Comparsas* and Carnival in the New Republic

1. The *corneta china* is actually a double reed brought to Cuba by Chinese indentured laborers in the late nineteenth century. It is associated primarily with the Santiago area, but in more recent times has been incorporated into *comparsa* groups in other parts of the island as well. For a recorded example, see the recent Gloria Estefan release *Mi tierra* (Epic / Sony ET 53807, 1993) which incorporates this instrument (or possibly a synthesized imitation) into the song "Tradición."

2. For some of the best visual documentation of *comparsa* groups from the 1930s, including photos of dancers, instrumentalists, costumes, and the *faroles* (lanterns), see Roig de Leuchsenring 1946.

3. *Carnival in Cuba* (recording, Folkways FE 4065, [1970s?]); *Congas por barrio* (recording, EGREM LD-4471, Havana, 1988); and Harry Belafonte, *Routes of Rhythm* (vol. 1, Rounder compact disc 5049, 1990).

4. Ortiz 1984, 44–45. Ortiz's article on the Día de Reyes celebrations contains extended descriptions of street revelry and music making in Havana of the 1840s, 1850s, and 1860s. It is translated in Bettelheim 1995.

5. "Innumerables grupos de comparsas de negros africanos recorren todas las calles de la capital: la turba es inmensa: su aspecto horroriza . . . El ruido que forman los tambores, los cuernos y los pitos aturde por doquiera los oídos del transeúnte: aquí se ve un falso rey lucumí en medio de su negra falanje: allí un gangá; allá otro de nación carabalí . . . y todos ellos soberanos de un día, cantan con monótono y desagradable sonido en lenguaje africano" (Pérez Zamora, in Ortiz 1984, 47). See Goodman 1873 for similar accounts of street celebrations in Santiago de Cuba.

6. These ideas remained the norm until at least the 1910s and 1920s in Cuba; see Moore 1994 for examples of related ideas in the writings of Fernando Ortiz.

7. Santiago de Cuba developed summer carnival traditions beginning in the late eighteenth century distinct from those of much of the rest of Cuba. See Pérez Rodríguez 1988.

8. "En los ambientes del salón burgués, se organizaban comparsas de jóvenes

blancos que se vestían con algún traje ... representativo. Muchas fueron las comparsas de blancos disfrazados de negros, bien con ridículos atavíos de un negrismo de etiqueta comercial, o copiando la vestimenta del negro sureño de los Estados Unidos. Igual fenómeno se recoge en el carnaval montevideano (León n.d., 24).

9. E.g., Diehl 1992, 19. Blackface carnival traditions have been observed in many other parts of Latin America as well. Aurolyn Luykx (personal communication) notes that blackface troupes are common in Bolivian carnivals in various forms. These include "African zambo" dancing, as well as *bufo*-type presentations performed by military personnel in loincloths. George Andrews discusses blackface groups in the nineteenth-century carnivals of Buenos Aires in *Afro-Argentines of Buenos Aires* (Madison: University of Wisconsin Press, 1980), 161.

10. See chapter 4 on *coros de guaguancó*, considered to be the most popular genre of underclass Afrocuban music and dance entertainment in the western half of the island before the popularization of *son* in the 1910s (León n.d. 25).

11. E.g., *El nuevo criollo,* 27 May 1905, 1.

12. "Todos los años, en los días de Carnaval, presenciamos escenas que desdicen de nuestra cultura y que hacen suponer que en una parte de nuestra población todavía ejercen influencia atavismos que están en pugna con la civilización. [paragraph] El espectáculo resulta ... repugnante: hombres y mujeres, perdida la noción del pudor, al son de música africana y cantando monótono estribillo, recorren en el tropel las calles reproduciendo en sus movimientos gestos que pueden ser lógicos en Africa salvaje, pero que son un contrasentido en Cuba civilizada ... aquellas [comparsas], las que, con pretexto del Carnaval reproducen en nuestras calles escenas salvajes, debieran ser prohibidas por atentatorias á la civilización, á la cultura y al buen nombre de Cuba" (unsigned article, *Cuba y América* 15 [16 March 1912], 8).

13. Castillo Boloy 1916, 4, mentions that the *baile de maní* was frequently incorporated into carnival parades in the 1910s. Ortiz 1981, 396–429, provides an extended description of this dance form.

14. "Una raza [los negros] que necesita para tomar posesión de los derechos que ayer supo conquistar en el campo de la revolución, levantar la vista hacia el cielo y decir 'soy hombre no soy cosa' ... los derechos no se consiguen ni en rumbas ni en comparsas, sino sintiéndose culto" (Castillo Boloy 1916, 4).

15. Angel de la Torre 1918, 1, 6. Fernández Robaina 1985 contains lists of additional articles from this period denouncing specific Afrocuban musical instruments and dance movements.

16. "El año 1913 se quiso que las comparsas salieran custodiadas por un Oficial de policía con los vigilantes a sus órdenes, si bien prohibiéndoles su paso por el Paseo de Martí ... y prohibiéndoles ... el empleo de instrumentos africanos o de sonido parecido, como tambores, güiros y maracas ... y que fueran marchando con danzas, es decir, prohibiéndoles 'bailar o hacer movimientos con el cuerpo al son de la música'" (Ortiz and Vasconcelos 1946, 140). See also Beruff Mendieta 1937, 18.

17. Ongoing tensions over *comparsas* existed even after 1916 (González 1973, 3).

The well-known *comparsa* song "Tira si va' a tirá, mata si va' a matá" (Shoot if you're going to shoot, kill if you're going to kill) dates from this period. It is said to have been written by *comparseros* who played carnival music in the streets despite prohibitions, daring the police with their lyrics and music to take action against them (ibid.).

18. E.g., the *Heraldo de Cuba*, 12 March 1916, 12, entitled "Se acabaron, por este año, las típicas y trágicas comparsas."

19. The *tango-congo* rhythm also bears a striking similarity to certain patterns in *toques de santo* associated with Yemayá (Scott McNitt, personal communication).

20. Issues of *comparsa* copyright arise for the first time during the 1910s as a result of the genre's commercialization. Anckermann copyrighted "Siembra la caña," clearly derived from the earlier Ramírez piece, under his own name, as well as "La chambelona" (to be discussed later). Many professional composers seem to have blatantly appropriated popular street music of the period and made it legally their own without any attempt to locate or recompense the original composers. Similar questions arise in the case of singer Miguelito Valdés and his copywriting of the *comparsa* piece "Los Dandys de Belén," written in the early 1940s by Chano Pozo (Cugat 1992). Valdés and Pozo were good friends, however, so the author would probably not have minded in this case (Leonardo Acosta, personal communication).

21. "Lo quiere todo el pueblo, lo quiere la nación / Batista presidente triunfará sin discusión"; "Ahí viene la aplanadora, Ahí viene la aplanadora, / con Prío adelante y el pueblo atrás."

22. See chapter 7. Many Afrocuban artists also wrote highly political congas during this later period, though they tended to be less frequently heard and performed. Light-skinned trumpeter Julio Cueva, for example, wrote congas in celebration of the defeat of Hitler in the mid-1940s (Cañizares 1991, 36).

23. See, for example, their version of "La chambelona," RCA Victor '78 #79397.

24. Robreño 1981, 81. Urfé 1955 has collected rare examples of political *comparsa* music recreated in the recording studio.

25. "Creé este ritmo para incorporarlo a una banda de circo donde tocaba, allá por Santiago de Cuba, en el año 1912. Este circo era el "Kentucky" . . . De Santiago vine con mi música para Las Villas. En el año 1916, siendo Menocal Presidente de la República, el Partido Liberal presentó la candidatura presidencial del doctor Alfredo Zayas y del Coronel Carlos Mendieta. En plena campaña política surgió mi música y con un conjunto que yo dirigía comenzaron a amenizarse los actos de la calle al son de 'La chambelona.' . . . la primera letra de 'La chambelona decía: 'Viva Gómez y viva Zayas / y el valiente coronel / Viva Sánchez del Portal y el cornetín Rafael' . . . Mi jefe y amigo José Miguel Gómez comprendió que 'La chambelona' estaba destinada a ocupar un lugar preferente en la política. Por eso me hizo llevar a La Habana con mi conjunto" (Fuentes n.d.).

26. Just as all political *comparsas* of the Liberals came to be called *chambelonas*, groups hired by the Conservative Party to play various renditions of "Tumba la caña" were frequently called *congas*.

tradition as the stylistic basis for a few early recordings they made with María Teresa Vera, apparently in 1918 (personal communication). See Díaz Ayala 1994b, 319.

11. Dedicated *santería* initiates were found among classically trained Afrocuban musicians, such as *danzón* orchestra leader Joseíto Valdés, of the Orquesta América, and singer Barbarito Diez.

12. Santiesteban 1985, 54, 331. Perhaps the most common salutation among friends in Havana today employs this term: "¿Qué volá, asere?," roughly translated as "What's happening, man?"

13. My thanks to Cristóbal Sosa for help in clarifying the usage of these terms in early *sones*.

14. Ignacio Piñeiro, "Iyamba Bero," is recorded on Columbia '78 #2421-X (93950).

15. The tendency to use ritual African lyrics in popular song reached its culmination in the 1950s with the recording of dance numbers by Celia Cruz and the Sonora Matancera such as "Yembe laroko" (see Suazo n.d.). This work consists of a complete *santería* liturgical chant in Yoruba arranged for dance band.

16. *Mulé* = white, *bibí* = black, *omó* = godmother or spiritual mother, the one responsible for introducing a devotee to the *santería* religion (Cristóbal Sosa, personal communication).

17. Bacallao 1994; López 1994. Countless authors refer to legislation specifically prohibiting *son* performance at this time, yet no one I interviewed has seen it personally or knows where to find it. My own attempts to locate such documents in the Archivo Nacional in Havana proved fruitless. It remains unclear whether *son* was actually banned by municipal decree or whether it merely became established practice for police officials and others to discourage its performance.

18. Bacallao 1994. Such incidents proved to be of little consequence to the members of this group because they had influential white patrons who could negotiate their release within a few hours.

19. Martínez Furé 1994. Fernando Ortiz began his personal collection of objects associated with Afrocuban cultural expression at this time by requesting them from the police (Rogelio Martínez Furé, personal communication).

20. Cañizares 1978, 41; Acosta 1993, 3. According to *danzón* musician Joseíto Valdés (1994), the USMC was based in offices at 516 San José Street, between Campanario and Lealtad. See Valdés Cantero 1988 on the USMC's activities between 1939 and the mid-1940s.

21. By 1938, Arriete and Collazo managed to convince musicians' unions to accept "orquestas típicas" such as Collazo's own Orquesta Gris as members, but "conjuntos, dúos, tríos y trovadores" were still not allowed to join (Collazo 1987, 175). At this later date, the ACCTI had established offices in the calle Blanco no. 116, Barrio de Colón.

22. The very first *son* recordings were made in 1917 by the Cuarteto Oriental under the direction of Carlos Godínez. The Cuarteto Oriental contained many of the musicians who later recorded as the Sexteto Habanero (Díaz Ayala 1994b, 324).

23. Arango 1994. Pedrito Aróstegui directed the house orchestra of the Pompillo

for many years in the 1930s, while the *conjunto* of Manolo Piñón provided *son* dance music.

24. As with earlier genres including the *danzón,* distinct forms of dancing developed in the process of *son* music's acceptance in new contexts. In ballrooms and other middle-class venues, *son* choreography tended to deemphasize pelvic movement and physical contact. Many dancers became proficient in both "high" and "low" styles and could switch between the two as needed (Martínez Furé 1994). Those in middle-class establishments who moved too suggestively or incorporated too many fancy *vueltas* would be admonished for using *pasillos de academia* (dance steps from the *academia*) by their peers (Linares 1992).

25. Otero (1954, 765, 769) provides some additional information on the history of these establishments. La Tropical dates from the 1880s, while La Polar was established in 1911.

26. Linares 1993. "Entonces Machado, el presidente, llevaba grupos de son a unos jardines de agua mineral que había en San Francisco de Paula, y entonces llevaba allí a sus amigas, a sus queridas y sus mujeres de mundo, y sus amigos políticos, a bailar el son. Y a lugares como ese iban los Mendoza, Paul Mendoza y los banqueros y la gente muy rica de la aristocracia."

27. Ruth Glasser comes to roughly the same conclusion in her analysis of race records in New York (1995, 137). She suggests that World War I may also have played a role by cutting off European trade and forcing companies to explore new markets and musical resources. But, as Steven Feld observes, ideological currents can also affect the marketplace by creating a demand for certain cultural products and images over others (personal communication).

28. All of these dance musics, for instance, are advertised in the *Diario de la Marina,* 4 July 1927, 2.

29. Collazo states that the first stations, including 2MG organized by the Salas brothers, began broadcasting as early as 1918 (1987, 29).

30. Blanco notes that the composition "Tres lindas cubanas," by Septeto Habanero director Guillermo Castillo, won first prize in the festival, held on 23 May, but fails to mention who organized it.

31. Parodies of *son* musicians appear in *Bohemia,* 9 January 1927, 32–33. The caricature, entitled "The Manzanillo Symphony," depicts a group of twenty or thirty Afrocuban musicians, either a *conjunto* or an *estudiantina,* performing on numerous instruments. The faces have been altered to give the impression of brutishness, and the technically unsophisticated nature of many of the instruments has been emphasized to make the "symphony" seem ridiculous.

32. "[El son] es un producto tan nuestro, tan auténticamente cubano, como puede serlo una danza o un bolero . . . Además, en lo que a expresión puramente lírica se refiere, el són . . . ha creado con sus letras un estilo de poesía popular, tan genuinamente criollo como pueden serlo las décimas guajiras . . . Toda una mitología antillana . . . vive en esas coplas" (Carpentier 1930, 151).

33. Rodríguez Domínguez 1978, 112. In the case of the Trío Matamoros, it is

unclear whether this resulted from contractual agreements or an outright swindle on the part of the company.

34. Díaz Ayala 1981, 171; see this author for more details about the history of the Sonora Matancera. The group is unique as a stylistic bridge between the theater orchestra and urban *conjunto*. When the Sonora first arrived in Havana in 1927, they found work in the Teatro Alhambra and in *academias*. Their later popularity and stylistic influence is partly the result of years of live performance as the Radio Progreso house band after 1931.

35. Some sources suggest Arsenio never played with the Sexteto Munamar (David García, personal communication). See Max Salazar, "Arsenio Rodríguez: Life Was Like a Dream" (*Latin Beat* 4, no. 2 [March 1994]: 12–17) and an article about Rodríguez in the *Encyclopedia of Latin American Music,* edited by Frank Figueroa (1995). Nevertheless, the information I gathered in Havana indicates that he did.

36. For a recorded example, see *Memories of Cuba: Orquesta Casino de la Playa (1937–44).* Tumbao CD TCD-003. Switzerland: Camarillo Music, Ltd., 1991.

37. Anacaona was an indigenous leader living in Haiti (Española) at the time of the conquest whom the Spanish tortured and killed despite her overtures of friendship (Ortiz 1965, 46, 68). In the twentieth-century Caribbean, Anacaona has become a symbol of creole pride and independence and is the subject of many songs.

38. Castro et al. 1994. The father of the Castro family was a Chinese immigrant shopkeeper who married a mulatto woman in the 1910s and settled in Lawton, Havana. After deciding to stay in Cuba, he changed his name from Li to Castro.

Chapter 5. Nationalizing Blackness

1. "Atravesamos, en efecto, por natural dictado de madurez histórica y por instinto de defensa contra el vasallaje económica a que nos viene sometiendo el imperialismo americano, un período de intensa afirmación de cubanidad" (Marinello 1929, 134).

2. "Descubierta por Colón en el siglo XV, por los ingleses en el siglo XVIII, por Humbolt y la intelectualidad criolla en el XIX, faltaba que Cuba se descubriera a sí mismo en el siglo XX y eso fue lo que sucedió. . . . Lo que política, social y culturalmente trajo el período de 1923 al 32 fue el espíritu de la época, y con él, la imperiosa necesidad de un cambio" (Fornet 1967, quoted in E. Martín 1971, 99).

3. Saumell, for instance, based some piano pieces on popular genres such as the *clave, guajira,* and habanera (Orovio 1981, 382).

4. See Pérez 1988, 178. The Teller Amendment, amending the declaration of war against Spain, was passed by Congress in 1898. It declared that the United States disclaimed "any disposition of intention to exercise sovereignty, jurisdiction, or control over [Cuba] except for pacification thereof" and asserted "its determination, when that is accomplished, to leave the government and control of the island to its people."

5. The exact amount of Cuban land held by the United States during this period is unclear. Authors who consider only arable land put the figure at over 75 percent, while those who discuss the total land surface of the country suggest that the United States controlled 20–30 percent. See Benjamin 1977, 19, 198.

6. Tiburicio Castañeda, "¡La tierra cubana ya no es de los cubanos!," *Diario de la Marina,* 26 July 1927, discusses the land appropriation issue; see also García Reyes 1928; Quilez 1928.

7. See for instance the commentary on Sindo Garay's "No se puede vivir aquí" and "Tratado de paz" in de León (1990, 55), and "Tiene caña quemá" by Lorenzo Hierrezuelo (León 1984, 128).

8. "Nuestra primera constitución había sido un calco de la Norteamericana; nuestras reformas educacionales . . . fueron propuestas por norteamericanos al comienzo de la República y luego bajo Machado . . . Nuestros Códigos Electorales han sido confeccionados por norteamericanos, nuestro periodismo ha seguido siempre los patrones norteamericanos; el fox trot ha abierto brecha por el territorio isleño; el cine, el cable y el radio nos ha ido imponiendo día a día el ritmo de la civilización comercializada norteamericana; nuestros Clubs y Círculos imitaban al Norte y a Europa olvidando a Cuba y desnaturalizando nuestras íntimas y más fecundas características nacionales . . . nuestra arquitectura seguía los trillos extranjeros, nuestros jóvenes mascaban chicle y fumaban cigarrillos rubios; nuestros hijos jugaban con jugetería norteamericana; los choferes manejaban absolutamente máquinas yanquis, nuestro deporte nacional era el 'base-ball'" (Arredondo 1939, 105).

9. E.g., Sánchez de Fuentes 1923, 1928c. This (racist) author derides jazz music because of its associations with North American blacks as well as its extranational origins. In this sense, he is more consistent than other middle-class listeners who rejected Afrocuban genres as "barbarisms," yet conveniently overlooked the black roots of jazz.

10. Benjamin 1977, 52–65. ABC revolutionaries included many prominent figures in Cuban literary and artistic circles, including Jorge Mañach and Francisco Ichaso, among others (see chapter 7).

11. *Bohemia* 28 (June 1931): 40–41, 54. Photos of corpses and mob retaliation against Machado's supporters after his exile appear in *Bohemia,* November–December 1933.

12. "Y entregados al baile . . . aún en los momentos como los actuales, de más agudas crisis políticas y sociales, parecen los cubanos pretender agotarse física y moralmente con el baile y el juego, en un arrebato suicida de locura colectiva, para anestesiar sus males, dificultades y desgracias" (Roig de Leuchsenring 1932, 80).

13. Rodríguez Domínguez 1978, 133; this song, Miguel Matamoros's "Bomba lacrimosa" (Tear gas bomb), was recorded in 1928 on RCA Victor '78 #46691-b.

14. Cañizares 1978, 49, 55. A rival symphony, the Orquesta Filharmónica de la Habana, began performing two years later under the Spanish conductor Pedro Sanjuan (Acosta 1993, 6). Musicians and composers associated with this group tended to be more progressive and involved in modern, experimental composition.

Most composers of the *afrocubanismo* vanguard had their works premiered by the Filharmónica (see chapter 7).

15. See Wright 1988, 110. Cuba Contemporánea members, who included Fernando Ortiz, José Antonio Ramos, Manuel Sanguily, and Enrique José Varona, came from diverse backgrounds such as law, journalism, and literature.

16. Ironically given its title, *El folk-lor en la música cubana* (1923) and other similar works by Sánchez de Fuentes deal almost exclusively with art music composition rather than "folk" musics.

17. The date of the Cienfuegos festival is unknown, but the Havana events took place in the Teatro Nacional on 16 March 1922 and 28 January 1923 (Díaz Ayala 1981, 104). These concerts were debated in the Cuban Senate, suggesting that they received government support (Collazo 1987, 44). See also the *Diario de la Marina*, 17 March 1922, 8, and 28 January 1923, 7.

18. "El estudio descriptivo encaminado a un fin de verdadera terapéutica social, de ciertas prácticas morbosas, como los actos de brujería y ñañiguismo, en que, en forma tan expresiva se manifiesta la baja vida popular" (del Morro 1923, 49).

19. "Desde hace tiempo, y en todos los tonos, se viene clamando entre nosotros por . . . un arte criollo, que tenga modalidad propia . . . Si por circunstancias geográficas, económicas y políticas de todos conocidas, necesitamos para no perecer como Estado y hasta como pueblo, conservar la lengua, la tierra y la economía, también nos hace falta tener arte en general, y literatura propios, como un medio más que con esos otros, contribuya al robustecimiento y engrandecimiento nacionales" (Roig de Leuchsenring 1927, 18).

20. See Agüero y Barreras on the decidedly limited influence of Siboney music on twentieth-century Cuba (1946, 118).

21. Debate over the origins of the "*areíto* de Anacaona" went on for decades, much of it written by Sánchez de Fuentes and Fernando Ortiz. Sánchez de Fuentes maintained through the 1930s that the *areíto* was written by the Siboneys, as Bachiller y Morales had earlier suggested. But in an exhaustive scholarly essay Ortiz demonstrated that Afrohaitians actually composed the piece and that its text as notated by Bachiller y Morales was derived from Congolese phrases used in Voudun ceremony (1965, 77–87).

22. Sánchez de Fuentes 1928b, 169; Grenet 1939, xxiv. To Sánchez de Fuentes, virtually all musical genres of European derivation in Cuba were influenced by autochthonous musics: "It is not unlikely that the formation of [the unique rhythms of the *danza, danzón,* and *contradanza*] manifest . . . aboriginal elements, as in the case of the *zapateo,* the *punto cubano,* and the *guajira* ("No es de extrañar que en la gestación de estos peculiares ritmos . . . hayan actuado, como hemos manifestado en otras ocasiones, elementos aborígenes, como en el Zapateo, en el Punto Cubano, y en la Guajira") (Sánchez de Fuentes 1928b, 169).

23. On the Montaner recording, see Martínez Malo 1988, 144. The Cueto version is on Victor '78 #81213-a, the Victor Orchestra on '78 #46154-a, and the Bing Crosby English adaptation on Belafonte, *Roots of Rhythm,* vol. 1 (Rounder CD 5049).

24. "Siboney, yo te quiero, yo me muero por tu amor / Siboney, en tu boca la miel

puso su dulzor / Ven aquí que te quiero y que todo tesoro eres tu para mí / Siboney, al arrullo de tu palma pienso en tí . . . Oye el eco de mi canto de cristal / No se pierda por entre el rudo manigual" (Lecuona 1929a; Montaner n.d.).

25. Curet Alonso's Anacaona" is especially noteworthy, given its enduring popularity and parallels suggested in the lyrics between indigenous struggles and those of the Puerto Rican independence movement.

26. These are printed in Anckermann 1942.

27. "¡Cuba! eres un portento de la invicta raza hispana / Mi España de ti se ufana . . ." (Simons n.d., 2).

28. "El movimiento iniciado por algunos compositores, favor de la música afrocubana provocó una violenta reacción por parte de los adversarios de lo negro. A lo afrocubano se opuso entonces lo guajiro, como representativo de una música blanca, más noble, más melódica, más limpia" (Carpentier 1946, 302).

29. "Para los denostadores de lo afrocubano, lo verdadero, lo útil, lo legítamente utilizable—casi con carácter de obligatoriedad—lo específicamente criollo dentro del folklore cubano, es la música del bohío blanco, recortada en el descolorido marco de un aria lacrimosa de Tosti, y las morbideces de una criolla-bolero (marca Donizetti)" (García Caturla 1929, 16).

30. "Sus carácteres físicas—enriquecidas y multiplicadas en su cruce con el blanco y el amarillo—, sus bailes, de un maliciado y encantador primitivismo, lo hacen movito de la mejor plástica. Su música puede llegar a ser lo que nos coloque con mejores títulos en el mapa-mundi de la nueva estética. Los ensayos musicales de nueva fisonomía con ritos afro-cubanos han iniciado una vía hecia [sic] lo esencialmente vernacular, es decir hacia lo universal" (Marinello 1930, 53).

31. "Ninguno de nuestros artistas creadores, nacidos y cultivados en nuestro suelo, gustó nunca de mojar sus pinceles, de modo determinado, en la gama africana. . . . No lo hizo el más sapiente de nuestros maestros, Ignacio Cervantes . . . No lo hizo White . . . no lo hizo Jiménez . . ." (Sánchez de Fuentes 1928b, 190). If one accepts the *cinquillo* as an Afrocaribbean-derived rhythm, this statement is clearly false. White's composition "La sella cubana," for instance, incorporates the *cinquillo* rhythm (Cristóbal Díaz Ayala, personal communication).

32. Some have noted the similarity between discourses about musical "universalization" and those associated with racial *blanqueamiento*. In both cases the goal involves movement away from "blackness" and toward Ibero-European norms. Conceptions of cultural evolution inform the perceived need to "whiten" Afrocuban music, while conceptions of racial evolution led to a desire to blend their physical features with those of Hispanics.

33. Examples include the Ignacio Villa composition "Drumi mobila"; the salon conga "Uno, dos, tres" by Rafael Ortiz; and the *afro* "Lupisamba e yuca ñame" by Sindo Garay (de León 1990, 193).

34. The obvious exception to this overall trend is Lecuona's "La comparsa" (1912), an Afrocuban-inspired work he composed as a teenager well before the period described above. Lecuona referred to "La comparsa" in interviews during the 1950s to justify the claim that he was the first *afrocubanista*.

35. "Hoy es la fiesta de Reyes, fiesta de loca alegría, noche de bella poesía y dulce esperanza y azul ilusión . . . "

36. Margarita Lecuona was a younger cousin of Ernesto and author of the *afros* "Tabú" and "Babalú" from the mid-1930s. For a partial listing of compositions by these authors, see Simons 1929; Grenet 1931, 1932, 1944; and Orovio 1981, 226; 1992, 492.

37. On Cosme and her performance career, see Collazo 1987, 75, 138, 173, 180.

38. Some of Villa's works have recently appeared on the compact disc *El inigualable Bola de Nieve* (EGREM CD-0011, Canada, 1992).

39. Examples of Villa's own work that incorporates conscious *bozal* misspellings of Spanish include the songs "Drumi mobila," an *afro* lulluby, and "Calota ta mori," an elegy about the death of a loved one.

40. Debuté y me tocó la suerte de que no me tiraran hollejos de naranja, ni piedras, ni nada . . . Me aguantaban. Yo seguí abusando de la gente, y hasta ahora estoy trabajando en eso" (Villa 1981).

41. *Cecilia Valdés* filled the theater for more than 100 consecutive performances (Robreño 1967, 79).

42. María la O was a musician and director of the famous Comparsa de Cocuyé in Santiago in the early nineteenth century (Zoila Lapique Becali 1993). Cecilia Valdés is also said to have been a real person who lived in Havana at roughly the same time, although less is known about her. Of course, authors freely added fictional details when writing about such women.

43. Roig n.d., 1; 1990. For the original cast, see Collazo 1987, 109.

44. See Cañizares 1987, 285–99, for a more comprehensive listing of Roig's works.

45. "No hay que ser negro lucumí, ni tampoco un esclavo ya / Para sentir ansias de gozá cuando resuena un bongó . . . Venga ritmo sabrosón, vamos todos a escuchar en la rumba blanca brujona."

46. For a complete listing of the original members, see Collazo 1987, 17, 88.

47. *Diario de la Marina*, 6 February 1937, 34

48. See *Memories of Cuba: Orquesta Casino de la Playa* (1937–1944). Tumbao Cuban Classics TCD-003. Switzerland: Camarillo Music, Ltd. On other jazz bands that played Afrocuban-influenced musics, see Acosta 1993; Díaz Ayala 1981; Blanco 1992; Collazo 1987.

49. *Diario de la Marina*, 12 January 1939, 19.

Chapter 6. The Rumba Craze

1. "Este es el 'siglo de la rumba.' . . . Se baila en los más empingorotados salones; los espectáculos más selectos la han escogido como uno de sus números coreográficos de mayor estimación y mejor gusto . . . en New York, París, Londres y Viena es la señora y tirana de los más refinados cabarets; y en su patria nativa ha sabido con el más cruel y tenaz despotismo cobrarse, en represalia, las repulsas y los desdenes de que la hicieron víctima propiciatoria, cuando era una pobrecita inocente y desconocida" (Villoch 1938, 12).

2. See Ignaza 1989 and Moore 1994. The clearest exposition of Ortiz's thoughts on

transculturation are presented in "Por la integración cubana de blancos y negros." *Estudios afrocubanos* 5 (1945–1946): 217–38.

3. On types of noncommercial rumba and associated rhythmic patterns, percussion instruments, dance movements, and melodies, see Gómez Yera 1964; Martínez Rodríguez 1977; Crook 1980, 1982; León 1984; Jahn 1989; Acosta 1991; and Daniel 1995. For recorded examples of noncommercial rumba, see Carlos Embale n.d., 1988, and tunes such as "Mi guaguancó" and "Chano Pozo" from Mongo Santamaría's *Afro Roots* (n.d.).

4. "Todo caben en ella; todos los ritmos constitutivos de la música cubana . . . Todo lo apto a ser admitido por un tiempo en 2 por 4, es aceptable por ese género que, más que un género, es un atmósfera. Esto sin contar que en Cuba no hay una 'rumba' sino varias 'rumbas' . . . la palabra 'rumba' haya pasado al lenguaje del cubano como sinónimo de holgorio, baile licencioso, juerga con mujeres del rumbo" (Carpentier 1946, 242). Interestingly, Carpentier defines rumba in these terms, yet later in the same book he denounces the diversity of musical forms that came to be associated with the term in the United States (ibid., 360).

5. "Quedan prohibidos los bailes titulados *El papalote* y *El yambú*, como así mismo todo el que no sea conocido su título, y que por su compás, ademanes y trajes indecorosos, fueran obscenos o puedan considerarse que infringen lo mandado en el particular; debiendo el funcionario que esté de servicio, dar cuenta al Jefe de Policía de lo que note respeto al particular" (Roche Monteagudo 1925, 588).

6. Franco 1961, 11. Franco notes that the Paris movement had its counterpart in Germanic countries as well. In particular, he cites L. Frobenius's *Der Schwarze Dekameron* (1910), *Volksmärchen und Volkdichtungen Afrikas* vols. 1–12 (1921–1928), and *Kulturgeschichte Africkas* (1933) as influential.

7. Paul Whiteman, Sidney Bechet, Vernon and Irene Castle, Jackie Coogan, Jeanette MacDonald, and Langston Hughes frequented Paris, as did African-American celebrities Buddy Gilmore and Louis Mitchell.

8. Quoted in Guirao 1938, xviii.

9. "Un producto infernal y diabólico, enviado por el demonio para arruinar a la humanidad . . . un arte de bárbaros, apta únicamente para exitar los fatigados y lúgubres sentidos de un público corrompido y decadente" (Casella 1929, 3).

10. "Cuya situación en la escala de la cultura ocupa apenas el modesto peldaño neolítico" (García Cabrera 1927).

11. The number of Cuban magazine articles of the period featuring Baker and similar artists is astonishing. Photos and/or commentary on Baker, for instance, appear in *Carteles,* April 1928, 21; *Carteles,* March 1928, 7; *Carteles,* 10 June 1928, 17; *Carteles,* 17 June 1928, 11. Information on the Folies Bergères and at least one of their Cuban tours can be found in *Bohemia* 19 (7 August 1927): 24.

12. Meluzá Otero 1945c. Many other white *rumbera* artists deserve mention here who became known internationally in the 1930s. For biographical information on Alicia Parlá, a dancer who worked closely with the orchestra of Justo Azpiazu between 1931 and 1934, see Dorschner (1995, 4e). Parlá's case is especially interesting

in that she began working with Azpiazu in New York by chance while living there in exile during the *machadato*. The orchestra had initially contracted an Afrocuban couple as dancers, but found that the Greenwich Village club where they intended to perform would not allow racially mixed acts. Eventually, Azpiazu sent the Afrocuban couple home and hired Parlá in their place. She had never danced any sort of rumba prior to her debut.

13. Rita Montaner, "Negrita"—Columbia '78 #3226-X (96681). See Lecuona n.d. 4.

14. "Rita Montaner . . . nos grita, a voz abierta, con un formidable sentido del ritmo, canciones arrabaleras, escritas por un Simons o un Grenet, que saben, según los casos, a patio de solar, batey de ingenio, puesto de chinos, fiesta ñáñiga y pirulí premiado. '¿Para qué invocar . . . esas lacras?', me preguntarán algunos . . . ¿Lacras? ¿Lacras las notas de color que constituyen una riquísima y sabrosa aportación folklórica? . . . ¡Pobres de los pueblos descoloridos e insípidos, que carecen de lacras análogas!" (Carpentier 1976, 2:90).

15. "Estoy de acuerdo en que ciertas costumbres primitivas, ciertos hábitos populacheros, surgidos en la ciudad o en el campo, resultan un peligro para la civilización de un país, cuando este país se encuentra todavía viviendo su Medioevo, sin carreteras transitables, sin tranvías y bebiendo de aljibe. Pero cuando se posee una de las más bellas capitales del mundo, cuando se cuenta con ferrocarriles y automóviles en número increíble . . . una nación como Cuba debe enorgullecerse de conservar todavía unas pocas notas de color local. ¡Cuidemos de [nuestra música] guajira, arrabalera y afrocubana! ¡Defendámosla contra sus detractores! ¡Amemos el son, el solar bullanguero, el güiro, la décima, la litografía de caja de puros, el toque santo, el pregón pintoresco, la mulata con sus anillas de oro, la chancleta ligera del rumbero . . . ¡Bendita sea la estirpe de Papá Montero y María la O! . . . ¡Cuando se ven las cosas desde el extranjero, se comprende más que nunca el valor de ese tesoro popular!" (ibid.).

16. See ibid., 2:98. The date of 1923, as given in this anthology, is clearly wrong; it probably should be 1932.

17. Muñoz Albuquere 1989. For a list of the players in this ensemble, see Collazo 1987, 31.

18. Simons wrote "El manisero" in 1922 at the request of Carpentier for a show to be presented in Spain which would feature Cuban folkloric genres dating from the nineteenth century, including the *pregón*. Collazo 1987, 41, 51, maintains that it was initially an instrumental piece, and first became popular in the Havana Yacht Club, where Simons often performed with his dance band. Rita Montaner apparently wrote lyrics for it a year or two later, and first performed it in its present form.

19. "Si una carne ves pasar vacúnala / si la quieres conquistar vacúnala . . . Porque eso del vacunao es lo que da resultao . . . "

20. [Ella:] "Comer quiero yo, comer quiero yo, tasajito con mojo crudo, yuca y quimbombó, y en el manigual después de almorzar a orillitas del Almendares juntos navegar . . . [él:] También tengo yo ganas de comer picadillo y arroz con huevo frito . . . te voy a llevar, te voy a llevar a orillitas de Almendares, china, pa' almorzar . . ."

21. See Perazzo 1988, 42, for a list of such performers, including Vincent López and Eugenio Noble.

22. Bastin and Crump 1991 and Carpentier 1976 both provide useful biographical information on Azpiazu. The Havana Casino Orchestra was apparently the first group to bring exhibition rumba dancers to the United States when they opened on 26 April 1930 at the Palace Theater in New York City. Azpiazu stands out for having been one of the first white bandleaders to accept dark-skinned Afrocubans in his ensemble (Roberts 1979, 98).

23. See King 1938. On the King band, see Claghorn 1973; Rust 1975.

24. Examples of such jazz and Dixieland versions recorded by the Havana Novelty Orchestra are Victor '78 #22597A and B. See Grenet n.d., 2.

25. "¿Cuántas clases de rumbas habrá por ahí, fantásticamente interpretadas? La rumba se ha convertido en un postulado musical del cual han nacido cien postulados más" (Avilés Ramírez 1932, 28–29).

26. "Y con imitaciones torpes como *Sweet Rosita* o *Speak Easy,* los yankees demuestran que ya han comenzado a ejercer sus apetitos imperialistas en el terreno de nuestra música, como los ejercieron ya en tantos otros, y que están bien dispuestos a desempeñar un arbitrario papel en invasión mundial de los aires cubanos, para adornarse una vez más, según vieja costumbre, con plumas prestadas" (Carpentier 1931, 18).

27. "La película es una americanada más, ahora nos tocó a nosotros hacer el ridículo" (Alburquere 1989, 4).

28. *Blue Book Guide to Cuba* (1938), 216. See also *Diario de la Marina,* 14 January 1937, 3.

29. Arango 1995. It is extremely difficult to gather information on the artists and venues associated with Cuban cabaret entertainment. In the interest of providing some basic information, the following is a partial list of *cabarets de tercera* of the period other than those listed above on the beaches in Marianao, and their respective locations: El Kursaal: Habana Vieja on the corner of Oficio and Teniente Rey, said to have had predominantly black clientele (Blanco 1992, 106; Leaf 1948); La Verbena: Playa district in the basement of the Cine Arenal at the corner of Avenues 41 and 26 (Acosta 1993, 14; Blanco 1992, 106; Collazo 1987, 86); El Infierno: Centro Habana on the corner of Barcelona and Amistad (Blanco 1992, 106; Collazo 1987, 87); the cabaret Tokío: Centro Habana on the corner of San Lázaro and Manrique, primarily a jazz locale (Acosta 1993, 18); the cabaret Royale on the corner of Prado and Neptuno (Acosta 1993, 20); and El Pirata: located in Cojímar (Acosta 1993, 21). (On *cabarets de primera,* see chapter 1.)

Cabarets in Marianao other than those listed above include La Playa, La Frita, El Panchín, La Choricera, and El Niche (Acosta 1993, 33). White entrepreneurs such as the Asturian Ramiro González played a prominent role in the creation of what became known as the "beach cabarets of Marianao," one of the areas with the highest concentration of venues featuring Afrocuban artists. The Marianao cabaret district existed through 1964, when they and all other privately owned businesses were outlawed by the socialist government.

30. Campoamor 1966, 26, mentions that although Shueg never performed abroad, he did appear in the films *Un extraño en la escalera* and, with Errol Flynn, *La pandilla del soborno*. See also Leaf 1948.

31. Cristóbal Sosa, personal communication. The commercial video release *Rumbas y comparsas de Cuba* from the 1970s (Havana, Mundo Latino) includes an interesting segment of traditional *abakuá* knife dancing.

32. The only dark-skinned *rumbera* in the Marianao cabarets recalled by informants was Xiomara Alfaro (Arango 1995).

33. Despite their fame, many *parejas de baile* whose photos appeared constantly in publications of the 1930s are now known to music historians only by their first names or stage names, and their careers still generate little interest. With the help of Lázaro Herrera I located Rivero's sisters and interviewed them, but I learned little about Ajón. An article in *Bohemia*, 15 August 1954, gives her real name and a few other details.

34. Information about Curbelo is taken from Padura Fuentes 1988, 8.

35. "Una mujer caribeña, sensual y pecadora . . . cuya tragedia surgía de la transgresión, en contra de su propia voluntad, do los cánones morales" (M. Martínez 1989, 40).

36. "Ideal de mujer para cumplimentar las represiones eróticas y los secretos anhelos del hombre promedio y su machismo autorizado, imagen de la belleza lúbrica codiciada y rechazada a la vez. Prototipo de amante perfecta, pero no de esposa" (ibid., 41).

37. This film starred Roberto Rey, Silvia Morgan, and Luís Arroyo, and featured a musical score by Obdulio Morales. Its plot is based on the unlikely pretext of a white Cuban explorer in sub-Saharan Africa coming across a village in which a white female orphan, Bella, is living. She tells of being abandoned as a child and having been raised since that time by an African tribe who has made her their queen. The explorer takes Bella back to Havana against her wishes, where her "savage" upbringing provides the pretext for extended "bump and grind" dance footage.

38. Fernández Robaina 1994. All of these artists are featured in *Show,* December 1955, 34–35.

39. "Una de las figuras cumbres de nuestra música y nuestra cultura cubana . . . uno de los más puros estilistas de la canción criolla y un profundo conocedor de los ritmos afrocubanos" (Radamés Giró, personal archives).

Chapter 7. Modernism and *Afrocubanismo*

1. "El joven compositor latinoamericano ha comprendido ya que . . . [ciertas] aportaciones étnicas, ciertos mestizajes, ciertos imperativos históricos, sociales . . . han marcado profundamente la formación de su sensibilidad. En busca de sus raices propias, el músico nuestro se agarra, entonces, a lo que más soluciones le ofrece: el folklore . . . Hay ahí una materia rica . . . recogido al estado bruto, donde existía por derecho propio. El acervo es excelente. Pero ahora . . . ¿qué hacer con él? . . . ¡Estilizarlo! . . . Elevar una expresión popular a la categoría universal, por medio del conocimiento, de la ciencia . . . cuando se ha 'etilizado' de esta manera, se obtienen

dos resultados a la vez: ser 'moderno' y ser 'nacional.' ¡Qué gran descanso!"
(Carpentier [1946] 1980, 259).

2. García Caturla n.d. 1; Roldán n.d. 1; León 1991b, 282. Most of their music
remains impossible to locate in recorded or score form. The albums cited contain
only a small fraction of their total output.

3. Cairo Ballester 1976, 1978, 1988.

4. "Creíamos que se podía mantener la vida pública cubana dividida en dos
zonas: la zona de la cultura y la zona de la devastación. Y creíamos que, ampliando
poco a poco, por el esfuerzo educador, la primera de esas parcelas—con artículos,
conferencias, libros y versos—acabaríamos algún día por hacer del monte, orégano"
(quoted in Cairo Ballester 1978, 140).

5. Information about this performance comes from an article in *Carteles,* 12
February 1928, 27.

6. Carpentier 1976, 93. Carpentier mentions that these festivals were organized by
Nicolas Slonimsky and included representatives from many Latin American
countries. Both the 1929 event and another in 1931 took place in the Salle Gaveau
and featured the Staram orchestra with Slonimsky conducting. Musical personalities attending included Sergei Prokofiev, Edgar Varèse, and Charles Ives. Roldán's
"Danza negra" received a warm reception in the first festival, singled out for praise
by Varèse and others (ibid., 94). García Caturla wrote his "Bembé" specifically for
the 1931 event at the request of Carpentier.

7. "Hemos adquirido la mercancía oscura en otros mercados estéticos y la hemos
hecho aforar en las aduanas sin percatarnos de nuestra realidad negra" (Guirao 1938,
xviii).

8. "La poesía negra que se cultiva en las Antillas hispánicas, en Colombia, en
Venezuela o en el Ecuador, no es en su origen otra cosa que poesía española. No es
sólo en el idioma que se vierte la emoción africanista, sino que el arranque creador
también nos ha venido de España" (Ballagas in Kutzinski 1993, 158).

9. Casella 1929, 3. Kutzinski 1993, 158, uses Stuart Hall's term *inferential racism* to
describe the "racist propositions" inscribed in many *afrocubanista* works, and the
unquestioned assumptions about race informing their attitudes.

10. "Este interés marcado de los artistas modernos por esa nueva escuela de
ritmo, que lleva forzosamente a un discurso sonoro rudo, franco, de contornos
angulosos, me ha obligado a pensar más de una vez en el inmenso tesoro que
malgastamos al no utilizar los más ricos recursos de nuestra música nacional. Si
bien la suave y acariciadora 'guajira', 'el bolero', 'la clave' . . . producen a la larga una
sensación invencible de monotonía por la uniformidad de sus acentos y el matiz
tenue de todas sus melodías, los elementos brutos y hasta ahora inexplotados de las
danzas populares, encierran . . . una potencia de ritmos formidables. [La música
afrocubana] podría estilizarse conservándose sus instrumentos y su fuerte sabor,
utilizando esa original y recia 'polirritmia', en creaciones simbólicas, de alto valor
estético, inspiradas directamente en nuestro 'folklore'" (Carpentier in Ballester 1988,
18).

11. Jaime Valls's sketches "Cabeza de mulata achinada" and "Rumba" are reproduced in *Social* 12, no. 12 (December 1927): 19.

12. Fernández de Castro served a brief jail term in 1927 because of his association with the Minoristas and their political activism, but later that year became director of the *Diario de la Marina* (Castillo Vega 1984, 17).

13. Palés Matos helped organize an association similar in many ways to the Minoristas in San Juan, P.R., known as "Los Seis" (Kutzinski 1993, 148). Latin American artists such as Luís Llorens Torres and Ildefonso Pereda Valdés also achieved international recognition for their use of *negrismo* subject matter during the same period.

14. *Atuei* ran from November 1927 to August 1928, and *La Revista de Avance,* March 1927–October 1930. The name *Atuei* is derived from that of the Siboney leader "Hatuey" and represents yet another example of the appropriation of indigenous symbolism in the twentieth century.

15. One such article appears in *Carteles,* 11 March 1928, 12.

16. Examples include editorials entitled "Directrices," *La Revista de Avance,* February 1929, 35–36, and March, 64–65.

17. I have seen no written analysis of this artist's work and know little about him except for fragments of information gathered at a display of his drawings in the Museo de Bellas Artes in the spring of 1994.

18. The Guirao poem first appeared in the *Diario de la Marina,* 8 April 1928.

19. Baguer 1988, 136. Numerous Afrocuban poets could be mentioned here, including Afrocubans Nicolás Guillén and Marcelo Arozarena, as well as Hispanics Vicente Gómez Kemp, Rafael Estenger, and Teofilo Radillo, a lyrical collaborator with Eliseo Grenet who co-authored the songs "Tata Cuñengue" and "Mercé."

20. Cuban blacks and mulattos involved in *vanguardismo* visual art include Wifredo Lam—son of a Chinese father and mulatto mother—Alfredo Peña ("Peñita"), and sculptor Ramos Blanco. Because Lam's work, although still extremely influential, did not address African and Afrocuban subject matter significantly until the early 1940s, it does not fit easily into a discussion of the early *afrocubanista* vanguard. Peña's and Ramos Blanco's creations, though competent, were considerably less influential. Peña's work is characterized by a prominence of political themes and the frequent absence of Afrocuban references. He probably did not share his white contemporaries' enthusiasm for *afrocubanismo,* as the overall attitude toward the movement among the black middle classes was negative.

21. Information about Valls is taken from an interview with his niece (Valls 1994).

22. "Música del bohío, la del batey, la del barrio bajo" (unsigned article in the *Diario de la Marina,* 5 April 1927).

23. "El primero de nuestros artistas que ha tomado la resolución . . . de consagrarse por completo a hacer obra cubana" (Roig de Leuchsenring 1927, 68).

24. This last work appeared in the *Revista de Avance* on April 15th, 1930. Valls's drawings have rarely been reprinted in anthologies of Cuban visual art. Most can only be accessed in archives in the Museo de Bellas Artes in Havana.

25. A black-and-white reproduction of "Antillas," for instance, appeared in

Carteles in June 1928, apparently sent to Havana by Carpentier. The *Revista de Avance* also printed "El triunfo de la rumba" on 15 January 1930.

26. "No quiero ocultarle que desde entonces me he quedado con la desagradable sensación . . . de que, al abandonar aquella manera de pintar, perdí la prenda. . . . Ahora mismo estoy hablando de aquello y todavía—¡han pasado más de treinta años!—siento desasosiego y amargura. . . . Si hubiera ido a conocer santeros babalaos, bembés, fiestas de negros y todo aquello de lo que Alejo me hablaba en París, tal vez hubiera encontrado . . . inspiración. Pero, dejando aparte la falta de tiempo, ¿cómo asistir solo para conocer todo lo mencionado si no sabía cómo comportarme en los lugares donde se encontraba? Y he dicho solo porque . . . no había una sola persona, entre las que yo trataba entonces, que me hubiera confesado su interés por conocer por dentro estos asuntos . . . Y estaba también el miedo a lo negro, el temor a las costumbres que, tal vez por ser casi desconocidas, o mal conocidas, eran tenidas por vulgares . . . no puedo dejar de mencionar que se daba el caso de aquellos—no tan pocos como usted, que no vivió la época, pudiera pensar—para quienes un negro era un delincuente, o, al menos, un delincuente en potencia" (Seone Gallo 1986, 193–94).

See also Martínez 1992 on Carlos Enríquez and Wifredo Lam, other artists who incorporated Afrocuban themes; and Ortiz 1950 on Lam.

27. Despite the importance rhetorically attributed to *afrocubanista* composers of the 1920s and 1930s, surprisingly little scholarship has been produced discussing their lives and works. Musical analyses of even the most famous compositions of the period are virtually nonexistent. Little is known about when such composers first became interested in Afrocuban street musics, the manner in which they studied them, the extent of their knowledge of street genres, and the elements of particular songs or rhythms that influenced their work.

28. "Blasfemia, la peor afrenta que se puede inferir a la música patria" (García Caturla 1929, 15).

29. If it were not for the establishment of the Orquesta Filharmónica by a small group of artists sympathetic to twentieth-century-style composition, the symphonic works of most *afrocubanistas* might never have been performed in Cuba (Asche 1983, 6).

30. Carpentier 1980, 278. A well-known essay by Sánchez de Fuentes (1928b) denying African influences in Cuban music is said to have resulted from controversy in the press over "Tres pequeños poemas" (ibid.).

31. "La obra nacional de engrandecer nuestra música no debe sacrificarse al interés bastardo de atraer al populacho—siempre dispuesto a la vulgaridad y a las regresiones—al reclamo de un tambor africano . . . Hora es ya de puntualizar nuestra personalidad musical . . . nuestro deber es moralizarla y nunca prostituirla" (Sánchez de Fuentes 1928c, 35).

32. "La rebambaramba" is based on the music and dance of nineteenth-century Día de Reyes celebrations, while "El milagro de Anaquillé" incorporates *guajiro* musical fragments, as well as those of *abakuá* origin. See Béhague 1979, 148–49, for

more information about "El milagro de Anaquillé." Carpentier 1946, 307–18, provides commentary on "Rítmicas" and "Motivos de Son."

33. Martínez Furé 1994 notes that "El milagro de Anaquillé" incorporates the melody of a sacred song to Yemayá entitled "Soku taniwo," meaning "Yemayá is the goddess of riches."

34. "Yamba-O" is a Carabali phrase which Carpentier translates as "loado seas" or "praise be unto you" in his novel *Ecué Yamba-O* from 1933 (Carpentier 1977).

35. H. González 1973. Caturla wrote "La rumba" with the intention that it be sung by Rita Montaner, although she apparently never did. Today "La rumba" is typically performed by Cuban orchestras without a vocalist, for reasons which remain unclear (H. González 1994).

36. Béhague 1979, 150. One of the most comprehensive studies of García Caturla's work is the extended essay "La obra musical de Alejandro García Caturla" by Adolfo Salazar. It appears in *Revista cubana* 11 (January–March 1938): 5–43.

37. Asche refers particularly to García Caturla's "Preludio corto" as a good example of a work incorporating polytonality and canonic imitation, and to Roldán's "Preludio cubano" as one quoting nineteenth-century Cuban art music. In this case the citation comes from the Santiago composer Laureano Fuentes Matons.

38. Given the popularity and broad dissemination of his work during his lifetime, it is striking that little has been written about Valdés, unlike Roldán and García Caturla. Helio Orovio's *Diccionario de la música cubana* from 1981 contains no entry for Gilberto Valdés, and the 1992 edition a brief entry. Valdés's absence from the first volume may reflect the fact that he did not support the 1959 revolution, and was excluded (against Orovio's wishes) along with dozens of other artists living in the United States.

39. The only copies I was able to find of this and most other works by Valdés are unpublished manuscripts in the archives of the Museo Nacional de la Música.

40. "Deduzco la inferioridad de la música de los siboneyes, aún comparándola con la de los negros africanos, no obstante estar ambos en la primera étapa de su evolución social" (Agüero y Barreras 1946, 115).

41. "Tiene hondos, muy hondos raíces: se remonta a los tiempos en que el hombre no había calibrado el sonido, no había divido sus vibraciones . . . Entonces . . . el hombre no hablaba, gritaba espontáneamente inflexiones" (Sanjuan 1930, 36).

42. "De carácter agreste y rudo como todos los cantos primitivos" (Simons 1927a).

43. "Si los aportes africanos son rudimentarios (tan rudimentarios como los indios . . .), es bien natural que sea así. . . . Rudimentarios, embrionarios casi, han sido todos los aportes musicales en los comienzos del arte . . . sus características melódicas, armónicas y rítmicas fueron aprovechadas luego por los grandes compositores para forjar sus obras maestras" (Simons 1927d, 42).

44. "En presencia de catecúmeno salvaje, el misionero despliega una política de conversión, en el justo significado del término. Suaviza sus instintos, afina su sensibilidad, lo educa, lo civiliza en fin" (Ichaso 1928).

45. "[Faltan] totalmente de sentido tonal, de 'plan' armónico basado sobre el cimiento histórico de la música europea . . . como una catedral que pretendiera elevarse sobre la arena. Precario edificio. Lo propio del negro no es la catedral, sino el bohío" (Salazar 1938, 12).

46. "Una música primitiva, música que parece hallarse en una etapa ancestral del arte, cuando . . . no existían aún las fórmulas de cocinar el arte en los conservatorios y en los tratados de composición"; "Una rumba mejor que las que se oyen en los solares, pero en el fondo, la misma cosa." (ibid., 16–17).

47. "En el Club Atenas se llegaba al absurdo de que las orquestas eran obligadas por la 'Comisión de Orden' a tocar valses, foxtrots, danzones o boleros, y se les prohibía terminantemente ejecutar rumbas, sones y mambos. Mientras tanto, los blancos de 'buena sociedad' se desarticulaban bailando la música de los negros, y la tradición exigía terminar la fiesta con una conga callejera" (Acosta 1993, 34).

48. Black and mulatto Cubans on the whole reject this term even today.

49. "Self-determination" (autodeterminación) refers to the proposal supported by early Communist Party leaders of creating a separate black nation for Afrocubans in Oriente Province; see chapter 1.

50. "Al mismo tiempo que la teoría de la 'auto-determinación' camina en Cuba la corriente de 'afrocubanismo.' Se hacen 'versos negros,' se hace 'arte negro,' se escriben 'artículos negros,' . . . se celebran actos y conmemoraciones referentes al negro o a lo negro . . . Y nada más absurdo, más confusionista, más desnaturalizador de los problemas de 'lo negro en nuestra nación' y 'el negro en nuestra realidad social,' que esa etiqueta injusta de 'afrocubanismo'" (Arredondo 1939, 107).

51. "Esa que pretende llamarse poesía negra, deja muy mal parado al negro, porque lo caricaturiza, desfigura sus trazos y lo presenta en un ambiente que no es el suyo, en un mundo en el cual los negros no viven ni quieren vivir" (ibid., 116).

52. "Una especie de fuga, una sublimación inconsciente de aquella actitud marginal en que creíamos deber y poder mantenernos. . . . Lo que nos rodeaba era tan sórdida, tan mediocre . . . que buscábamos nuestra redención espiritual elevándonos a planos ideales, o complicándonos el lenguaje que de todas maneras nadie nos iba a escuchar" (quoted in Cairo Ballester 1978, 140).

Conclusion

1. E.g., Victoria Eli Rodríguez's discussion of "mono ethnicity" (1995, 91).

2. See, for instance, "What Color Is Black?" Newsweek, 13 February 1995, 62.

3. Anthropologist Nadine Fernández told one such joke to me that was popular in Havana in 1993, a result of the appointment of Afrocuban Esteban Laso to head the Communist Party in Oriente: "What is the difference between Paris and Santiago de Cuba?" Answer: in Paris they have the Mona Lisa, and in Santiago they have the mono [monkey] Laso." See also Feijóo 1987, 105–08.

4. Thompson made such comments at a public lecture in 1993 at the University of Texas, Austin.

5. Slurs of this sort referring to "los negros" often come from individuals of mixed racial background who would be considered black in the United States.

6. "Por medio de esos elementos afrocubanos, queríamos reaccionar contra la sensiblería, contra la languidez, contra la melodía sin nervio ni estructura. La reacción era, tal vez, excesivamente radical, como suele serlo toda reacción. Pero era un medio de orientar el público hacia géneros distintos creando en él una conciencia nueva de la diversidad de su folklore y de las posibilidades sinfónicas que ese folklore ofrecía. . . . Claro está—y puedo confesarlo ahora—que no nos ilusionábamos demasiado acerca de las posibilidades de lo afro-cubano. Sabíamos que un folklore, por rico que sea, no puede alimentar eternamente a un músico que habrá de situarse, tarde o temprano, ante los problemas eternos de la música universal" (Carpentier 1944, 4–5).

7. "Puede haber un compositor que no trabaje con estos elementos folklóricos . . . Si este compositor no persigue vanas entelequias ni un universalismo sin raices, sino que produce de acuerdo con un estado de sensibilidad que es producto legítimo de su medio cubano . . . su música podrá ser tan cubana como la del que trabaje directamente con nuestro folklore" (Ardévol 1945, 4).

8. One of the first examples is the Santero album (Panart LD-2060) featuring traditional *batá* drummers Jesús Pérez, Trinidad Torregrosa (one of Fernando Ortiz's primary musical informants), and others in addition to singers Cruz, Valdés, and Caridad Suárez.

9. "La 'afromanía' ha querido revalorizar elementos folklóricos negros, o supuestamente negros; y en este género de proceder se han echado al olvido verdaderas creaciones de la tierra y la nación, que están pereciendo bajo la rudeza de los ritmos de los instrumentos de percusión" (Martín 1954, 650).

10. See Martínez Furé, in Manuel 1991, on attitudes of the 1960s socialist government toward Afrocuban street culture. The article does not reflect Martínez Furé's own views, despite what he says. It was written during a period of intense intellectual repression by the government during which he could publish only by espousing the views of the Communist Party.

11. Re-released on *Superexitos: bailables cubanos*. Areíto/EGREM cassette #C-141. Havana, 1993.

12. Mercedita Valdés, *Aché*. Areíto/EGREM cassette #C-230. Havana, 1992. This cassette is a second re-release of one made in Santiago de Cuba in 1985.

GLOSSARY

abakuás: Groups of predominantly Afrocuban men belonging to secret social groups, also called *ñáñigos.* These organizations derive from African traditions in the Cameroon area. *Abakuá potencias,* or brotherhoods, have been described as "cults of masculinity." Their ceremonies incorporate singing and drumming as integral elements.

Academias de baile: Dance academies, working-class recreational institutions associated with dance, musical entertainment, and prostitution. Popular in Cuba through at least the 1940s, they derive from similar nineteenth-century venues called *casas de cuna. Academias de baile* are of fundamental importance to the early popularization of the *son* in Havana.

afro: A musical genre first popularized in Cuba during the 1920s and 1930s that makes overt lyrical and musical reference to Afrocuban culture. *Afro* lyrics include allusions to *santería* ceremony, African deities, or descriptions of slave life in the nineteenth century. They tend to be written in *bozal* speech and frequently incorporate the two-measure *tango-congo* rhythm mimicking the drumming of nineteenth-century Kings' Day celebrations.

afrocubanismo: Afrocubanism, an artistic movement of the 1920s and 1930s similar in many respects to the Harlem Renaissance. The works of this period, while often written by white, middle-class artists, typically took their inspiration from black working-class street culture.

afrocubanista: A member of the *afrocubanismo* movement, or pertaining to the *afrocubanismo* movement.

afrocubano/afrocubana: Afrocuban.

agrupaciones de guaguancó: See *coros de guaguancó.*

areíto: A sacred form of expression among Cuba's indigenous, pre-conquest population involving music, communal dancing, singing, and ritual consumption of tobacco and alcohol.

atraso: Backwardness, a term used in the early twentieth century among Cuba's middle classes to describe African-derived culture and its perceived detrimental effects on the nation. *Santería* ritual, traditional rumba performance, *abakuá* ceremony, and similar practices were often denounced as manifestations of *atraso.*

autodeterminación: Self-determination, a term applied to the proposal by Cuban Communist Party leaders in the 1920s and 1930s to create a separate nation for Afrocubans in Oriente Province rather than accept them as citizens in the existing Republic.

babalaos: Male, primarily Afrocuban, religious leaders who specialize in predicting the future and soliciting divine intervention with the help of their Yoruban-derived patron saint, Orula.

baile de maní: Peanut dance, one of many African-derived dance forms common in late nineteenth-century Cuba and a precursor of *rumba columbia.* It was performed to the sound of *yuka* drums (derived from the Congo region) by a circle of male dancers surrounding a lead dancer. Its choreography involves belligerent gestures and blows inflicted by the leader, while the others defend themselves while continuing to dance.

bando: Government decree, ordinance.

bandola: A Spanish-derived string instrument similar to the guitar.

barracones: Slave barracks.

barrio: Neighborhood, city district; sometimes a lower-class area or slum.

batá drums: A set of three sacred, double-headed drums used in *santería* ceremony. In decreasing order of size, they are: *iyá, ikónkolo,* and *itótele* (Yoruban names).

beguine/biguine: An early twentieth-century dance music genre from Martinique and Guadeloupe.

bembé: An informal devotional event observed by many practitioners of African-derived religions in Cuba. *Bembés* are organized around music and dance performances in praise of the *orichas* (African deities). Food and drink are also ritually offered on an altar, then consumed by participants at the end of the evening.

blanco/blanca: White.

blanconazo/blanconaza: See *mulato blanconazo.*

bongó: The Cuban term for the bongo drum consisting of two single-headed drums of slightly different size fastened together in a wooden frame. The smaller drum is called the *macho* or male, the larger drum the *hembra* or female.

bonkó: A long, single-headed drum performed during *abakuá* ceremonies. One performer plays the head of the drum with his hands, while another beats on the shell of the instrument near the base with wooden sticks.

botao: A dance movement performed by women in traditional *rumba guaguancó* in which the *woman* takes a step away from her partner and covers her groin.

botija: Also *botijuela.* A bass instrument made from a ceramic jug associated with Cuban *conjuntos de son* before about 1925. Typically, the jug originally contained olive oil imported from Spain.

bozal: A term often used to describe the broken Spanish of recently arrived African slaves, and by extension that of free blacks with little formal education. *Bozal* speech was an important element in works written for the Cuban blackface theater, adding to the humor of sketches involving the *negrito*. It is also heard in many *afro* compositions of the 1920s and 1930s.

brujería: Witchcraft, a term used for many years to refer to all forms of African-derived religious activity in Cuba.

cabaret de primera: First-class cabaret, a large establishment with a wealthy, white clientele and a diversity of stage acts offered each evening.

cabarets de segunda/tercera: Second- and third-class cabarets, cheaper and more modest in size than *cabarets de primera,* they accepted Afrocubans as patrons and performers more frequently.

cabildos: Afrocuban social groups of the nineteenth century that were an important means of perpetuating African cultural traditions in Cuba. With the permission of colonial authorities, slaves and free blacks from virtually every West African ethnic group formed *cabildos* to help newcomers adapt to the new environment.

cachumba: A secular Afrocuban dance form popular in the nineteenth century. As with related genres such as the *caidita* and *cangrejito,* there is little documentation about the dance.

caidita: See *cachumba.*

calypso: A genre of popular song from Trinidad associated with carnival celebrations with English, French, and occasionally West African lyrics. Lyrics are often improvised and may be humorous, bawdy, satirical, or political in nature.

carrozas: Carnival parade floats.

casas de cuna: Centers of music, dance, and prostitution in nineteenth-century Cuba. They were frequently owned and managed by mulatto women, themselves former prostitutes. *Casas de cuna* provided important areas of social contact across racial and class lines.

catedrático: See *negrito.*

cervecerías: Beer factories, among the first commercial venues to contract *conjuntos de son.* Large *cervecerías* in Havana such as La Polar and La Tropical staged concerts for the working classes in outdoor beer gardens beginning around 1900.

chachachá: A genre of ballroom dance music popularized in Cuba in the early 1950s that developed out of the *danzón, danzonete,* and *son.* It was performed primarily by *charanga* ensembles.

charanga: A dance ensemble (also called *charanga francesa*) that developed in the early twentieth century out of the *orquestas típicas.* Initially, they included many horns and wind instruments in addition to the *timbal,* bass, piano, violin, and *güiro,* but later horns were replaced by more violins and a flute. *Charangas* performed primarily *danzones, danzonetes,* and *chachachás.*

chéquere: An African-derived musical instrument consisting of a dried gourd around which a net with seeds, nuts, or beads is fastened. The net is pulled or manipulated over the gourd, creating percussive sounds. The gourd itself can also be struck on the bottom, producing a clear, resonant tone.

chismosa: The gossip, a variant of the *mulata* stage personality developed in the Cuban blackface theater.

cinquillo: A five-beat rhythmic pattern characteristic of the *contradanza* and *danzón*. It is said to have been brought by French colonists and their servants fleeing Haitian slave insurrections in the 1790s. *Cinquillo* rhythms are also found in the music of Puerto Rico and Dominican Republic.

clarina: The female lead singer of *coros de clave,* Afrocuban music groups of early twentieth-century Havana.

clave: A two-measure repeating figure, found in virually all Cuban music, that provides a rhythmic foundation. The term can also refer to a variety of these rhythms (such as the *clave* pattern associated with the *son*), as well as an instrument, the *clave* sticks on which many *clave* rhythms are performed, and occasionally to the vocal genre most often performed by turn-of-the-century *coros de clave.*

comparsas (also *congas*): Afrocuban carnival bands. Similar groups were organized by *cabildos* in the nineteenth century that performed on Kings' Day (6 January). In recent years, *comparsas* are formed by residents of neighborhoods in Havana, Santiago, and other cities. Each group has approximately thirty members and includes drummers, horn players, singers, and dancers.

comparsero/comparsera: A performer in a *comparsa* group.

conga: A term that can mean (1) a woman of Congolese origin; (2) pertaining to the Congo; (3) a campaign melody written for the Conservative Party; (4) traditional *comparsa* music (from the Bantu term *maconga,* or song); (5) a *comparsa* band; (6) a *conga* drum of any type; and (7) the jazz-influenced dance music (derived from stylized representations of street *congas* in Cuban blackface theater) incorporating some traditional *comparsa* rhythms that became popular in Europe and the United States during the "conga craze" of the mid-1930s.

conga drum: A stave drum patterned after African percussion instruments but created by the Afrocuban community. *Conga* drums come in various sizes, of which many musical genres incorporate two or three. The drum with the deepest tone is often called the *caja;* the smaller drums are the *conga* or *tumbadora* (terms that can also apply to all *conga* drums) and the *quinto* or *salidor.*

conguero: A *conga* drum player.

conjunto de son: A common term used in the 1920s and 1930s to describe the six- or seven-member bands playing *son* music. Such groups included *tres,* guitar, maracas, bongo drums, *clave, botija* or acoustic bass, and sometimes trumpet. *Conjunto* more recently refers to any smaller dance band playing *son* music, often with an electric bass and the addition of *conga* drums and/or additional horn players.

contradanza: A nineteenth-century ballroom dance genre, similar to square dance, derived from the English country dance and the courtly French *contredanse.* This genre was popularized in Cuba in the late eighteenth century by Haitian colonists fleeing slave insurrection.

copla: Couplet.

coros de clave: Afrocuban choral ensembles common in the late nineteenth and early twentieth centuries that contributed to the development of the modern *son.* Frequently, singers accompanied themselves on instruments such as the *viola* (a small bass or banjo without strings used as a percussion instrument), guitar, *clave,* harp, and *botija.*

coros de guaguancó: A more percussive form of the *coro de clave* that often incorporated the drums associated with traditional rumba; they were also known to include European instruments.

costumbrismo: An artistic movement that emphasized the quaint or humorous elements of everyday life and prevailing customs. *Costumbrista* works for the blackface theater frequently emphasized Afrocuban music, dance, and street slang.

costumbrista: One affiliated with the *costumbrismo* movement; pertaining to *costumbrismo.*

criolla: A middle-class Cuban vocal genre, similar to the *canción,* that borrows heavily from European parlor music and art song of the early twentieth century. The *criolla,* typically in moderate 6/8 time, contains lyrics that allude to Cuba's natural beauty or other nationalist themes.

cuarteta: Quatrain.

danzón: An instrumental dance genre that was developed in Matanzas during the late nineteenth century out of the *danza* and *contradanza* and first popularized in black middle-class *sociedades de color. Danzones* are typically in duple meter and are danced by a couple. In the nineteenth century, ensembles that performed them were called *orquestas típicas;* in the early twentieth century they were performed by *charangas.* The popularization of the *danzón* corresponded closely to the final years of war against Spain. After 1898, *danzones* became an important national symbol.

danzonero: A performer of *danzones.*

danzonete: A subgenre of the *danzón* that became popular in Cuba in the late 1920s. It differs from the *danzón* only in that it incorporated vocal melodies and also occasionally a *son*-derived *montuno* section.

décima: A form of sung poetry (formally composed or improvised) and a subgenre of *música guajira,* the music of rural Hispanic farmers. The metrical form, first developed in medieval Spain, consists of ten eight-syllable lines with the *espinela* rhyme scheme *(abbaaccddc).* Melodies associated with *décimas* are stylized and formulaic, while the lyrics are of primary importance.

diablitos: Male Afrocuban dancers (also called *íremes*) who performed during Kings' Day events of the nineteenth century in masks and full-body raffia costumes. This African-derived tradition was perpetuated primarily by *abakuá* initiates. Municipal repression of *abakuás* and Afrocuban dance in the early twentieth century resulted in the decline of the tradition.

Día de Reyes: Kings' Day (Epiphany, 6 January), a holiday throughout much of the nineteenth century when slaves and free blacks were allowed to dance, sing, and play percussion instruments in the streets. The Día de Reyes was essentially a form of segregated carnival, in that most Afrocubans were not allowed to participate in pre-Lenten carnival celebrations.

diálogo: Dialogue, a term used in the comic theater to describe comic sketches recorded on '78 RPM records in the early twentieth century.

diatonic scale: Seven-tone scale, the traditional major scale of Western classical music.

ecué/ekué: A sacred friction drum used in the ceremonies of *abakuá* groups. The instrument is hidden from view so that even most initiates never see it being played.

ejército permanente: Permanent army, a national military force created with the aid of the United States during the first years of the Republic to help assure political stability in Cuba. José Miguel Gómez employed the *ejército permanente* against Afrocuban protesters in the Little War of 1912 (Guerrita del Doce). Afrocuban soldiers employed in this force also helped popularize the *son* genre in Havana at about the same time.

Escalera conspiracy: In the mid-1840s, one of the most brutal periods of repression of the Afrocuban community in Cuban history, an alleged plot among the black middle classes to foment slave rebellion gave rise to imprisonment, torture, and execution of thousands of citizens.

españoles: Spaniards.

estudiantinas: Bands of strolling student musicians who performed mostly in eastern Cuba near Santiago. They were among the first groups to perform *son* music in urban areas using both traditional string and percussion instruments, as well as others such as cello, flute, violin, and *timbal.*

farándula: A term for all those associated with popular entertainment—musicians, dancers, actors, and models. The *farándula cubana* might translate roughly as the Cuban entertainment industry, or the stars of popular culture.

farol: Lantern, a name given to the fancy parade standards with colored lanterns attached to them carried by *comparsa* ensembles during carnival celebrations.

gallego: Galician Spaniard. In the blackface theater, the *gallego* had a comical Spanish accent, a strong attraction to mulatto women, and an inability to dance.

guaguancó: One of the best known and most commonly performed subgenres of traditional rumba (also called *rumba guaguancó*). It is similar to earlier forms such as the *yambú* in that its choreography represents a stylized enactment of attempted sexual conquest. The *guaguancó* was adapted at the turn of the century for the *teatro vernáculo* and as cabaret entertainment after the 1930s.

guajira: A subgenre of the *son,* associated with rural areas, that is performed in a moderately slow duple meter and features the guitar and *tres* or *bandurria,* maraca, and cowbell, among other instruments. Its lyrics often celebrate the beauty of the Cuban countryside.

guajirismo: An artistic movement of late nineteenth- and early twentieth-century Cuba that adopted the rural Hispanic peasant and related cultural forms as symbols of the nation. It was manifested in poetry, literature, song lyrics, and visual art.

guajiro/guajira: Rural Hispanic farmer, peasant; pertaining to the *guajiro* or *guajiro* culture.

guapo: Brave, prone to violence and bullying; also, an individual given to violent outbursts of anger. The term, often associated with Afrocubans, can also mean handsome or elegantly dressed.

guaracha: A working-class, Afrocuban genre of vocal (and often dance) music that developed in the nineteenth century and was popularized through the *teatro vernáculo.* In this century *guarachas* have been heavily influenced by the Cuban *son,* differing from other *sones* in being faster in tempo and incorporating bawdy or satirical lyrics.

Guerrita del Doce: The Little War of 1912, a massacre of thousands of Afrocuban protesters in Oriente Province by the *ejército permanente* under orders of President Gómez. Most of the victims were members of the Independent Party of Color (PIC), a political organization devoted to equal rights for blacks and mulattos. The Congress had denounced the PIC as racist and declared it illegal earlier that year.

güiro: Gourd scraper, an Afrocuban percussion instrument created from a notched dried gourd scraped by a stick. Similar instruments can be found in Puerto Rico, the Dominican Republic, and elsewhere.

habanera: A Cuban vocal music and dance genre derived from the *danza* that reached the height of its popularity in the late nineteenth century. It is performed in a moderate 2/4 meter, incorporates major-minor sectional modulations, and is associated with a unique isorhythmic pattern (the habanera rhythm). This genre became popular in Argentina, influencing the development of the tango.

habanero/habanera: A Havana native; pertaining to Havana.

indigenismo: An artistic movement, common to a number of Latin American countries in the late nineteenth and early twentieth centuries, that adopted indigenous groups and culture as symbols of the nation. In Cuba, many who advocated independence from Spain in the 1870s and 1880s expressed themselves through *indigenismo* poetry celebrating Siboney and Arawak culture.

indio/india: One whose physical features suggest some indigenous ancestry; pertaining to Indians or indigenous groups.

isleño: Someone born in Cuba (as opposed to Spain); pertaining to the island.

jaba'o: A light-skinned Cuban with Negroid hair and/or facial features.

Ladder Conspiracy: See Escalera conspiracy.

ladino: A term applied to early emigrants of African ancestry who came to Cuba directly from Spain. *Ladinos* spoke an ornate form of Andalusian Spanish and wore fancy clothing. Their speech and dress is said to have influenced representations of the free Afrocuban community in the *teatro vernáculo.*

lamento: Slave lament, a slow, melancholy song of a slave who cries out for freedom. The genre, popular among *afrocubanismo* composers of the 1920s and 1930s, often featured a *tango-congo* rhythm in the accompaniment and *bozal*-style lyrics. Many appeared in *zarzuela* productions.

Liberales: Members of the Cuban Liberal Party of the early twentieth century.

liceos: See *sociedades de color.*

machadato: The period from 1928 to 1933 associated with escalating violence between forces loyal to Gerardo Machado and those attempting to topple his government.

mambi/mambises: Soldiers in the Cuban Wars of Independence against Spain, most of whom were Afrocuban.

maraca: A Cuban percussion instrument traditionally made from small dried gourds into which seeds or similar objects are placed.

María la O: A beautiful, semi-mythical *mulata* figure immortalized in many popular songs as well as a *zarzuela* of the same name by Ernesto Lecuona. María la O was a musician and director of the famous Comparsa de Cocuyé in Santiago in the early nineteenth century. Little else is known about her.

marímbula: An African-derived instrument used to provide a bass accompaniment in some early *conjuntos de son. Marímbulas* are constructed from large box resonators with a hole cut in them allowing sound to escape. Near this opening a number of steel metal strips are fastened. *Marímbula* players sit on the box itself and pluck the strips of metal, each of which has been tuned to a particular pitch.

marquillas: Fancy cigar labels with colorful and highly detailed illustrations that often depicted interactions between Afrocuban women and white men. They were an important form of *costumbrismo* art.

maxixe: Turn-of-the-century Afrobrazilian dance music associated with urban areas and played in a moderate duple meter. It is danced by a couple.

Minorismo: An elite, academic, pan-artistic movement of the *afrocubanismo* period, roughly synonymous with *vanguardismo.* Advocates of the most progressive tendencies of the day, Minoristas aspired to reconcile the *afrocubanismo* aesthetic with that of experimental modernism.

Minorista: A member of the Minorismo movement; pertaining to the Minorismo movement.

montuno: Pertaining to the mountains or the countryside. Also, the final section of a *son* composition, characterized by a cyclic, African-derived formal structure, prominent improvisation, and call-and-response interaction between a chorus and a vocal or instrumental soloist.

moreno: Mulatto, with coffee-colored skin.

mozambique: A style of Cuban dance music invented by Pedro Izquierdo (Pedro el Afrokán) in the early 1960s and used in carnival celebrations. It is characterized by a fusion of rhythms associated with *comparsa* bands and others derived from *santería* ceremony.

mulata del rumbo: A nineteenth-century term for free women of color who enjoyed parties and were sexually promiscuous. Many frequented or managed *casas de cuna.*

mulato/mulata: Mulatto, of mixed Caucasian and Negro ancestry. In the blackface theater (and later in the *zarzuela*) the *mulata* was an important stock character, the epitome of sexual attractiveness, with the *negrito* and the *gallego* competing for her attention. Variations include the *mulata borracha* (the drunkard), the *mulata chismosa* (the gossip), and the *mulata sentimental* (a maudlin figure).

mulato blanconazo: A mulatto that can pass for white.

música guajira: Country music, a generic term for various types of music and dance heavily influenced by Spanish traditions that are performed primarily in rural areas by white/Hispanic farmers. See *guajiro.*

ñáñigo: See *abakuá.*

negra lucumí: An African woman of Yoruban descent. In the blackface theater, she is a witch, a mystic figure who predicts the future and casts spells.

negrismo: See *afrocubanismo.*

negrista: Black, pertaining to or influenced by Afrocuban aesthetics.

negrito: "Little black man," with the *mulata* and *gallego,* a stock character of the *teatro vernáculo.* Invariably played by a white actor in blackface, the *negrito* is a buffoon similar to those featured in U.S. minstrel shows. Subcategories include the *negro bozal* (a recently arrived slave who speaks poor Spanish), the *negro catedrático* (pretentious, semi-educated slave), the *negro calesero* (coach driver–slave), the *negro guarachero* (fun-loving slave), and the *negro jaranero* (a troubador).

negro/negra azul: "Blue" black, a very dark-skinned black.

negros curros: Gaudily dressed free blacks. *Curro* initially referred to someone from southern Spain. In nineteenth-century Cuba it became closely associated with an Afrocuban subcultural group that imitated the clothing and speech styles of *ladinos,* Afro-Andalusians brought to Cuba as slaves who were believed to dress outlandishly.

Obatalá: The male Yoruban *oricha* of creation, creativity, wisdom, and spiritual clarity.

Ochún: The female Yoruban *oricha* of beauty and physical love. Ochún is usually depicted as a *mulata* rather than a *negra.*

opera seria: An Italian term for opera with serious or tragic subject matter. It has three acts, whereas comic works have one or two acts.

orquestas de baile: Dance orchestras.

orquestas típicas: The most common ballroom dance ensembles of nineteenth-century Cuba, containing primarily European instruments such as the violin, acoustic bass, clarinet, trombone, and cornet, as well as the *timbal* and occasionally the *güiro.*

orichas: African ancestor deities. In Cuba, each *oricha* is equated with a particular Catholic saint believed to be a manifestation of the same god.

Oyá: The female Yoruban *oricha* of storms and cemeteries; the guardian of the dead.

paila: Percussion instrument; also *paila criolla.* See *timbal.*

papolote: A nineteenth-century subgenre of the traditional rumba.

pardo: Dark black, of very dark skin.

pareja de baile: Cabaret dance couple. Many entertainment venues of the 1930s featured these pairs of male and female dancers in sketches depicting various forms of stylized Afrocuban dance, especially the *rumba guaguancó.*

pasillo: A Colombian ballroom dance, similar to the waltz, performed in 3/4 time.

pasillos: Dance steps.

paso doble: A music and dance genre from Spain in duple meter that enjoyed great popularity in Cuba in the early twentieth century. It was especially common in dances sponsored by the *sociedades españolas.*

peninsular: Someone born in Spain; pertaining to the Iberian peninsula.

posada: Inn or hostel. In Cuba, *posadas* are low-budget hotels where a couple can rent a room for a short time to have sex.

potencia: Secret social organization (also called a *plante*) created by *abakuás.*

pregón: Musical cries of street vendors used to attract customers, a tradition that comes from Spain and is found throughout Latin America. In Cuba, commercial songs based on *pregones* were bawdy, double entendre compositions first popularized in the blackface theater. Beginning in the 1920s, lyrics patterned after the *pregón* also appeared in *sones* and other dance music. See Díaz Ayala 1988.

punto cubano: A subgenre of *música guajira* (music of rural Hispanic farmers), primarily a form of instrumental string music played on the *laúd, tres,* and *bandurria* (guitarlike instruments developed in Cuba) as well as the guitar, and accompanied by maracas or other hand-held percussion. It often accompanies improvised vocal performance.

quintero: The drummer playing the *quinto* or highest-pitched *conga* drum of the traditional rumba ensemble. The *quintero* is usually the best performer of the group, expected to improvise constantly over the relatively static rhythms of the other instruments.

ritmo yesá: Yesá (also *iyesá*) rhythm. Any one of a number of rhythmic patterns associated with Yesá drumming, a sacred, Yoruban-derived musical tradition in Cuba.

rumba: A heavily African-influenced form of secular entertainment unique to Cuba. Traditional rumba is a complex and highly improvisatory form involving performance on various percussion instruments, song, and dance. It developed in the mid-nineteenth century in the provinces of Havana and Matanzas. Many subgenres and regional variants exist.

rumba de fantasía: Fantasy rumba, a reference to the stylized rumba shows presented in Cuban cabarets beginning about 1930. These acts often incorporated some musical and choreographic components from noncommercial rumba, but tended to fuse them with the music and dance associated with jazz, the *son,* classical ballet, and other traditions.

rumba guaguancó: See *guaguancó.*

rumba yambú: See *yambú.*

rumbera: A female dancer performing stylized rumba and other dances for audiences as part of cabaret shows. The *rumbera* figure was popularized internationally beginning in the 1930s through Mexican and Cuban films.

rumbero: A male musician or dancer of traditional rumba.

sainete: A one-act comic play that served as the basis for most works performed in the Cuban blackface theater.

salsa: The commercial name (literally, "sauce") for dance music, largely of Cuban origin, that is promoted and performed by Latino communities in New York, Puerto Rico, Colombia, and throughout the world since the early 1970s.

samba: A form of Afrobrazilian dance music popularized in the early twentieth century and closely associated with carnival celebrations in Rio de Janeiro and elsewhere.

santería: A term used in Cuba to refer to various syncretic religious practices fusing West African and Catholic elements. Such traditions are far from marginal, representing the most widespread form of religion practiced in the country. Properly speaking, *santería* refers only to Yoruban-influenced worship, which is the most common, while *palo monte, espiritismo,* and related terms apply to those influenced by other African culture areas. Music and dance play a central role in all *santería* worship.

sartenes: Frying pans. Aside from their traditional use in the kitchen, they serve as *comparsa* instruments during carnival season. *Comparsero* musicians fasten two or more to a frame and strike them with spoons or metal rods.

sociedades de color: Afrocuban social clubs, also called *liceos.* These establishments existed throughout the island until 1959, when they were outlawed by the revolutionary government.

sociedades españolas: Spanish social clubs, each devoted to a particular region in Spain, that accepted as members those who could trace some ancestry to that area. In Havana, they became large, powerful organizations, some with tens of thousands of members, that sponsored musical events and thus had a strong impact on artistic life. They remained racially segregated for many years.

solar: Large urban tenement, a multi-story building for poorer families, typically built around a central patio.

son: A highly syncretic genre of dance music created by Afrocuban performers in eastern Cuba towards the end of the nineteenth century. In terms of its form, lyrical content, and instrumentation, the *son* demonstrates the fusion of both African and European elements. It first achieved national recognition in the 1920s. The *son* has become a powerful symbol of Afro-Hispanic cultural fusion and Cuban nationalism.

sonero: A performer of *sones.*

sucu-sucu: A subgenre of the *son* that developed on the Isle of Pines in the late nineteenth century. It differs from other rural *sones* only in that its lyrics are often improvised during performance and that it incorporates both *conga* drums and a machete scraped with a knife as percussion instruments.

syncretic: Used to describe forms of expression demonstrating the fusion or blending of cultural traditions, often derived from distinct ethnic groups.

tahona: A nineteenth-century Afrocuban music and dance genre considered to be a precursor of the modern rumba.

tango: A generic term for African-derived dance in nineteenth-century Cuba. The term also applied to wandering groups of Afrocuban musicians who performed in Kings' Day celebrations.

tango africano: A nineteenth-century name for slave dance or African dance.

tango-congo: This term was used by middle-class Cubans to describe the music, dance, and rhythmic patterns executed by slaves while parading through the streets on Kings' Day in the nineteenth century. During the Wars of Independence, stage shows incorporating parodied versions of such expression began to appear in the blackface theater that featured a distinct "*tango-congo* rhythm." This two-measure pattern, illustrated in chapter 3, represents a simplified imitation or parody of actual *tango-congo* music. In the 1920s and 1930s, many musicians employed the *tango-congo* rhythm in *zarzuelas* and *afro* compositions for the salon. It continues to appear in popular songs to this day.

teatro vernáculo: Vernacular theater, a common name for the Cuban blackface theater. It is also referred to as *teatro bufo* (comic theater), *teatro criollo* (creole theater), *teatro de variedades* (vaudeville or variety show), or simply *los bufos*. In the 1920s and 1930s, blackface *sainete* sketches alternated on stage with musicians, dancers, recited poetry, and silent movie shorts.

tertulia: Informal gathering of friends or colleagues to discuss issues of common interest.

timbal: A percussion instrument (also called the *paila,* or kettle) developed by Afrocuban performers in military bands and street ensembles during the nineteenth century. The instrument consists of one or two round metal single-headed drums similar in shape to the snare drum. It is played with sticks both on the head and on the shell or *cáscara. Timbales* first gained national popularity in *danzón* orchestras (substituting for the timpani) and in the blackface theater as a means of parodying African drumming.

timbalero: A performer on the *timbal.*

tonadilla: A Spanish form of comic musical theater that influenced the development of the Cuban *teatro vernáculo*. It flourished in Spain from the mid-eighteenth through the early nineteenth centuries.

toque: Drum rhythm used in *santería* ceremony. Many distinct *toques* exist with their own unique sound, and each is associated with a particular *oricha* or deity.

toques de santo: Sacred Afrocuban musical performances that serve as the liturgical basis of *santería* ritual. They are performed instrumentally and as an accompaniment to singing and dancing. Pieces must be performed in a predetermined order, each praising a major deity.

tres: A small guitarlike Cuban instrument with three double courses of metal strings used in many *conjuntos de son.*

tresillo: A rhythmic musical figure consisting of three beats falling over one 4/4 measure: two dotted quarter notes followed by a quarter note.

trigueño/trigueña: Wheat-colored, swarthy, one of the many subtle terms used by Cubans to categorize each other racially. It may or may not imply some Afrocuban ancestry.

trova: Traditional popular song (also *vieja trova*) performed by street musicians *(trovadores)* and other working-class artists that first became nationally popular at the turn of the century. The earliest *trova* singers, from Santiago de Cuba, were central to the development of bolero music. Despite its humble origins, *trova* repertory demonstrates the clear stylistic influence of Italian opera and other classical genres.

trovador: Troubador, a performer of *trova.*

tumbadora: See *conga* drum.

"vaca gorda" years: The "fat cow" years, ca. 1914–1920, a period of economic prosperity caused by high international sugar prices during World War I.

vacunao: A dance movement in traditional *rumba guaguancó* in which the man makes a sudden thrust of his pelvis toward his partner, attempting to touch her.

vals: Waltz.

vanguardia: The middle-class artistic vanguard of the 1920s and 1930s, roughly synonymous with the Minoristas.

vanguardismo: See Minorismo.

vanguardista: A member of the artistic avant-garde; also, progressive, modern, experimental, related to the artistic avant-garde.

vieja trova: See *trova.*

vigüela/vihuela: An Iberian-derived string instrument, similar to the lute, used in eastern Cuba in the early years of the Spanish colony.

viola: A percussion instrument used in some *coros de clave* and related ensembles at the turn of the century. The Afrocuban *viola,* which bears no similarity to its European counterpart, was a banjo or small acoustic bass with the strings removed that was used as a percussion instrument by a player striking it with the hands.

yambú: A form of Afrocuban music and dance predating (yet similar in many respects to) the *rumba guaguancó.* It is performed at a slower tempo, and its dance movements are often mimetic.

zafra: Sugar harvest; by extension, any major source of income. Before 1959, many referred to government *"botellas"* or sinecures as the "second *zafra,"* and tourism as the "third *zafra."*

zamba: An Argentine scarf dance in 6/8 time derived from Spanish genres and typically performed on the guitar.

zapateo: Also *zapateado.* A Spanish-derived dance music genre in 3/4 or 6/8 time performed primarily on the guitar and other string instruments. *Zapateo* dancing emphasizes movement from the knee down only, fancy footwork, and stomping of the heels.

zarzuela: Nationalist light opera. The *zarzuela* was originally a form of Spanish musical theater, but Cuban artists adopted the genre as their own beginning in the mid-1920s. A majority of Cuban *zarzuelas* written during the *afrocubanismo* period continue to be performed today. They are typically set in the nineteenth century and make reference to everyday life in colonial Havana as well as to slave culture. *Zarzuela* plots almost invariably revolve around a sensual *mulata* figure who attracts multiple suitors.

REFERENCES

Abbreviations for Research Centers in Havana

ANC	Archivo Nacional de Cuba, Compostela #906 e/ San Isidrio y San Parado, Habana Vieja
BNJM	Biblioteca Nacional José Martí, Plaza de la Revolución, Plaza
CIDMUC	Centro de Investigación y Desarrollo de la Música Cubana, calle G #505 e/ 21 y 23, Vedado
COU	Centro Odilio Urfé, calle G #251 esq. Línea, Vedado
IH	Instituto de Historia, Palacio de Aldama, Habana Vieja
MBA	Museo de Bellas Artes, Palacio de Bellas Artes, Habana Vieja
MNM	Museo Nacional de la Música, Copdevila #1 e/ Habana y Aguiar, Habana Vieja
RHC	Radio Habana Cuba, Infanta y 25, Vedado
RP	Radio Progreso, Infanta y 25, Vedado

Books and Articles

Abascal, Horacio. 1930. "La obra científica de Israel Castellanos." *Revista bimestre cubana* 24, no. 2 (November–December 1930): 199–209.

Abril, Julio. 1916. "La 'Columbia Gramophone Co.'" *Bohemia* 7, no. 21 (May 1916): 26–28.

Acosta, Leonardo. 1982. *Música y descolonización.* Mexico City: Presencia latinoamericana.

———. 1983. *Del tambor al sintetizador.* Havana: Editorial Letras Cubanas.

———. 1991. "The rumba, the guaguancó and Tío Tom." In *Essays on Cuban Music: North American and Cuban Perspectives*, edited by P. Manuel, 51–73. Lanham, Md.: University Press of America.

————. 1993. "Cuba be, Cuba bop. A History of Jazz in Cuba." Manuscript. Forth-coming from Fundación Musicalia, Puerto Rico.

Acosta, Loló. 1950. "Se Marcha la 'Perla Negra.'" *Carteles* 31, no. 6 (5 February 1950): 22–24, 88.

Acuña Lazcano, Tomás. 1938. "A la nación cubana." *Adelante* 3, no. 34 (March 1938): 7–8, 20.

Agüero y Barreras, Gaspar. 1946. "El aporte africano a la música popular cubana." *Estudios afrocubanos* 5: 115–28. Havana: Sociedad de Estudios Afrocubanos.

Aguilar, Luis E. 1972. *Cuba 1933: Prologue to Revolution*. Ithaca: Cornell University Press.

Anderson, Benedict. 1983. *Imagined Communities: Reflections on the Origin and Spread of Nationalism*. London: Verso.

Andrews, George Reid. 1980. *Afro-Argentines of Buenos Aires*. Madison: University of Wisconsin Press.

Antelo Martínez, Crisel, et al. 1984. "Opiniones de la populación sobre el carnaval habanero." *Memorias del II simposio de la cultura de la Ciudad de la Habana*. Havana: Prov. de Cultura.

Ardévol, José. 1945. "Posición del compositor cubano actual." *Conservatorio* 5 (October–December): 3–8. Havana: Conservatorio Municipal de la Habana.

Arnaz, Desi, Jr. 1976. *A Book by Desi Arnaz*. New York: William Morrow.

Arredondo, Alberto. 1936. "El negro y la nación." *Adelante* 1, no. 10 (March 1936): 6. [BNJM]

————. 1937a. "Dos palabras más sobre el negro y la nación." *Adelante* 2, no. 10 (January): 7–8, 11. [BNJM]

————. 1937b. "El arte negro a contrapelo." *Adelante* 3, no. 26 (July): 5–6, 20.

————. 1938. "Eso que llaman afrocubanismo musical." *Adelante* 3, no. 35 (April): 5–7. [BNJM]

————. 1939. *El negro en Cuba*. Havana: Editorial Alfa.

Arredondo, Enrique ("Bernabé"). 1981. *La vida de un comediante*. Havana: Editorial Letras Cubanas.

Asche, Charles Bryon. 1983. "Cuban Folklore Traditions and Twentieth Century Idioms in the Piano Music of Amadeo Roldán and Alejandro García Caturla." DMA treatise, University of Texas, Austin.

Attali, Jacques. 1989. *Noise: The Political Economy of Music*. Trans. B Massumi. Minnesota: University of Minnesota Press.

"Autores de la música popular: Gilberto Valdés." N.d. [1950s] *Cubamena*: 40. [MNM]

Averill, Gage. 1994. "Anraje to Angaje: Carnival Politics and Music in Haiti." *Ethnomusicology* 38, no. 2 (spring–summer): 217–48.

Avilés Ramírez, Eduardo. 1932. "La rumba, baile mundial." *Bohemia* 24, no. 2 (10 January): 28–29.

Baguer, Néstor E. 1988. *Apuntes sobre un creador: José Zacarías Tallet*. Havana: UNEAC.

Bakhtin, Mikhail. 1968. *Rabelais and His World*. Cambridge: MIT Press.

Ballagas, Emilio. 1934. *Cuaderno de poesía negra*. Santa Clara, Cuba: Imp. La Nueva.

————. 1935. *Antología de la poesía negra hispanoamericana*. Madrid: M. Aguilar.

Barnet, Miguel. 1966. *Biografía de un cimmarón*. Havana: Academia de Ciencias Sociales.

Barral, G. 1932a. "Hace 25 años que Lecuona es Compositor." *Bohemia* 24, no. 7 (14 February): 38.

———. 1932b. "Una nueva embajada de arte cubano." *Bohemia* 24, no. 6 (7 February): 38.

———. 1954. "Recuerdos de 'Alhambra' en la muerte de Villoch." *Bohemia* 46, no. 47 (21 November): 66–68, sup. 10, 76.

Bauman, Richard, and Charles Briggs. 1990. "Poetics and Performance as Critical Perspectives on Language and Social Life." *Annual Review of Anthropology* 19: 59–88. Palo Alto: Annual Reviews, Inc.

Béhague, Gerard. 1979. *Music in Latin America: An Introduction*. Englewood Cliffs, N.J.: Prentice-Hall.

Benjamin, Jules R. 1977. *The United States and Cuba: Hegemony and Dependent Development, 1880–1934*. Pittsburgh: University of Pittsburgh Press.

———. 1990. *The United States and the Origins of the Cuban Revolution: An Empire of Liberty in an Age of National Liberation*. Princeton: Princeton University Press.

Beruff Mendieta, Antonio. 1937. *Las comparsas populares del carnaval habanero, cuestión resuelta*. Havana: Molina y Cía.

Betancourt, Juan René. [1940?]. *Doctrina negra: La única teoría certera contra la discriminación racial en Cuba*. Havana: P. Fernández y Cía.

Betancourt y García, Ramón. 1936. "Igualdad de derechos." *Adelante* 1, no. 8 (January 1936): 9.

Bettelheim, Judith, ed. 1993. *Cuban Festivals: An Illustrated Anthology*. Hamden, Conn.: Garland Publishing.

Blanco, Jesús. 1992. *80 años del son y soneros en el caribe*. Caracas: Fondo Editorial Trapykos.

Blue Guide to Cuba. 1938. Havana: Roger Le Febure Publishers.

Blum, Stephen. 1991. "Prologue: Ethnomusicologists and Modern Music History." In *Ethnomusicology and Modern Music History*, edited by S. Blum et al., 1–22. Chicago: University of Illinois Press.

Borbolla, Carlo. N.d. "Rumbita no. 1, no. 2, no. 3, danza no. 3, son no. 11." Manzanillo, Cuba: Impresión y fotograbado "El Arte."

Bourdieu, Pierre. 1977. *Outline of a Theory of Practice*. New York: Cambridge University Press.

———. 1984. *Distinction: A Social Critique of the Judgement of Taste*. Trans. Richard Nice. Cambridge: Harvard University Press.

Buchanan, Donna Anne. 1991. "The Bulgarian Folk Orchestra: Cultural Performance, Symbol, and the Construction of Identity in Socialist Bulgaria." Ph.D. diss., University of Texas, Austin.

Bynum, Caroline Walker. 1987. "Women's Symbols." In *Holy Feast and Holy Fast: The Religious Significance of Food to Medieval Women*, 277–96. Berkeley and Los Angeles: University of California Press.

Cairo Ballester, Ana. 1976. *El movimiento de veteranos y patriotas. Apuntes para un estudio ideológico del año 1923*. Havana: Editorial Arte y Literatura.

———. 1978. *El grupo Minorista y su tiempo*. Havana: Editorial de Ciencias Sociales.

————. 1988. "La década genésica del intelectual Carpentier (1923–1933)." In *Letras. Cultura en Cuba,* edited by A. Cairo, 3–38. Havana: Editorial Arte y Educación.

Calderón González, Jorge. 1986. *María Teresa Vera.* Havana: Editorial Letras Cubanas.

Calero Martín, José, et al., eds. 1929. *Cuba musical. Album-resumen ilustrado de la historia y de la actual situación del arte en Cuba.* Havana: Imprenta Molina.

Callejas, Bernardo. 1965. "Esta crónica es casi en serio: trata de la historia del carnaval." *Hoy,* 17 March 1965, 5.

Campoamor, Fernando G. 1966. "Chori." *Bohemia* 58, no. 13 (April): 24–27.

Cañizares, Dulcila. 1978. *Gonzalo Roig.* Havana: Editorial Letras Cubanas.

————. 1991. "Julio Cueva: el rescate de su música." Pamphlet. Havana: Editorial Letras Cubanas.

Carbonell, Walterio. 1961. *Crítica: Como surgió la cultura nacional.* Havana: Author.

Carles Batlle, Miguel. 1991. Liner notes for *Xavier Cugat and His Orchestra, 1940–1942.* Tumbao CD TCD-002. Switzerland: Camarillo Music Ltd.

Carpentier, Alejo. 1930. "Los valores universales de la música cubana." *Revista de la Habana* 2, no. 5 (May): 145–54.

————. 1931. "La rumba de amor en el 'Casino de París.'" *Carteles* 17, no. 40 (6 December): 18, 66.

————. 1944. "La música cubana en estos últimos 20 años." *Conservatorio* 1, no. 2 (January–March): 2–7. [BNJM]

————. 1946. *La música en Cuba.* Mexico City: Fondo de Cultura Económica.

————. 1976. *Crónicas.* 2 vols. Havana: Editorial Arte y Literatura.

————. 1977. *Ecue-Yamba-O. Novela afrocubana.* Havana: Editorial Arte y Literatura.

————. 1980. *Ese músico que llevo adentro,* vol. 3. Havana: Editorial Letras Cubanas.

Casal, Lourdes. 1988. "Race Relations in Contemporary Cuba." In *The Cuban Reader,* edited by Philip Brenner et al. New York: Grove Press.

Casella, Alfredo. 1929. "La música necesaria." *Musicalia* 7 (July–August 1929): 2–5. [BNJM]

Castellanos, Israel. 1914a. "El tipo brujo." *Revista bimestre cubana* 9, no. 5 (September–October): 328–44.

————. 1914b. "Evolución del baile negrero en Cuba." *Vida nueva: revista mensual de higiene y ciencias sociales* 6, no. 7 (July): 150–53. Havana: Imprenta de Rembla, Bouza y Cía. [BNJM]

————. 1916. *La brujería y el ñañiguismo desde el punto de vista médico-legal.* Havana: Impresa de Lloredo y Cía. [BNJM]

————. 1927. "Instrumentos musicales de los afrocubanos." *Archivos del folklore* 2, no. 3 (October): 193–208.

————. 1928. "El diablito ñáñigo." *Archivos del folklore* 3, no. 4 (December): 27–37. Havana: Cultural.

Castellanos, Jorge, and Isabel Castellanos. 1987. "The Geographic, Ethnologic, and Linguistic Roots of Cuban Blacks." *Cuban Studies* 17 (1987): 95–110.

Castellanos, Lázara. 1990. *Víctor Patricio Landaluze.* Havana: Editorial Letras Cubanas.

Castillo Boloy, Estanislao. 1916. "Afilerazos: Palpitaciones de la raza de color: crónica escrita para negros sin taparrabos, mestizos no arrepentidos y blancos de sentido común." *La prensa* 8, no. 76 (16 March): 4.

Castillo Faílde, Osvaldo. 1964. *Miguel Faílde, creador musical del danzón.* Havana: Editora del Consejo Nacional de Cultura.

Castillo Vega, Marcia, and Rosa González Alfonso, comp. 1984. *Indice analítico del suplemento literario del Diario de la Marina (1927–30).* Havana: Editorial Academia.

Chávez Alvarez, Ernesto. 1991. *El crimen de la niña Cecilia. La brujería en Cuba como fenómeno social (1902–25).* Havana: Editorial de Ciencias Sociales.

Claghorn, Charles Eugene. 1973. *Biographical Dictionary of American Music.* New York: Parker.

Collazo, Bobby. 1987. *La última noche que pasé contigo: 40 años de la farándula cubana.* Puerto Rico: Editorial Cubanacán.

Coplan, David B. 1985. *In Township Tonight: South Africa's Black City Music and Theater.* New York: Longman.

Corrigan, Philip, and Derek Sayer. 1985. *The Great Arch: English State Formation as Cultural Revolution.* New York: Basil Blackwell.

"Cronología de Carlos Enríquez." N.d. Unpublished. Museo de Bellas Artes archives, Havana.

Crook, Larry Norman. 1980. "The Cuban Rumba." M.A. thesis, University of Texas, Austin.

———. 1982. "A Musical Analysis of the Cuban Rumba." *Latin American Music Review* 3, no. 1 (spring–summer): 95–123.

Cruz, Mary. 1974. *Creto Gangá.* Havana: Instituto Cubano del Libro.

Cugat, Xavier. 1948. *Rumba Is My Life.* New York: Didier.

Dalhaus, Carl. 1980. "Nationalism and Music." In *Between Romanticism and Modernism.* Trans. M. Whittall, 79–101. Berkeley: University of California Press.

Daniel, Yvonne. 1989. "Ethnography of the Rumba: Dance and Social Change in Contemporary Cuba." Ph.D. diss., University of California, Berkeley.

———. 1995. *Rumba, Dance, and Social Change in Contemporary Cuba.* Bloomington: Indiana University Press.

De la Fuente, Alejandro. 1995. "Race and Inequality in Cuba, 1899–1981." *Journal of Contemporary History* 30, no. 1 (January): 131–68.

De la Torre, Miguel Angel. 1918. "Las comparsas trágicas." *Heraldo de Cuba* 4, no. 68 (8 March): 1, 6.

De León, Carmela. 1990. *Sindo Garay: Memorias de un trovador.* Havana: Editorial Letras Cubanas.

Del Morro, Juan. 1923. "La sociedad del folklore cubano." *Revista bimestre cubana* 18: 47–52.

———. 1929. "Cultura, no raza." *Revista bimestre cubana* 24, no. 5 (September–October): 716–20.

Demaison, André. 1938. "Nunca me conmovió tanto Africa como escuchando a Gilberto Valdés." *Estudios Afrocubanos* 2, no. 1: 151–55.

Deschamps Chapeaux, Pedro. 1971. *El negro en la economía habanera del siglo XIX.* Havana: UNEAC.

Despaigne Chueg, Raimundo. 1939. "¿Cómo debe resolverse el problema racial cubano en la nueva constitución?" *Adelante* 4, nos. 44–45 (February): 11.

Díaz Ayala, Cristóbal. 1981. *Música cubana del areyeto a la nueva trova.* San Juan, P.R.: Editorial Cubanacán.

———. 1988. *Si te quieres por el pico divertir. Historia del pregón musical latinoamericano.* San Juan, P.R.: Editorial Cubanacán.

———. 1994a. Liner notes for *Cuarteto Machín,* vol. 1: *1931–32.* Harlequin compact disc HQCD 24. West Sussex, England: Interstate Music Ltd.

———. 1994b. *Cuba canta y baila: discografía de la música cubana.* Vol. 1: *1898–1925.* San Juan, P.R.: Fundación Musicalia.

Diehl, Kiehla. 1992. "Tempered Steel: The Steel Drum as a Site for Social, Political, and Aesthetic Negotiation in Trinidad." M.A. thesis, University of Texas, Austin.

Doctrina del ABC. Manifiesto-programa de 1932 y otros documentos básicos. 1942. Havana: Publicaciones del Partido ABC.

Dorschner, John. 1995. "Las 1,000 noches de gloria de Alicia Parlá." *El Nuevo Herald* (Miami), 25 March 1995, 4E.

Eli Rodríguez, Victoria. 1995. "Cuban Music and Ethnicity: Historical Considerations." In *Music and Black Ethnicity: The Caribbean and South America,* edited by G. Béhague. New Brunswick, N.J.: Transaction Publishers.

Erlmann, Veit. 1991. *African Stars: Studies in Black South African Performance.* Chicago: University of Chicago Press.

Estrada Mora, N. 1900. Ordinance, "Ayuntamiento de la Habana." *Gaceta de la Habana: Periódico oficial del gobierno* 62, no. 82 (6 April): 655. [IH]

Evans, Walker. 1989. *Cuba 1933.* New York: Pantheon Books.

Fanon, Frantz. 1952. *Black Skin White Masks: The Experiences of a Black Man in a White World.* New York: Grove Press.

Faya, Alberto. 1993. Paper presented at a conference entitled "Música, africanía y nación," Vedado, Havana, 23 August.

Feijóo, Samuel. 1987. *El negro en la literatura folklórica cubana.* Havana: Editorial Letras Cubanas.

Feld, Steven. 1988. "Notes on World Beat." *Public Culture Bulletin* 1 (fall 1988): 31–37.

———. 1995. "From Schizophonia to Schismogenesis." In *Music Grooves,* edited by C. Keil and S. Feld, 257–89. Chicago: University of Chicago Press.

Fernández de Castro, José Antonio. 1935. *Tema negro en las letras de Cuba (1608–1935).* Havana: Ediciones Mirador.

Fernández Robaina, Tomás. 1985. *Bibliografía de temas afrocubanas.* 2nd ed. Havana: Biblioteca Nacional José Martí.

"Fiestas populares de canto y baile en la zona central de Cuba, en el poblado de Sancti Spiritus." N.d. [1970s]. Unsigned manuscript, archives of Radio Habana Cuba.

Figueroa, Frank, ed. 1995. "Arsenio Rodríguez." *Encyclopedia of Latin American Music.*

Fiske, John. 1989a. *Understanding Popular Culture.* Boston: Unwin Hyman.

———. 1989b. *Reading the Popular.* Boston: Unwin Hyman.

Fornet, Ambrosio. 1967. *En blanco y negro.* Havana: Instituto del Libro.

Foster, Robert J. 1991. "Making National Cultures in the Global Ecumene." *Annual Review of Anthropology* 20:235–60.

Franco, José L. 1961. *Afroamérica*. Havana: Publicaciones de la Junta Nacional de Arqueología y Etnología.

———. 1963. *La conspiración de Aponte*. Havana: Consejo Nacional de Cultura, publicaciones del Archivo Nacional LVIII.

Fuentes, José Lorenzo. N.d. "Murió el verdadero autor de 'La chambelona.'" Unidentified newspaper article. [MNM]

Galán, Natalio. 1983. *Cuba y sus sones*. Valencia, Spain: Pre-Textos.

Gálvez, Zoila. 1940. "Una melodía negra." *Estudios afrocubanos* 4, nos. 1–4: 23–26.

García, Francisco. 1969. *Tiempo muerto: memorias de un trabajador azucarero*. Havana: Instituto del Libro.

García, Marina, ed. 1980. *Diccionario de la literatura cubana*. Vol. 1. Havana: Editorial Letras Cubanas.

García Agüero, Salvador. 1937a. "Presencia africana en la música nacional." *Estudios afrocubanos* 1, no. 1: 114–27.

———. 1937b. "Valor complejo de la música de Gilberto Valdés." *Social* 21, no. 3 (March): 30, 57, 61.

García Cabrera, Enrique. 1927. "El futurismo considerado como un retroceso." *Diario de la Marina*, 7 August, 42.

García Caturla, Alejandro. 1929. "Posibilidades sinfónicas de la música afrocubana." *Musicalia* 7 (July–August): 15–17. Havana: Maresa y Reyes.

———. 1931. "The Development of Cuban Music." In *American Composers on American Music*, edited by Henry Cowell, 173–74. Stanford, Calif.: Stanford University Press.

———. 1978. *Correspondencia*. Intro. María Antonieta Henríquez. Havana: Editorial Arte y Literatura.

García Garófalo, Juan M. 1930. "Los orígines del son 'Mamá Inés.'" *Archivos del folklore* 5, no. 2 (June): 160–63.

García Pérez, Severo. 1927. "Nacionalismo y costumbrismo." *Revista de Avance* 1, no. 11 (15 September): 282–83, 297.

Garcíaporrúa, Jorge. 1974. "Eduardo Sánchez de Fuentes." Pamphlet. Havana: Biblioteca Nacional José Martí.

García Reyes, F. 1928. "Alrededor del problema social en Cuba." *Carteles* 11, no. 9 (26 February): 26.

Garrido, Pablo. 1937. "Presencia y conquista del ritmo negro." *Adelante* 3, no. 27 (August): 5–6, 20.

Geertz, Clifford. 1973. *The Interpretation of Cultures*. New York: Basic Books.

Giralt, José Antonio. 1920. "La sociedad 'Pro-Arte Musical.'" *Bohemia* 11, no. 13 (28 March): 12.

Glasser, Ruth. 1995. *Music Is My Flag: Puerto Rican Musicians and Their New York Communities 1917–1940*. Berkeley: University of California Press.

Gómez Yera, Sara. 1964. "La Rumba." *Cuba* 3, no. 32 (December): 58–67. Havana: Empresa Consolidada de Artes Gráficas.

Góngora Echenique, M. 1928. "La escuela municipal de música." *Carteles* 11, no. 15 (8 April): 26–27, 48.

González, Hilario. 1978. "La rumba, de Alejandro García Caturla." *Música* 38:3–19. Havana: Casa de las Américas.

González, Hilario, and María Antonieta Henríquez. 1995. "Ernesto Lecuona: Fisonomía de lo cubano." *La Gaceta de Cuba* September–October: 12–18.

González, Jorge Antonio. 1986. *La composición operística en Cuba*. Havana: Editorial Letras Cubanas.

González, Reynaldo. 1992. *Contradanzas y latigazos*. Havana: Editorial Letras Cubanas.

González Torres, Julio M. 1935. "Societarias." *Adelante* 1, no. 5 (October): 12–13.

Goodman, Walter. 1873. *The Pearl of the Antilles, or, An Artist in Cuba*. London: H. S. King.

Grenet, Eliseo. 1942a. "Mis triunfos en Europa." *Guitarra* 3, no. 4 (July): 14–17.

Grenet, Emilio. 1939. *Popular Cuban Music: 80 Revised and Corrected Compositions Together with an Essay on the Evolution of Music in Cuba*. Havana: Carasa y Cía.

Gross, Bertram. 1980. *Friendly Fascism: The New Face of Power in America*. New York: M. Evans.

Guanche, Jesús. 1983. *Procesos etnoculturales de Cuba*. Havana: Editorial Letras Cubanas.

Guerra, Armando. 1938. "Presencia negra en la poesía popular cubana del siglo XIX." Paper presented at the Sociedad de Estudios Afrocubanos at the Club Atenas, 19 April. Havana: Editorial Alfa.

Guillén, Nicolás. 1980. *Motivos de son*. Intro. Marta Aguirre. Havana: Editorial Letras Cubanas.

Guirao, Ramón, ed. 1938. *Orbita de la poesía afrocubana 1928–1937*. Havana: Ucar, García y Cía.

Hagedorn, Katherine J. 1995. "*Anatomía del Proceso Folklórico:* The 'Folkloricization' of Afro-Cuban Religious Performance in Cuba." Ph.D. diss., Brown University.

Hall, Stuart. 1979. "Culture, the Media and the 'Ideological Effect.'" In *Mass Communication and Society,* edited by J. Curran et al. London: Sage Publications.

———. 1981. "Notes on Deconstructing the Popular." In *People's History and Social Theory,* edited by by Rafael Samuel, 227–40. London: Routledge and Kegan Paul.

Hallorans, A. O. 1882. *Guarachas cubanas. Curiosa recopilación desde las más antiguas hasta las más modernas*. Madrid: Imp. de A. Pérez.

Hebdige, Dick. 1987. *Hiding in the Light: On Images and Things*. New York: Comedia-Routledge.

———. 1989. *Subculture: The Meaning of Style*. New York: Comedia-Routledge.

Helg, Aline. 1991. "Afro-Cuban Protest: The Partido Independiente de Color, 1908–1912." *Cuban Studies* 21 (1991): 101–21.

———. 1995. *Our Rightful Share: The Afro-Cuban Struggle for Equality, 1886–1912*. Chapel Hill: University of North Carolina Press.

Hernández, Armando. 1936. "El negro, la cultura y la revolución." *Adelante* 2, no. 13 (June): 8. [BNJM]

Hernández de Cervantes, Calixta. 1935. "Zoila Gálvez." *Adelante* 1, no. 5 (October): 17–18. [BNJM]

Hobsbawm, Eric. 1972. "Some Reflections on Nationalism." In *Essays in Memory of Peter Nettl: Imagination and Precision in the Social Sciences,* edited by T. J. Nossiter et al., 385–406. London: Faber and Faber.

———. 1987. *The Age of Empire 1875–1914.* New York: Random House.

Hobsbawm, Eric, and Terence Ranger, eds. 1983. *The Invention of Tradition.* Cambridge: Cambridge University Press.

Hokosawa, Shuhei. 1994. "Rumba in Japan in the 1930s." Paper presented at the annual meeting of the International Association for the Study of Popular Music in Havana, Cuba, 13–20 October.

Homenaje a Eliseo Grenet. 1966. Havana: Consejo Nacional de Cultura.

Ichaso, Francisco. 1928. "La rembambambara." *Revista de avance* 2 (15 September): 244–46. Havana: Editorial Hermes.

Ignaza, Diana. 1989. *Transculturación en Fernando Ortiz.* Havana: Editorial de Ciencias Sociales.

"Industrias cubanas: características de la gran cervecería La Tropical." 1932. *Diario de la Marina. Número Centenario.* Havana: Ucar, García y Cía.

Jacobs, Glenn. 1988. "Cuba's Bola de Nieve: A Creative Looking Glass for Culture and the Artistic Self." *Latin American Music Review* 9, no. 1 (spring–summer): 18–49.

Jahn, Jahnheinz. [1961] 1989. *Muntu. African Culture and the Western World.* New York: Grove Weidenfeld.

Johnson, R., et al. 1982. *Making Histories: Studies in History-Writing and Politics.* London: Centre for Contemporary Cultural Studies.

Jones, LeRoi (Imiri Baraka). 1963. *Blues People: The Negro Experience in White America and the Music That Developed From It.* New York: William Morrow.

Kapferer, Bruce. 1989. "Nationalist Ideology and a Comparative Anthropology." *Ethnos* 54: 161–99.

Keil, Charles. 1985. "People's Music Comparatively: Style and Sterotype, Class and Hegemony." *Dialectical Anthropology* 10:119–30.

Kutzinski, Vera M. 1993. *Sugar's Secrets: Race and the Erotics of Cuban Nationalism.* Charlottesville: University Press of Virginia.

Lancís, Ricardo R. 1922. "Resolución." *Gaceta Oficial de la República de Cuba* 20, no. 121 (22 November): 11346–47. [ANC]

Lapique Becali, Zoila. 1974. "Figura musical de Eduardo Sánchez de Fuentes." Pamphlet. [BNJM]

———. 1979. *Música colonial cubana,* vol. 1: *1812–1902.* Havana: Editorial Letras Cubanas.

"Las comparsas." 1912. *Cuba y América* 15 (16 March): 8.

Leaf, Earl. 1948. *Isles of Rhythm.* New York: A. S. Barnes.

Leal, Rine. 1980. *Breve historia del teatro cubano.* Havana: Editorial Letras Cubanas.

———. 1982. *La selva oscura: de los bufos a la neocolonia,* vol. 2. Havana: Editorial Arte y Literatura.

Lechuga Hevia, Carlos M. 1946. "Recordando el pasado. Luz Gil, ex-reina de la Habana alegre." *Bohemia* 38, no. 41 (13 October): 32–33, 81–82. [BNJM]

Lekis, Lisa. 1960. *The Dancing Gods.* New York: Scarecrow Press.

León, Argeliers. N.d. *La fiesta del carnaval en su proyección folklórica.* Havana: Consejo Nacional de Cultura. [MNM]

———. 1961. Program notes for the Festival de Folklore, Teatro Nacional de Cuba, 20 January. Havana: Ministerio de Educación. [COU]

———. 1984. *Del canto y el tiempo.* Havana: Editorial Letras Cubanas.

———. 1985. "La fiesta del carnaval." *Temas* 6: 37–64. Havana: Ministerio de Cultura.

———. 1991a. "Notes Towards a Panorama of Popular and Folk Musics." In *Essays on Cuban Music: North American and Cuban Perspectives,* edited by P. Manuel.

———. 1991b. "Of the Axis and the Hinge: Nationalism, Afro-Cubanism, and Music in Pre-Revolutionary Cuba." In *Essays on Cuban Music: North American and Cuban Perspectives,* edited by P. Manuel, 267–82.

Le Riverend, Ada Rosa, ed. 1984. *Diccionario de la literatura cubana.* 2 vols. Havana: Editorial Letras Cubanas.

Le Riverend, Julio, ed. 1973. *Orbita de Fernando Ortiz.* Havana: UNEAC.

Levine, Lawrence. 1988. *Highbrow Lowbrow: The Emergence of Cultural Hierarchy in America.* Cambridge: Harvard University Press.

Lezcano, José Manuel. 1991. "African-Derived Rhythmical and Metrical Elements in Selected Songs of Alejandro García Caturla and Amadeo Roldán." *Latin American Music Review* 12, no. 2 (fall–winter): 173–86.

Linares, María Teresa. 1970. Introduction to *Cuba: la música popular.* Havana: Instituto del Libro.

Linnekin, Jocelyn. 1992. "On the Theory and Politics of Cultural Construction in the Pacific." *Oceanea* 62: 249–95.

Lipsitz, George. 1990. *Time Passages: Collective Memory and American Popular Culture.* Minneapolis: University of Minnesota Press.

Löfgren, Orvar. 1989. "The Nationalization of Culture." *Ethnologia Europaea* 19:5–23.

López, Alvaro. 1979. "Estudio complementario." In *Teatro Alhambra: antología,* edited by Eduardo Robreño, 651–702. Havana: Editorial Letras Cubanas.

López, Oscar Luís. 1981. *La radio en Cuba: Estudio de su desarrollo en la sociedad neocolonial.* Havana: Editorial Letras Cubanas.

López Segrera, Francisco. 1989. *Cuba: cultura y sociedad.* Havana: Editorial Letras Cubanas.

Loza, Steven Joseph. 1979. "Music and the Afro-Cuban Experience: A Survey of the Yoruba Tradition in Cuba in Relation to the Origins, Form, and Development of Contemporary Afro-Cuban Rhythms." M.A. thesis, University of California, Los Angeles.

Mañach, Jorge. 1925. "La crisis de la alta cultura en Cuba." Paper presented at a meeting of the Sociedad Económica de Amigos del País. Havana: Imprenta "La Universal." [BNJM]

———. 1927. "Vanguardismo: la fisonomía de las épocas." *Revista de Avance* 1, no. 2 (30 March): 18–20.

Manuel, Peter. 1988. *Popular Musics of the Non-Western World: An Introductory Survey.* New York: Oxford University Press.

———. 1991a. "Salsa and the Music Industry: Corporate Control or Grassroots Expression?" In *Essays on Cuban Music: North American and Cuban Perspectives,* edited by P. Manuel, 27–47.

———. 1991b. "Musical Pluralism in Revolutionary Cuba." In *Essays on Cuban Music: North American and Cuban Perspectives,* edited by P. Manuel, 283–312.

———. 1994. "Puerto Rican Music and Cultural Identity: Creative Appropriation of Cuban Sources from Danza to Salsa." *Ethnomusicology* 38, no. 2 (spring–summer): 249–80.

Marinello, Juan. 1929. "Vértice del gusto nuevo." *Revista de avance* 3 (15 May): 130–38. [BNJM]

———. 1930. "Sobre la inquietud cubana 2." *Revista de avance* 4, no. 43 (15 February): 52–54. [BNJM]

———. 1936. "Acción y omisión." *Adelante* 2, no. 15 (August): 7, 10. [BNJM]

Martí, José. 1959. *La cuestión racial.* 2nd ed. Biblioteca Popular Martiana no. 4. Havana: Editorial Lex.

Martín, Edgardo. 1971. *Panorama histórico de la música cubana.* Havana: Cuadernos CEU, Universidad de la Habana.

Martín, Juan Luís. 1954. "El folklore afrocubano." Libro de Cuba: Edición conmemorativa del cincuentenario de la República, 1902–1952, y del centenario del nacimiento de José Martí, 1853–1953, 646–50. Havana: Publicaciones Unidas.

Martín, Juan Antonio. 1937. "Falsa interpretación afrocubana." *Adelante* 3, no. 25 (June): 7. [BNJM]

———. 1938. "El afrocubanismo y nuestra cultura." *Adelante* 3, no. 32 (January): 11. [BNJM]

Martínez, Juan A. 1992. "Afrocubans and National Identity: Modern Cuban Art, 1920–1940s." *Athanor* 11. Tallahassee: Florida State University.

Martínez, Mayra A. 1989. "Rumberas en México." *Revolución y cultura* 11 (November 1989): 40–45.

Martínez, Orlando. 1989. *Ernesto Lecuona.* Havana: UNEAC.

Martínez Furé, Rogelio. 1966. "Tambor." *Cuba,* February 1966, 40–47.

———. 1991. "Tambor." In *Essays on Cuban Music: North American and Cuban Perspectives,* edited by P. Manuel, 27–47.

Martínez-Malo, Aldo. 1988. *Rita la única.* Havana: Editorial Abril.

Martínez Rodríguez, Raúl. 1977. "From the 'Columbia' to the "Guaguancó." *Direct From Cuba* 168 (1 May). Havana: Prensa Latina.

———. 1986. "Ignacio Villa y Fernández, Bola de Nieve. En su 75 aniversario de natalicio y 15 de fallecido." Pamphlet. Havana: Ministerio de Cultura, Museo Nacional de la Música.

———. 1987. "Blanquita Becerra (1887–1987). Centenario de su nacimiento." Pamphlet accompanying an exposition in September 1987. Havana: Museo Nacional de la Música.

Masud, Félix Roberto. 1980. "Cuban Nationalism." In *Canadian Review of Studies in Nationalism,* edited by Thomas Spira, 3:82–89.

Meintjes, Louise. 1990. "Paul Simon's Graceland, South Africa, and the Mediation of Musical Meaning." *Ethnomusicology* 34, no. 1 (winter): 37–73.

Meluzá Otero, F. 1945a. "La vida de Carmita Ortiz. Narrada por Alberto Garrido." *Carteles* 26, no. 21 (27 May): 22–23. [BNJM]

———. 1945b. "La vida de Carmita Ortiz. Narrada por Alberto Garrido." *Carteles* 26, no. 22 (3 June): 22–23, 30–31. [BNJM]

———. 1945c. "La vida de Carmita Ortiz. Narrada por Alberto Garrido." *Carteles* 26, no. 23 (10 June): 30–31. [BNJM]

Middleton, Richard. 1990. *Studying Popular Music.* Philadelphia: Open University Press.

Mintz, Sidney W., and Sally Price, eds. 1985. *Caribbean Contours.* Baltimore: Johns Hopkins University Press.

Moore, Carlos. 1988. *Castro, the Blacks, and Africa.* Los Angeles: UCLA Center for Afro-American Studies.

Moore, Robin. 1990. "'Primitivism' and Afrocuban Music: Developmental Parallels." *Caribbean Studies Journal* 7, nos. 2–3 (winter–spring): 181–88.

———. 1994. "Representations of Afrocuban Expressive Culture in the Writings of Fernando Ortiz." *Latin American Music Review* 15, no. 1 (spring–summer): 32–54.

———. 1995. "The Commercial Rumba: Afrocuban Arts as International Popular Culture." *Latin American Music Review* 16, no. 2 (fall–winter): 165–98.

Muñoz Alburquere, Carmelina. 1989. "Moisés Simons Rodríguez: Centenario de su nacimiento." Havana: Ministerio de Cultura. [MNM]

Neuman, Daniel M. 1991. "Epilogue: Paradigms and Stories." In *Ethnomusicology and Modern Music History,* edited by S. Blum et al., 268–77. Chicago: University of Illinois Press.

Orovio, Helio. 1981. *Diccionario de la música cubana. Biográfico y técnico.* Havana: Editorial Letras Cubanas.

———. 1992. *Diccionario de la música cubana. Biográfico y técnico,* 2nd ed. Havana: Editorial Letras Cubanas. [Contains additional entries for Cubans who left the country after 1959.]

Ortiz, Fernando. 1924. "La decadencia cubana." Paper presented at a meeting of the Sociedad Económica de Amigos del País, 23 February. Havana: Imprenta "La Universal."

———. 1929a. "Los afrocubanos dientimellados." *Archivos del folklore* 4, no. 1 (March): 16–33.

———. 1929b. "El estudio de la música afrocubana." *Musicalia* 5 (January–February 1929): 169–74.

———. 1934. "La poesía mulata: presentación de Eusebia Cosme." *Revista Bimestre Cubana* 34, nos. 2–3 (September–December 1934): 205–13.

———. [1935] 1992. *The Xylophonic Clave of Cuban Music: An Ethnographic Essay.* Trans. V. Boggs. Havana and New York: Editorial Letras Cubanas and City University of New York Graduate School.

———. [1938] 1992. "Palabras al lector." In *El sistema religioso de los afrocubanos,* edited by Rómulo Latachañeré, vii–xxxvi. Havana: Editorial de Ciencias Sociales.

———. 1939. "La cubanidad y los negros." *Estudios afrocubanos* 3, nos. 1–4.

———. 1950. *Wifredo Lam. Su obra vista a través de significados críticos.* Havana: Imp. P. Fernández y Cía.

————. 1952. "La transculturación blanca de los tambores de los negros." *Archivos venezolanos de folklore* 1, no. 2 (July–December): 235–65.

————. 1965. *La africanía de la música folklórica de Cuba.* Havana: Editora Universitaria [1950].

————. [1950s] 1981. *Los bailes y el teatro de los negros en el folklore de Cuba.* Havana: Editorial Letras Cubanas.

————. 1984. *Ensayos etnográficos,* selección de M. Barnet y A. L. Fernández. Havana: Editorial de Ciencias Sociales.

Ortiz, Fernando, and Ramón Vasconcelos et al. 1946. "Las comparsas populares del carnaval habanero." *Estudios afrocubanos* 5 (1940–1946): 129–47.

Otero, Juan Joaquín, et al., eds. 1954. *Libro de Cuba: Edición conmemorativa del cincuentenario de la República, 1902–1952 y del centenario del nacimiento de José Martí, 1853–1953.* Havana: Publicaciones Unidas.

Padura Fuentes, Leonardo. 1987. "Chori: vida, pasión y muerte del más célebre timbalero cubano." *Granma,* 1 February, 7.

————. 1988. "Carmen con y sin nostalgia." *Juventud rebelde,* June 26, 8–9.

Paquette, Robert L. 1988. *Sugar Is Made With Blood: The Conspiracy of La Escalera and the Conflict between Empires over Slavery in Cuba.* Middletown, Conn.: Wesleyan University Press.

Paredes, Américo. 1958. *With His Pistol in His Hand: A Border Ballad and Its Hero.* Austin: University of Texas Press.

París, Rogelio. 1966. "¡No cambia, señores!" *Cuba,* February: 58–61.

Peña, Manuel. 1985. *The Texas-Mexican Conjunto.* Austin: University of Texas Press.

Peraza, Fermín. N.d. "Vidas Cubanas: Grenet." Unidentified magazine article, 1950s? [MNM].

Pérez, Louis A. 1986. *Cuba Under the Platt Amendment, 1902–1934.* Pittsburgh: University of Pittsburgh Press.

————. 1988. *Cuba: Between Reform and Revolution.* New York: Oxford University Press.

————. 1992. *Slaves, Sugar, and Colonial Society: Travel Accounts of Cuba, 1801–1899.* Wilmington, Del.: Scholarly Resources, Inc.

Pérez Perazzo, Alberto. 1988. *Ritmo afrohispano antillano 1865–1965.* Caracas: Publicaciones Almacenadoras.

Pérez Rodríguez, Nancy. 1988. *El carnaval santiaguero.* 2 vols. Santiago de Cuba: Editorial Oriente.

Piñeiro Díaz, José. 1977. "Centenario de Jorge Anckermann 1877–1977." Pamphlet. Havana: MNM.

Pinto, Angel C. 1937. "Una aclaración." *Adelante* 3, no. 25 (June): 10–11. [BNJM]

Plantinga, Leon. 1984. "Nationalist Music." *Romantic Music.* New York: Norton, 341–404.

Pompey, Francisco. 1928. "Tres artistas cubanos en París." *Carteles* 11 (8 April): 23, 56. [BNJM]

Popular Memory Group. 1982. "Popular Memory: Theory, Politics, Method." In *Making Histories: Studies in History-Writing and Politics,* edited by Richard Johnson, G. McLennan, B. Schwarz, and D. Sutton, 205–52. Minneapolis: University of Minnesota Press.

Portuondo, José Antonio. 1972. "Landaluze y el costumbrismo en Cuba." *Revista de la Biblioteca Nacional José Martí* 63, no. 1 (January–April): 51–84.

Portuondo Calá, Romilio A. 1937. "Sobre el problema negro." *Adelante* 3, no. 25 (June): 12. [BNJM]

Quilez, Alfredo T. 1928. "Defensa económica." *Carteles* 11, no. 16 (15 April): 11. [BNJM]

Quintana, Jorge. 1954. "Humara y Lastra: 100 años al servicio comercial de Cuba." *Bohemia* 46, no. 23 (6 June): 64–65, 75–76. [BNJM]

Ralston, Shawn Leigh. 1991. "Afrocuban Resistance, Protest, and Organization in the Nineteenth and Twentieth Centuries." M.A. thesis, University of Texas, Austin.

Ramírez, Arturo. 1943a. "Nuestra farándula: Carmita Ortiz." *Carteles* 24, no. 41 (10 October): 6–9. [BNJM]

———. 1943b. "Nuestra farándula: Blanca Becerra." *Carteles* 24, no. 50 (12 December): 6–9. [BNJM]

Ramírez, Santos. N.d. 1. "Historia de las agupaciones 'Azules.'" Leaflet. [MNM].

———. N.d. 2. "Leyenda de la Comparsa 'El Alacrán.'" Leaflet. [MNM].

Randel, Don Michael, ed. 1986. "Nationalism." *The New Harvard Dictionary of Music*, 527.

Rego, Oscar. 1985. "Arquímedes Pous." *Bohemia* 77, no. 5 (1 February): 16–19. [BNJM]

Robbins, James. 1989. "Practical and Abstract Taxonomies in Cuban Music." *Ethnomusicology* 33, no. 3 (fall): 379–90).

Roberts, John S. 1979. *The Latin Tinge: The Impact of Latin American Music on the United States.* New York: Original Music.

Robreño, Eduardo. 1961. *Historia del teatro popular cubano.* Havana: Oficina del Historiador de la Ciudad.

———. 1981. *Cualquier tiempo pasado fue.* Havana: Editorial Letras Cubanas.

Robreño, Eduardo, ed. 1979. *Teatro Alhambra: antología.* Havana: Editorial Letras Cubanas.

Robreño, Gustavo. 1942. "El arroyo que murmura: génesis de un canto popular." Introduction to sheet music edition of a song by the same title by Jorge Anckermann. Havana: Talleres del Sr. Jesús Sandomingo Mercaderes. [MNM]

Roche Monteagudo, Rafael. 1925. *La policía y sus misterios en Cuba*, con prólogo por Dr. Felipe González. 3rd ed. Havana: La Moderna Poesía. [BNJM]

Rodríguez Domínguez, Ezequiel. 1978. *Trío Matamoros: treinta y cinco años de música popular.* Havana: Editorial Arte y Literatura.

Roig de Leuchsenring, Emilio. 1919. "La ocupación de la República Dominicana por los Estados Unidos y el derecho de las pequeñas nacionalidades de América." Paper presented at a meeting of the Sociedad Cubana de Derecho Internacional, 28 January. Havana, Imprenta Siglo XX. [BNJM]

———. 1920. "La doctrina Monroe y el pacto de la Liga de Naciones." Havana: Imprenta Siglo XX. [BNJM]

———. 1922. "La enmienda Platt, su interpretación primitiva y su aplicación posterior hasta 1921." Paper presented at the fifth annual meeting of the Sociedad Cubana de Derecho Internacional, 4 March. [BNJM]

———. 1923. "Análisis y consecuencias de la intervención norteamericana en los asuntos interiores de Cuba," pamphlet. Havana: Imprenta Siglo XX. [BNJM]

———. 1925. "La colonia sobreviva, Cuba a los veintidos años de la república." Lecture, 11 April. Havana: Imprenta Siglo XX. [BNJM]

———. 1927. "Un animador de tipos afrocubanos." *Social* 12, no. 12 (December): 18–19, 68, 94. [BNJM]

———. 1928a. "Cubanismo, sinónomo de anti-intervencionismo." *Carteles* 11, no. 16 (15 April): 18, 43. [BNJM]

———. 1928b. *La Habana de ayer, de hoy y de mañana.* Havana: Sindicato de Artes Gráficos. [BNJM]

———. 1932. "Bailando junto al abismo." *Social* 17, no. 9 (September): 12–13, 80. [BNJM]

———. 1946. "Las comparsas carnavalescas de la Habana en 1937." *Estudios afrocubanos* 5 (1940–1946): 148–73.

Roldán, Amadeo. 1933. "The Artistic Position of the American Composer." In *American Composers on American Music,* edited by Henry Cowell, 175–77. Stanford, Calif.: Stanford University Press.

Roldán Aliarte, Esteban, ed. 1940. *Cuba en la mano: enciclopedia popular ilustrada.* Havana: Ucar, García y Cía. [BNJM]

Root, Dean L. 1972. "The Pan American Association of Composers (1928–1934)." *Yearbook for Inter-American Research* 8: 49–70.

Roquelosabe, U. 1931. "Quisicosas. La rumba invade Europa." *Carteles* 17, no. 14 (13 December), 30, 55. [BNJM]

Rose, Phyllis. 1989. *Jazz Cleopatra: Josephine Baker in Her Time.* New York: Random House.

Rosell, Rosendo. 1992. *Vida y milagros de la farándula de Cuba.* 2 Vols. Miami: Ediciones Universales.

Ruiz, Ramón Eduardo. 1968. *Cuba: The Making of a Revolution.* New York: Norton.

Rust, Brian. 1975. *The American Dance Band Discography 1917–1942.* 2 vols. New York: Arlington House.

Saco, José Antonio. [1830s] 1960. *El juego y la vagancia en Cuba.* Havana: Editorial Lex.

Sáenz Coopat, Carmen. N.d. [1990?]. "Amadeo Roldán." Liner notes to *Amadeo Roldán.* Areíto LP #LD-4131. Havana: EGREM.

Salazar, Adolfo. 1938a. "El movimiento africanista en la música de arte cubana." *Estudios afrocubanos* 2, no. 1: 3–18. Havana: Sociedad de Estudios Afrocubanos.

———. 1938b. "La obra musical de Alejandro García Caturla." *Revista cubana* 11 (January–March 1938): 5–43.

Salazar, Max. 1994. "Arsenio Rodríguez: Life Was Like a Dream." *Latin Beat* 4, no. 2 (March): 12–17.

Sánchez, Luís Alberto. 1936. "Sobre el desdén del negro y por el negro." *Adelante* 2, no. 16 (September): 5–6. [BNJM]

Sánchez de Fuentes, Eduardo. 1923. *El folk-lor en la música cubana.* Havana: Imprenta "El Siglo XX."

———. 1928a. "El danzón." *Social* 13, no. 12 (December): 32, 77, 83. [BNJM]

———. 1928b. "Influencia de los ritmos africanos en nuestro cancionero." In *Evolución de la cultura cubana 1608–1927,* edited by José Manuel Carbonell, 18:155–202. Havana: Imprenta "El Siglo XX."

———. 1928c. *Folklorismo: artículos, notas y críticas musicales.* Havana: Molina y Cía.

———. 1932. "Bailes y canciones." *Diario de la Marina. Número centenario,* 101–02. Havana: Ucar, García y Cía.

———. 1938a. "La música aborigen de América." Paper presented at the inaugural session of the Academia de Artes y Letras, 22 October. Havana: Molina y Cía.

———. 1938b. "La música cubana y sus orígenes." *Boletín latino-americano de música* (Bogotá) 4 (October 1938): 177–82.

———. 1940. "Panorama actual de la música cubana." Paper presented at the innaugural session of the Academia Nacional de Artes y Letras, 16 December. Havana: Molina y Cía.

Sánchez Roca, Mariano. 1960. "Nota introductaria." In *J. A. Saco, El juego y la vagancia en Cuba,* 5–10. Havana: Editorial Lex.

Sanjuan, Pedro. 1930. "Posibilidades artísticas en la música africana." *Diario de la Marina,* 20 April, 36. [BNJM]

Santiesteban, Argelio. 1985. *El habla popular cubana de hoy. Una tonga de cubichismos que le oí a mi pueblo.* Havana: Editorial de Ciencias Sociales.

Schloss, Andrew. 1982. Liner notes to *The Cuban Danzón: Its Ancestors and Descendents.* Folkways LP #FE 4066. New York: Foklways Records and Service Corp.

Schwartz, Rosalie. 1977. "The Displaced and the Disappointed: Cultural Nationalists and Black Activists in Cuba in the 1920s." Ph.D. diss., University of California, San Diego.

Scott, Rebecca. 1985. *Slave Emancipation in Cuba: The Transition to Free Labor, 1860–1899.* Princeton: Princeton University Press.

Seoane Gallo, José. 1986. *Eduardo Abela cerca del cerco.* Havana: Editorial Letras Cubanas.

Serviat, Pedro. 1986. *El problema negro en Cuba y su solución definitiva.* Havana: Editora Política.

Simons, Moisés. 1927a. "La 'guajira montuna' o 'punto cubano.'" *Diario de la Marina,* 24 June, 33. [BNJM]

———. 1927b. "Música cubana." *Diario de la Marina,* 26 June, 42. [BNJM]

———. 1927c. "Teatros y artistas: una polémica musical." *Diario de la Marina,* 7 July, 8. [BNJM]

———. 1927d. "Una polémica musical: respuesta al maestro Sánchez de Fuentes." *Diario de la Marina,* 7 August, 42. [BNJM]

Soloni, Félix. 1963. Program notes to *La casita criolla,* published as part of the II Festival de Música Popular Cubana. Havana: Consejo Nacional de Cultura. [COU]

Spence, Jonathan D. 1984. *The Memory Palace of Matteo Ricci.* New York: Viking/Penguin.

Stevenson, Robert. 1976. *Music in Aztec and Inca Territory.* Berkeley: University of California Press.

Tellería, Nefertiti. 1977. "50 aniversario del Septeto Nacional." Program notes for the performance held in the Palacio de Bellas Artes, Havana, February. [MNM]

Thompson, E. P. 1967. "Time, Work-Discipline, and Industrial Capitalism." In *Past and Present* 38:56–97.

Thompson, Robert Farris. 1983. *Flash of the Spirit: African and Afro-American Art and Philosophy*. New York: Vintage Books.

Torgovnick, Marianna. 1990. *Gone Primitive. Savage Intellects, Modern Lives*. Chicago: University of Chicago Press.

Urfe, Odilio. 1982. "La música folklórica, popular y del teatro bufo." *La cultura en Cuba socialista*, 151–73. Havana: Editorial Letras Cubanas.

———. 1984. "Music and Dance in Cuba." In *Africa in Latin America: Essays on History, Culture, and Socialization*, edited by Moreno Fraginals. New York: Holmes and Meier, Inc.

Urrutia, Gustavo. 1932. "Raza y nación: aportaciones del negro en Cuba." *Diario de la Marina, Número Centenario*. Havana: Ucar, García y Cía.

———. 1935a. "Influencia del arte negro." *Adelante* 1, no. 3 (August): 8–9, 11. [BNJM]

———. 1935b. "Cuba, el arte y el negro II." *Adelante* 1, no. 6 (November): 9, 20. [BNJM]

———. 1935c. "Cuba, el arte y el negro III." *Adelante* 1, no. 6 (September): 9. [BNJM]

Valdés, Mercedita. 1993. Paper presented at the Casa de las Américas, Vedado, Havana, 17 August.

Valdés Cantero, Alicia. 1988. *El músico en Cuba. Ubicación social y situación laboral en el período 1939–1946*. Havana: Editorial Pueblo y Educación.

Varona, José Enrique. 1930. Letter to the editor. *Revista de Avance* 4, no. 47 (15 June): 161–62. [BNJM]

Vasconcelos, Ramón. 1916. "Al primer tapón, zurrapas." *La prensa* 8, no. 67 (7 March): 4. [BNJM]

Vázquez Díaz, Ramón, et al. 1988. *La vanguardia: Surgimiento del arte moderno en Cuba*. Havana: Museo Nacional, Palacio de Bellas Artes.

Vázquez Millares, Angel. 1964. *Carnaval de la Habana: desarrollo histórico*. Havana: Comisión organizadora del carnaval de la Habana.

Villareal, J. Jerez. 1935. "El elemento de color en la formación de la cultura cubana." *Adelante* 1, no. 1 (June): 12–13, 20. [BNJM]

Villoch, Federico. 1938. "La rumba de Lina Frutos." *Carteles* 32, no. 36 (4 September): 1–12. [BNJM]

———. 1945. "Viejas postales descoloridas: la orquesta de Alhambra y sus danzones." *Diario de la Marina*, 2 December, 37. [BNJM]

Villoch, Federico, and Jorge Anckermann. 1933. *"La gloria del solar," sainete lírico en un acto*. Libretto by Federico Villoch and Pepín Rodríguez, music by Jorge Anckermann. Archives, Centro Odilio Urfé, Alhambra collection no. 58.

Wade, Peter. 1993. *Blackness and Race Mixture: The Dynamics of Racial Identity in Colombia*. Baltimore: Johns Hopkins University Press.

West, Cornel. 1988. *Prophetic Fragments*. Grand Rapids, Mich.: Eederman's.

Widdess, Richard. 1992. "Historical Musicology." In *Ethnomusicology: An Introduction*, edited by H. Meyers, 219–37. New York: Macmillan.

Williams, Brackette F. 1991. *Stains on My Name, War in My Veins: Guyana and the Politics of Cultural Struggle*. Durham: Duke University Press.

Williams, Raymond. 1977. *Marxism and Literature*. New York: Oxford University Press.

Wright, Ann. 1988. "Intellectuals of an Unheroic Period of Cuban History, 1913–23. The 'Cuba Contemporanea' Group." *Bulletin of Latin American Research* 7, no. 1: 109–22.

Zea, Leopoldo. 1986. "Negritude e indigenismo." *Ideas en torno a Latinoamérica,* 2:1341–55. Mexico City: Universidad Nacional Autónoma de México.

Printed and Recorded Music

Acebal, Sergio. 1918. "Mala gandinga." *Diálago y canto* performed by Sergio Acebal and F. de Campo. Columbia '78 #C 3291 (82175).

Anckermann, Jorge. 1898. *Album de cantos y bailes cubanas para piano y canto y piano solo.* New Orleans: L. Grunewald [MNM].

———. N.d. 1. "A Maceo." *Clave* sheet music, unpublished. [MNM]

———. N.d. 2. "Canción tropical." *Clave* sheet music from the *zarzuela El triunfo de la clave.* Havana: Anselmo López. [MNM]

———. N.d. 3 [1910s]. "Conga mandinga." *Tango-congo* from the *zarzuela El superhombre.* [Archives, MNM]

———. N.d. 4. "Cubita de mis amores." Rumba sheet music, unpublished. [MNM]

———. N.d. 5 [1920s]. "Las notas de mi son." *Son* sheet music. Havana: Tipografía musical. [MNM]

———. N.d. 6. "El negro Pancho." Conga sheet music, unpublished. [MNM]

———. N.d. 7. "Mercé." Rumba sung by Blanca Becerra and Adolfo Colombo. Brunswick '78 #40406. Recorded in Cuba. [MNM]

———. 1913. "Siembra la caña." *Tango-congo* sheet music from the *sainete La casita criolla.* Havana: Anselmo López. [MNM]

———. 1916. "La danza de los millones." Fox-trot sheet music for piano and voice. Havana: Anselmo López. [MNM]

———. 1918. "Sin pan y sin luz" and "Cuba en la guerra." Columbia '78 disc #C3428 and 82284. [MNM]

———. 1942. *Doce cantos escolares del maestro Jorge Anckermann.* Sheet music. Havana: Talleres del Sr. Jesús Sandomingo Mercaderes. [MNM]

Anckermann, Jorge, and Sergio Acebal. 1918. "Congos de Luvine." *Diálogo y rumba* performed by Luz Gil and Sergio Acebal, with piano accompaniment. Columbia '78 #C3356 (82220). [MNM]

Anckermann, Jorge, and Manuel María Delgado. N.d. "Varadero." Rumba–fox-trot sheet music for voice and piano. [MNM]

Aragón, la Orquesta. 1992. *The Heart of Havana,* vol. 1, Rafael Lay, director. RCA compact disc #3204-2-RL. New York: BMG Music, Inc. (Tropical series).

Bastin, Bruce, and Charlie Crump. 1991. *Don Azpiazu.* Harlequin compact disc HQCD 10, with liner notes. West Sussex, England: Harlequin.

Belafonte, Harry, producer. 1990. *Routes of Rhythm,* vols. 1–2. Rounder CD #5049–50. Cambridge: Cultural Research Communications, Inc.

Caesar, Irving, and Oscar Levant. N.d. "Lady Play Your Mandolin." Rumba-fox trot performed by the Havana Novelty Orchestra. Victor '78 #22597-A. [MNM]

Calloway, Cab. [1930–1931] 1982. "Doin' the Rumba." *Mr. Hi-De-Ho.* Universal City, Calif.: MCA cassette #MCAC-1344. Jazz Heritage Series.

Casas Romero, Luís. N.d. "Estela." *Criolla* performed by the Orquesta Casas. RCA Victor '78 #77843. [MNM]

Casino de la Playa, Orquesta. 1991. *Memories of Cuba: Orquesta Casino de la Playa 1937–44.* Tumbao CD TCD-003. Switzerland: Camarillo Music Ltd.

Cruz, Celia. 1991. "Bemba colorá." *Celia Cruz: The Best.* Globo Records CD #80587. Miami: Sony, Inc.

Cuarteto Machín, vol. 1: *1931–32.* Harlequin compact disc HQCD 24. West Sussex, England: Interstate Music Ltd.

Cugat, Xavier. 1992. *Xavier Cugat and His Orchestra, 1940–1942.* Tumbao compact disc TCD-002. Switzerland: Camarillo Music Ltd.

Embale, Carlos. N.d. *Carlos Embale.* Areíto LP #LD-3810. Havana: EGREM.

———. 1988. *Todavía me queda voz.* Areíto LP #LD-4297. Havana: EGREM.

Espígul, Ramón. N.d. 1 "Entra sin miedo, negra." *Diálogo* performed by Dulce María Mola and Ramón Espígul. RCA Victor '78 #46224-b. [MNM]

———. 1916. "El Ford." *Diálogo y canto* performed by Ramón Espígul and Lola Mayorga. RCA Victor '78 #72650-a. [MNM]

Estefan, Gloria. 1993. *Mi tierra.* Epic CD # EX 53807. New York: Sony Records.

Garay, Sindo. N.d. [1928]. "Lupisamba o yuca y ñame." *Afro/tango-congo* sung by Rita Montaner. Columbia #3324-X (97354).

García Caturla, Alejandro. N.d. [1990?]. *Alejandro García Caturla.* 2 vols. Areíto LP #LD-4129–30. Havana: EGREM. (A recorded anthology of his works by the Orquesta Sinfónica Nacional and Coro Nacional.)

Grenet, Eliseo. N.d. 1. "¡Ay! Mamá Inés." *Danzón* sheet music. Havana: Excelsior Music Company. [MNM]

———. N.d. 2. "Ay Mama Ines." Rumba–fox-trot version of the Grenet original by the Havana Novelty Orchestra. Victor '78 #22597-B. [MNM]

———. N.d. 3. "Camina pa' 'lante." Conga arranged by E. Vázquez, performed by the Lecuona Cuban Boys. Vocalists: A. Bruguera and Chiquito Oréfiche. *Lecuona Cuban Boys*, vol. 2. Harlequin compact disc HQCD 7. West Sussex, England: Harlequin Records. [MNM]

———. N.d. 4. "Hatuey." *Danzonete* arranged by O. Calvet. Victor '78 #46983-b. [MNM]

———. 1932a. "La comparsa de los congos." *Motivo afrocubano* sheet music for piano. New York: Southern Music Publishing Co. [MNM]

———. 1932b. *Mamá Inez* [sic]: *American Adaptation of the Greatest of all Cuban Rumbas.* Sheet music, English lyrics by L. Wolfe Gilbert. New York: Edward B. Marks Music Corp. (In Spanish and English)

———. 1942b. "Náñigo." Sheet music for piano. Havana: Robbins Music Company of Cuba. [MNM]

———. 1946. "Himno a nuestra Patrona, Santísima Virgen de la Caridad del Cobre." Havana: n.p. [MNM]

Grenet, Eliseo, and Nicolás Guillén. N.d. "Yambambó." *Compositores cubanos.* Areíto LP #LD-3346. Havana: EGREM.

Grenet, Eliseo, and Teofilo Radillo. 1931. "Tata Cuñengue." *Tango-congo* sheet music for piano. [MNM]

Grenet, Eliseo, and Teofilo Radillo. 1944. "Facundo." *Tango-congo* sheet music for piano. New York: Southern Music Publishing Co. [MNM]

Grillo, Frank. 1989. *Machito and His Afro-Cubans—1941*. Palladium compact disc PCD-116. Europe: Tecval Memories.

Irakere, Grupo. N.d. *Irakere,* vol. 1: *Selección de éxitos 1973–78.* Havana: Areíto/EGREM cassette C-4003.

King, Henry. 1938. *Ten Famous Rumbas Played by Henry King and His Orchestra.* Decca five-record set recorded in Los Angeles, 21 July. Record numbers DLA 1331A-1340A.

Lecuona, Margarita. 1934. "Tabú." *Afrocubano* sheet music. New York: Southern Music Publishing Co.

———. 1939. "Babalú." *Motivo afrocubano* sheet music. New York: Southern Music Publishing Co.

Lecuona, Ernesto. N.d. 1 [1927]. "La conga se va." *Danza* sheet music. Havana: Lecuona Music Co.

———. N.d. 2 [1929?]. "Canto Siboney." *Capricho* sung by Margarita Cueto. RCA Victor '78 #81213-A (43965).

———. 1928a. "Negrita." *Danza* sheet music. [MNM]

———. 1928b. "El calesero." *Couplet* sung by Rita Montaner. Columbia '78 #2964-X (96269).

———. 1928c. "Canto Siboney." *Capricho* sung by Rita Montaner. Rereleased on *Rita Montaner: Rita de Cuba.* Tumbao CD #TCD-046. Switzerland: Camarillo Music Ltd., 1994.

———. 1929a. *Obras.* Album No. 3. Havana: Lecuona Music Co. [MNM]

———. 1929b. "Canto indio." Sheet music for voice and piano, unpublished. Originally from *La flor del sitio.*[MNM]

———. 1930. "Los enamorados." Sheet music reduction of the *serenata* from the *zarzuela María la O.* Havana: Molina y Cía. [MNM]

———. 1939. "Negra me muero." *Capricho* sheet music for piano and voice. Havana: Cándido G. Galdo. [MNM]

———. [1950s]. *Rosa la china, sainete lírico en un acto.* Libretto by Gustavo Sánchez Galarraga, music by Ernesto Lecuona. Madrid: Montilla Records. No record number. [RHC]

———. 1955. *Lecuona Plays Lecuona: The Great Songs of the Revered Composer.* RCA LPM-1055. Camden, N.J.: RCA Victor.

López, Israel ("Cachao"). 1977. "Dos." Salsoul LP Sal-4115. New York: Mericana Record Corp.

López, Regino. 1919. "La brujería." Comic dialogue recorded on RCA Victor '78 #77458-A. [MNM]

Matamoros, Miguel. 1928. "Bomba lacrimosa." *Bolero-son* performed by the Trío Matamoros. RCA Victor '78 46691-B.

Montaner, Rita. N.d. *Homenaje a Rita Montaner.* Areíto LP #LDA-3336. Havana: EGREM.

———. 1994. *Rita Montaner: Rita de Cuba.* Tumbao CD #TCD-046. Switzerland: Camarillo Music Ltd.

Monteagudo, H. 1924. "El melonero." *Diálogo y pregón,* performed by Arquímedes Pous, Conchita Llauradó. Columbia '78 C-4153 (93207). [MNM]

Moré, Beny. N.d. *Pare . . . Que llegó el bárbaro.* New York: Discuba LPD-501 [1950s].

Palmieri, Eddie. 1992. *Llegó la India.* Soho Sounds compact disc #CD-80864. Miami: Sony Records, Inc.

Pello el Afrokan. 1988. *Congas por barrio: Grupo Pello el Afrokan,* dir. Pedro Izquierdo. Areíto/EGREM LP LD-4471, Havana. (Recordings of traditional *comparsa* music).

Piñeiro, Ignacio. N.d. 1. *Sones cubanos: Septeto Nacional de Ignacio Piñeiro.* New York: Seeco LP #SCLP 9278.

———. 1923. "Iyamba Bero." *Clave ñáñiga* performed by Cruz, Bienvenido, and Villalón. Columbia '78 #2421-X (93950).

———. 1992. *Ignacio Piñeiro and His Septeto Nacional.* Tumbao compact disc TCD-019. Switzerland: Camarillo Music, Ltd. [1928–1930].

Pous, Arquímedes. 1917. "Las mulatas del Bam-Bay." *Diálogo y canto* performed by Sánchez Pous and Conchita Llauradó with orchestral accompaniment. Columbia '78 #C 2986 (48362). [MNM]

———. N.d. 2. "El negro Galleguito." Performed by Blanca Vázquez and Arquímedes Pous. Columbia '78 #C2493 (37956). [MNM]

Prado, Pérez, and Orchestra. 1990. *Havana 3 AM.* New York: Tropical series/RCA cassette 2444-4-RL [1950s].

Rodríguez, Arsenio. N.d. "Yo nací de Africa." Sound recording from the archives of Radio Progreso in Havana.

Roig, Gonzalo. N.d. 1 [1932]. "Canto de la esclava." Aria from the *zarzuela Cecilia Valdés,* sung by Aida Pujol and chorus with the Orquesta Gonzalo Roig. Discos Camafo LP #2091 FJM-CV-PT.6, side 5. [MNM]

———. N.d. 2. "Po po po." *Tango-congo* from the *zarzuela Cecilia Valdés,* sung by Ruth Fernández with the Orquesta Gonzalo Roig. Discos Camafo LP #2089 FJM-CV-PT 2. [MNM]

———. 1945. "Lamento negroide." *Capricho afrocubano* sheet music for voice and piano. Havana: Melodías Cubanas, s.a. [MNM]

———. 1990. *Cecilia Valdés.* Centenario de Gonzalo Roig. Areíto 2-LP set #LD 4675–76. Havana: Estudios de Grabaciones y Ediciones Musicales (EGREM).

Roldán, Amadeo. N.d. [1990?]. *Amadeo Roldán.* Areíto LP #LD-4131. Havana: EGREM. (A recorded anthology of his works by the Orquesta Sinfónica de la Habana and Coro Nacional.)

Sánchez, José "Pepe." N.d. "La música de Pepe Sánchez." Liner notes by Odilio Urfé. Santiago de Cuba: Siboney/EGREM LP LD-315.

Sánchez de Fuentes, Eduardo. N.d. "Tú." Habanera performed by Rosario García Orellana with orchestral accompaniment. RCA Victor '78 #30814-a. [MNM]

———. 1974. *Eduardo Sánchez de Fuentes. Centenario 1874–1974.* Two-LP set of compositions by Sánchez de Fuentes. Ramón Calzadilla, baritone, Juan Espinosa, pianist. Havana: Areíto/EGREM LD-3405.

Santa Cruz, Carlos. N.d. "Malanga dice." *Guaracha* performed by Orlando "Cascarita" Guerra and the Orquesta Casino de la Playa. RCA Victor LP 23-0904-B. Recorded in Cuba. [MNM]

Santamaría, Mongo. N.d. *Afro Roots*. 2-LP set, Prestige PR 24018. Berkeley, Calif.: Fantasy Records.

Simons, Moisés. N.d. 1. "Con picante y sin picante." *Sonsonete-pregón callejero* sheet music for piano. Havana. [MNM]

———. N.d. 2. "Me siento cubana." *Capricho cubano* sheet music for piano. Havana: Vda. de Carreras & Co. [MNM]

———. 1929. *Album "Simons." 25 composiciones cubanas del maestro Moisés Simons.* Sheet music. Havana: Molina y Cía. [MNM]

Strachwitz, Chris, ed. N.d. *La historia del son cubano: Sexteto Habanero*. Vol. 2 of *The Roots of Salsa*. Folklyric Records LP #9054. El Cerrito, Calif.: Arhoolie.

Strachwitz, Chris, and Michael Avalos, eds. 1991. *Sextetos Cubanos: sones 1930*. Arhoolie Folklyric compact disc CD #7003. El Cerrito, Calif.: Arhoolie Productions, Inc. (Selected recordings of the Sexteto Munamar, Sexteto Machín, Sexteto Nacional, and Sexteto Matancero.)

Suazo, Blanco. N.d. "Yembe laroko." *Guaracha* performed by Celia Cruz and the Sonora Matanzera. Seeco '78 #7141B (SR 1935).

Superexitos: bailables cubanos. 1993. EGREM cassette anthology #C-141. Havana: EGREM.

Urfé, Odilio, comp. 1955. *Festival in Havana: Folk Music of Cuba*. New York: Riverside Records RLP 4005. World Folk Music Series.

Valdés, Gilberto. N.d. 1. "Evocación negra." Song for piano and voice, unpublished. [MNM]

———. N.d. 2. "Bembé." *Danza lucumí* for piano and voice. Havana: Ediciones "New Rhythm." [MNM]

———. 1937. "Ilenkó-Ile'nbé." Overture for piano, voice, and orchestra, unpublished manuscript score. [MNM]

———. 1938. "Rumba." Composition for piano and voice, unpublished manuscript score. [MNM]

———. 1939. "Vamo a bailá mercé." Conga written for the film *Mi tía de América*. Havana: Havana Music Supply Co.

———. 1940a. "Guaguancó." Composition for orchestra and voice, unpublished manuscript score. [MNM]

———. 1940b. "Mango, mangüe." *Pregón* for voice and piano, unpublished manuscript score. Dedicated to Rita Montaner. [MNM]

———. 1941a. "Ecó." *Pregón* sheet music for voice and piano. Havana: Cándido G. Galdo. [MNM]

———. 1941b. "Que vengan los rumberos." Rumba sheet music for voice and piano. Havana: Cándido G. Galdo.

Valdés, Mercedita. 1992. *Aché*. Areíto cassette #C-230. Havana: EGREM.

Villa, Ignacio ("Bola de Nieve"). 1981. *Bola de Nieve: en memoriam*. Havana: EGREM LP #LD-3978. [CIDMUC]

Voces eternas del bolero: grabaciones históricas de 1907–1934. 1990. LP anthology with unsigned liner notes. Mexico City: Asociación mexicana de estudios fonográficos, 1990.

Interviews

All interviews were conducted by the author.

Acosta, Leonardo. 1992. Vedado, Havana, 13 August. (Musicologist)

Alvarez, René. 1994. Vedado, Havana, 4 April. (*Son* musician)

Arango, Gilberto ("Sagüita"). 1995. Mariano, Havana, 31 May. (Cabaret worker)

Arcaño, Antonio. 1992. Reina, Havana, 16 July. (Bandleader)

Bacallao, Francisco. 1994. Centro Habana, 12 January. (Son of a founding member of the Septeto Habanero)

Bolívar, Natalia. 1996. Miramar, Havana, 13 October. (Author)

Castro, Olga, Ondina Castro, Ada Castro, and Alicia Castro. 1994. Lawton, Havana, 19 January. (The Castro sisters, members of the Orquesta Anacaona)

Fernández Robaina, Tomás. 1992. Vedado, Havana, July. (Author)

———. 1993. Atarés, Havana, 9 December.

———. 1994. National Library, Havana, 6 April.

González, Hilario. 1994. Nuevo Vedado, Havana, 14 April. (Composer)

Hernández Cuesta, Florencio ("Carusito"). 1994. Centro Habana, Havana, 13 March. (*Son* player)

Herrera, Lázaro. 1993. Reina, Havana, 13 September. (Trumpet player of the Septeto Nacional)

———. 1994a. Reina, Havana, 8 January.

———. 1994b. Reina, Havana, 7 February.

Herrera, Natalia. 1994. Playa, Havana, 21 February. (Dancer)

Hierrezuelo, Reynaldo. 1994. Centro Habana, Havana, 2 March. (*Son* musician)

Jimeno, Tomás, 1992. Centro de Investigación y Desarrollo de la Música Cubana in Vedado, Havana, 3 August. (Percussionist and music teacher)

Lapique Becali, Zoila. 1993a. Playa, Havana, 11 September. (Author)

———. 1993b. Playa, Havana, 1 October.

Linares, María Teresa. 1992. Vedado, Havana, 2 August. (Musicologist)

———. 1993. Vedado, Havana, 21 December.

López, Oscar Luís. 1994. Vedado, Havana, 23 February. (Radio historian)

Martínez Furé, Rogelio. 1994. Vedado, Havana, 20 January. (Ethnographer)

Martínez Rodríguez, Raúl. 1993. Vedado, Havana, 7 November. (Musicologist)

Matamoros, Miguel. N.d. [1960s]. Recorded interview, archives of Radio Habana Cuba.

Mora, Adelaida. 1995. Marianao, Havana, 31 May. (Dancer)

Orovio, Helio. 1996. El Vedado, Havana, 26 September. (Musicologist)

Quiñones, Serafín ("Tato"). 1992. Playa, Havana, July. (Ethnographer of the UNEAC)

Rey, Julio. 1994. Museo Nacional de la Música, Havana, 10 February. (Actor)

Reyes, José ("Pepe"). 1994. Vedado, Havana, 22 March. (Researcher for the Centro Odilio Urfé)

Rivero, Hilda, and Raquel Rivero. 1994. Reina, Havana, 5 April. (Sisters of dancer René Rivero)

Robreño, Eduardo. 1994. Vedado, Havana, 4 March. (Theater historian)

Rocillo, Eduardo. 1993. Offices of Radio Progreso, Havana, August. (Radio personality)

Sosa, Cristóbal, 1994. Centro Habana, Havana, 25 February. (Radio journalist for Radio Habana Cuba)

Suárez, Senén. 1994. Vedado, Havana, 11 January. (Music historian and bandleader)

Valdés, Joseito. 1994. Guanabacoa, Havana, 10 January. (Director of the Orquesta Ideal)

Valls, Avelina Alcalde. 1994. La Víbora, Havana, 14 April. (Niece of painter Jaime Valls)

INDEX

Boldface type indicates a photograph or illustration.

Valorize

bricolage — 113

Grenet — 78
A2 Pimy

Library of Congress Cataloging-in-Publication Data

Moore, Robin, 1964–
    Nationalizing blackness : afrocubanismo and artistic revolution in Havana, 1920–
1940 / Robin Moore
        p.   cm. — (Pitt Latin American series)
    Includes bibliographical references (p.   ) and index.
    ISBN 0-8229-4040-x (cloth : acid-free paper). — ISBN 0-8229-5645-4 (pbk. : acid-
free paper)
    1. Popular music—Cuba—African influences.   2. Blacks—Cuba—Music.
3. Popular culture—Cuba—African influences.   I. Title.   II. Series.
ML3486.C8M66   1997
781.63'089'9607291—dc21   97-21045